HARVARD HISTORICAL STUDIES

HARVARD HISTORICAL STUDIES

BRITISH POLICY AND THE TURKISH REFORM MOVEMENT

A Study in Anglo-Turkish Relations

1826-1853

BY

FRANK EDGAR BAILEY

NEW YORK

Howard Fertig

1970

TO THE MEMORY OF MY FATHERS
FRANK EDGAR BAILEY
ROBERT HOLMES CUSHMAN

FOREWORD

THOUGH forewords are very much out of favor with modern scholars at the moment, I have decided to include one, partly to maintain an old convention in this ever more convention-less world, but largely to justify myself before that corps of patient, tireless workers, the librarians, for adding another volume to their already creaking shelves. Although the subject is highly specialized and for that reason of no significance for the general reader, nevertheless it does have a purpose which I hasten to explain at the beginning in case my reader never arrives as far as my conclusion.

The Turkish reform movement in the decades prior to the outbreak of the Crimean War is treated to a limited degree in almost all the general histories of the Ottoman Empire in the nineteenth century, and is also the subject of at least two significant monographs, namely, Ed. Engelhardt, *La Turquie et le tanzimat, ou Histoire des Réformes dans l'Empire Ottoman depuis 1828 jusqu'à nos jours*, 2 vols., Paris, 1882–1884, and G. Rosen, *Geschichte der Türkei vom dem Siege der Reform in Jahre 1826 bis zum Pariser Tractat vom Jahre 1856*, 2 vols., Leipzig, 1866–1867. Yet, no author has approached the reform movement in the Ottoman state from the exclusive viewpoint of how far the Sultans were inspired or encouraged by the western nations. That the attitude of the western European states, particularly France and England, was significant in achieving a partial rejuvenation of imperial Turkey is suggested by several authorities, yet, modern writers for the most part have not probed deeper than a study of the diplomatic problems in which the western nations were involved. To correct this deficiency as far as British influence was concerned is the sole justification for this work. A similar study of the later period of the *tanzimat* to appear under the title, *Great*

Britain and the Reform Period in Turkey, 1856–1878, is now
in progress by Miss Grace Grove, Swansea, Wales. Together,
it is hoped, these two books will present a complete picture of
British influence on the modernization of one state outside of
her own immediate sphere.

The attempt of the Ottoman Empire in the nineteenth century to correct its worst abuses and restore its former vitality
before complete disintegration took place has been known for
long as the *tanzimat.* Literally translated this word means
"beneficent legislation," which may be interpreted either as a
return to an ancient system long corrupted, or as the installa-
tion of a new order. In this study I have looked upon the
tanzimat as a forward movement, an attempt to westernize an
oriental power, and in my study of Anglo-Turkish relations
between the years 1826 and 1853, I have attempted to maintain as my focal point the influence of the British government
on the reforms promulgated by Sultan Mahmoud II and his
successor Abdul Medjid. Certain factors inherent in the subject have made the maintenance of this ideal difficult. First,
England's policy, as it affected Turkey, was so entwined with
her Mediterranean and Indian policies, to isolate it completely
was impossible; also, it has not always been easy to differentiate between British attitude towards the internal development
of Turkey and her purely diplomatic and commercial relations
with that power. In order to place the problem of Britain and
the reform movement in its correct setting, some account of
the more important diplomatic events of the period, especially
the crises of 1833 and 1839–1841, was necessary, though they
have been treated fully in monographs by Professors Rodkey,
Swain, and Mosely.

The Introduction, dealing with the state of the Ottoman
Empire in the first quarter of the nineteenth century, the general theme of which has been done many times, has been included for several reasons, the chief of which was to form a
setting for the problem to be examined. Moreover, such a survey not only indicates the great need of reform in the Sultan's

dominions, but by comparing the status of Turkey prior to 1826 with its condition on the eve of the Crimean War, the extent to which the *tanzimat* was successful during the period can be measured. The reform movement was essentially Turkish in origin, growing out of the needs of the time, and any study of British influence on its continuation is out of balance without a glance at prevailing conditions, the obstacles to reform, and the earliest attempts of the Sultans to overcome those obstacles. As a survey of the extent, organization, and weaknesses of the Ottoman Empire, this chapter makes no pretense at completeness. No more has been attempted here than to outline briefly the principal problems of the Turkish state which had to be corrected, if it was to survive as a strong power in Europe. This chapter is based entirely on secondary materials. Subsequent chapters are the result of research carried on in England in 1933 and 1935, and for the conclusions arrived at, as well as any errors of omission or commission, the author accepts full responsibility.

It will be immediately obvious to the reader acquainted with Britain's Near Eastern policy prior to 1853 that I have attempted to bring into small compass a far-reaching and elusive subject. Moreover, it is a difficult subject of historical investigation, and the further one goes with the materials the greater the feeling of inadequacy. I am fully aware of the deficiencies of this study, the affairs untreated, the questions unanswered. However, this book may have some value in throwing light on a new aspect of British foreign policy in the years before the outbreak of the Crimean War. If it should once again focus attention on the importance of the economic background of Britain's policy in this period, I shall feel that I did not write in vain.

The subject of British influence on the Turkish reform movement was first suggested to the writer by Professor William Leonard Langer, Coolidge Professor of History, Harvard University. His profound scholarship has been an inspiration throughout the preparation of this book. I am also deeply in-

debted to my good friend, Professor N. Neilson of Mount
Holyoke College, whose criticisms of the style and form of this
book have helped to make it more readable than it otherwise
would be. To Pace and Wade, and the other archivists in the
Public Record Office in both its London and Canterbury reposi-
tories, to the Librarians of the Board of Trade, Whitehall, and
the Customs House my sincere gratitude; also, to Widener Library, Harvard University, so generous in its loans of books,
and in particular to Mr. Robert H. Haynes, Assistant Librarian,
for his many courtesies, I wish to express my thanks. I am
indebted to the University of Chicago Press for permission to
use material from my article, "The Economics of British Foreign Policy," published in the *Journal of Modern History* in
December, 1940; to the Harvard University Press for permission to quote from A. H. Lybyer's *The Government of the
Ottoman Empire in the Time of Suleiman the Magnificent;* to
Longmans, Green & Co. for a quotation from H. L. Hoskins'
British Routes to India; to the Macmillan Company for quota-
tions from J. H. Clapham's *An Economic History of Modern
Britain*, vol. I, and from the *Cambridge History of British Foreign Policy*, vol. II; to Methuen and Co., Ltd., for a quotation
from G. R. Porter's *Progress of the Nation;* to the Oxford University Press, London, for a quotation from T. W. Arnold's
The Caliphate; and to the Stanford University Press for quota-
tions from V. J. Puryear's *International Economics and the
Diplomacy of the Near East*. Finally, to my wife, Carolyn
Cushman Bailey, without whose constant encouragement this
book would never have been produced, I am most truly grateful.

F. E. B.

WASHINGTON, D. C.
October, 1942

CONTENTS

TABLES

CHARTS

BRITISH POLICY AND THE TURKISH
REFORM MOVEMENT

ABBREVIATIONS

B. T.   Original manuscripts in the library of the British Board
           of Trade (Gt. Russell Street, Whitehall), or in the Board
           of Trade series in the Foreign Office records

F. O.   Foreign Office records

P. R. O.   British Public Record Office (London)

Customs.   Customs reports housed in the Public Record Office, Lon-
           don and Canterbury repositories

INTRODUCTION

ALTHOUGH the discrediting title, "the sick man of Europe," was not conferred upon the Ottoman state until the nineteenth century, observers in the Levant had long been aware of the anemic condition which possessed the once great Turkish Empire. The Ottoman Empire had reached the high point of its development under Suleiman, the Magnificent,[1] 1520–1566, but with his demise the state over which he had ruled began to decline in power. The fact that this vast assemblage of people held together during the next four centuries (i.e. until 1918) is far more surprising and much less easily accounted for than the dismemberment of the empire which has been the work of the last one hundred and fifty years. For several decades after 1566 the Empire appeared to have considerable strength, due largely to the momentum generated by Suleiman and his forbears.

The decline of Turkey which began toward the latter part of the sixteenth century had a variety of causes, the most important of which was the weakness of the successive rulers, and the loss of drive due to the completion of their conquests. As soon as the Turks became a sedentary people they became less of a menace to Europe, because destructive forces immediately began to work within their domains.[2] To be sure there were periods in the eighteenth and nineteenth centuries when the Porte seemed to show signs of its old power, but the place among the powers which Suleiman had won was never again reached.

[1] The best description of the Ottoman state at the peak of its greatness will be found in A. H. Lybyer, *The Government of the Ottoman Empire in the Time of Suleiman the Magnificent*, Harvard University Press, Cambridge (Mass.), 1913.

[2] "The growth, the splendour, and the decline of the Ottoman Empire have always been in direct relation with its military strength." A. Djevad Bey, *État*

About the middle of the eighteenth century, during the reigns of Osman III (1754–1757) and Mustapha III (1757–1774), Turkey was relatively prosperous, due to the fact that the weakness of the sultans was outweighed in large measure by the efforts of an intelligent and able Grand Vizir, Razhib Pasha. The death of Razhib in 1763 came as a prelude to the attacks of Russia which almost spelled the end for Turkey.

In the nineteenth century the Ottoman Empire stiffened after Mahmoud IInd's destruction of the Janissaries in 1826, an act which opened an era of reform which continued intermittently until 1878. With these two exceptions, the decline had been steady since the middle of the sixteenth century. Though many writers have traced the course of Turkish history through this period, nevertheless, a brief sketch of the extent, population, government, social organization, and the needed reforms of the Ottoman Empire at the opening of the nineteenth century seems an appropriate introduction to the reform movement, or *tanzimat*. From such a survey the reader can determine to what extent the Turkish Empire was "a vast organism dying in parts and by inches." [3]

At the opening of the nineteenth century the Ottoman Empire was one of the largest states in Europe, not to mention the Sultan's extensive holdings in Asia and Africa.[4] European Turkey alone extended from the Dniester river on the northeast westward to the Dalmatian coast, and southward to the tip of the Morean peninsula, and included also Crete and most of the Aegean islands.

The first three decades of the nineteenth century witnessed several important losses from this territory. Bessarabia, the territory between the Dniester and Pruth rivers, was lost in

---

militaire Ottoman depuis la fondation de l'Empire jusqu'à nos jours, Paris, 1882, p. 6.

[3] W. S. Davis, *A Short History of the Near East*, New York, 1934, p. 278.

[4] According to Ubicini, Turkey possessed in 1876, 371,950 sq. kilometers of territory in Europe, 2,075,220 sq. kilometers in Asia, and 925,330 sq. kilometers in Africa, or a total of 3,372,500 sq. kilometers. Cf. M. A. Ubicini, *État présent de l'Empire Ottoman*, Paris, 1876, Introd., pp. 10–11. By adding the losses of the previous seventy-five years one can estimate its area in 1800.

1812, a very serious forfeiture, because, although the Porte still controlled the Danube delta, and thereby the whole Danubian basin, Russia, by the annexation of this province, advanced one step further in her march towards Constantinople. The Serbs, as a result of the revolution begun in 1804, acquired an autonomous position in the Ottoman Empire by the Treaty of Bucharest, May 16, 1812,[5] which they maintained until their complete independence was finally recognized by the Treaty of Berlin, July 13, 1878.

Costliest for the Sultan, however, was the Greek War for Independence, 1821–1829, for thereafter the Morean peninsula south of the Arta-Volo line,[6] Euboea, and the Cyclades were free and independent of the Sultan. Moldavia and Wallachia, over which Russia had secured a protectorate in 1774, remained a bone of contention for almost a century. By the treaty of Adrianople it was provided that these provinces should remain Turkish, but subject to Russian supervision.[7] Having lost Bessarabia and Greece outright, and retaining merely nominal control over Serbia, the principalities, and Crete,[8] the Ottoman Empire in Europe in 1839 consisted of Turkey proper, Bulgaria, Thrace, Thessaly, Macedonia, Bosnia, Herzegovina, Albania, Montenegro, and the islands of Chios, Samos, Lemnos, and Lesbos.

The same disintegrating forces, namely, the revolts of the subject peoples and the imperialism of the great powers, were at work, though to a far less degree, in Asiatic Turkey. Asia Minor (i.e. Anatolia, and the six vilayets known as Armenia)

[5] Privileges acquired by the Serbs in the treaties of Bucharest (May 16, 1812), Akerman (October 7, 1826), and Adrianople (September 14, 1829) were reaffirmed by Article 28 of the Treaty of Paris, March 30, 1856.

[6] After considerable negotiation this boundary was decided upon July 21, 1832. Cf. C. W. Crawley, *The Question of Greek Independence, a Study of British Policy in the Near East, 1821–1833*, Cambridge (England), 1930, Ch. 14.

[7] After the Crimean War the powers substituted for the Russian protectorate a collective guarantee (Article 22 of the Treaty of Paris, 1856), and this arrangement held until the independence of Rumania was recognized by the Treaty of Berlin (Article 43) in 1878.

[8] Crete, governed by Mehemet Ali 1822–1840, was restored to the Sultan by the Convention of July 15, 1840.

remained a part of the Turkish Empire throughout its existence. The first and undoubtedly the most important loss of
territory in the non-European half of the empire was Egypt,
which became *de facto* autonomous under Mehemet Ali in 1808,
though it was considered a part of the Sultan's domain until
Britain established her protectorate there in 1914.[9] After 1808
Mahmoud continued to look upon Mehemet Ali as his vassal,
though Mehemet for his part grew more and more independent,
until in the last years of the Sultan's reign both lord and vassal
were in death throes over the issue. Intervention by the powers
was finally necessary to protect the Sultan, and preserve Syria
and Arabia for the crumbling Turkish state. Tripoli remained
Turkish until annexed by Italy in 1912; Tunis became a
French colony in 1881, France acquiring her original foothold
in Algeria in 1830.[10] Thus, it can be seen that the Ottoman
Empire in the nineteenth century was difficult to rule not only
because of its size and extent, but also because Turkey was
not one nation, but "an agglomeration of nations."[11]

There are many other facts, however, which must be considered to understand completely the perplexing problem of
maintenance not to mention reform of that "agglomeration of
nations" known as the Ottoman Empire. These extensive dominions were inhabited by more than thirty millions of people.
It is impossible to determine with precision the total population
of the Sultan's domain both because of the absence of population records, and because parts of the Sultan's territories

[9] Egypt's status in the nineteenth century has been well defined as that of a
"semi-autonomous entity under the final suzerainty of the Sultan." Though the
Sultans continued to invest the rulers of Egypt with their power, they really
had no final authority over their Egyptian vassals. Cf. V. A. O'Rourke, *The
Juristic Status of Egypt and the Sudan*, Baltimore, 1935, pp. 29, 35.

[10] It might be said that Algeria, Tunis, and Tripoli were to all intents and
purposes free at the beginning of the nineteenth century; they completely disregarded the Sultan, their suzerain, and since he had no powerful fleet it was
almost impossible to subject them to his law.

[11] M. A. Ubicini, *Letters on Turkey*, 2 vols., London, 1856, vol. I, Introduction, p. 11. For a contemporary description of the various peoples of the Ottoman Empire, see Le Baron Antoine Juchereau de Saint Denys, *Histoire de
l'Empire Ottoman, 1792–1844*, 4 vols., Paris, 1844, Vol. I, pp. 1–23.

changed hands frequently, being lost entirely or merely remaining under the nominal control of the Sultan.[12] Urquhart estimates that in 1833 there were twelve millions in European Turkey and Greece alone, while other guesses range from seven to twenty-two millions.[13]

Urquhart's explanation of the difficulties of ascertaining the population of Turkey, and the manner in which he reached his conservative estimate are worth noting. "Previous to the last Russian war," he writes in 1833, "the Porte entertained the most extravagant notions as to the population of the country. It trusted to its old registers, or admitted unscrupulously the swollen estimates of the different bouluc bashis, beys, and pashas, who by lengthening their muster-rolls endeavored to increase their own importance. But the passage of the Balkans has quickened their sight, and awakened energy with apprehension, statistical details have been demanded throughout the whole country, and these can easily be detected from the municipalities. The governors and pashas of late appointment can all read and write, and seem to have taken up statistics with spirit." [14] Urquhart bases his estimate of twelve millions in European Turkey on the proposal of the Grand Vizir in 1827 to organize 300,000 men, "drafted from the Mussulman population, taking one man from fifteen souls, which would give a Mussulman population of 4,500,000 . . . the Mussulman population never exceeds one-third of the Christian." [15]

---

[12] Ubicini estimates 13,487,000 people in European Turkey in 1866, 16,463,000 in Asiatic Turkey, and 750,000 under the Sultan's control in Africa. Ubicini, *État présent de l'Empire Ottoman, op. cit.,* p. 18.

[13] David Urquhart, *Turkey and Its Resources: Its Municipal Organization and Free Trade; the State and Prospects of English Commerce in the East, the New Administration of Greece, Its Revenue and National Possessions,* London, 1833, p. 270. In 1841 missionaries estimated seven millions in European Turkey. *Missionary Herald,* vol. 37, 1841, p. 71.

[14] Urquhart, *Turkey and Its Resources,* p. 271.

[15] Urquhart, *op. cit.,* p. 272; Urquhart classified the population by race and language, which he believes "preferable to uncertain territorial subdivisions," or to ranging them under the definite heads of Christians and Turks:

Osmanlis — Turkish race and language, all Mussulman 700,000

Greeks — Hellenic race and language, all Christians 2,050,000

Albanians — Skipertar race and language, two-thirds Mussulman 1,600,000

The population of Anatolia, Syria, Arabia, Tripoli, and Algeria about 1800 is almost impossible to estimate. Mehemet Ali claimed approximately six million souls as his subjects, and since Egypt was the most populous of the Turkish Asiatic and African provinces, one can get some idea of the total number of the Sultan's non-European subjects; ten to twelve million seems a rather conservative estimate. Thus, if one computes the total population for the whole Turkish Empire in 1800 at approximately thirty million people, he is within reasonable bounds.[16]

To classify this population sharply into Mussulmans, i.e. descendants of the original Ottoman invaders, and non-Mussulmans or *rayahs* (Greeks, Jews, Christians, pagans), is oversimplification of a very difficult problem. The Ottoman government itself was really responsible for this classification according to religious faith, because for tax and recruiting purposes it usually separated the followers of Mohammed from those who declared some other faith. Many western writers have continued to use these groupings, much to the detriment of the Turks as rulers. Although all admit the Turkish government to be a kind of politico-religious state, one should not thereby imply that non-Mussulmans were not tolerated within the Sultan's dominions. To be sure, *rayahs* were looked upon as inferiors by all the followers of Mohammed, and many were the humiliations which they suffered because of their inferior

Sclavonic race and dialects — one-third Mussulman, two-thirds Christian	6,600,000
Vlachi Greek Church	600,000
Other races — Gypsies (200,000); Jews (250,000); Armenians (100,000); Franks, etc. (50,000)	600,000
	12,150,000
Moldavia and Wallachia	1,500,000
Total	13,650,000

[16] For further information on population, see David Ross, *Opinions of the European Press on the Eastern Question*, London, 1836, p. 309; E. H. Michelsen, *The Ottoman Empire and Its Resources*, London, 1853, pp. 138-139; A. Besse, *L'Empire Turc*, Paris, 1854, p. 91; Ubicini, *Letters*, vol. I, Letter #1. M. D'Ohsson, *Tableau général de l'Empire Ottoman*, 7 vols., Paris, 1788-1791.

position, yet in few cases was their treatment more unfair than
that received by protestants in many western catholic states or
by unbelievers in some Calvinistic communities at an earlier
period.

Western writers have too often confused Christianity with
civilization and toleration. An interesting study might be made
of Turkey as the haven for peoples oppressed in some of the
supposedly more civilized states, such as the Jews who in the
nineteenth century crossed the borders of the Ottoman state in
their flight from Russia, or the Hungarians who during the
revolution of 1848 were given refuge within Turkish territory.
There is ample proof from the writings of missionaries, travellers, and observers of life in the Levant that the Mussulmans
were rarely as hard with the *rayahs* as some of the renegade
Christians who for political reasons had gone over to Islam.
For these reasons the present writer intends to use this distinction of Mussulman and non-Mussulman merely as a convenient
division in explaining the social structure of the Ottoman state.

It would really be more correct to separate the population
of the Ottoman Empire into three categories rather than two as
is usually done. The first group, small in number yet more important, consisted of the Mussulmans who managed the affairs
of Turkey, employed either in the departments of the government, the army, or in the faith, namely, the vizirs, defterdars,
pashas, and ulemamen.[17] A second element, larger than the
first and chiefly important from the economic viewpoint, was
that which consisted of Jews, Franks, Greeks, and Armenians,
who were the directors of industry, commerce, and banking.[18]
The remainder of the population constituted the third group;

[17] Approximately three and a half million or about one-tenth of the total
population were of this official class according to Marshal Marmont, *The Present
State of Turkey*, London, 1839, p. 95.

[18] Marmont suggests that this element in the population made reform difficult both because they were regarded by many old Turks as potential enemies
of the state, and also because they opposed a regenerated Turkey which might
further limit their power. "We may reasonably ask," he writes, "by what
circumstances, or process the Turkish Empire can be reconstructed, or restored?
The base on which it was founded has disappeared, and we cannot expect that

here are found the poorer classes, chiefly peasants and artisans, those who bore the brunt of the burdens, the majority of whom were Christians. The first group is the most important, since they were the ones responsible not only for the condition of Turkey at the beginning of the nineteenth century, but also for the success of any reforms which might later occur. In a brief survey it is impossible to discuss adequately the social organization of the Ottoman state. Moreover, since in Turkey, as in any semi-feudal state, to distinguish sharply between the social and governmental organization is impracticable, I shall pass directly to an outline of how this vast territory was governed.

The Ruling Institution [19] or government of the Ottoman Empire consisted of the Sultan [20] and his family, officers of the household, executive officers of the government, the standing army, and the young men being educated for positions in the army, court, and the government. But since the Ottoman state at the beginning of the nineteenth century was essentially an autocracy, the center of power was naturally the seraglio,[21] or palace of the Sultan. Here the Sultan met his advisors, formulated his policies, and issued many of the decrees which ruled the state. Equally important in practice was the government palace, or Sublime Porte,[22] a building not far removed from the seraglio, where the Grand Vizir resided, and where some of the other important ministers maintained their offices. Here also met on occasion the Supreme Council of the Empire, which

the Christians, who form a majority of the population of European Turkey, will take part in the combinations required to regenerate this country, and thus prolong their state of bondage." *Ibid.*, p. 98.

[19] Lybyer, *op. cit.*, p. 36.

[20] Originally meaning power or authority, the word *sultan* soon came to be used for the man who had assumed that power and authority. T. W. Arnold, *The Caliphate*, Oxford University Press, London, 1924, p. 202. For a discussion of the powers of the Sultan, see Ubicini, *Letters*, vol. I, Letter #6.

[21] An excellent description of the seraglio, the palace school, etc., will be found in Barnette Miller, *Beyond the Sublime Porte*, New Haven, 1931.

[22] In the literature on nineteenth century Turkey the term "Porte" is often loosely used to refer either to the Sultan and his government, or to either one or the other. In the strictest sense it should be used only to designate the administrative bureaucracy of the Ottoman government.

assisted the Sultan in administrative as well as advisory capacity. The Divan,[23] as this council was called, was composed of the Grand Vizir,[24] who, as first lieutenant of the Sultan, managed the civil affairs of the government, the Reis Effendi whose duties corresponded to those of a minister of foreign affairs in western cabinets, the Seraskier or commander-in-chief of the army, the Capitan Pasha or admiral of the fleet, and several defterdars, the chief of whom was comparable to a secretary of the treasury,[25] the others managing finances, trade, and interior affairs.[26]

Though in theory appointed by the Sultan on the merit basis, these officials of the central government often purchased their positions, bribery and corruption being rampant in direct proportion to the weakness of the sultans.[27] During Mahmoud IInd's reign there was less dishonesty in high places than in

[23] The grand conseil d'état composed of all the ministers, the *ulema*, and pashas in and around Constantinople rendered advice on general problems; for administrative purposes beylerbeys, pashas, and military officials from outlying districts were often called in for advice and instruction. This larger council was in no sense a *mejliss* or assembly for legislative purposes. Juchereau de Saint Denys, *op. cit.*, II, 33. Originally the Sultan presided over the Divan in person; in due course this task was turned over to the Grand Vizir whose position then became comparable to that of prime minister. W. L. Wright, *Ottoman Statecraft, the Book of Counsel for Vezirs and Governors*, Princeton, 1935, p. 23. When Selim III (1789–1807) reorganized the council, the power of the Grand Vizir was weakened. After the revolution of 1807–1808 the Grand Vizirs tried in vain to reestablish their power, but Mahmoud resumed the old practice of sitting with his ministers in council to learn their advice. R. Walsh, *A Residence in Constantinople*, 2 vols., London, 1836, II, 307. During the last years of Mahmoud's reign, however, he became more autocratic and dictatorial, and as a result the council was weakened. In 1839 Abdul Medjid restored the council with the Grand Vizir in a powerful position over it. Juchereau de Saint Denys, *op. cit.*, II, p. 32.

[24] For a valuable survey of the power and authority of the Grand Vizir, cf. Wright, *op. cit.*, ch. I, pp. 64–86.

[25] *Ibid.*, ch. III, pp. 94–109.

[26] The mechanics of the Ottoman government are well described in D'Ohsson, *op. cit.*, vol. VII, bks. 1–9. See also Juchereau de Saint Denys, *op. cit.*, II, 23–42. The relation of the officers of the central government to the local officials is graphically portrayed in Crawley, *The Question of Greek Independence*, Appendix VI.

[27] Under the weakest sultans bribery was found in all phases of the government, from the highest to the lowest offices. Cf. Wright, *op. cit.*, ch. II, pp. 87–93.

many of the previous periods, the Sultan having perceived that
simony had weakened the central government, and that Turkey's decline as a great power was coincident with the increasing influence of the harem, which was the clearing house for
much of the bribery. Of course this does not mean that corrupt
practices did not exist in Mahmoud's reign, nor that he was entirely free from favorites, but for the most part he depended
upon the advice of able men such as Bairactar, his principal
minister at the beginning of his reign, Pertev-Effendi, the Minister of Home Affairs, or Reschid Pasha, the Minister of Foreign Affairs during a part of the *tanzimat* period.

The Grand Vizir, in theory a kind of prime minister, was
usually a man of wealth, often closely related to the Sultan by
way of marriage with one of the Sultan's daughters. His power
varied according to the character of the Sultan. During the
latter part of Mahmoud's reign the Sultan himself managed
the office.[28] At times too the Grand Vizir was forced to share
his authority with the Sheik-ul-Islam who was the chief of the
ulema, the learned men of the realm who interpreted the laws.
Venerated by the people because of his religious-legal capacity
and regarded very highly by the *ulema*, the Sheik was often
able to oppose the wishes not only of the Grand Vizir but also
of the Sultan himself. As regards the other officials near to the
Sultan their functions were largely what their titles imply and
call for no further elaboration.

Though such a system of central administration resembles
that of certain other strong monarchies, in practice it was far
from being an efficient despotism. "The firmans," wrote Ross,
"do not obtain on their first promulgation, the prompt and
minute observance that laws obtain in European governments,
with ponderous, complicated, and oppressive machinery, the
very constitution of the Turkish government, prevents it, and

[28] One of Abdul Medjid's early acts was to restore the Grand Vizir to his
rightful position in the government. For further details on this office, and other
ministers of the central government see Ubicini, *Letters*, vol. I, Letter #2, and
Besse, *op. cit.*, pp. 63–90.

this simple fact proves, how absurd it is to apply the sweeping and vague term of despotism to the Turkish government." [29] If one examines the local administration,[30] one is further convinced of the truth of this statement.

Under Selim III (1789–1807) the empire was divided into twenty-six vilayets [31] or provinces, each of which was ruled by a beylerbey [32] or pasha [33] of at least three horse-tails. These vilayets were in turn divided into military districts or sandjaks, ruled by an aga or military governor, and these into livas or pashaliks, which were managed by lesser pashas, often called beys, of one horse-tail.[34] A few of the livas were managed by governors appointed for life, though the majority of the pashas received annual appointments, and if a pasha knew how to play the political game, he could be sure of controlling the same pashalik for many years.

A provincial pasha had extensive powers as an administrator, and was a judicial officer as well, having power of life and death over his subjects. He maintained an elaborate court, in most respects a miniature of the Sultan's at Constantinople; he had his own army which he used to keep the peace in his territory, though it was subject to the Sultan's summons at any time; he

[29] Ross, *op. cit.*, p. xx.

[30] Ubicini, *Letters*, I, 45–47.

[31] Called eyalets until reorganized and limited in number by Selim III. Mahmoud II further reduced the number of vilayets to nineteen by 1833, and the number of sandjaks to two hundred and forty. Cf. Crawley, *The Question of Greek Independence*, Appendix VI.

[32] D'Ohsson, *op. cit.*, VII, 276–277.

[33] The title pasha, literally meaning chief, was sometimes applied to all governors of the subdivisions of the empire, though the provincial governors were usually called beylerbeys or vizirs. The title is often found after the names of important administrative officials as well. In the latter sense it was the highest official title of honor which might be conferred by the Sultan, in some respects not unlike the European titles of nobility. It was not, however, hereditary, nor was it attached to possessions like a feudal title, nor did it give rank to the wife of the man so honored. After the World War the title was used for military men entirely, and finally abolished in 1934. Cf. *Encyclopedia of Islam*, vol. 3, pp. 1030–1033.

[34] Beys flaunted one horse-tail, pashas two, and vizirs three; grand vizirs were allowed five, and the Sultan alone seven horse-tails. Cf. Crawley, *op. cit.*, Appendix VI, and T. Thornton, *The Present State of Turkey*, 2 vols., London, 1809, I, 155–156n.

had his own tax-collectors, his treasurers, in fact in more ways
than one the pasha was a local sultan comparable with the
great lords of a feudal state. Their power was so extensive that
it was the great ambition of most Turkish officials to one day
control a pashalik. Often this ambition was satisfied by means
of money which could be had from the Greek or Armenian
bankers. The bankers having established a client in a pashalik
continued to be the real power behind the throne, making exorbitant demands of the pasha which he in turn passed on to his
subjects.[35] Thus the system which in itself was reasonably
sound was weakened by these non-Turk rulers who were often
more merciless with the people than the Turks themselves.

The criticism is frequently made that the independence which
the pashas exercised was the greatest obstacle to good government. In some cases the independence of the pashas made for
prosperity in the provinces,[36] but the indirect relationship of
ruler and those ruled was a great source of weakness in the
Ottoman Empire. Yet, when one reflects on the size of the
Turkish state and the number of people it contained, one concludes that close relationship of government and citizen would
be a problem in any state of the same magnitude. The pasha
system in practice, however, greatly enhanced this difficulty.
As long as the pashas transmitted their annual dues to the
Porte, the Sultans cared but little how they ruled their provinces, unless their rule was so distasteful to the people as to
cause revolt.

According to Ross, "government leaves to custom, to habits,
to opinion, and to local necessities the direction of the greater
part of the interests of the people. Its sovereignty is only exercised in higher spheres, and presses not upon individual existence. It is content to exist under the sanction of laws which in
principle are unchangeable." [37] Often the pashas did not under-

---

[35] Frequently the pashalik itself was purchased by Greek or Armenian men
of wealth who reaped a harvest from the taxes of the district.

[36] A. Slade, *Records of Travel in Turkey and Greece,* 1829–1831, 2 vols.,
London, 1833, I, 333.

[37] Ross, *op. cit.*, p. 13.

stand what was expected of them by the Sultan, and he in turn did not realize how they treated his subjects in their districts. Revolts against the Sultan were frequent, partly because of the insatiable ambition of the pashas, and also because the people were out of touch with the central authority at Constantinople. "The will of the Sultan was disobeyed, because it is not known to the governed as well as the governors." [38] The Hatti Sherif of 1839, a proclamation for the people as well as the governors, was aimed to correct this fault.

Lack of knowledge of the Sultan's will was, however, but one reason for the misgovernment which existed in the Ottoman Empire at the opening of the nineteenth century. As has already been pointed out, many of the Sultan's pashas were indifferent to his wishes so imbued were they with their own strength and importance. To overcome this independence the Sultan needed a strong, efficient force to carry out his decrees, in short an army which could impress his will upon the recalcitrant and disobedient governors.

The Sultan's army [39] was not small compared with those of other powers in Europe at the same time. The number of men enrolled has received varied estimates, some of which are as high as 300,000. Even though this figure were known to be correct, it would not prove its strength, because only a small proportion of the men listed on the army rolls were trained fighters; [40] moreover the army as a whole was not reliable, because of its lack of discipline.[41] This weakness was more important with respect to domestic affairs in time of peace than in time of foreign war. When attacked by some outside power, the Turks generally rallied to the Sultan's banner, and because they were naturally good warriors, they usually offered stiff

[38] Ross, *op. cit.*, p. xix.
[39] Juchereau de Saint Denys, *op. cit.*, I, 343–401.
[40] Probably 40,000 men in the first quarter of the nineteenth century. Ross, *op. cit.*, p. 309.
[41] For a detailed account of the state of the Ottoman Empire with special emphasis on its defenses by an army man, see Marmont, *op. cit.*, and *Foreign Quarterly Review*, vol. 24, #48, London, 1840, pp. 395 ff.

resistance. In peace time, however, the Sultan found extreme difficulty in commanding a force sufficient to maintain order among the people and to enforce his decrees.[42] This weakness of the military organization of Turkey has long been considered one of the two great evils of the Ottoman system, the other being the defective appointment and control of the provincial governors.[43]

A third vulnerable spot in the Turkish state was its tax system. In order to maintain a state of Turkey's proportions a great deal of money was necessary, and as a result there grew up several forms of taxes, public taxes, *avanias* or extortions of the pashas, corvées, not to mention various communal taxes for each municipality and its environs.[44] One of the most critical observers on the state of the Ottoman Empire in the early nineteenth century, David Urquhart, has reduced the revenues of general application to five heads. "First. Poll-tax, divided into three classes, *edna, evsat, als,* . . . and fixed at ten, six, and three *leonines* or *piasters*, on adult males not professing the Mohammedan religion (i.e. rayahs). . . . Second. Land tax, one tenth of the produce, or by assessment; the tenth is either paid to the government or affected to military fiefs; a portion of these applied to the support of the governors, the remainder to the body of spahis; 450,000 men are thus calculated to be supported. The tributary lands are farmed at from one third to one half of the net produce. Third. *Nouzouli* and *avarisi*, assessed taxes in towns where the population is not agricultural. Fourth. Customs (gumruk), three per cent on foreign commerce, export and import; internal transport duties at gates of

---

[42] If regular paid troops had been instituted, this would not only have improved the army, but also would have broken down the religious distinctions between the *rayahs*, who paid the *Kharatch* instead of performing military service, and the Mussulman subjects who were on call at any time in the event of war.

[43] Cf. ante, pp. 13–15.

[44] John MacGregor, *Commercial Statistics, a Digest of the Productive Resources, Commercial Legislation, Customs Tariffs, Navigation, Port, and Quarantine Laws, and Charges, Shipping, Imports and Exports, and the Monies, Weights, and Measures of All Nations Including All British Commercial Treaties with Foreign States,* 4 vols., London, 1847–1848, II, 180.

towns and bridges. Fifth. Excise upon gunpowder, snuff, wine, and duties on various articles of late introduction, chiefly established to meet the expenses of the new organization under Selim the third." [45] To this list should also be added the *ichtisab* or indirect taxes.[46]

Aside from the number of taxes and their amounts, the mode of collection was a common grievance. The usual method of collecting taxes was by farm (ilitzam), each tax being auctioned off to the highest bidder. Ilitzam, first instituted in the fifteenth century under Mohammed II (1451–1481), had undergone many changes by 1800. According to Urquhart, "the farms have been increased, diminished, and subdivided, new branches of revenue have been introduced, and old ones newly appropriated; and all those modifications have applied to the subdivisions of the revenue, both generally and territorially. In some districts, certain of the ilitzam are farmed, as a matter of course, yearly by the pasha — in others there are farmers for life; in some districts, there are distinct farmers for the different branches, in others the whole taxes are at once compounded for; but all these distinctions vanish in practice, which resolves itself, . . . into a sum of so much demanded from each district or village, which the peasants are allowed to collect as they please; the mode may therefore vary in each village, but the object in all, is to adjust taxation to property." [47] One need

---

[45] Urquhart, *Turkey and Its Resources*, pp. 86–87. Cf. also Juchereau de Saint Denys, *op. cit.*, I, 401–414. The poll tax or *Kharatch* was paid by the *rayahs* (non-Mussulman subjects) in lieu of military service; a few Turks paid this also, though the great majority were expected to defend their country in case of need. "Of all the imposts, that of the Kharatch or Capitation tax, although moderate in its amount, was the most burdensome to the Rayahs on account of the mode of its collection. As this tax is attached to the individual, the slightest abuse in the mode of collection immediately assumes the form of a serious attack on individual liberty, which, as we have already stated, is here the object of much more real respect, than is commonly imagined." Ross, *op. cit.*, p. 86.

[46] Trade licenses, stamp duties, postage, tolls, and mines and fisheries taxes.

[47] Urquhart, *Turkey and Its Resources*, p. 86. Urquhart, who looked upon the municipal administrations as the most efficient in Turkey, the one ray of hope for better government, thought they should be given complete control of finances. "The local and municipal expenses, independent of arbitrary exactions,

scarcely add, after such an admirable description, that the object was seldom attained.[48]

As has already been indicated, the pashas were supreme in their provinces, yet they seldom supervised the management of their districts themselves, administrative functions usually being delegated to a subordinate, or mutzelim. Taxation was one of the functions so delegated.[49] In Smyrna, for example, the mutzelim managed the taxes in the most arbitrary fashion. He farmed out the amounts desired, collected through his agents the tenth of the produce, dismissing without redress any proprietor's complaint against the exorbitant exactions, and often punishing the plaintiff by demanding, not a tenth, but one sixth or even a fifth of his annual production. "The same oppression and mismanagement prevails throughout the whole of the pashaliks," writes Marshal Marmont, "as each pasha wrings from those dependent on him everything that he can obtain for his own profit." And not only did the mutzelims ravage the fortunes of the landed proprietors; they also sapped the power of the sovereign, for "not even a fourth part of what is levied reached the coffers of the Sultan." [50] Tax diversion by officials in turn led to debasement of the coinage, and an increase in the number and amounts of taxes, and at times even to the confiscation of property, until, in the early part of the nineteenth

amount at the very lowest, to three times the sum received by the government; and I have no doubt the people would be benefited if the government were to quadruple its demands, allowing the municipal authorities the entire management of the finances." *Ibid.*, p. 87.

[48] Though ilitzam was limited in the nineteenth century, it was not entirely abolished until the establishment of the Turkish Republic in 1918 when direct collection of all taxes was instituted. Cf. Wright, *op. cit.*, p. 98n.

[49] For a brief discussion of the revenues of the pashas, see Thornton, *op. cit.*, I, 156–160.

[50] Marmont, *op. cit.*, pp. 189–190. Because of the inadequacy of statistics it has been impossible to determine the sum total of *miri* or general public revenue, nor of the *hazue*, or revenue derived from the domain lands of the Sultan, from tributes paid by Mehemet Ali and others, the Danubian principalities, presents of the various pashas and functionaries. The admission of the Sultan in the official announcement of the Hatti Sherif de Gulhané (as it appeared in the Turkish Gazette) that an inquiry was necessary to determine the amounts paid in by each district would indicate that accurate accounts had not been kept up to that time.

century, the amount which a man paid to his government in taxes was almost one half his total earnings.[51] Here was a difficult problem, the settlement of which both for the Sultan's and his subjects' benefit involved a fundamental change of governmental administration.

Taxes could not be lowered as long as the multitude of officials dependent on them remained. In the early part of the last century there existed in the Ottoman Empire countless offices, the origin of which had long been forgotten. Under the title "functions of the divan" these offices maintained a corps of retainers far out of proportion to the duties they performed. Subdivision and specialization accounts for some of these posts, but many of the older ones had no relation to each other or to the divan as a whole. Such a situation was bad enough from the political viewpoint of efficient government, but it was also a problem of economics. The treasury already burdened beyond measure could not suffer the drain these offices made upon it; reform would have meant greater efficiency in administration as well as economy, but such a change was all the more difficult because of the number who benefited from the old system.[52]

A fourth problem, one which was peculiar to the Ottoman state, was the relation of the Ruling Institution to the Moslem Institution,[53] a problem which in some respects was similar to the church-state question in western states. In fact, if not in theory, the Sultan was a more powerful ruler because of his

---

[51] William Miller, *The Ottoman Empire, 1801-1913*, Cambridge, 1913, p. 18. Davis considers this too moderate an estimate, decidedly an understatement. Davis, *op. cit.*, p. 279.

[52] "The Government of Constantinople, like that of every other country which has not undergone reform for a long series of reigns, had insensibly been encroached upon by what we denominate as sinecures. Hence, the machinery of the system became considerably complicated, while the treasury was overburdened with expenses, which impeded its operations. Much courage was necessary to institute examination into this labyrinth, and more still to remove all the superfetations which obstructed the free action of the machine. . . ." Ross, *op. cit.*, p. 98.

[53] Composed of the grand mufti or Sheik-ul-Islam who was minister of religion and public law, the *ulema*, local muftis, and dervishes. Cf. Lybyer, *op. cit.*, pp. 36-37.

relationship with the Moslem Institution. A glance at the origin
of the Sultan's title of caliph is the best way of understanding
the relationship of the two.

It is occasionally stated, on the basis of some of the older
accounts of the institutions of the Ottoman Empire,[54] that since
the early sixteenth century the Sultanate and the Caliphate
were one, Selim I having assumed the rights and duties of the
last Abassid caliph, Mutewwekil Al Allah, in 1517, by declaring himself the successor of Mohammed, the religious head of
the Moslem world. The fact that the Sultan's claim to the
Caliphate was weak, because neither Selim nor his successors
were Koreish,[55] is explained away by saying that the power and
splendour of Selim's son, Suleiman, caused his religious subjects to overlook the usurpation, and later when the power of
the sultans waned, time and tradition made up for the absence
of legal claim to the position, until finally practically no devout
Mohammedan questioned the Sultan's headship of the Moslem
religion.

Nothing could be further from the truth than this interpretation. Actually the Sultanate and the Caliphate were not one
and indivisible; the office of caliph was not assumed by Selim I
in 1517, and the title was not always used by the Sultans.[56] In
fact, the Caliph was not primarily a religious functionary;
though he might perform religious deeds, he was "preeminently
a political functionary." [57] According to Arnold, an outstanding authority on the subject, the title caliph "passed from the
supreme authority who used to nominate the Sultana, to any
Sultan who cared to assume the designation once held to be

[54] D'Ohsson, op. cit., I, 269–270; Thornton, op. cit., I, Introduction, xciii.
According to D'Ohsson, Mohammed on his death intrusted the care of Medina
to one of his most devoted disciples, who assumed the title of caliph, i.e. lieutenant or successor, and thus originated the Abassid line. Cf. D'Ohsson, op.
cit., I, 214.
[55] Most noble of all the Arab tribes because of the fact that the Prophet
himself was a member of this group. Ibid., I, 269.
[56] Suleiman seldom used the title of caliph, attaching little importance to it.
Lybyer, op. cit., p. 150.
[57] Arnold, op. cit., p. 17.

unique." [58] In proof, he points out that minor sovereigns had long used the title to enhance their dignity when Murad I, about 1362, assumed the honor.[59] "The Caliph," writes Arnold, "is the 'prince of the faithful,' the universal monarch of the Musalmans, not the head of the Mohammedan religion; in respect of dogma and ritual he is a simple believer, obliged to observe the traditional doctrine as preserved by the ulema. He is defender of the Moslem faith, an enemy of heresy, just as European emperors, kings, and princes were defenders of the faith and the extirpators of heresy in past ages." [60] The fact that the Sultan is often spoken of in official firmans as Padishah [61] of Islam is still further evidence that the Ottoman rulers merely regarded themselves as defenders of the faith. The belief long held that the Mohammedan theocracy was superimposed upon the feudal autocracy of the Ottomans in 1517 [62] no longer has any supporters, but this is not to deny the fact that as Caliph the Sultan was a more powerful person, because of the support which his subjects rendered him religiously, as protector of Islam, when they disagreed with him politically. Traditionally, then, the Sultans did possess the power of the ancient caliphs in addition to that which they claimed as head of the Ruling Institution.[63]

From another point of view, however, the dual nature of the Sultan's power was a source of weakness rather than strength. As defender of the faith, the Sultan necessarily had to act in accord with the interpreters of the Koran, the *ulema*.[64] These "learned men," educated in the medreses or seminaries attached to the mosques, pursued a lengthy and laborious training,[65]

[58] *Ibid.*, p. 129.
[59] *Ibid.*, pp. 118, 130.
[60] *Ibid.*, p. 200.
[61] From Persian Pad, meaning protector, and shah, ruler. Cf. Wright, *op. cit.*, p. 64.
[62] Thornton, *op. cit.*, I, Preface, xix.
[63] Lybyer, *op. cit.*, p. 150.
[64] Ubicini, *Letters*, vol. I, Letter #4; Juchereau de Saint Denys, *op. cit.*, I, 321–343.
[65] Walsh, *op. cit.*, II, 452; Thornton, *op. cit.*, I, 29.

after which they devoted their lives to a study of the Koran and its many commentaries. Highly respected by devout Moslems because of their sacred duties, they exercised considerable power through their chief, the Sheik-ul-Islam, whose acts were at times regarded as having equal weight with those of the Sultan. Convinced that any change would ruin their religious hold over the people, the *ulema* tended to oppose all reform. Their motto, — "meddle not with things established; borrow nothing from infidels, for the law forbids it," — was a constant check on a wise ruler's power.[66] Moreover, by 1800 this body held a very important position in the state. If, for example, a Sultan was overthrown by a revolution, the new Sultan was forced to secure the *ulema's* legal sanction for his accession. The *ulema* had become, in fact, a kind of Supreme Court, responsible for all matters relating to justice,[67] and herein lay their danger. Since they were more interested in their religious duties, they neglected their civil functions, allowed disorder to reign in the courts of law below them, and thus contributed to arbitrary, tyrannical, chaotic government.

Nevertheless, the existence of the *ulema* was as nothing compared to the other religious difficulty which existed in Turkey. The Moslem subjects in the Ottoman Empire were only a fraction of the total population. Of the non-Moslem groups the largest was the Christian population, most of whom, at the opening of the nineteenth century, were followers of the Greek Orthodox faith. As long as these people were guided by their own church organization, all went well, but in 1766–1767 the last two Patriarchates (those of Ochrida, i.e. Macedonia, and Ipek, Serbia) were suppressed by Mustapha III, and the See of Constantinople was made supreme. For many years the Sultan and the Greek Patriarch worked together to control the

---

[66] Ubicini, *Letters*, I, 133, 111.

[67] The cadi or judges for the small towns and the mollahs, who might correspond to municipal judges, were chosen from their ranks. Walsh, *op. cit.*, II, 452. For a detailed description of the ulema as judges of the law as well as students of the Koran, see D'Ohsson, *op. cit.*, I, 257, 482–616; Slade, *Records of Travel in Turkey and Greece*, pp. 119–125.

Mohammedan-Orthodox population within the empire's bound-
aries. There was always present, however, the possibility of
friction, because an increase in the authority of one limited the
power of the other. Finally in 1822, when the Patriarch seemed
to sympathize with the rebellious Greeks, open conflict took
place, eventually resulting in the murder of the Patriarch, an
event which merely spurred the Greeks on in their revolt and
irritated the other Slavic-Orthodox groups. Since religion was
still a very important factor among the Near Eastern peoples,
the close union of religious and political power in the hands of
the Sultan was a constant source of weakness in the Ottoman
state.[68]

Brief as this survey of the Ottoman government at the opening of the nineteenth century is, certain facts are obvious. An
improved administration, a closer relationship between the governors and the governed, an efficient and just tax system, a
more extensive judiciary, and finally a force which could maintain order at home, protect the state from foreign enemies without, and insure the execution of the Sultan's decrees within the
state must be established and maintained. For the empire to
continue in the present state only spelled death. Marmont compared the declining state of Turkey to the human body, "in
which death begins at the extremities, the last struggles for life
being at the heart." [69] If one confined his investigation to Constantinople, one might be convinced that the Ottoman Empire
was far from death, but the further one goes from the capital,
the more certain appears the impending break-up. Yet, before
the most minor reforms could be made, a cancerous growth
which thrived on the general debility of the state, namely the
Janissary Corps, had to be removed.

The Janissaries [70] had long formed by far the most difficult

[68] The fact "that as a nation the Ottoman Turks remained Mohammedan,
. . . has constituted the real tragedy of the Turk! Bound hand and foot by that
scholastic Mohammedanism, . . . they could not amalgamate the subject Christian peoples, already confirmed in nationalism by the events of centuries."
Lybyer, *op. cit.*, pp. 8–9.   [69] Marmont, *op. cit.*, p. 7.
[70] "The term 'Janissary' is derived from the corruption of the words 'yeni

internal problem of the Ottoman state.[71] This praetorian guard probably dates from the fourteenth century; few writers agree as to the time and manner of its establishment.[72] Whatever its origin, by the sixteenth century, the Janissaries had become the private guard of the Sultan made up of robust Christians garnered from the various provinces,[73] well-trained, well-paid, well-fed, and forbidden to marry lest family responsibilities hinder its primary task of protecting the Sultans. The successors of Suleiman relaxed the rigid rules governing the Corps, recruited Turks as well as Christians (1584), permitted marriage, and even allowed sons of Janissaries to carry on in the guard (1574).[74] Later Sultans heaped other privileges on their private guards, privileges which became a source of future trouble, for when later Sultans restricted their rights, the Janissaries became sullen and mutinous. Under Murad IV (1622–1640) dewshirme was given up,[75] the Corps was limited entirely to Turks, and the hereditary principle of membership was definitely established. From that time on it became more and more

---

cheri" which, in the Turkish language meant 'new soldiers.' " Marmont, *op. cit.*, p. 33; *Encyclopedia of Islam*, II, 572.

[71] Wright, *op. cit.*, pp. 39–42, 45, 110–115; Lybyer, *op. cit.*, pp. 91–97.

[72] Whether the Corps was begun by Murad in 1362 or by Bayezid in 1389 was a moot question among the older writers, the majority of whom favored 1362. Cf. Thornton, *op. cit.*, I, 226; Slade, *Records of Travel in Turkey and Greece*, I, 300; Marmont, *op. cit.*, p. 33; H. A. Gibbons, *The Foundation of the Ottoman Empire, a History of the Osmanlis up to the Death of Bayezid I (1300–1403)*, Oxford, 1916, pp. 117–121; D'Ohsson believes the Corps existed in 1330; cf. D'Ohsson, *op. cit.*, VII, 311. Modern scholars make little attempt to establish the exact date of the origin of the Corps, suggesting in place of the old theories that the Janissaries were an outgrowth of the Bektashi order of dervishes. Cf. W. L. Langer, and R. P. Blake, "The Rise of the Ottoman Turks and its Historical Background," *American Historical Review*, vol. 37, #3, April, 1932, pp. 497–499.

[73] The process of impressing Christians for the Corps was known as "Dewshirme." Cf. *Encyclopedia of Islam*, I, 952. Any member of the Ruling Institution might be recruited by this method. Wright, *op. cit.*, p. 24. Impressment does not account for the origin of the Janissaries, however, since it was "only gradually and irregularly resorted to, . . ." Cf. Langer and Blake, *op. cit.*, p. 504.

[74] Wright, *op. cit.*, pp. 39–40.

[75] The last instance of the use of dewshirme was in 1637, though the regulations providing for it were not abolished until 1750. Wright, *op. cit.*, p. 39.

an organization of political intrigue, more intent on serving its own selfish interests than in fulfilling its duties to the state.[76]

In the course of the next two centuries the Corps continued to increase numerically [77] which of course made it more of a political force in the nation. There was no corresponding increase in the service which it rendered the state, however. In fact, discipline was more difficult to exact as the numbers increased, and as it began to have authority throughout the Empire. In proportion as it declined as a fighting force, it became more corrupt, more luxury-loving, more of a burden on the state. All manner of fraudulent and corrupt practices were traceable to the Janissary Corps. Arrogant of their privileges, they opposed every attempt to reform the state; in this they sought and often received the support of the *ulema* and other conservative forces favoring the *status quo;* [78] in a word, the Janissaries were the curse of good government, and their power in Turkey was most indicative of the weakness of the Sultan's administration.[79]

[76] The murder of Othman II in 1622 by members of the guard shows to what extent the aims of the Corps had been reversed. Cf. Juchereau de Saint Denys, *op. cit.*, III, xiii.

[77] It is estimated that more than 100,000 Janissaries were registered in 1825, two thousand of whom were regular soldiers, the remainder being armorers, boatmen, butchers, bakers, etc., each group of which was organized as a separate guild. Wright, *op. cit.*, p. 41. Thornton's figure of 40,000 in 1800 is unquestionably an underestimate, and does not include many of the hangers-on. Thornton, *op. cit.*, I, 226.

[78] Ubicini, *Letters*, Introduction, p. 7; Walsh, *op. cit.*, II, 265, 309–310.

[79] The writer has found but one nineteenth century observer of Turkish affairs who saw any good in the Janissary Corps. Slade, who travelled in Turkey and Greece in 1829–1831, maintained that the Janissaries were a much maligned organization; that they were not a cancer of the whole empire, but merely to the government at Constantinople because of their proximity to the seraglio; that in one respect they performed one of the tasks that western parliaments performed, in that they prevented the ruler from becoming too despotic. Corruption within the administration, for which the Janissaries were not responsible, was far more harmful to the empire, he maintained, than the existence of this special body of troops. Cf. Slade, *Records of Travel in Turkey and Greece, op. cit.*, I, 139, 306–309, 321. Slade's remarks need not be taken too seriously, however, because a few pages earlier he contradicted the above with the statement: "In fine, rapid as has been the decline of the Ottoman Empire since victory ceased to attend its arms, I venture to assert, that it would have

The first Sultan to realize the strength of the Janissaries was Murad IV (1622–1640). At one time he considered replacing the guard with regular troops. The casual observer might wonder that he did not succeed, since the Corps numbered little more than 40,000 men at the time; but it must be remembered that this corrupt, disunited, bribe-ridden organization would unite in the face of opposition and could present a strong front against anyone intent on depriving it of its privileges. It is interesting to note that it was during Murad's reign that the Corps succeeded in becoming a strictly Turkish hereditary body (with the abolition of dewshirme). While its existence was the greatest source of weakness in the Ottoman regime, eventually its "excess of arbitrary power" brought about its downfall.[80] But meanwhile all reforms had to wait until the nation was purged of this rebellious group which virtually ruled the state.[81]

The first ruler worthy of the title, "reform Sultan," [82] was Selim III (1789–1807). The earlier attacks of Russia and Austria which left the Turkish Empire in a rather hopelessly

---

been tenfold more rapid but for the privileged orders — the derebeys and the ulema. Without their powerful weight and influence — effect of hereditary wealth and sanctity — the Janissaries would long since have cut Turkey in slices, and have ruled it as the Mamelukes ruled Egypt." *Ibid.*, p. 125. It would appear that, since Slade visited the Near East after the Corps had been destroyed, yet before Mahmoud's early reforms began to bear fruit, his remarks represent a desire for a return to the old order of things about which he knew very little first hand. It is significant also that this defense of the Janissaries does not appear in his second book, *Turkey, Greece, and Malta*, published in 1837. On the contrary this volume is largely a plea for England to assist Turkey in reforming herself in order to be able to throw off the Russian yoke.

[80] ". . . the gradual awakening of the ancient Ottoman institutions has been principally occasioned by the constantly increasing influence, during a long series of years, of the military oligarchy of the Janissaries. This *imperium in imperio* absorbed all the powers of the state, pressing equally on the authority of the prince, and on the rights of the people. This powerful body, however, owed its destruction to the excess of its arbitrary power, . . ." Ross, *op. cit.*, p. 34.

[81] The extent of its power in the early nineteenth century is well portrayed in the manner in which it deposed Selim III, set up Mustapha IV, and when he was overthrown, placed certain conditions on Mahmoud II which he was forced to accept. See *supra*, pp. 28–29.

[82] Selim III "laid the corner-stone of reform in Turkey." Ubicini, *Letters*, II, 422.

disorganized state unveiled many of the evils which were ruin-
ing the country.[83] Ambition to rule a strong state or none he
early espoused the cause of reform. The military power was his
special interest as it was that of earlier and succeeding sultans.
Through his minister Hussein Pasha he planned a complete
regeneration of the army and navy. Fortresses were repaired,
foreign army instructors were called in (chiefly Frenchmen;
the British were called upon for advice concerning the navy),
military schools were established. Selim had hopes of establishing a new army corps modelled after those of western
Europe which in time might supplant the hated Janissaries. In
1793 a new military regulation, which had been suggested by a
reform council established shortly after he ascended the throne,
decreed that a new corps of 12,000 men, the *nisami* by name,
was to be established; this was to consist of volunteers, since
conscription was opposed by the populace at large as well as
by the Janissaries, and was to be given the best training that
western officers could provide. This noble experiment failed,
however, when few men volunteered for this new unit.[84]

The failure of this scheme, very dear to Selim's heart, and
one which was undoubtedly foiled by the machinations of the
Janissaries, merely intensified his hatred of this body. Selim's
attitude toward the Janissaries is nowhere better evinced than
in the beginnings of the Serb revolt in 1804. That he gave direct
encouragement to the *rayahs* in that area to rise against the
Janissaries who were oppressing them beyond endurance is
generally accepted.[85] Although successful in this particular instance (a doubtful triumph since the Serbs under the leadership of Kara George, having suppressed the Janissaries, turned
against the Sultan himself), Selim could accomplish nothing of

[83] Mustapha III (1757–1774) was convinced by the Russian victories of the
need of adopting western methods and in 1770 sought the council of Baron de
Tott for that purpose, but the Sultan's death in 1774 cut short any hoped for
reforms. Cf. V. Bérard, "Réforme Ottomane," *Revue de Paris*, vol. 5, September
1, 1908, p. 199.

[84] Public opinion did not support the new army, but was still loyal to the
Janissaries, as was the *ulema*. Juchereau de Saint Denys, *op. cit.*, II, 269.

[85] Davis, *op. cit.*, p. 288.

lasting importance in the face of the resistance of the Janissaries.[86] It must be said of this first reforming Sultan that although his attempts were well-meant, he lacked the courage to
deal ruthlessly with his enemies. His ideas were good, but his
methods lacked force as well as tact. An examination of his
army reforms shows that he failed to take into account the
traditions, religious prejudices, and racial differences of his
people. From another point of view his failure merely proves
the strength of the old Turks and the Janissaries. Finally, in
May, 1807, the Janissaries rose against this Europeanizing
ruler,[87] deposed him, and placed Mustapha IV at the head of
the government.[88]

Mustapha IV, conservative by nature, as well as being the
puppet of the reactionary Janissaries, immediately exorcised
all the reforms of his predecessor.[89] For the short space of a
few months Mustapha's reign appeared serene, but there was
trouble brewing beneath the surface. Resentful of Mustapha's
weakness the Europeanized army officers, under the leadership
of Mustapha, the Bairactar,[90] Pasha of Rustchuk, began a
counter-revolution.[91] Following the deposition of the Sheik-ul-
Islam and eight of his supporters (*ulema*-men) Bairactar

[86] Slade, in his attempt to defend the Janissaries, maintained that Selim III
was not a sincere reformer; that he merely sought to westernize his state in
order to enhance his despotism; that the Janissaries merely aimed to prevent the
establishment of a complete autocracy. Slade, *Records of Travel in Turkey and
Greece*, p. 314.

[87] "Le sultan Selim était susceptible de sentiments éléves; mais, trop peu con-
fiant en lui-même et ne voyant autour de lui que des hommes tremblants, plus
disposés à se cacher qu'à la defendre, il partageait la terreur générale." Juchereau de Saint Denys, *op. cit.*, II, 190.

[88] For an authentic account of the revolution which lasted from May, 1807
until July, 1808, see Juchereau de Saint Denys, *op. cit.*, vol. II, ch. 6–9; see also
M. J. Bastelburger, *Die militarischen Reformen unter Mahmoud II*, Gotha,
1874, ch. 2; C. MacFarlane, *Constantinople in 1828*, London, 1829, pp. 296–308;
and J. M. Jouannin, *Turquie*, Paris, 1853, pp. 373–382.

[89] Jouannin, *op. cit.*, p. 374.

[90] Marmont describes him as "proud and haughty, . . . a man of energy and
courage, . . . a great character," in spite of his being "profoundly ignorant."
Marmont, *op. cit.*, pp. 43–44.

[91] The threat of a Russian invasion enabled Bairactar to raise an army of
over 12,000 men. Juchereau de Saint Denys, *op. cit.*, II, 173.

stormed the Seraglio, July 8, 1808. Though the assault was successful, the rebels were disappointed to find that before surrendering the reactionaries had murdered the deposed Sultan, Selim III, who had been imprisoned by Mustapha IV.[92] Mustapha IV was deposed, and his nephew, Mahmoud II, the first Sultan really deserving of the title, reformer, was established as the ruler of the Ottoman state.

Mahmoud IInd's first year was anything but successful from the point of view of rejuvenating the declining Ottoman power. He appointed Bairactar Grand Vizir, and set out to carry out the reforms proposed by his inspiring predecessor Selim III, particularly to destroy the Janissaries who had been responsible for the revolution and his friend's death. One of his first acts was to have Mustapha IV put to death since he was the symbol of the opposition movement. The Grand Vizir, believing that the situation was under control, disbanded his private army prematurely; the Janissaries immediately revolted again, and in the course of the trouble Bairactar was killed.[93] Without his able assistant Mahmoud II was at the mercy of the opposition, who dictated the conditions under which they would suffer his remaining in power, the general nature of which was that he lay aside any hopes of restoring or carrying further the reform measures of Selim III.[94] Such was the inauspicious beginning of the thirty-one year reign of Mahmoud II.

Though forced to knuckle to the reactionaries, Mahmoud did not surrender his reforming spirit to the opposition, and in the next thirty years great changes occurred in the internal structure of the Ottoman state, the most important of which was the complete destruction of the Janissary Corps in 1826. No less than eighteen years of his reign passed before Mahmoud was able to take this all-important step, a step which made his later

[92] Cf. Barnette Miller, *op. cit.*, pp. 209–210.

[93] Jouannin, *op. cit.*, p. 382.

[94] This victory for the Janissaries in 1808 was the real cause of their ruin eighteen years later. They became so overbearing in the years following their 1808 triumph that they lost the support of the *ulema* and the people. Juchereau de Saint Denys, *op. cit.*, II, 269.

reforms and those of his successor, Abdul Medjid, possible. A brief sketch of Mahmoud's character and ability may help to explain how he could wait so long, and how he was eventually successful in the task which had proved too great for his predecessors.

Mahmoud II (1808–1839) was one of the most energetic, dominating sultans of the nineteenth century. Though possessed of a great will common to all autocrats, a will which often made for hasty action, on the whole he exercised good judgment as to the kind of changes which should be made, and how they should be accomplished.[95] At times he seems particularly astute, carrying through his plans with the finesse of a Cavour or a Bismarck. An indefatigable worker, he often managed several departments of the Divan himself, and always held his ministers directly responsible to him for their acts.[96] Here he made the mistake, typical of all absolute rulers, of keeping too much to himself; yet, it must be said in his favor, that his concealment of his plans until he was strong enough to make them effective was one of the reasons why he is today regarded as one of the great reformers of modern Turkey.[97]

Where and how he acquired these characteristics is not known; in fact, we know practically nothing of his early life up to the time he ascended the throne of Osman in 1808. That he was born in 1786, the son of Sultan Abdul Hamid I, that he received special training from Sultan Selim III, his closest friend, and that he suffered imprisonment during Mustapha

[95] For a description of Mahmoud's character, see Bastelburger, *op. cit.*, ch. I; Slade, *Records of Travel in Turkey and Greece, op. cit.*, I, 113–114. Slade admired Mahmoud though he regarded him as a dangerous innovator. Mahmoud's obstinacy and determination, says Slade, led to an "increase of personal power, . . . but has accelerated the decline of his empire more than the actions of five of his predecessors, . . ." *Ibid.*, p. 113. Cf. also Walsh, *op. cit.*, II, 312. Walsh, chaplain of the British embassy 1820–1827 and 1831–1832, is more sympathetic with Mahmoud. He writes in 1832 that Mahmoud has given up his "ruthless and unsparing cruelty" for a "humane and kindly disposition," though he still possesses "insatiable avarice." *Ibid.*, p. 285.

[96] F. O. 78/209, Canning to Palmerston, #12, March 7, 1832.

[97] This characteristic is seen in the manner in which he finally destroyed the hated Janissary Corps. Cf. *post*, pp. 33–35.

the IVth's short reign are about the only facts historians have been able to discover; Mahmoud's early life is but one of the many things which still remains hidden in the seraglio.

More important than his early training, however, for the role he was to play during the three decades of his reign, was his innate ambition, his determination to make of the Ottoman Empire a strong state, a state which would not stand out in such violent contrast to that of his illustrious predecessor, Suleiman the Magnificent. To place the Ottoman state on an equal basis with the other nations of Europe, he realized he must continue the process of reform begun by Selim III; he must adopt western ideas and forms. But before that was possible, he must become an absolute monarch, free from the domination of the enemies of reform, especially the Janissaries.

The circumstances of Mahmoud's accession to the throne convinced him at the start that the abolition of the Janissaries was the most needed reform. The domination of this group was as unbearable to Mahmoud as the power of the Streltsi was to Peter the Great, and the Sultan longed to follow the Tsar's example and eradicate it completely. Yet, he was aware of how real their power was in Turkey, and how important it was to proceed cautiously.[98] The first act which can in any sense be considered a reform was his improvement of the military schools established at Constantinople by Selim III for the purpose of training army officers in the European manner. In this small way he began to create the military force which was to prove the undoing of the Janissaries some twenty years later. By the time the Janissary Corps had been supplanted by this new army,[99] military efficiency had become one of his principal objectives. Stratford Canning observed this fact on his visit to Constantinople in 1831–1832. Writing in March, 1832 he states: "The great end and aim of the Sultan's exertions is the

---

[98] Mahmoud undoubtedly was aware of the fact that the revolution of 1808 had strengthened the Janissaries, yet this did not weaken his determination to crush them. J. E. DeKay, *Sketches of Turkey in 1831–1832*, New York, 1833, pp. 236, 238.

[99] There were approximately 12,000 men in this army in 1828.

formation of a military force, capable of maintaining his authority at home, and of enabling him to recover the station, which he has lost for the present, with respect to Foreign Countries." [100] Mahmoud continued this policy during his last eight years. Thus, throughout his reign, Mahmoud pursued the same military policy, which began in such a small way immediately after his accession in 1808.

Mahmoud's reform policy was hindered by a number of factors in the first years of his reign. In 1809 Russia attacked Turkey with new energy and continued to press Mahmoud until the Tsar was forced to turn his attention to Napoleon in 1812. To pursue reforms in a period of war was almost impossible. Furthermore, the principal minister, the man who had really placed Mahmoud on the throne, Bairactar Pasha, was dependent upon some of the stronger pashas, especially the beylerbeys of Anatolia and Roumelia, and only with their support could any renovation in the armed forces of the empire take place. The death of Bairactar in 1809 removed a most able assistant, and the loss was so keenly felt by the Sultan that he shelved the reorganization of the military for the moment.

In the ensuing years, although firmly convinced that Europeanization was the one means of saving his tottering empire, Mahmoud moved forward slowly. His insistence on certain minor changes, however, hurt rather than helped his cause. Had his knowledge of Europe been more extensive and direct, he would not have pushed some of his ideas to excess, though perhaps this was due more to an inherent desire for change than to a lack of knowledge of European conditions. For example, his decrees regarding the dress of his soldiers, and the adoption of European saddles for his cavalrymen, saddles which completely altered the national mode of riding, are two reforms which the Sultan adopted without careful consideration as to the psychological effect on the men, or the fact that the training of raw recruits would have to be completely altered, and

[100] F. O. 78/209, Canning to Palmerston, #12, March 7, 1832.

thereby delayed.[101] These, as many of Mahmoud's schemes for Europeanizing his state, met the immediate opposition of the "old Turks," many of whom were important functionaries in the government.[102] But more important than any of these obstacles was the continued power of the Janissary Corps. Each time he attempted a reform which he thought would strengthen his state he came face to face with the fact that this praetorian guard must be destroyed once and for all before any lasting changes could be made.

In spite of Mahmoud's anxiety to whip the high-handed Janissaries, he proceeded with much more caution than his predecessors, in fact with more caution than was characteristic of him at any other time during his reign. For almost twenty years the Janissaries had obstructed every reform act on the part of the Sultan, especially those which partook of westernization; more than once they had dictated policies to the ruler, all of which was anathema to an autocrat like Mahmoud II. The failure of the Janissaries to suppress the rebellious Greeks, together with the threatening attitude of Russia in 1825–1826 undermined what little faith many Turks still had in the traditional bodyguard. Some of the most devoted supporters of the Janissaries, especially the *ulema*, rallied to Mahmoud as the head of the state when his future was thus threatened.[103]

At the same time the demonstration of power by Mehemet's Europeanized forces convinced Mahmoud that reforms could be delayed no longer, and he began to make preparations, not to annihilate the Janissaries as circumstances later determined, but to merge them into a new army corps [104] which he could

---

[101] Marmont, *op. cit.*, p. 332.

[102] Mehemet Ali had become the Sultan's model. Mahmoud squeezed money from his subjects for these new improvements most of which ran completely counter to Turkish ideas. Thus did he irritate the people in two ways.

[103] Juchereau de Saint Denys, *op. cit.*, IV, 3; S. Lane-Poole, *The Life of the Right Honorable Stratford Canning, Viscount Stratford de Redcliffe*, 2 vols., London, 1888, I, 424.

[104] The new troops were given the name of eshkendji, i.e. active soldiers. This was especially irritating to the Janissaries who had originally been honored with this title. See *Encyclopedia of Islam*, II, 574.

control. The nucleus of this new army consisted of volunteers from the regular army, new enlistments,[105] and to this was to be added any members of the Janissary Corps who were willing to join. The new army was provided with the most modern equipment, and placed under the tutelage of Egyptian drill masters. Immediately the Janissaries objected to the new army, and began to think of revolt.[106]

On June 12, 1826 Mahmoud ordered the new army which had been assembled to begin regular drill. The Janissaries, believing that Mahmoud was preparing a force to destroy them, overturned (June 15, 1826) their soup kettles, a signal for open revolt. Mahmoud sent a mission to the Corps, which had shut itself up in its barracks, offering pardon if they would immediately cease their rebellion, disperse quietly, and accept his intentions. The Janissary reply to this token was to put the members of the mission to death, and demand also the heads of the chief ministers.

When the Sultan learned of this, his wrath knew no bounds. He consulted with the *ulema*, who sympathized with him, and they offered to bring out the standards, and pronounce anathema on all those who refused to range themselves under the sacred symbols. The people quickly rallied to the defense of their Sultan against the Janissaries who had done nothing but harass them in one way or another for years past. Assured of the public's support, Mahmoud then ordered a contingent of his regular troops under Hussein Pasha [107] to destroy the in-

[105] About 2,000 men. Cf. Lane-Poole, *op. cit.*, I, 421. For a description of new corps, see Juchereau de Saint Denys, *op. cit.*, IV, 10–13.

[106] The best accounts of the revolution which followed will be found in: Juchereau de Saint Denys, *op. cit.*, IV, 3–48; Jouannin, *op. cit.*, pp. 25–26; DeKay, *op. cit.*, pp. 239–241; MacFarlane, *op. cit.*, pp. 316–322; Slade, *Records of Travel in Turkey and Greece*, pp. 136–138; Bastelburger, *op. cit.*, ch. 4; G. Rosen, *Geschichte der Turkei vom Siege der Reform im Jahre 1826 bis zum Pariser Tractat vom Jahre 1856*, 2 vols., Leipzig, 1866–1867, I, 3–8; Lane-Poole, *op. cit.*, I, 417–426; A. Vicomte de La Jonquière, *Histoire de l'Empire Ottoman depuis des origines jusqu'au traité de Berlin*, Paris, 1881, pp. 120–122.

[107] "A man of plain common sense, of determined resolution, and of great bodily strength." Lane-Poole, *op. cit.*, I, 424. Hussein Pasha was an aga of the corps who supported the Sultan when his confreres threatened revolution. Marmont, *op. cit.*, p. 33.

surgents.[108] The estimates of the number of Janissaries killed in the ensuing struggle varies from several hundred to as many as thirty thousand.[109] A fair estimate would probably be from five to six thousand.[110] On June 17 an Imperial Firman declared the Corps abolished,[111] and its members outlaws. Thus was the power of the Janissary Corps broken at a stroke, and men looked forward to a progressive future.[112]

Two significant facts should be noted in connection with the destruction of the Janissaries. First, no effective reform was possible as long as they existed. Now with their power broken, the ground was cleared for the erection of a more stable state based on permanent foundations. Second, it should be emphasized that this first great reform which presupposed all the others was essentially a Turkish reform. Nowhere have I been able to find any semblance of outside influence either in the conception or execution of this great step.

Mahmoud's destruction of the Janissaries was immediately followed by an attempt to create a modern Europeanized army. He could do very little at this time, however, because he shortly became involved in a war with Russia rising out of the Greek

[108] Marmont gives an excellent description of the struggle in Constantinople on June 15th and following. He estimates that three hundred were killed in battle; the captured leaders of the revolt were executed, making a total of five hundred. How many were destroyed by the burning of the barracks is not known. *Ibid.*, pp. 31 ff.

[109] Between 25,000 and 30,000 says Juchereau de Saint Denys, *op. cit.*, IV, 37. Slade's estimate is 20,000 to 25,000. Slade, *Travels in Turkey and Greece*, *op. cit.*, I, 138. 20,000 Janissaries and their adherents, according to Walsh, were exterminated. Walsh, *op. cit.*, II, 265.

[110] Canning believed 6,000 were killed outright and more than 18,000 exiled to Asia in the first fortnight following the revolt. Lane-Poole, *op. cit.*, I, 423. These figures seem more reasonable than any others.

[111] Lane-Poole, *op. cit.*, I, 421.

[112] "There is no denying," wrote Canning on August 12, 1826, "that the opinions of respectable men, as far as they can be ascertained, are in favour of the change. . . ." "The Concurrence of the Ulema must have a powerful effect on the people at large." *Ibid.*, I, 423–424. On the other hand so many families were affected by this "awful visitation," as Canning called it (Lane-Poole, *op. cit.*, I, 423), that, afraid of what Mahmoud might do next, they tended to oppose change of any kind. Outside of Turkey the destruction of the Janissaries was reagrded with so much "surprise and admiration" that the hatred of the Sultan was for the moment submerged, but soon Phil-Hellenism returned in full swing. *Ibid.*, I, 427.

insurrection. Until the signing of the Treaty of Adrianople
(1829) Mahmoud's energies were wasted abroad. The Russian
war ended, the Sultan once again took up the cause of reform,
completing his army reform and repairing where necessary the
disruption caused by the war. He also struck for an efficient
civil service which seemed to him as important as a modern
army, and he began in earnest the centralization of his power
by destroying the semi-independent feudal vassals.

The first group to be abolished were the feudal cavalry
known as Spahis. Having eradicated the Janissaries and begun
a new standing army, the Sultan no longer felt dependent on
this group of warriors.[113] Mahmoud confiscated the military
fiefs [114] upon which their power rested, and placed their former
vassals under the civil governors. Equally rebellious were the
derebeys (Princes of the Valley),[115] who had become independent about 1700 when the central government's power was
weak. The derebeys in Armenia and Anatolia were a real
menace. Their "number and audacity increased in proportion
as the central power decayed," until they were "in possession
of nearly three fourths of the territory of the Empire, so that
the authority of the Sultans, . . . was almost confined to the
immediate precincts of Constantinople." [116] By abolishing
these feudal groups,[117] Mahmoud strengthened the central gov-

[113] The hereditary proprietors of these titles had long ceased to render military service, yet they still cherished their baronial privileges, often defying the
Sultan and going so far as to resist his officials with force in defense of what
they considered their rights.
[114] Some of these ziamets and timars dated back to the Conquest (1453).
In Suleiman's time there were as many as 3,192 large fiefs (ziamets) and more
than 50,000 small ones. In the early nineteenth century less than a thousand
estates remained in European Turkey, and approximately fifteen hundred in
Asia Minor.
[115] Originally officials of the Porte, the derebeys had gradually become vassals
of the Sultan. Cf. *Encyclopedia of Islam*, Vol. I, p. 945. Derebeys paid tribute
and troops in case of war; many of them could raise 1–20,000 men. For this
reason some observers deplored their destruction. Cf. Slade, *Travels in Turkey
and Greece*, I, 116–117; Walsh, *op. cit.*, II, 125–309.
[116] Ubicini, *Letters*, Introduction, p. 4. In 1800 the Sultan possessed but two
provinces in Asia Minor, the remainder being under these feudal lords. Cf.
Encyclopedia of Islam, I, 945.
[117] Mahmoud dispossessed the derebeys as he had the Spahis and placed their
lands under the control of governors. Walsh, *op. cit.*, II, 309.

ernment even as the western rulers had done during the fifteenth and early sixteenth centuries.

Such a policy had its disadvantages as well as its benefits.
Undoubtedly many able and loyal vassals were destroyed together with the weak and corrupt, a material loss [118] in return
for a gain in principle. Yet in spite of this, and in spite of the
fact that this policy of centralization eventually led to conflict
with his strongest vassal, Mehemet Ali of Egypt, who on two
different occasions seriously threatened the very existence of
the Ottoman Empire, critics all agree that the policy was a
sound one, and Mahmoud must be credited with beginning it.
Mahmoud's successors were more the masters of their own
house (though the empire shrunk in the process) as a result.

Other reforms of this period which should be mentioned
were Mahmoud's attempt to regulate the dervishes,[119] and the
reorganization of the central authority itself. The Sultan's
council was simplified, both for economy and efficiency, by the
removal of many useless officials. Attempts were made to improve the rayah's condition and to establish equality before the
law, but these met with little success.[120] Other decrees provided for the further adoption of European dress, especially
the substitution of the fez for the turban, and the shaving of
beards.[121] While some of these may seem to have been minor

[118] As Marmont wrote in 1834, "The great 'Timers' or fiefs, which existed in
Asia, and were wisely governed, furnished the Empire, in time of war, with
twenty thousand good cavalry; but the Sultan has destroyed these fiefs, and as
his agents cannot exercise over the population the same degree of authority that
the original owners possessed, he neither receives troops nor money from these
districts, which are a prey to disorder." Marmont, *op. cit.*, p. 93.

[119] For a description of these troublesome mendicants, see *Encyclopedia of
Islam*, I, 949–951; D'Ohsson, *op. cit.*, I, 310, and IV, 616–686. The dervishes
had long been used by the Janissaries to block reforms by instigating revolts
among the fanatic Moslems. Mahmoud had the leaders of the Bektachi order
executed, its buildings razed, and the members exiled. Mahmoud allowed some
of the better orders to continue, those which were not foreign to ideals of
Ulema. Jouannin, *op. cit.*, p. 407; Thornton, *op. cit.*, II, 123. The Sultan was
not as thorough in this task, as in the destruction of the Janissaries with the
result that they remained insolent and continued to oppose his modern ideas.
Ubicini, *Letters*, I, 106–107.   [120] Ubicini, *Letters*, II, 111.

[121] Juchereau de Saint Denys, *op. cit.*, IV, 40–46; Jouannin, *op. cit.*, pp.
407 ff.; Slade, *Records of Travel in Turkey and Greece*, II, 140–141; Walsh, *op.
cit.*, II, 276–278.

reforms, nevertheless, they do show Mahmoud's anxiety, like that of Peter the Great of Russia a century before, for western civilization. Incidentally, one might add that the effect of these reforms on the "old Turks" was comparable to that of Peter's similar hasty reforms in the great Slav state.[122] The immediate result was weakness through loss of morale, but this was eventually overcome, however, in the course of the following decades.

In all these reforms the foreign inspiration is evident, yet the Sultan was not directly inspired by conditions in France, Germany or Britain, but indirectly by the success of these changes in Egypt. The Greek War not only brought to light the many weaknesses within his own dominions, but it also made the Sultan aware of how his vassal Mehemet Ali had been forging steadily ahead, and he attributed Mehemet's success to his early adoption of western methods. By 1824 Mahmoud was determined to pursue the same course. Thus, since there is no proof that any of the changes mentioned above were sponsored by western states, one must conclude that the *tanzimat* was essentially Turkish in origin, though as will be shown in later chapters, once started, it was encouraged [123] by western states interested in Turkey's improvement. As for England, at this time she was not particularly interested in Turkish affairs, certainly to no such degree as she was a few years later. Britain did not fully awaken to the importance of the Ottoman Empire's geographical, political, and economic position in Europe until 1833 when Russia threatened England's position in the Near East by signing with Turkey the Treaty of Unkiar Skelessi.

[122] Mahmoud was regarded as a giaour (infidel) by the old Turks for his treatment of Dervishes, and for his preference for western forms. Ubicini, *Letters*, vol. I, Introduction, p. 8.

[123] Cf. *supra*, Chapters 4–6.

CHAPTER I

BRITAIN'S NEW INTEREST IN TURKEY, 1833 [1]

BRITAIN's policy [2] of maintaining "the territorial integrity of the Ottoman Empire" has long been accepted as an integral part of her foreign policy throughout the whole of the nineteenth century. Several attempts [3] have been made to correct this false impression, but it has continued to persist. When and for what particular reasons did the protection of Turkey become a cardinal principle of British foreign policy? Though not generally recognized, in the first quarter of the nineteenth century the British Public in general and the Foreign Office in particular had very little interest in the affairs of Turkey. The attitude of the British Foreign Office with respect to Near Eastern affairs underwent a profound change in 1833. The event which marks this new interest on the part of the Foreign Secretaries, as well as a large portion of the British populace,

[1] Some of the material in this and the chapter which follows appeared in my article "The Economics of British Foreign Policy" published in the *Journal of Modern History*, vol. XII, no. 4 (December, 1940), and is reprinted here with the permission of the University of Chicago Press.

[2] The most authoritative recent treatments of British policy in the Near East prior to 1855 are: H. W. V. Temperley, *England and the Near East: The Crimea*, London, 1936, and V. J. Puryear, *England, Russia, and the Straits Question, 1844–1856*, Berkeley, 1931. Professor Puryear's *International Economics and the Diplomacy of the Near East, a Study of British Commercial Policy in the Levant, 1834–1853*, Stanford University Press, Stanford, 1935, adds little to his earlier diplomatic study of the problem.

[3] In addition to the accounts already noted, mention should also be made of F. S. Rodkey's *The Turco-Egyptian Question in the Relations of England, France, and Russia, 1832–1841*, Urbana, 1921, and J. E. Swain's *The Struggle for the Control of the Mediterranean prior to 1848, a Study of Anglo-Turkish Relations*, Boston, 1933. The following articles were also useful: R. L. Baker, "Palmerston and the Treaty of Unkiar Skelessi," *English Historical Review*, vol. 43 (1928), pp. 83–89; C. W. Crawley, "Anglo-Russian Relations, 1815–1840," *Cambridge Historical Journal*, Cambridge University Press (1929), vol. 3, pp. 47–73; and F. S. Rodkey, "Lord Palmerston and the Rejuvenation of Turkey, 1830–1841," *Journal of Modern History*, I, (December, 1929), 570–593, and II, (June, 1930), 193–225.

was the crisis of 1833, in particular the signing of the Treaty
of Unkiar Skelessi between Russia and Turkey by which the
Ottoman Empire virtually became a protectorate of the great
Russian state.[4] It is the purpose of the present chapter to explain the somewhat abrupt change from the passive indifference
to affairs in the Near East to active interference in favor of
the Turks, a program which was followed for more than two
decades, i.e. as long as Palmerston and Stratford Canning held
important positions in English diplomacy.

Various explanations have been advanced for Britain's interest in prolonging the life of "the sick man of Europe."
Possession of territory in the Mediterranean is the most usual
answer to the question; yet, Britain had been a Levantine
power since 1815, when the Vienna Congress granted her protective rights over the Ionian Islands. These possessions were
never regarded as exceptionally valuable and were finally ceded
to Greece in 1864. As far as Gibraltar (acquired 1704) and
Malta (annexed in 1800) were concerned, these outposts of
the Empire achieved their greatest significance after the opening of the Suez Canal in 1869. Since that date British interest
in the Near East and the Mediterranean has been paramount.

More fundamental underlying causes for the new importance
of the Ottoman Empire in British policy were the steady improvement in trade relations with the Turkish state, and the
evolution of new methods of transportation to the distant ports
of the Empire and the world. As will be pointed out more fully
in a later chapter the constant increase in exports after 1825
to Constantinople, Smyrna, Beirut, Salonica, and Trebizond, —
to mention only the most important ports under Turkish control, — compelled even the most conservative Britishers to
recognize the significance of the Sultan's dominions to the economic prosperity of the British Isles. Moreover, the development of steam-propelled transports in the second and third

---

[4] Prior to 1833 "Britain had played a defensive role in the Near East." The
Treaty of Unkiar Skelessi tended to "focus British attention and concern on the
Mohammedan countries of the Mediterranean." H. L. Hoskins, *British Routes
to India*, Longmans, Green & Co., New York, 1928, p. 146.

decades of the last century made a shorter route with convenient stopping places for fuel and water necessary; as the Mediterranean began to replace the Cape as the more direct pathway to Asia and India, Turkey, because of her geographic position, took on new importance. In the first decades when the Mediterranean route was used it was less economical than the all-water Cape route, largely because of the overland portages at Suez or through Syria to the Tigris and Euphrates rivers, but the possibilities of a new means of transportation, namely, the railroad which had already proved itself in England, kept alive the new interest in the eastern Mediterranean until the canal became an actuality.[5] The perfection of ocean steamships, steam river-boats, and the railroad combined to make the Near East a half-way house to India.

Until the protection of her own interests became paramount British anxiety for "the territorial integrity of the Ottoman Empire" was slight. Only in so far as a rupture of the *status quo* in the Near East might cause a realignment of powers in Europe and possibly war, was the English foreign office interested in Turkey prior to 1825. Pursuance of this policy partly explains how Britain first became involved in Turkish affairs. To maintain the *status quo* England would necessarily have been forced to support the Sultan against his rebellious subjects, the Greeks, "an act entirely counter to her political and intellectual philosophy." [6] From 1822 to 1826 the foreign office vacillated. Finally, in 1826, partly because of the influence of the Phil-Hellenes in England, though more largely due to the bungling diplomacy of the Duke of Wellington, George Canning found himself definitely involved in an attempt to force mediation of the dispute between the Sultan and his Greek subjects, a policy which culminated in one of the most embarrassing incidents of the nineteenth century, the Battle of Navarino Bay. In the ensuing Russo-Turkish war, which finally

[5] Hoskins, *op. cit.* Mr. Hoskins' treatment of this problem leaves little to be desired; he examines the problem from the political and diplomatic as well as from the geographical and economic points of view.

[6] Swain, *op. cit.*, p. 47.

achieved freedom for the Greek state by the Treaty of Adrianople, Britain was hardly more than an observer.

The result of her observations was a new interest in Turkey
as one of the members of the European family of nations.
Hoskins describes this most succinctly as follows:

In 1827 there was much vacillation and doubt as to what should
be British attitude toward the Turkish Government. That Power
had long been courted because it could give commercial privileges or
withhold them at pleasure. Likewise it could grant or refuse rights
of passage to India by any of the nearer routes and its fiat was un-
challenged. But the Battle of Navarino — the most enlightening of
a series of significant events — suddenly lifted the veil and disclosed
to Great Britain and to the world at large not a powerful Empire,
but a weak, disintegrating state, honeycombed with corruption,
stricken with poverty, disorganized and disunited, and incapable of
any long or consistent course of action. The Ottoman Empire had
become little more than a loose confederation, although its traditions
still gave its government a prestige quite out of proportion to its real
strength.

In the face of this revelation, British attitude had to be revised.
The first impulse was to stand aside and permit the forces of disruption to complete their work. Religious and moral forces in England, active at the time, strongly contributed to this tendency. After
the Russo-Turkish War, however, with both Russian and France
strong in the eastern Mediterranean, the alternative policy was
adopted at London, and the determination to protect and preserve
the Turkish state and particularly its capital, Constantinople, became
a corner stone of British foreign policy for the next half century.[7]

While the Greek episode was enlightening to many Britishers,
few really appreciated the significance of the demise of "the
sick man of Europe." Only the most far-seeing diplomats, Stratford Canning for example, perceived in 1829 or 1830 what the
break-up of Turkey would mean to Britain. Palmerston, who
had become Foreign Secretary in 1830, was new at the diplomatic game, having been associated with the war department

---

[7] Hoskins, op. cit., p. 135. Swain supports this view in the statement that
"the setback which the British experienced in 1829 (i.e. Greek freedom) did not
alter their belief or their determination that Turkey should be kept intact."
Swain, op. cit., p. 52.

prior to this time. Moreover, the Foreign Secretary's attention was confined to events nearer home, namely the Belgian crisis. That his interest in the Ottoman Empire was not aroused until he learned of the Treaty of Unkiar Skelessi is now a well-established fact, and one which has never yet been stressed sufficiently.[8]

The year 1833 is a more accurate starting point for the new policy with respect to Turkey for in that year several happenings focused the attention both of the public and the Foreign Office on the Near East. First, it was not until the middle thirties that a large body of traders with extensive financial interests at stake began to press for a more active policy, through such journals as *Blackwood's*, the *Edinburgh Review*, and the *Quarterly*. Trade with the Ottoman state had not been substantial enough until that time to warrant their asking the government to intervene in behalf of the Turks. Second, as steam navigation grew in popularity in the Mediterranean, transportation across the land areas of the Near East became more desirable. Though a wide difference of opinion existed as to which was the best route and how it could be conquered most economically, all recognized the importance of Turkey's geographical position. But the fact that British influence in the Near East was not seriously threatened until 1833 was most important. Mehemet Ali's defeat of the Sultan's forces at Koniah was climaxed when Russia secured a dominating position in the affairs of the Porte by means of the Treaty of Unkiar Skelessi, July 8, 1833. The Russo-Turk treaty caused to become fixed a policy toward which Britain had been tending for several years. Palmerston was shocked into action by the events of 1833. That this experience was one of the great lessons of his diplomatic career and the real basis for the policy he pursued during the following decades is seen as one explores the episode in detail.

[8] "If Russia had freed Greece in 1829, she enslaved Poland in 1830; this was the turning point for Whig Principle. The dividing line for Palmerstonian policy was rather the Treaty of Unkiar Skelessi; for in these matters Palmerston was

The Greek War for Independence, which had been the occasion for Mahmoud's destruction of the Janissaries, the first and most significant step in his reform program, also precipitated trouble between the Sultan and his most powerful vassal, Mehemet Ali, a struggle which out-lived Mahmoud, and indirectly enhanced the whole reform movement in the Ottoman state. Mahmoud II did not fare well in his early attempts to subdue the rebellious Greeks.[9] His army was not a small one, but it was poorly organized, with little or no discipline, and few able generals. To defeat the Greeks on land was impossible with such an inefficient army. The Sultan's navy was even worse. Far inferior to that of the Greek merchants' fleets, at times it was barely able to insure sufficient supplies coming in to Constantinople. An efficient fleet was absolutely necessary to keep the sea-ways open to the capital, and to bring in troops from outlying parts of the empire to subdue the recalcitrant Greeks.

Though Mehemet Ali of Egypt, the Sultan's vassal, possessed a fleet,[10] Mahmoud hesitated to call upon him, because to do so would be to exhibit his weakness to all his subjects. Finally in 1824, despairing of the outcome of the war up to that time, he reluctantly asked Mehemet Ali for his assistance. Mehemet immediately complied, the next year sending his son, Ibrahim Pasha, a very able general, with an army of 17,000 men trained in the latest European fashion. The successes of this force are well known to every student of the Greek Rebellion. Mahmoud had purchased his vassal's assistance with the promises of Crete

---

no Whig but a true Canningite." Crawley, "Anglo-Russian Relations, 1815–1840," *op. cit.*, p. 49.

[9] The delusion which had long prevailed as to the power of the Turkish Empire, a delusion which was their greatest protection and strength, was destroyed by the success of the early nineteenth century revolutions, especially the Greek Revolution, 1821–1829.

[10] Mehemet Ali's fleet, though inferior numerically to that of the Sultan, was much better equipped and manned. Cf. Canning's *Memorandum*, Appendix I, p. 240. After 1829, the ships which had been lost in the Greek War, especially at Navarino, were replaced, and others were added until by 1837 Mehemet again had a sizable and powerful navy. Cf. H. H. Dodwell, *The Founder of Modern Egypt; a Study of Mohammed Ali*, Cambridge (England), 1931, pp. 73, 223.

and part of the Morean peninsula,[11] a very high price which he later regretted, and which was the chief bone of contention between the two rulers for the next fifteen years.

That the Sultan and his vassal would eventually come to blows over this bargain of desperation was certain because of the nature of the two men. Mahmoud and Mehemet shared some of the same characteristics — especially acquisitiveness, and stubbornness.[12] A man of vision and energy, Mehemet Ali is well described as the Napoleon of the East, the greatest easterner since Suleiman the Magnificent. An Albanian by birth, he began as a successful tobacco merchant in Salonica. In 1798 he went to Egypt as an officer in the *bashi bazouks* to fight against Napoleon. No mere adventurer, Mehemet soon perceived his opportunity to make use of the high position he had won in the army. Within seven years (1805) he had achieved the coveted position of Pasha of Egypt, the richest pashalik in the whole Ottoman Empire. He continued his policy of playing the Mameluke Beys against the other opposition parties in that confused country (eventually destroying the Beys in 1811), until he was the sole ruler of Egypt, responsible only to his suzerain, Mahmoud II. During this time, however, Mehemet did not limit his efforts to political maneuvering entirely. He improved agricultural conditions, stimulated business and commerce, and built up a large and efficient army and navy with which he was able to extend his rule up the Nile as far as Khartoum, over the Wahabis in Arabia, and the tribes to the west.

Mehemet Ali believed that a great king was one who knew how to use both the sword and the purse, and his whole policy was built around that idea. He was forever drawing the sword

[11] Mahmoud promised to surrender Crete outright, whereas the Morea was to be governed by Ibrahim Pasha in the Sultan's name. Cf. J. A. R. Marriott, *The Eastern Question*, Oxford, 1917, p. 188.
[12] Dodwell's biography of Mehemet Ali is by far the best study in English covering the whole life of the Egyptian. Mehemet's rise in Egypt is fully treated in S. Ghorbal, *The Beginnings of the Egyptian Question, and the Rise of Mehemet Ali*, London, 1928.

to fill his purse, with which he extended and reorganized his army and generally built up his country. His intervention in favor of Mahmoud in 1825 had been made on that principle. Mahmoud adhered somewhat to the same policy, but he never was as successful in fulfilling it. After the defeat by Russia in 1829, a defeat which cost him the Greek state, the Sultan was in no mood to surrender more territory to the Pasha of Egypt. He realized his position as precarious, and gave no attention to making good his rash promises of 1824. He went even further, and entertained in his heart the fond hope of depriving Mehemet Ali of his independence, and once again bringing him into complete subjection to Constantinople. Thus these two rulers glared at each other for three years, each hoping to forestall the aims of the other; finally in 1832–1833 Mehemet openly rebelled and for a time threatened the very existence of his sovereign's state.

From the point of view of Egypt the Turco-Egyptian crisis of 1833 [13] had its immediate cause in the French occupation of Algiers in 1830. When the French seemed to have gained a definite foothold in Algeria, Mehemet Ali turned his face from the west to the east. Syria, not only nearer to his Egyptian domains, but also not separated by vast desert stretches, was much more suitable ground for expansion. Moreover, control of Syria was becoming an absolute necessity, since for years it had provided a place of asylum for Mehemet's enemies.[14] For these reasons, about the middle of the year 1832, Mehemet Ali ordered his son, Ibrahim Pasha, into Syria. Mahmoud's forces were speedily defeated and the Pashalik of Acre was incorporated within the Egyptian Empire.

Had Ibrahim's forces now turned back, there would never have resulted the crisis of 1833, and the new attitude of the powers resulting therefrom. But the Egyptian army continued its march through Syria, and into Asia Minor as far as Koniah.

[13] For a brief account of the 1832–33 crisis, cf. Swain, op. cit., pp. 89 ff.; a fuller account can be found in F. S. Rodkey, *The Turco-Egyptian Question.*

[14] The Pasha of Acre freely admitted those who opposed Mehemet's Egyptian administration.

Ibrahim even hoped to go on to Constantinople, but his father advised caution, lest the great powers be unduly aroused. The Sultan, panic-stricken by the rapid progress of Mehemet's forces, appealed both to England [15] and France for assistance in sparing his capital from his unruly subject, but both nations were so involved in settling the recent Belgian crisis that they paid little heed.

Stratford Canning, who had but recently returned from a special mission to the Porte, frantically urged his government to go to the rescue, but the new reformed parliament was faced with domestic issues, and international events nearer home blinded the Foreign Office to the real importance of the crisis in the Near East.[16] Palmerston later admitted (August 28, 1833) that the Sultan had appealed to Britain in November, 1832 for "maritime assistance," but he explained that "it would have been impossible to have sent to the Mediterranean such a squadron as would have served the purpose of the Porte. . . ." [17] "If England had thought fit to interfere, the progress of the invading army would have been stopped, and the Russian troops would not have been called in; but although it was easy to say, after events had happened, that they were to be expected, yet certainly no one could anticipate the rapidity with which they had succeeded each other in the East." [18]

In despair after the rout at Koniah and the refusals of France and England to succor him, Mahmoud sent a frantic call for help to his former enemy, the Tsar, and here the appeal was

[15] Immediately following the fall of Acre, Namic Pasha, a major general of the imperial guard, was sent to England to secure naval assistance on the coast of Syria. F. O. 78/212, Mandeville to Palmerston, October 18, 1832. Palmerston received his request for aid November 3, 1832, Hansard, *op. cit.*, vol. 22, 1834, p. 321.

[16] Crawley, "Anglo-Russian Relations," *op. cit.*, p. 55.

[17] Hansard, *Parliamentary Debates*, London, 1833, 3rd series, vol. 20, p. 900. Belgian and Portuguese problems were important issues in Palmerston's mind in 1832, and both these affairs called for the use of a part of the English fleet.

[18] *Ibid.*, vol. 19, p. 579. This statement was made in the House of Commons on July 11, 1833. When the Foreign Secretary learned of the Russian treaty, his regret at his inaction was even greater. For further defense of his actions in 1833, see Palmerston's speech of March 17, 1834, *ibid.*, vol. 22, pp. 318–349.

not in vain. In fact the reply of the Tsar's Foreign Minister was so prompt that Mahmoud, — sensing a trap, hesitated to accept the proffered assistance.[19] By February, 1833, however, the Sultan was so alarmed by Mehemet's advances that he was ready to welcome the Russians, preferring to risk them in their new role of friend rather than enemy.[20] The Tsar immediately dispatched seven ships of the line bearing a force of forty thousand men which within a few weeks was encamped on the Asiatic shores of the Bosphorus.

The presence of Russian armed forces so close to the Ottoman capital forced the French and English Foreign Offices to cooperate,[21] and they offered mediation. When the Egyptian ruler announced dissatisfaction with the suggested settlement,[22] France and Britain tried to exert pressure on the Sultan (by means of a naval demonstration) to make peace. Eventually (May 3, 1833) the Sultan decided to relinquish Adana as well

[19] In December, 1832 Mahmoud had refused the Tsar's offer of fifty thousand men, believing that it was naval support he needed more than anything else. After the defeat at Koniah, however, the Sultan, ready to accept whatever assistance he could get, approved the second proposal of Russia, presented through General Mouravieff. F. O. 78/222 Mandeville to Palmerston, December 31, 1832; and F. O. 27/463 Granville to Palmerston, No. 27, January 21, 1833.

[20] For an excellent account of how the Russians changed their policy from one of forceful annihilation of the Ottoman Empire to one of peaceful penetration toward Constantinople between the years 1827 and 1833, see S. M. Gorianov, *Le Bosphore et les Dardanelles*, Paris, 1910, pp. 25–81.

[21] Palmerston had at first refused the French offer of a joint settlement of the problem, because he feared that De Broglie had designs on the Near East. As a matter of fact the French Foreign Minister, though sympathetic with Mehemet, did not regard the destruction of the Turkish Empire with favor. Close cooperation between France and England at an earlier date might well have made Russian intervention unnecessary and thereby have maintained the *status quo* in the Near East. Swain, *op. cit.*, p. 92. Talleyrand, who was on a special mission to London concerning the Belgian crisis at that time, was struck by "the extreme coldness with which for the last three months the English Government has received all our overtures relative to Eastern Affairs, . . ." Talleyrand to De Broglie, March 22, 1833, quoted in C. M. de Talleyrand-Perigord, Prince de Benevent, *Mémoires*, 5 vols., New York, 1891–1892, vol. 5, p. 94. Talleyrand gives an excellent picture of the attitude of the British Government towards the Eastern Question at this time, especially the Foreign Minister's indecision, and his inability to lead his cabinet in favor of joint mediation. *Ibid.*, vol. 5, pp. 67–95.

[22] Mehemet wanted Adana; the substitution of Aleppo or Damascus was not satisfactory. F. O. 78/222, Mandeville to Palmerston, No. 61, March 31, 1833.

as Syria, and the peace of Kutahia [23] was signed.[24] The Russians immediately began to withdraw their forces, and the crisis seemed to have passed without a rupture. This amicable state of affairs was not long-lived, however, for it was shortly learned unofficially that two days before the Russian evacuation was completed, they had arranged and the panicky Sultan had signed the Treaty of Unkiar Skelessi (July 8, 1833), a treaty which placed the Sultan in the lap of the Tsar, and what was more important, a treaty which completely reversed the policies of the western powers, especially that of England.[25]

The Treaty of Unkiar Skelessi,[26] which was to last for eight years, consisted of six articles. After declaring for perpetual peace and amity between Russia and the Ottoman Empire, the treaty provided for mutual assistance in case the independence of either power was endangered. As such it was purely a defensive alliance. The most important feature of the treaty, however, was a secret article, which was not officially communicated to the British Foreign Office until January 16, 1834, but of which they were aware several months before that date. This secret article released the Turks from furnishing men or arms to Russia in case she was attacked, but provided that for this release Turkey would promise to close the straits at Russia's command. The secret article reads as follows:

In virtue of one of the clauses of Article I of the Patent Treaty of Defensive Alliance concluded between the Imperial Court of Russia

[23] G. F. von Martens, *Nouveau Recueil de traités d'alliance, . . . depuis 1808 jusqu'à présent*, 16 vols., Gottingue, 1817–1842, XVI, 18–20.

[24] For an excellent summary of the 1833 crisis, see Hoskins, *op. cit.*, pp. 143 ff.

[25] In one sense the British were in part responsible for the signing of the Unkiar, treaty, though they did not realize it at the time. Lord Ponsonby was new at his post, having arrived at Constantinople (May 1, 1833) but two days before the treaty of Kutayia was signed. Ponsonby learned, May 10, 1833, that Sir Pulteney Malcolm had been ordered to hold his fleet off the Dardanelles, but in no event to enter the Straits without orders from the Admiralty. F. O. Turkey 78/220, Palmerston to Ponsonby, 10 May 1833. The Porte recalling Admiral Duckworth's forcing of the Straits in 1807, misjudged Britain's intention of protecting Constantinople from Mehemet, and therefore considered the treaty with Russia was necessary.

[26] E. Hertslet, *The Map of Europe by Treaty*, 4 vols., London, 1875–1891, no. 168, II, 925 ff.

and the Sublime Porte, the two High Contracting Parties, are bound to afford to each other, mutually substantial aid, and the most efficacious assistance, for the safety of their respective dominions. Nevertheless, His Majesty the Emperor of all the Russias, wishing to spare the Sublime Ottoman Porte the expense and inconvenience which might be occasioned to it by affording substantial aid, will not ask for that aid, if circumstances should place the Sublime Porte under the obligation of furnishing it. The Sublime Porte, in place of the aid which it is bound to furnish in case of need according to the principal of reciprocity of the Patent Treaty, shall confine its action in favour of the Imperial Court of Russia to closing the Strait of the Dardanelles, that is to say, to not allowing any foreign vessel of war to enter therein, under any pretext whatsoever.

Interpretation of the phrase "closing the Strait of the Dardanelles" was one of the most controversial points in the months immediately following July, 1833, and so it has remained for more than a century.[27] The diplomats of 1833 were well aware that by this treaty Russia had at length acquired what she had been seeking for more than half a century, namely, a protectorate over the decadent Ottoman state, based on Turkey's pledge to close the Dardanelles to "any foreign vessel of war," "under any pretext whatsoever," which might "favour the Imperial Court of Russia." Yet few contemporaries assumed that since the entrance of Russian warships into the Bosporus and the Sea of Marmora was not mentioned, Russia had the right of egress from the Black Sea. This misunderstanding was the result of analyses made after the crisis and curiously enough has survived until our own time.[28]

Gorianov, who is perhaps more responsible for this misconception than any other writer on the subject, maintained that since the treaty of Unkiar Skelessi reaffirmed all existing treaties between Russia and Turkey, Russia, by article 7 of the

[27] The acceptance of Mr. Philip E. Mosely's interpretation of the treaty of Unkiar Skelessi by the foremost authorities on the subject will undoubtedly finally settle this very moot question. Cf. P. E. Mosely, *Russian Diplomacy and the Opening of the Eastern Question in 1838 and 1839*, Cambridge (Mass.), 1934.

[28] Rosen, *op. cit.*, I, 186–189; N. Jorga, *Geschichte des Osmanischen Reiches*, 5 vols., Gotha, 1908–1913, V, 372.

Russo-Turkish Treaty of September 23, 1805, had the right to send her ships into the Mediterranean at will.[29] Recently the Russian materials have been reexamined and a point which the great Russian archivist and historian overlooked has been established, namely, that, since the treaty of 1805 was denounced by Turkey in 1806, it could not have been reaffirmed in 1833.[30] "The secret article on the Straits," writes Mosely, "did not contain any provisions contradictory to the principle, maintained by the Porte, of closing the Straits to all warships. . . ."[31] Thus, while Russia was able to prevent warships from entering the Black Sea, she did not secure in 1833 the right to send her warships into the Mediterranean.[32]

Another question which caused much trouble during the thirties was raised by the phrase "in case of need." Did this mean that Russia might demand that the strait be closed at all times or merely when Russia was at war? A contemporary French army officer, Marshal Marmont, who had travelled extensively in Russia and the Near East, interpreted this to mean exclusion of all war vessels, except those of the contracting parties, at *all* times. Writing in 1835, he said: "From the letter of the treaty, and its secret article, it has been generally considered that the exclusion of foreign ships of war from the Dardanelles would only take place in the commonly understood 'case of need,' of the existence of hostilities between the contracting parties (Turkey and Russia), and any other maritime

[29] Gorianov, *op. cit.*, pp. 43-44.
[30] Mosely, *op. cit.*, p. 13.
[31] *Ibid.*, p. 11. The principle referred to constitutes the ninth article of the Anglo-Turkish treaty of 1809 which states that "As ships of war have at all times been prohibited from entering the Canal of Constantinople, namely, in the Straits of the Dardanelles and of the Black Sea; and as this ancient regulation of the Ottoman Empire is in future to be observed towards every Power in time of peace, the Court of Great Britain promises on its part to conform to this principle." Though this principle had been accepted for many years, it was first formulated in writing in this Treaty of 1809. Cf. J. W. Headlam-Morley, *Studies in Diplomatic History*, London, 1930, p. 224. Of course neither the Anglo-Turkish treaty of 1809 nor the treaty of Unkiar Skelessi affected any but ships of war. Merchant ships might pass the Straits at any time for the usual fee. Hansard, *op. cit.*, vol. 22, 1834, pp. 324-325.
[32] Temperley, *The Crimea*, p. 414, note 109.

powers; but the spirit adopted and acted upon carried the principal to the exclusion at *all* times, of the ships of war of *all* nations, but those of Turkey and Russia. . . ." [33] Gorianov, writing seventy-five years later, basing his conclusion on the preface of the treaty of 1833, holds much the same view, but "it is the clauses of the treaty, not the general preface, which have force in international law." [34] In the minds of the Russian diplomats who arranged the treaty, this broad interpretation did not exist. The treaty of 1833 was merely a separate guarantee within the old principle, formulated in 1809, and provided only for assistance from Turkey when Russia was at war with some other power. [35]

If Russia did not believe in 1833 that she had the right of egress into the Mediterranean, and if she understood the treaty to be only effective when she was attacked by some outside power, what advantage did the great Slav state derive from this new arrangement with Turkey? According to Mosely, Russia's primary motive in making the treaty of July 8th was "to secure recognition from the Porte of her paramount interest in Turkey and of her previous right of intervention, to the exclusion of the alliance and intervention of the Powers." [36] Russian policy since 1829 had been one of preserving the Ottoman Empire from "premature dissolution until more favorable circumstances should permit Russia to take the share appropriate to her as the most powerful neighbor." Friendship with Turkey had to be maintained, "since it was preferable that the Straits be in the hands of a weak and officially amicable government rather than in those of any European state." The only reasonable conclusion that can be made is that while the immediate advantages of the treaty were slight, the "potential advantage to Russia" was very great, in that "in accustoming the Porte to the position of vassal" Russia had "prepared the way for a repetition of the 1833 expedition." [37]

---

[33] Marmont, *op. cit.*, p. 53.
[34] Mosely, *op. cit.*, p. 13.
[35] Mosely, *op. cit.*, p. 15.
[36] *Ibid.*, p. 20.
[37] *Ibid.*, pp. 8–9, 21, 23; cf. also Temperley, *The Crimea*, p. 413, note 106.

As will be pointed out later,[38] a "repetition of the 1833 expedition" was just what Palmerston was most anxious to forestall, since the firm establishment of a Russia protectorate over Turkey would be detrimental both to British connections with India and to her trade with the whole Near East. The Foreign Secretary's immediate concern, however, was the problem of the Straits. In his opinion the treaty of 1833 was a direct abrogation of the Anglo-Turkish treaty of 1809, and he immediately protested. Britain's protest, presented by Lord Ponsonby, August 26, 1833, concluded with the statement that "if the stipulations of that treaty (Unkiar Skelessi) should hereafter lead to the armed interference of Russia in the internal affairs of Turkey, the British government will hold itself at liberty to act upon such an occasion, in any manner which the circumstances of the moment may appear to require, equally as if the Treaty above mentioned were not in existence." [39]

The government of Louis Philippe sent an equally emphatic protest, expressing its dissatisfaction with the treaty. This protest was communicated to the Russian government by the French Chargé d'Affaires at St. Petersburg, Monsieur I. de LaGrene, as follows:

The undersigned, Chargé d'Affaires of his Majesty, the King of the French, is instructed to express to the Cabinet of St. Petersburg, the profound affliction which the French Government has experienced on learning the conclusion of the Treaty of the 8th of July last between his Majesty the Emperor of Russia and the Grand Signior. In the opinion of the King's Government, that Treaty imparts to the mutual relations of the Ottoman Empire and of Russia a new character, against which all the powers of Europe have a right to pronounce themselves. The undersigned is therefore instructed to declare, that if the stipulations of that act were hereafter to bring on an armed intervention of Russia in the internal affairs of Turkey, the French Government would hold itself wholly at liberty to adopt such a line of conduct as circumstances might suggest, acting from that moment as if the said treaty existed not. The undersigned is also desired to inform the Imperial Cabinet that a similar declaration has been de-

[38] See *supra*, ch. 4.
[39] Hertslet, *op. cit.*, II, 928n.

livered to the Ottoman Porte by His Majesty's Ambassador at Constantinople.

(Signed)   I. de LaGrene [40]

Nesselrode's reply is significant:

The undersigned has received the note by which M. I. de LaGrene, Chargé d'Affaires of his Majesty the King of the French, has communicated the deep regret which the conclusion of the Treaty of the 8th of July, between Russia and the Porte, has caused the French Government, without stating at the same time either the motives of that regret or the nature of the objections to which that Treaty may give rise. The undersigned cannot be acquainted with them — still less can he understand them. *The Treaty of the 8th of July is purely defensive: it has been concluded between two independent powers, exercising the plentitude of their rights, and it does no prejudice to the interests of any state whatever.* What could, therefore, be the objections which other powers might deem themselves justified in raising against such a transaction? How, above all, could they declare that they consider it of no validity, unless they have in view the subversion of an empire which the Treaty is destined to preserve? But such cannot be the design of the French Government. It would be at open variance with all the declarations it made in the last complications in the East. The undersigned must, therefore, suppose that the opinion expressed in M. de LaGrene's note rests upon incorrect data, and that, when better informed by the communication of the Treaty which the Porte has recently made known to the French Ambassador at Constantinople, his Government will rightly appreciate the value and usefulness of a transaction concluded in a spirit as pacific as it is conservative.

That act changes, indeed, the nature of the relations between Russia and the Porte; for, to a long enmity, it makes relations of intimacy and confidence succeed wherein the Turkish Government will henceforth find a guarantee of stability, and, if need be, means of defence calculated to ensure its preservation. It is in this conviction, and guided by the purest and most disinterested intentions, that his Majesty the Emperor is resolved on faithfully fulfilling, should the occasion present itself, the obligations which the Treaty of the 8th of July imposes upon him, acting thus as if the declaration contained in M. de LaGrene's note did not exist.

(Signed)   Nesselrode [41]

---

[40] Marmont, *op. cit.*, p. 302.
[41] *Ibid.*, p. 303.

The British Foreign Office, which had not been actively interested in Turkish affairs since Navarino, was given somewhat of a jolt when it learned the terms of the Treaty of Unkiar Skelessi. The Foreign Secretary, Lord Palmerston, had not yet learned the art of quickly sizing up a given situation, and what is more important, he did not know exactly what action to take in order to forestall foreign influence and keep England's position uppermost in Turkey. The Palmerston of 1833 was by no means the Palmerston of 1839 or 1841. In spite of his long service in various subordinate positions of the Tory Cabinets since 1809, in spite of his devout aim to become a disciple of his illustrious predecessor, George Canning, it must be admitted that during the first years of his long reign over the Foreign Office he seemed to be groping about, a little uncertain as to what was the best course to follow. In this he was not unlike the great Bismarck during the first years of his long regime as head of the Prussian state some thirty years later; whether wisely or no at least Bismarck acted promptly; [42] herein Palmerston failed in 1833.

Palmerston's failure to act promptly in 1833 was not due to his lack of knowledge of the Turkish problem. Hardly had he assumed office when the liquidation of the Greek War was before the powers. In this affair Palmerston supported the Greeks, but this was by no means a disavowal of his statements concerning the integrity of the Sultan's domains. Acting on the advice of his agent, Stratford Canning, Palmerston had fostered the independence of Greece, "partly because he sympathized with Hellenic aspirations, partly because he felt that the strength and essential integrity of the Turkish Empire would be maintained rather than injured by the removal of this inflammatory appendage." [43] On this basis he had agreed to the extension of the limits of Greece in 1831. In 1832, however, Palmerston did not look upon the continued disintegration of

[42] Cf. Bismarck and Polish Revolt of 1863.

[43] *Cambridge History of British Foreign Policy*, 3 vols., Cambridge University Press, Cambridge (England), 1922–1923, II, 289.

the Ottoman Empire as a major diplomatic problem. "To judge from the absence of French and British ambassadors at the Porte," [44] sarcastically remarked the opposition *Times*, "and from the official silence maintained on the subject by the governments connected with the Mediterranean, one would have supposed that the decisive battle of Koniah was the first event of the war, and that this *dénouement* of an extraordinary drama came upon western Europe with all the surprise of novelty." [45]

The year 1832 found Palmerston more interested in events nearer home, in particular the question of the independence of Belgium. "The truth seems to be," concludes R. L. Baker, "that the swift succession of events in the Near East caught Palmerston preoccupied, unprepared, and belated." [46] In a letter to Ponsonby, December 6, 1833, Palmerston recognizes his lack of preparedness for the Russian *coup* six months before. "Preparations," wrote Palmerston, "however, have been made, and are still making, to enable H. M. Gov't. to deal with future circumstances according to the view which may be taken of the exigencies of the moment." [47]

Palmerston's unpreparedness did not result from lack of warning from his agents in Constantinople. As early as August 9, 1832 Stratford Canning [48] reported that the Porte, having

[44] Canning, having finished his mission on the Greek question, left Constantinople August 11, 1832. Ponsonby, due to circumstances at Naples where he had been ambassador, did not arrive at Constantinople until May 1, 1833. Chargé d'Affaires Mandeville was acting ambassador during the interim. The French ambassador, Roussin, reached Constantinople February 17, 1833.

[45] *London Times*, May 7, 1833.

[46] Baker, "Palmerston and the Treaty of Unkiar Skelessi," *op. cit.*, p. 85. Swain holds somewhat the same view. "Palmerston's Mediterranean policy, for a time, lacked precision. He agreed with the traditional policy of preserving the Ottoman Empire from the ravages of greedy powers, but he was slow in realizing that there was any immediate danger." Swain, *op. cit.*, p. 75. Cf. also Crawley, "Anglo-Russian Relations," *op. cit.*, p. 55. Ponsonby's original instructions, dated December 11, 1832 (he was appointed November 9, and accepted November 29, 1832), should prove valuable in establishing definitely the truth of these statements. The instructions are conspicuously absent from both the ambassadorial and consular materials.

[47] F. O. 78/220, Palmerston to Ponsonby, No. 23, December 6, 1833.

[48] Canning was in Constantinople from January 28 to August 11, 1832 for the purpose of securing the Sultan's assent to the final terms of Greek settlement.

more confidence in Britain than any other power, had made direct proposals for an alliance. Though Canning was aware that the Sultan sought support in suppressing Mehemet Ali he did believe "that those Powers whose interests are at all involved in its (Turkey's) fate should lose no time in adopting towards it a steady systematic course of policy in one sense or the other." [49] Again in December, 1832 Stratford Canning, sensing the predicament of the Porte in its relations with Mehemet Ali and Russia, begged the Foreign Minister to pursue a more active policy in the eastern Mediterranean. Motivated by a deep regard for the Sultan and his people, and well aware of what the victory of Mehemet would mean to British commerce, Stratford advised that the defeat of the Sultan would so weaken his empire that it would not only render further encroachments by Russia more easy, but also would retard the internal improvements "essential to the maintenance of his (the Sultan's) independence." [50] "In one respect, however, the prospect is clear," concluded Canning. "Let Mehemet Ali succeed in constituting an Independent State, and a great and irretrievable step is made towards the dismemberment of the Turkish Empire. That Empire may fall to pieces at all events; and he must be a bold man who would undertake to answer for its being saved by any effort of human policy. But His Majesty's Government may rest assured that to leave it to itself is to leave it to its enemies."

Canning's warning, however, fell on deaf ears. The Foreign Secretary felt that if matters were allowed to run their course both the Sultan and Mehemet Ali would soon exhaust their resources and arrange a reasonable settlement of their diffi-

[49] F. O. 78/211, Canning to Palmerston, August 9, 1832.
[50] F. O. 78/211, Canning to Palmerston, December 19, 1932. This Memorandum of Canning's provides not only a candid picture of the situation in the Near East, but also the cool indifference with which the ambassador's report was received at the Foreign Office. Although this document has been printed before (*Cambridge History of British Foreign Policy*, II, 638, and in Crawley, *op. cit.*, Appendix 5), I include it here as Appendix I, because the marginal notations in Palmerston's own handwriting so well explain the lack of a definite Near Eastern policy prior to 1833.

culties. Palmerston's lack of interest was naturally anathema to a man like Canning. The marginal notation which typified Palmerston's attitude at the time was in the form of a question: "Is not the unwieldy extent of the Turkish Empire one great check to the improvement of its industry and resources and possibly one great cause of its external weakness?" [51] At the very moment the Foreign Secretary pondered this question, the Sultan's forces were being severely defeated at Koniah (December 21, 1832); this defeat was followed by the unsuccessful appeals to Paris and London, and eventually the acceptance of the protecting arm of the Tsar. Palmerston breathed easier when the Russian troops began to evacuate, following the settlement of Kutahia.

Ponsonby's report [52] of a probable alliance between Russia and Turkey awakened Palmerston with a start. He immediately despatched a letter to Ponsonby, August 7, 1833,[53] instructing him to advise the Sultan against any form of alliance with Russia, which England could but regard as a cessation of confidence. If a treaty had already been signed, Ponsonby by all means was to prevent its ratification. This dispatch reached Ponsonby several days after the final ratifications had taken place. Thus, Palmerston's inactivity in Mediterranean affairs in the previous two years, due in part to the fact that he had not yet fully comprehended the magnitude of his tasks, made it possible for France to make extensive gains in northern Africa, and Russia to extend her influence over the coveted Straits, gains which seriously threatened the new route to India.[54]

When the Russo-Turkish treaty became known,[55] thinking

[51] Appendix I, p. 239.

[52] Ponsonby reported July 10, 1833 that he possessed a copy of the convention signed July 8th between Russia and Turkey. At this time he did not know about any secret articles but he surmised the existence of such. F. O. 78/223, Ponsonby to Palmerston, No. 32, July 10, 1833. Copy of Treaty enclosed in Ponsonby to Palmerston, No. 35, July 12, 1833, F. O. 78/224.

[53] F. O. 78/220, Palmerston to Ponsonby, No. 15, August 7, 1833.

[54] Palmerston "was not easily convinced that both France and Russia furthered their interests, Russia with the Sultan and France with Mehemet Ali, at the expense of the British." Swain, *op. cit.*, p. 88.

[55] *Morning Herald*, August 21, 1833.

Englishmen were quick to perceive its real significance. David Urquhart looked upon the alliance of July 8, 1833 as "an offensive treaty against England, and an abrogation of the treaty between England and Turkey of 1809." [56] Another contemporary blamed the British government for the sorry state of affairs in the Ottoman Empire and the necessity of such an arrangement with a strong power. "It was not until the Russians," he writes, *"not being able to awaken us* — came forward themselves, that we began to rub our eyes and wonder at seeing the eagle hovering over the minarets of Constantinople: — so that in very truth, we — we alone — are responsible for the present state of affairs in that quarter." [57] In October, 1833, three months before the treaty was officially announced [58] the *London Times* expressed the hope that this arrangement which gave the Russian Tsar *carte blanche* in Turkish affairs would be resisted with vigour by all the Powers.[59]

These censures of the actions of the Foreign Minister, while not immediately effective, are worth noting because they forced Palmerston to prepare a definite policy with respect to Turkey and keep to it during the ensuing years. For the moment, however, Palmerston was not prepared to counteract the effect of the treaty, so he pursued a policy of watchful waiting. The moment of hesitation in Palmerston's policy as regards the preservation of the Ottoman Empire did not last longer than a few months. By the end of the year, determined to prevent Russia from intervening in Turkish affairs under the terms of the Unkiar treaty, the Foreign Secretary was especially vigilant lest the Sultan, by some overt act, should provide the Tsar with the necessary pretext for intervention. "The great object of the British Government," wrote Palmerston on October 2,

[56] David Urquhart, *Sultan Mahmoud et Méhémet Ali Pasha* (quoted in Ross, *op. cit.*, p. 382).

[57] "Reflections on the Domestic and Foreign policy of Great Britain since the war" by a British Merchant, *Quarterly Review*, London, 1833, vol. 49, p. 527.

[58] Treaty of July 8th was not officially announced until January, 1834, though it had been ratified by the two powers in September, 1833, due to vagueness of Porte's copy of Treaty.

[59] *London Times*, October 16, 1833.

1833, "is the maintenance of peace, . . . we are averse to any great changes in the relative distribution of political power because such changes must either be brought about by war or must have a tendency when effected to produce war." [60] In December, 1833, he instructed Ponsonby to do everything in his power to prevent Mehemet Ali from swerving from his momentarily peaceful policy, lest he become "the instrument of Russia, to work out his own degradation," and that of Turkey as well, because Palmerston was convinced that Russia's treaty with Turkey was but one step in her "aggrandizement toward the South." [61]

Palmerston urged Ponsonby to use his influence to persuade [62] the Sultan that Britain was the truer friend of Turkey, since her interest in the Ottoman state was not motivated by any territorial acquisitiveness. "Conveniences and dangers might be avoided," he warned, "by reverting to the ancient policy of the Porte; and by looking for aid to England, instead of leaning upon a powerful and systematically encroaching neighbor." [63] Through Ponsonby, Palmerston cleverly insisted upon an elucidation by the Sultan of certain doubtful points in the Porte's version of the treaty,[64] with the purpose of bringing

[60] F. O. 78/226, Palmerston to Campbell, October 2, 1833. Palmerston had strengthened his understanding with France following the Munchengrätz convention of September 18, 1833 in order to counter balance this Austro-Russian rapprochement. With the aid of France he hoped to maintain the *status quo*.

[61] F. O. 78/220, Palmerston to Ponsonby, No. 23, December 6, 1833. This document has been published by R. L. Baker in the *English Historical Review*, XLII, 83–89. The method of carrying out the general policy outlined in this dispatch was worked out by Palmerston and his cabinet during the next two years. This dispatch is significant as the first expression of the British government's views on the affairs of the Near East, following the startling events of 1832–33, and also because it is the basis for the policy pursued during the next six years. Cf. also F. O. 65/206, Palmerston to Bligh, No. 101, December 6, 1833.

[62] Ponsonby, shortly after his arrival in Constantinople, secured contact with the Mahmoud through the embassy physician, Dr. MacGuffog, and one Vogorides, "the Prince of Samos," two men who had been used by Canning as intermediaries in the solution of the Greek question in 1832. F. O. 78/225, Ponsonby to Palmerston, "Secret," December 19, 1833.

[63] F. O. 78/220, Palmerston to Ponsonby, No. 23, December 6, 1833.

[64] *Cambridge History of British Foreign Policy, op. cit.,* vol. II, Appendix C, p. 639. Palmerston knew that the copy of the Treaty of July 8, 1833, com-

home to the Sultan the fact that Britain recognized him as a
vassal of the Tsar. Palmerston's protests having gone unheeded, he immediately began to work out detailed plans for
circumventing the influence of the Tsar, and within five years
Britain's prestige in the Near East was much improved.[65]

Thus, the crisis of 1833, which marked a new low in the
steady decline of the Ottoman Empire, was really a blessing
in that it brought about a more active policy upon the part of
Britain, and through the rivalry of England and Russia, Turkey was greatly improved in the next decade. Palmerston, who
had previously looked upon the Near East as of no great importance, now began to consider it as the mainspring of his
whole Mediterranean and Indian policy. The Treaty of Unkiar
Skelessi had shown him how far British influence in Turkey
had declined, and he was determined to improve it.[66] Every
phase of the Near Eastern question was examined,[67] and measures were designed to win the favor of the Sultan as well as to
encourage the reform movement already in progress in Turkey.
Palmerston recognized only too well that as long as Russia
controlled the Straits, and thereby Constantinople, she held a
dominating position in the Eastern Mediterranean, and he
never rested peacefully until the hated Treaty of Unkiar was
no more, and British influence had replaced that of Russia.

Fear of Russia [68] was not the only reason, however, which
caused Palmerston to make the Near East an integral part of
his foreign policy during the next two decades. British policy
in the nineteenth century was motivated by a variety of influ-

---

municated to the Foreign Office by the Porte, was defective, because Ponsonby
had transmitted to London on July 12, 1833 a true copy of the Patent Treaty
and the Secret Article which he had secured from unofficial sources. F. O.
78/224, No. 35, Ponsonby to Palmerston "confidential," July 12, 1833.

[65] See Chapter IV.

[66] "The British policy of maintenance of Turkey, the beginnings of which go
back to 1791, was made a reality after Unkiar Skelessi." Puryear, *International
Economics, op. cit.*, p. 15.

[67] *Ibid.*, p. 133.

[68] Cf. "The Diplomacy of Russia," *British and Foreign Review*, vol. I, no. 1,
1835, pp. 126 ff.

ences, — political, religious, humanitarian, and last but by no means least, economic. The need of new outlets for the increased production of the factories at home was always a driving force in the policy pursued by the Foreign Office. If Turkey was to be free and independent, she must receive sympathetic support from some other power than Russia; encouragement of the reform movement already in progress was one of the best methods of undermining Russia's influence and thereby making the Porte self-sufficient. Moreover, a strong Turkey would insure an outlet for British produce as well as a source of supply for certain useful raw materials.

CHAPTER II

THE OTTOMAN EMPIRE AND THE EXPANSION OF BRITISH COMMERCE AND INDUSTRY AFTER 1815

ECONOMIC NATIONALISM was more far-reaching after the close of World War I than in any previous period of history. Practically all the major powers in the world today pursued policies far removed from any concept of economic interdependence. Several states boasted autarchy as their governing economic principle, and those that did not were nevertheless proceeding toward that ultimate goal; the difference was merely one of degree. Yet, economic nationalism was not new; merely the terminology and the degree to which it was carried was new; economic advantage had long been the guiding star of European foreign offices. It is not always easy, however, to differentiate between economic and political motives in the foreign policy of any one particular state. Historians and economists are equally prejudiced in their viewpoints; the historian, viewing the whole past, tends to see certain historical facts as the causes of economic trends, while many economists, on the other hand, are convinced that economic conditions determine a nation's history. To strike an even balance is almost impossible.

The development of British foreign policy in so far as it is related to Near Eastern affairs in the period between the Greek War for independence and the Crimean War is one of the best examples of the interrelation of history and economics. In 1827 George Canning, the British Foreign Minister, though accidentally and reluctantly, intervened in cooperation with Russia in behalf of the Greeks who sought freedom from the Ottoman Turk, yet twenty-five years later Palmerston and Russell were ready to risk war to prevent the final disintegration of the Turkish Empire. This lack of continuity, which amounted to almost a reversal of British policy, cannot be explained by glib allusions to the weaknesses of the cabinet system of government, nor by the statement that Palmerston was the exact opposite of his illustrious predecessor. As a matter of fact, Palmerston prided himself on being a disciple of Canning, and like him opportunistically fitted his policy to his nation's needs. Moreover, it is now well-established that British policy during the years that Palmerston dominated the foreign office was not always constant. Palmerston was more or less indifferent to the future existence of the Ottoman Empire when he took office, yet when he left it the welfare of Turkey was one of the most important aspects of his many-sided program. The explanation of this diplomatic inconstancy is found in large measure in economic facts, in short, in the development of Britain's overseas trade with Turkey in the twenty-five years prior to the outbreak of the Crimean War. The policy of watchful guidance for Turkey's territorial integrity which was pursued for more than twenty years after 1833 is explained in large measure by the fact that the British people recognized the real importance of Turkey to their economic prosperity and to their access to India. Traders and travellers who visited the Near East in ever-increasing numbers in the 1830's and 1840's returned with stirring accounts of Turkey's economic and strategic importance to the British Empire. For the first time the maintenance of the "territorial integrity of the Ottoman State" had real meaning to all Britishers.

As a pathway to the East the Mediterranean took on new significance in the second quarter of the nineteenth century.[1] The new interest in the Mediterranean route which showed itself in the 1830's resulted from certain industrial changes of the preceding era. In order to manage the new factories at maximum efficiency a constant stream of raw materials was necessary, while manufactured goods had to be speeded to the

---

[1] In spite of the fact that Britain's first contacts with India had been by way of the Mediterranean and the overland route, from the time that Drake and Cavendish circled the globe until the 1830's the Mediterranean held second place to the Cape route. Hoskins, *op. cit.*, p. 1.

markets to make way for new production. The exchange of raw materials for manufactured goods, especially where food-stuffs were involved, called for a shorter, more efficient and more speedy means of transportation to India and the East.[2] The new steam vessels were speedier and more dependable than sailing ships, but for long voyages so much fuel and water were needed there was little space left for cargo. A shorter passage with frequent stops for supplies was indispensable.

As early as 1784 a few English traders, the chief of whom was George Baldwin, saw the possibility of a cheaper route to India by way of the Mediterranean and the Isthmus of Suez,[3] but it was not until 1830 that English surveyors and scientists seriously considered an all-water route to India via Egypt.[4] The reports of their findings, printed by order of Parliament,[5] aroused so much interest that the House of Commons established a Select Committee to consider a shorter route to India.[6] Agitation for the canal across the Isthmus increased in the following decade. The distance from England to India by way of Suez was little more than one-third that of the Cape route,[7] and this appealed to the small independent traders as well as the great companies.

Had the canal not met with such strong opposition in the Foreign Office, it is quite possible that it would have been undertaken much earlier than it was, and as an English enterprise.

[2] The voyage around the Cape occupied from five to eight months, and though the passage of the first steamship, the *Enterprize*, from an English port to Calcutta in 113 days by way of the Cape was considered a feat, it was not fast enough. Moreover, this route was a most hazardous one; often whole cargoes were lost in storms encountered in the African seas, and ship-owners worked in constant fear of pirates. Hoskins, *op. cit.*, p. 94.

[3] *Ibid.*, p. 7.

[4] Swain, *op. cit.*, p. 86. "General European exhaustion following the long wars and lack of motive for the development of new routes to the East made for a policy of laissez-faire in eastern matters. Besides, the Cape route with the new way station at Table Bay sufficed for English transportation needs." Hoskins, *op. cit.*, p. 129.

[5] Parl. Papers, 1834, Reports. Committees, Steam Navigation to India, vol. XIV, pp. 1–234, and Appendices, pp. 1–197.

[6] Hansard, *op. cit.*, 3rd series, XXIV, 142.

[7] Hoskins, *op. cit.*, p. 88.

Palmerston opposed the canal project from the start, declaring that it was not only a physical impossibility but a politically dangerous undertaking as well.[8] To Palmerston a canal in such a position would become a second Bosporus with all its accompanying difficulties. He considered a railway across the Isthmus more practical as well as much cheaper.[9]

That Palmerston did appreciate, however, the need of more direct communication with India is shown by the fact that he was an ardent supporter of the Euphrates development projects.[10] Communication with India via the Euphrates and the Persian Gulf appeared not only more direct,[11] but that route also would avoid the dangers of the Red Sea as well as the southwest monsoon which swept the Arabian Ocean for four months of the year. All these arguments were used by Palmerston to strengthen his opposition to the canal project which carried with it so many political difficulties. In pursuing this line of thought Palmerston was representative of an earlier era which frowned upon the railway and the expensive inefficient ocean steamship. River transportation had proved its effectiveness on the Rhine and Danube; why should it not be extended to the Tigris and Euphrates, asked Palmerston and the opponents of the canal.[12] Yet, more important than any of these

[8] Hansard, op. cit., 3rd series, CXLVI, 1043–1044. To the British ambassador at Constantinople Palmerston wrote in 1851: "A ship canal from the Mediterranean to the Red Sea, if such a work were practicable, would be a different thing; and it is needless to point out how such a work, changing as it would the relative position of some of the maritime powers of Europe toward each other, would involve the possibility of political consequences of great import and might seriously affect the foreign relations of the Turkish Empire." Palmerston to Canning, July 24, 1851, F. O. 78/411.

[9] Swain, op. cit., p. 136. On February 8, 1847, Palmerston wrote to Murray his agent in Egypt, urging him to inform the Pasha of the costliness and impracticability of a canal, pointing out "that the persons who press upon the Pasha such a commercial scheme (as the canal), do so evidently for the purpose of diverting him from the railway which would be perfectly feasible and comparatively cheap." (F. O. 97/411.)

[10] Hoskins, op. cit., p. 155.

[11] Early surveys incorrectly announced this to be shorter than via Suez, with the result that it came to be known as the direct route, whereas Suez went by the misnomer "overland route." Ibid., p. 154.

[12] Ibid., p. 148, note 57.

ideas in Palmerston's mind was his belief that the political situation in the Near East after 1833 made the Euphrates route the only feasible one. This explains why he exercised such caution lest by any word he might lend governmental sympathy to the canal supporters, and thereby aggravate an international problem already critical.[13] Thus, if he favored the route which was more directly under the Sultan's control, because he then enjoyed the friendship of Mahmoud II,[14] the reverse is equally true, — his interest in a shorter route to India via Syria and Mesopotamia strengthened his desire to befriend and support the Sultan's empire against those who would destroy it.

There is little need of carrying this survey of trade routes further. Enough has been said to demonstrate that from the point of view of protection of her Asiatic interests, British foreign policy in the Near East after 1833 was largely determined by the geographic position of the Ottoman Empire. Yet, the extreme fear of Russia and the anxiety for the route to India were not the only reasons why Englishmen had a new interest in the Ottoman Empire in the second quarter of the last century; Turkey itself was an important factor in the commercial prosperity of the United Kingdom, and the effect of this expansion of trade with the Ottoman dominions on the policies of the foreign secretaries is worth noting. Before discussing Anglo-Turkish trade in the decades prior to the Crimean War, however, a few remarks on British commerce in general after 1825 are pertinent.

The first decade and a half of the nineteenth century was a period of almost constant warfare with the French Emperor, but in spite of this fact, it was also an era of steadily increasing trade for Great Britain. That the course of the Industrial Revolution was altered by two decades of European conflict no one will deny, yet the burdens of economic displacement were

---

[13] Hansard, *op. cit.*, 3rd series, CXLVII, 1652–1662, 1676–1683. Occupation of Aden by Britain in 1839 did not necessarily mean that Palmerston had been convinced by the supporters of the canal. Throughout this period Palmerston opposed the canal as impractical and politically dangerous.

[14] Hoskins, *op. cit.*, p. 147.

not borne equally by all classes in England, nor by every member of an economic group. While the working classes felt the hardships of war in the low wages they received, and the high prices they paid for food and clothing, the landed element as a whole thrived on the domestic conditions which the war did not alter, namely, increased rents, the benefits of the enclosures, and the comparatively low taxes. The middle classes regarded the war on the continent with mixed feelings. While some of the smaller traders were ruined by the loss of certain markets, a result of the Emperor's Continental System, on the other hand many of the new manufacturers and exporters were carrying on an ever-increasing trade with the hitherto unappreciated markets in Africa, India, and especially South America. During the later years of the Napoleonic period English merchants, confident that peace would bring even greater prosperity, persuaded the manufacturers to expand their businesses in order to take advantage of the situation which peace would afford. How this over-production brought on one of England's worst economic depressions in the years immediately following the Congress of Vienna is a story well-known to all students of nineteenth century English history.

By 1825, however, the surplus manufactures had been liquidated, and in spite of the commercial crisis of 1825–1826,[15] caused largely by speculation and unsound hasty expansion, the two logical results of the industrial changes of the eighteenth century stood out after 1825 in bolder relief than ever before; not only was a greater premium placed on raw materials, but also merchants, who had been forced by the Continental System to find new markets for their manufactured articles, now recognized the possibilities of world trade. Competition with the other European states, however, for both markets and raw materials was not as keen in the decades following the Greek War as it was to become half a century later when all Europe,

[15] L. Levi, *History of British Commerce, 1763–1870*, London, 1870, ch. 4. J. H. Clapham, *An Economic History of Modern Britain*, 3 vols., Cambridge University Press, Cambridge, 1927–1932, I, 272–273.

Germany in particular, began to develop industrially and commercially. England during the first half of the nineteenth century enjoyed a near-monopoly of international trade. Her problem was to find new markets for the flood of made-up

CHART I

TOTAL EXPORTS AND IMPORTS OF THE UNITED KINGDOM,
BY VALUE, 1825–1853

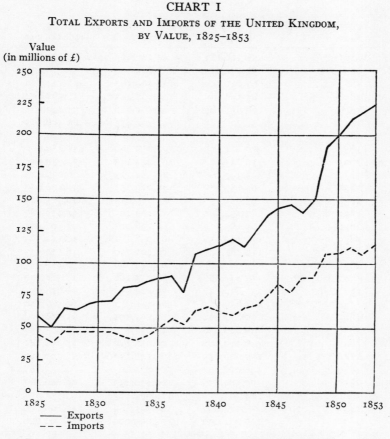

Value
(in millions of £)

——— Exports
– – – Imports

goods which constantly poured from the mills. A glance at the foreign trade of Britain after 1825 bears out the above statements.

Unfortunately no accurate figures exist for the total exports and imports of the United Kingdom during the twenty-eight years, 1825 to 1853,[16] but Table 1 and accompanying chart indicate the degree of expansion of British commerce.

TABLE 1

OFFICIAL VALUE OF EXPORTS AND IMPORTS OF THE UNITED KINGDOM, 1825–1853 *

Year	Official Value Exports	Official Value Imports	Trade Balance
1825	£ 56,320,182	£ 44,208,803	£ 12,111,379
1826	51,042,023	37,813,890	13,228,133
1827	62,052,755	44,908,173	17,144,582
1828	62,734,635	45,167,443	17,567,192
1829	66,838,127	43,995,286	22,842,841
1830	69,700,748	46,300,473	23,400,275
1831	71,431,490	49,727,828	21,703,662
1832	76,070,148	44,610,546	31,459,602
1833	79,821,110	45,944,426	33,876,684
1834	85,397,268	49,364,733	36,032,535
1835	91,157,783	49,029,334	42,128,449
1836	97,611,856	57,296,045	40,315,811
1837	85,779,568	54,762,285	31,017,283
1838	105,165,479	61,258,013	43,907,465
1839	110,190,656	62,048,121	48,142,535
1840	116,481,005	67,492,710	48,142,535
1841	116,902,887	64,444,268	52,458,619
1842	113,841,802	65,253,286	48,588,516
1843	131,832,947	70,214,912	61,618,035
1844	145,956,654	74,449,374	70,507,280
1845	150,877,902	85,297,508	65,580,394
1846	148,609,056	75,934,022	72,675,034
1847	146,172,008	90,921,866	55,250,142
1848	150,996,040	93,547,134	57,448,906
1849	190,010,394	105,874,607	84,135,787
1850	197,309,876	100,460,433	96,849,443
1851	214,391,017	110,679,125	103,711,892
1852	219,545,699	109,345,409	110,200,290
1853	242,072,000	123,099,000	118,893,000

* William Page, *Commerce and Industry, Tables of Statistics for the British Empire from 1815*, London, 1919, Table 23, p. 70. The incompleteness of the figures in the Customs ledgers has made it necessary to fall back on the above table which is based on customs tariffs of the United Kingdom, 1800–96, *Parl. Papers*, 1898 (c. 8706); though not as accurate as the Customs Reports, it is nevertheless expressive of the great rise in overseas trade between 1825 and 1853.

[16] Exports are listed in Customs ledgers in official values (according to rates

It will be noted from the foregoing table that the total exports of the United Kingdom increased some £185,000,000 in the twenty-eight years prior to 1853, while total imports increased almost £79,000,000.[17] Since these represent official values (according to the rates of 1696), better evidence of the expansion of British industry in these three decades can be found in a comparison of the exports of certain manufactured articles and some of the principal imports of raw materials at the beginning and end of the period. For example, cotton goods which were the chief export of Britain during this era,[18] increased almost 100 per cent, rising from £18,788,016 in 1825 to £34,763,792 in 1855. Iron and steel output increased sevenfold, while hardware and cutlery almost doubled. Woolen manufactured goods, another staple export of the United Kingdom, increased more than two million pounds in thirty years.[19] The average declared value of exports for the United Kingdom for the years 1825 to 1830 was £42,913,654; for the period 1850 to 1855 the average was £129,013,568. This was all the more significant when one considers that price levels were falling due to more efficient methods of production.

Imports of raw materials also show great increases in this period. In 1825 the United Kingdom imported 1,829,379 lbs. of raw silk; thirty years later this item equalled 6,618,862 lbs. Imports of sheep and lamb's wool increased 50 per cent 1825–1855, while cotton wool rose from 226,052,135 lbs. in 1825 to

---

of 1696) for all years except 1849 and 1850, in which years they are listed in declared values. Export ledgers for 1846 and 1853 contain no abstracts. Import ledgers lack abstracts for the five years 1847 to 1851. Imports were likewise listed in official values (until 1870). According to John Marshall, *A Digest of Accounts of Population, Production, Revenue, . . . of the United Kingdom of Great Britain and Ireland* . . . , London, 1833, p. 65, the real value of exports and imports was about 70 per cent of the official value.

[17] These are official values, about 30 per cent larger than real values. Clapham's figure of £25,000,000 increase in exports is a very conservative one. Cf. Clapham, *op. cit.*, I, 476. It would probably be nearer £42,000,000 in declared value.

[18] Cotton goods made up almost half of Britain's total exports in this period. Cf. Tables 1–7, Appendix II.

[19] For intervening five-year periods cf. Tables 2–4, Appendix II.

907,676,094 lbs. in 1855.[20] English imports increased at the
rate of 3½ per cent per annum from 1826 to 1846, rising to
6 per cent per annum in the next quarter of the century.[21]
From 1825 to the outbreak of the Crimean War, British exports surpassed imports on an average of £20,000,000, beginning as low as £12,000,000 in 1825, and rising to approximately
£119,000,000 favorable trade balance in 1853.

That the horizons of the British merchant were broadened
by this steady expansion of trade no one can deny. The point
of view of the Foreign Office, which was more and more forced
to hear the complaints of the trader and assist him in market-
ing his goods, likewise became more extensive. Thus, it was no
mere coincidence that this period of rapid economic development in Britain was also the period in which her interest in the
welfare of the Ottoman Empire was greatest, for Turkey from
1825 to 1855 was one of England's best customers. In order to
appreciate the importance of Turkey as an outlet for England's
ever-expanding trade, the situation on the continent is enlightening.

In the second quarter of the nineteenth century England's
trade with the European states was limited, due to the barriers
which were raised there in order to foster their own industrial
development.[22] France which began to realize the possibilities
of industry and commerce after 1825, took the lead in this
respect. Textiles, both yarns and fabrics, were absolutely
barred until 1834, when these and certain other prohibitions
were replaced by duties. The German Zollverein, while not

[20] Cf. Tables 8 and 14, Appendix II. For intervening five-year period cf.
Tables 9–13. Since imports are listed in official values, I have compared quantities rather than import values.

[21] A. L. Bowley, *Short Account of England's Foreign Trade in the Nineteenth
Century*, London, 1905, p. 39.

[22] "That part of our commerce which, being carried on with the rich and
civilized peoples of Europe, should present the greatest field for extension, had
fallen off in a remarkable degree. Our average annual exports to Europe were
less in value by nearly 20 per cent, in the five years from 1832 to 1836, than
they were in the five years that followed the close of the war; . . ." G. R.
Porter, *Progress of the Nation*, Methuen & Co., London, 1836, rev. ed., 1912,
p. 482. Cf. also Clapham, *op. cit.*, I, 476–480.

specifically prohibiting English goods, did tax foreign manufactures, and though its duties were not heavy in the beginning, there was a tendency to move upwards. Trade channels with the Germanies existed however, via Belgium, Holland, and the Hanse Towns, and states not members of this economic league, which carried goods across Europe to the Austrian and Russian frontiers. To keep these channels open was "the prime object of British commercial diplomacy." [23] In the same way the Austrian lands [24] were protected by high tariffs, one of which (1833) prohibited some sixty-nine articles and levied exorbitant duties on as many as sixteen hundred items. The Russian tariff of 1833, which replaced the absolute prohibition of all foreign manufactures established in 1810, prohibited more than three hundred articles; this became the basis of Russian tariff policy until 1844. Yet, as has been pointed out, there was a steady increase in the outward flow of goods from English factories. Where were these manufactures sold?

Britain's Asiatic and African possessions consumed large quantities, as did the new South American markets, but large and frequent ship-loads of manufactured products went out to the Turkish ports as well.[25] According to Clapham, "while the German market remained stagnant, and the French market shut, the markets of the Turkish Empire and of the East were in brisk motion. Between 1839 and 1849, — half way through the early railway age and about its close; both years of normal good trade, whose figures would fall on or near the ascending line of exports, — the plain cotton goods shipped overseas more than doubled (380 to 795 million yards); those shipped to India and Ceylon and to the Turkish Empire more than trebled. . . ." [26]

Table 2 and accompanying chart indicate the true importance of the Levant trade in this period.

[23] Clapham, *op. cit.*, I, 480.
[24] Hungary was not included in the Habsburg tariff in the period under study.
[25] The South American markets, won from Spain when their colonies revolted during the Napoleonic period, practically balanced Britain's losses on the Continent until 1835. Cf. Puryear, *International Economics, op. cit.*, p. 108.
[26] Clapham, *op. cit.*, I, 481–482.

BRITISH POLICY AND TURKISH REFORM

TABLE 2

OFFICIAL VALUE OF EXPORTS FROM THE UNITED KINGDOM TO TURKEY
COMPARED WITH IMPORTS INTO THE UNITED KINGDOM
FROM TURKEY, 1825–1853

Year	Exports *	Imports †	Trade Balance
1825	£ 1,079,671	£1,207,172	£ 127,501
1826	1,104,897	818,516	286,381
1827	1,078,920	598,650	480,270
1828	423,151 ᵃ	731,943	308,792
1829	1,394,588	431,062	963,526
1830	2,745,723	726,065	2,019,658
1831	2,113,928	759,797	1,354,131
1832	2,091,590	654,146	1,446,444
1833	2,450,204	643,958	1,806,246
1834	2,467,944	741,280	1,726,664
1835	2,706,591	879,089	1,827,502
1836	3,649,925	1,030,110	2,619,815
1837	2,747,807	841,395	1,906,412
1838	4,672,720	789,118	3,883,602
1839	3,578,561	1,196,430	2,382,131
1840	3,673,903	1,240,812	2,433,091
1841	3,630,792	1,212,749	2,418,043
1842	4,688,207	1,168,036	3,520,171
1843	5,440,941	1,243,759	4,197,182
1844	7,688,406	1,292,989	6,395,417
1845	7,620,140	1,465,972	6,154,168
1846	....	1,071,340 ᵇ	....
1847	7,619,106	....	....
1848	11,186,524	....	....
1849	2,373,669 ᶜ	....	....
1850	2,515,821 ᶜ	....	....
1851	7,479,175	....	....
1852	8,489,100	2,252,283	6,236,817
1853	....	3,050,518	....

* Customs 9/12–24 and Customs 8/47–81; no abstracts for 1846 and 1853.
† Customs 4/20–50; no abstracts for 1847–1851 and 1854.
ᵃ Blockade effective from October, 1828.
ᵇ Exclusive of Moldavia and Wallachia.
ᶜ Declared values only.

The foregoing table does not give a complete picture of Anglo-
Turkish trade prior to the outbreak of the Crimean War, both
because of the incompleteness of the records upon which it is
based, and because of the variation in the way in which values

were listed. Moreover, it is obvious that the Turkish trade was a very small proportion of Britain's total commerce.[27] Nevertheless, it does indicate that the favorable trade relations which

CHART II

TRADE OF THE UNITED KINGDOM WITH TURKEY,
BY VALUE, 1825–1853

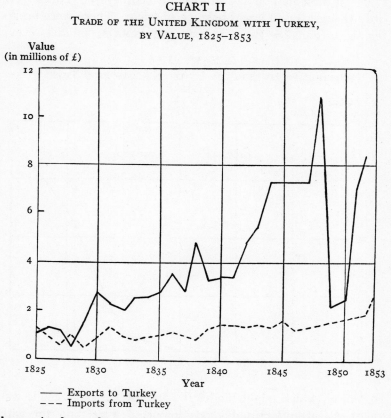

Value
(in millions of £)

Year

——— Exports to Turkey
– – – Imports from Turkey

began in the early 1830's were worth continuing. The very fact that between 1825 and 1852 exports to Turkey increased eight-fold (reaching a high of £11,186,524 in 1848) while imports, after returning to the 1825 level in 1836, remained relatively steady, gave England a most favorable trade balance in the two decades prior to the Crimean War.[28] By 1845 six million

[27] See Table 1, p. 70.
[28] Beginning with an unfavorable trade balance in 1825, on the eve of the

pounds sterling was available from this one source alone for reinvestment and expansion, not only in the Levant trade, but in the various parts of the world.

In the first half of the nineteenth century the Turks gave little thought to an equal balance of trade. There were no attempts to equalize their imports and exports; in fact, every

CHART III

WHEAT IMPORTED INTO THE UNITED KINGDOM FROM TURKEY,
1825–1855

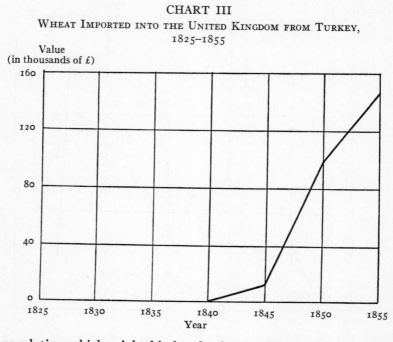

regulation which might hinder the free exchange of goods was shunned. Manufactured goods imported were paid for with agricultural produce, and the country was forced to increase its production in proportion to its need of foreign articles.[29] The fact that Turkey paid her creditors with products valued

---

Crimean War (1852) the balance in England's favor was more than twenty-one times greater than it had been twenty-six years before (1826).

[29] Ross, *op. cit.*, p. 291. Turkey did not balance the manufactures imported with her grain as is generally stated. As a matter of fact, wheat ranked eighteenth in importance on the list of Turkish exports to Britain until 1845. After

in their own currency tended to reduce the sum total of the nation's resources, since the exchange was always against them.[30] For this same reason the repeal of the Corn Laws in 1846 was not as beneficial to the Turks as it was to some of the other grain producing states.

A large proportion of the Turkish balances were paid in bullion or specie.[31] Since they did not resort to borrowing until about 1850 [32] depreciation of the currency was necessary in order to produce the needed specie to meet their annual payments.[33] Devaluation of the Ottoman currency, which in turn caused an ever-increasing price level, raised havoc with Turkish finance and tended to weaken the whole economic structure of the Empire to a degree a less rich country could not have withstood.[34] From the British viewpoint, however, as long as there remained investment sources, the transfer of gold was very beneficial. This explains why the business element in England was so anxious to maintain amicable relations with the Ottoman state in the first half of the nineteenth century. In order to appreciate the real significance of Britain's trade with Turkey in this period, a glance at the Turkish side of the picture is equally important.

The Ottoman Empire in the nineteenth century was primarily an agricultural country.[35] Its products were chiefly those of the soil, tobacco, grains, cotton wool, sheep and lamb's wool, valo-

---

the repeal of the Corn Laws it became the fourth most important export in 1850 and in 1855 it was second. Cf. Appendix II, Tables 12, 13, and 14.

[30] Engelhardt, *op. cit.*, I, 100.

[31] Paid in London in sterling, a great disadvantage to the Turks. Ubicini, *Letters*, I, 301n.

[32] D. E. Blaisdell, *European Financial Control in the Ottoman Empire; a Study of the Establishment, Activities, and Significance of the Administration of the Ottoman Public Debt*, New York, 1929, p. 27.

[33] Sixty million piastres (£552,000) in paper currency was issued in 1841. Ubicini, *Letters*, I, 299.

[34] Abuse and lack of currency was particularly hard on the agricultural classes which provided the products with which to secure foreign manufactured goods. *Ibid.*, p. 330.

[35] Ubicini, *Letters*, I, 307–338. For the influence of geography and climate on agriculture, cf. L. J. Gordon, *American Relations with Turkey; an economic interpretation*, Philadelphia, 1932, pp. 74–81.

nia, etc.[36] Yet, the Turkish state was never a self-contained unit, both because agriculture was never developed to the point of complete self-sufficiency[37] and because of the almost total absence of manufactured articles. Turkey's dependence upon outside states for manufactured goods later proved her undoing, because it led to exploitation by the more advanced states which Turkey was not able to prevent by counter-competition. It must be admitted, however, that the great variety of her soil-products was one of the reasons why Turkey so long survived her weak governmental administration within and the frequent attacks of neighboring states from without.

Except for the silk manufactures of Brusa there was little or no industry in Turkey prior to 1850. The industrial revolution in the sense of changes in methods of production and distribution has only come to Turkey in recent times, and then largely through foreign exploitation.[38] The Turks remained content with the easier method of trading the products of the soil and small luxury articles for manufactured necessities. More specific reasons for Turkey's industrial backwardness were the lack of capital, the limited resources of coal and iron, and the absence of protective tariffs to encourage industry. Thus, the traditional dependence on outside sources (encouraged by foreign traders), together with the character of the people, satisfied with the usual necessities of life, tended to keep industry in the handicraft stage, — small shops employing a few men. Turkey's foreign trade, and in particular her commercial relations with Britain to 1855, cannot be understood apart from the above facts.

The most cursory study of Turkish commerce proves that

[36] Other products were: rice, honey, olive oil, fruits and vegetables, wine, opium, flax, hemp, silk, sugar-cane, timber, resin, turpentine, cattle, gold, silver, iron, tin, lead, salt, and marble, sponges, and fish. The predominance of soil-products is most striking.

[37] Lack of knowledge, dearth of labor, want of capital, and poor transportation and communication were the reasons for Turkey's agricultural deficiencies. Ubicini, *Letters*, vol. I, Letter #15, pp. 307–338.

[38] To effect a real industrial system and thereby make Turkey self-sufficient was one of the aims of the late Mustapha Kemal, Ataturk Ghazi.

the Turks as a people were not a nation of traders. That as individuals they drove shrewd bargains no traveller in Turkey would dispute, but collectively, when compared with some of the western states, they appear most un-commercial. The fact that the majority of merchants and bankers in Turkey were not Turks but Armenians, Greeks, Franks, or Jews, is but one instance. The complete absence of any protective system is an even more striking example of their commercial backwardness. From the time of Suleiman, the Turks allowed foreign goods to enter their country freely.[39] A 3 per cent ad valorem duty on imports and a small anchorage fee were the only taxes on foreign trade.[40] On the other hand the Turks suffered an export duty of 12 per cent on native products.[41] Why the Turkish government reversed the usual action of tariffs has never been fully explained. Even the need of more money to manage their ever-growing governmental administration was not enough to induce them to change their traditional tariff policy. Instead of introducing a tariff for revenue purposes only the government preferred to increase taxes or depreciate the currency. When these methods were not sufficient, rather than borrow,[42] the Sultan debased the coinage still further, thereby subjecting the people to double taxation.

While such a commercial system as has just been described spelled backwardness for Turkey, it meant wealth for English tradesmen. It was no wonder then that they exerted all the pressure they possibly could upon the Foreign Office to act in behalf of Turkey to prevent such a valuable market from being lost to other powers, especially Russia. One of the most ardent

[39] In almost every case the dues levied on British ships were lower than those charged Ottoman vessels. Firmans to pass the Bosporus and the Dardanelles could be procured by British captains for approximately the same fee as Turkish masters paid. F. O. 78/358, Cartwright to Ponsonby, September 11, 1839.

[40] An additional tax of 2 per cent was levied on the consumer of the foreign goods, thereby making a total tax of 5 per cent. J. R. McCulloch, *A Dictionary, Practical, Theoretical and Historical, of Commerce and Commercial Navigation,* London, 1834, p. 394.

[41] Seller paid 9 per cent; buyer 3 per cent. *Ibid.,* p. 394.

[42] The problem of international loans and foreign indebtedness did not become acute until the last quarter of the nineteenth century.

advocates of the advantage to Britain of a free and independent Turkey, David Urquhart, expressed the sentiments of many of his countrymen in his many books and pamphlets, in particular his *Turkey and Its Resources* written in 1833. His conclusion to his chapter on the "Commercial Resources of Turkey" was an appeal in which many joined.

Turkey [wrote Urquhart] is a country having three thousand miles of coast still remaining, and a territory of five thousand square miles, under the happiest climate, possessed of the richest soil, raising every variety of produce, having unrivalled facilities for transport, abounding in forests and mines, opening innumerable communications with countries further to the East with all which our traffic is carried on in English bottoms, where labour is cheap, where industry is unshackled, and commerce is free, where our goods remand every market, where government and consumers alike desire their introduction. But all the advantages that may accrue to us from so favorable a state of things, is contingent on her internal tranquillity and political re-organization. Here is a field for diplomatic action of the noblest and most philanthropic character, where our interests are so much at stake as to call forth our most strenuous exertions, and where that interest is so reciprocal as to involve no selfish motives, and to introduce no invidious distinctions.[43]

What of the antecedents of this commerce which was so important from 1825 to 1853? Before treating specifically the articles of commerce between the two countries, and the ports visited by the "English bottoms," it seems pertinent to treat briefly the background of British trade in the Levant in the years before 1825. Anglo-Turkish commerce antedated Anglo-Turkish political relations by more than two centuries. England, like most of the western states in the Middle Ages, had been a market for the Genoese traders bringing goods from the Levant, but commercial intercourse in the real sense of the term did not begin until the second half of the sixteenth century. By 1579 English merchants were recognized at Constantinople, and two years later the Levant Company was established.[44]

[43] Urquhart, *Turkey and Its Resources*, pp. 216–227.
[44] The Levant Company was reincorporated and given a new charter by James I in 1605, just five years after the East India Company, which always

English trade in the Near East improved under this organization and by 1700 had surpassed that of the French in spite of Richelieu's and Colbert's efforts to strengthen French commerce in that area. The Levant Company existed until 1826, but since it was an open or regulated company, i.e. dependent on the government for protection,[45] the British government had been forced to enter into many entangling capitulations and articles of peace in the seventeenth and eighteenth centuries.[46]

While steady progress had been made since the early seventeenth century, it was not until 1753 that the ships of the Levant Company were free to enter any Turkish port for the uniform fee of £20, instead of the fees which varied from 25 to 50 pounds according to the good-will of the local pasha. In 1758 all territory within the company's sphere of influence was placed under an embargo against foreign importations which gave the company a virtual monopoly in certain areas.[47] Finally, a decree of the Sultan (October 20, 1799) gave to British merchants the long-sought privilege of commerce on the Black Sea.[48] All these rights and many others were eventually confirmed in the Treaty of the Dardanelles, concluded January 5, 1809,[49] which provided for freedom for British ships on the seas surround Turkey, the right to enter any port for stores, safety, etc., protection of British nationals in all trading centers, the right to maintain consuls in some of the lesser ports, and generally that all Britishers should have the same rights and privileges as the French or other traders. The reason for

---

overshadowed it in importance, received its charter. E. Lipson, *Economic History of England*, 3 vols., London, 1915–1931, II, 335–352. For a recent treatment of the Levant Company, see A. C. Wood, *The History of the Levant Company*, London, 1935.

[45] For the difference between open or regulated companies and joint stock companies, cf. McCulloch, *op. cit.*, pp. 386–389.

[46] For a complete list of capitulations, cf. Lewis L. Hertslet, ed., *A Complete Collection of the Treaties and Conventions, . . . as They Relate to Commerce and Navigation*, 30 vols., London, 1840–1924, II, 346–369. Brief summary of same in McCulloch, *op. cit.*, pp. 1349–1350.

[47] MacGregor, *op. cit.*, II, 65.

[48] *Ibid.*, p. 30.

[49] Hertslet, *op. cit.*, II, 371.

this clarification and restatement was that during the period of the revolution, English merchants had secured control of most of the foreign trade in Turkey from the French, and they needed adequate protection in their new field. Such was the situation when the end of the wars on the continent made Turkey one of the most important outlets for British production.

Thus, the establishment of peace in 1815 and the liquidation of the problems raised by the war allowed British commerce and industry to go forward. A shorter and quicker means of transportation to the distant portions of the empire and the world which supplied both the raw materials and the markets for this new expansion became a prime necessity. Moreover, since the Turkish Empire lay directly across the principal routes to India and the East, England became more and more aware of the dangers which the Sultan faced both within and without his vast yet rapidly disintegrating empire. Yet, this was but one reason for English anxiety for the "sick man" after 1833. In an era of ever-increasing economic activity the direct trade between England and the Ottoman Empire,[50] due in part to the prohibitions and restrictions which existed in the European markets, was equally important.

In the two decades after 1830 Britain sold more and more goods in the Levant until by 1850 Turkey was surpassed only by the Hanse Towns and Holland as an outlet for British manufactures. Italy, France, Russia, and the Austrian territories were all less significant than the Ottoman Empire, Russia by more than a million pounds. The importance of the Ottoman Empire in British trade is shown by Table 3.

Thus, as was so often true of foreign policies in general in the nineteenth century (British policy in particular), self-interest was one of the primary motives for Britain's determination to

[50] Direct trade between England and Turkey was enhanced by the modification of the Navigation Laws, June 25, 1821, removing trade restrictions with Turkey as well as Russia. Cf. Hansard, *op. cit.*, new series, V, 1289–1310.

maintain the Ottoman state.[51] A more detailed examination of the various articles exchanged between England and Turkey, as well as a study of the principal trade centers of the Turkish Empire, will provide more specific proof of the place of the

TABLE 3
DECLARED VALUE OF EXPORTS FROM THE UNITED KINGDOM, 1850 *

Hanse Towns	£6,755,000
Holland	3,542,000
Turkey	2,811,000
Italy	2,791,000
France	2,401,000
Russia	1,455,000
Austrian Territories	607,000

* Levi, *op. cit.*, p. 562. The declared value of British exports to Turkey in 1850, as shown in the customs reports, was £2,515,821.

Ottoman state in British trade, and correlatively her importance in British foreign policy in the decades prior to the outbreak of the Crimean War.

[51] "Commercial opportunity for foreigners in free-trade, non-competing Turkey, . . . was one of the principal reasons for the British policy of maintenance of the Ottoman Empire, . . . especially after the signature of the Russo-Turkish alliance of Unkiar Skelessi in 1833. . . ." Puryear, *International Economics, op. cit.*, p. 1.

CHAPTER III

ANGLO–TURKISH TRADE, 1825–1855 [1]

THOUGH the tables of exports and imports [2] are the best proof of the importance of the Ottoman Empire in British trade, a few remarks on the nature of British exports to and imports from Turkey in the three decades preceding the Crimean War may not be irrelevant here. Two facts stand out in the most cursory analysis of the appended tables: first, the great increase in the number of articles exported to and imported from Turkey; these prove beyond question that Turkey was one of Britain's important outlets for manufactured goods as well as a significant source for raw materials. Of equal significance was the steady predominance of agricultural products coming into Britain from the Levant, while the goods exchanged were primarily manufactured products.

A comparison of the exports to Turkey in the years 1825 and 1855 is the best proof of the relative importance of the Levant trade to British commercial activity as a whole. In 1825, for example, the number of articles valued at one hundred pounds or more exported to Turkey was twenty-eight. This figure was not passed until 1845, but from that date on the increase was very rapid, especially in the years 1850 to 1855 when the number of articles exported increased from thirty-nine to eighty-four. This sudden upturn was due to certain developments of that half-decade. One of the new items in 1855, for example, was naval stores. That one-third of the total production of these articles went out to Turkey in 1855 was due, no doubt,

[1] While recognizing that the year 1855 was by no means a normal year, due to the Crimean War, nevertheless it has seemed more feasible to use that date rather than 1853 (as in the previous chapter) in view of the fact that my other tables were for each fifth year and 1855 marks the end of three decades.

[2] Tables 1–14, Appendix II.

to the increased needs resulting from the Crimean War. Another example is the case of telegraph materials. The extension of the telegraph to Constantinople necessitated the purchase in 1855 of £71,000 worth of telegraph wires, while the total production of this article in the United Kingdom amounted to only £163,737.

There were few changes in the general character of the export trade, however, manufactured goods predominating throughout the whole three decades. It is interesting to note that no foodstuffs were exported to Turkey in 1825,[3] but, in 1855, thirteen of the forty-five new articles listed in that year were foodstuffs, some of which were of considerable importance. For example, one-third of the provisions produced in Britain in 1855 were exported to the Ottoman state, as well as one half of the salt pork, and one fifth of the beef. Yet, of the total eighty-four items, more than sixty of them must be classed in the category of manufactured goods.

The single most important manufactured article which held first place during the whole thirty years was cotton cloth. After cotton, in order of importance, came refined sugar, iron and steel (exclusive of ore), woolens, i.e. yarn and manufactures, unwrought tin, and hardware and cutlery.[4]

Turkey became an important outlet for English textiles during the Napoleonic period. At that time England's rivals, Austria and Switzerland, were unable to compete with Britain's more substantial output.[5] After 1815 Britain was able to maintain control of this new market because of the steady lowering price levels which a larger market and more efficient methods of production made possible. Transport costs notwithstanding, British merchants were able to sell cottons, for example, on the Turkish frontier cheaper than the neighboring Austrian traders.[6] While Turkey imported but a small part of the total

[3] Items valued at less than one hundred pounds were not considered in this survey of the Customs ledgers.

[4] For quantity and value of these articles exported from the United Kingdom, see Appendix II, Tables 1–7.   [5] McCulloch, *op. cit.*, p. 395.

[6] Urquhart, *Turkey and Its Resources, op. cit.*, p. 170.

production of cottons in England (approximately one thirty-eighth) in 1825, it became a very significant outlet in the next three decades. Britain produced some eighteen million pounds worth of cottons, yet the quantity sent to Turkey was valued

CHART IV

Total Cotton Goods Exported from the United Kingdom
to Turkey, 1825–1855

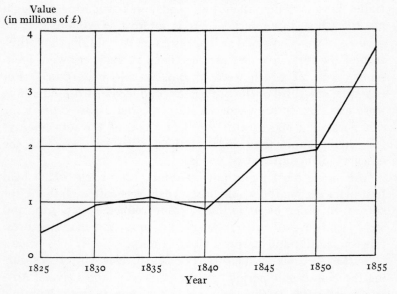

at £490,413 in 1825. In the next five years cottons exported to Turkey almost doubled, and a steady increase followed until in 1855 when the total production was valued at £34,763,792, well over £3,000,000 was the return from this item sold in Turkey, or approximately one ninth of the total production.[7]

Largely because of the climate and habits of the Turks, the Ottoman state was not an equally important outlet for English woolens. Yet, the exports of woolen yarn and manufactures increased seventeen-fold, from £8,318 in 1825 to £142,772 in 1855. One notes a decrease in 1840, after several years of in-

[7] Cf. Tables 1 and 6, Appendix II.

creased consumption of English woolens. This is partly explained by the fact that Carcassone and Austrian woolens, dyed to suit the Turkish taste, were becoming really competitive. The British manufacturers did not study the oriental desires as

CHART V

WOOLENS EXPORTED FROM THE UNITED KINGDOM TO TURKEY,
1825–1855

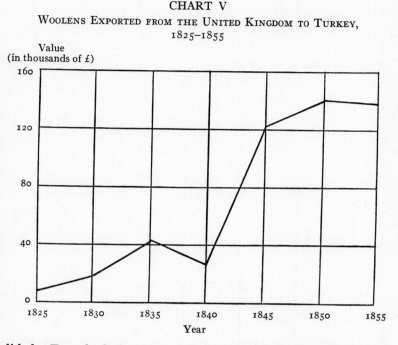

Value
(in thousands of £)

Year

did the French, Swiss or Germans, and when the cheaper English woolens fell off in total production as they did in 1840, it made it easier for the other traders to press their dyed-to-order products.

In some respects the tables of exports are most deceiving. For example, in 1825 refined sugar was second on the list of exports to Turkey, but due to extreme increases in certain items by 1855 it was seventeenth, yet the actual quantity sold to the Turks increased from 10,930 cwt. to 14,149 cwt. in the three decades. Thus, instead of Turkey consuming but one thirty-eighth of British refined sugar as in 1825, due to a decrease in the total production of this product from almost 400,000 cwt. to slightly over 40,000 cwt., Turkey imported almost one-third of all the sugar refined in Britain in 1855. The figures for iron and steel are equally elusive. Here we find an increase from

CHART VI

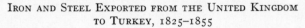

IRON AND STEEL EXPORTED FROM THE UNITED KINGDOM TO TURKEY, 1825–1855

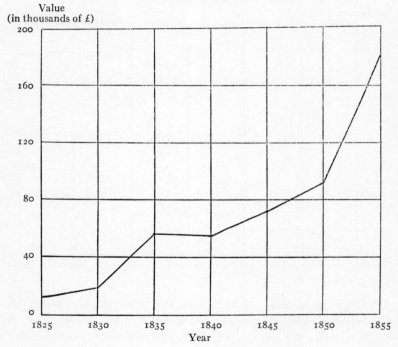

£12,527 in 1825 to £187,017 in 1855,[8] which is largely accounted for by the increased price of iron and steel; the actual quantity of this product sent to Turkey merely advanced from 6,223 tons in 1830 (no quantity figure for 1825) to 20,439 tons in 1855, little more than a three-fold increase.

[8] Consumption of British iron seems to have been little affected by the increased production of the Samakoff mines, near Philippopolis, which produced a cheaper grade of iron, except in the year 1842. Cf. MacGregor, *op. cit.*, II, 89.

Likewise Turkey imported but a small percentage of British unwrought tin in 1825 (about one seventeenth of total produced); by 1855, however, she took almost one-fifth of the production of that article. Tin plates exported to Turkey increased five-fold in the same period; and hardware and cutlery exports to Turkey jumped from 914 cwt. to 8,330 cwt., while the total production little more than doubled. The importance of Turkey as an outlet for British manufactured goods seems abundantly clear.

Aside from the principal exports to Turkey mentioned above most of the other items increased, though to a more limited degree. There were only three items which declined in importance over the three decades. Lead and shot went down steadily, until, by 1850, it amounted to only £179 in the Turkish trade.[9] While this was about one twenty-fifth of the 1825 figure (£4,495), it will be noted that the total exports of lead and shot dropped from £239,788 to £36,534 in the same period. Military stores fell off abruptly in the years 1825 to 1830, and never thereafter were valued at more than £547 which figure it touched in 1845. The number of watches exported to Turkey decreased almost fifty per cent in the thirty years after 1825, but due to the advancing prices of this item, the Turkish market was equally valuable in 1855 with the 1825 outlet. Yet these decreases were slight compared to the increases, and were more than made up for by the new items which appear in 1855, such as tarpaulins, half of which were manufactured for the Turkish trade, or tobacco, more than half of which was exported to Turkey to be mixed with their own production.

When one turns to Britain's imports from Turkey, the whole picture is seen in better perspective. The most important imports from Turkey in order of importance were madder root, raw silk, raisins, sheep and lamb's wood, and valonia. In 1825 Turkey was also an important source for cotton wool and yarn, camel and mohair yarn, and opium, but other sources developed

---

[9] In 1855 the Ottoman Empire used £813 worth of this British export out of some £44,447 worth exported, or about one fifty-fifth of the total production.

for these materials in the next three decades.[10] The predominance of agricultural products imported from Turkey is at once noted. Of the sixteen articles listed in 1825 no more than four could be catalogued as partial manufactures; the number

CHART VII

MADDER ROOT IMPORTED INTO THE UNITED KINGDOM
FROM TURKEY, 1825–1855

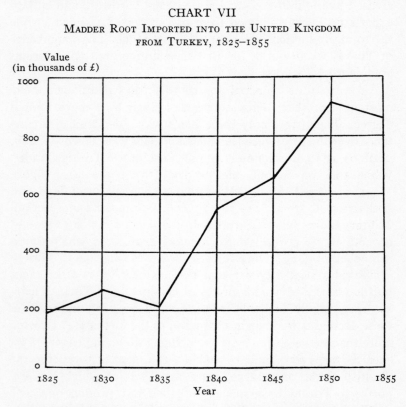

Value
(in thousands of £)

of manufactured articles remains fixed through the next three decades, but the total number of imports increased to thirty-nine.

While Turkey's exports to the United Kingdom were primarily soil-products, they included not only foodstuffs and

---

[10] India, Egypt, and the United States were the principal sources of raw cotton by 1840. For the decline of the Levant as a source of raw cotton, see Appendix II, Tables 8–14.

luxury articles but raw materials for the manufacturers as well. One of the most important in this last category was madder root,[11] used in the dying of textiles. In 1825 England imported 21,910 cwt. of madder root from Turkey or almost 50 per cent

CHART VIII

SILK IMPORTED INTO THE UNITED KINGDOM FROM TURKEY,
1825–1855

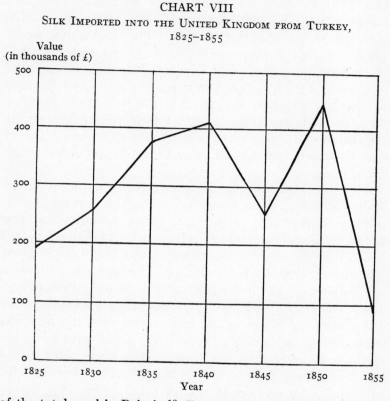

of the total used in Britain.[12] From 1840 on, madder root was Turkey's chief export to England, Turkey supplying more than half the amount used in 1855.

Turkey was also an important source of raw silk, an item

[11] For quantity and value of these items imported into the United Kingdom, see Appendix II, Tables 8–14.

[12] In my study of imports I have compared quantities in each case, because Imports were listed in Official Values, which was the usual evaluation until 1870. Real values were approximately 70 per cent of Official Values.

which ranked third in the list of imports in 1825, and rivalled madder root in most of the years studied until it dropped to fifth place in 1855. In 1825 Turkey produced one-third of all the raw silk consumed in the United Kingdom, ranking second only to Italy. Italy was displaced by France by 1840 as a source of raw silk, and Turkey was having difficulty in withstanding the competition of the East India Company for second place. By 1845 Turkey supplied England with more than half of the raw silk used, but the opening of certain Chinese ports as a result of the first Opium War added the necessary impetus to place the Far East well ahead of the Near East. In 1850, Turkish producers almost equalled their former figures, but the entrance of Egypt into the market in 1855 forced Turkey once again into fourth place, after China, Egypt, and the East India Company.

The steady increase in the consumption of raisins in the United Kingdom [13] was a boon to the Turkish growers and exporters. Turkey was the principal source for raisins in 1825, but by 1830 Spain had taken the lead which it held until 1855.[14] From that time on raisins varied from fifth to tenth place. The amount of sheep and lamb's wool imported into Britain increased from sixty-three million pounds to more than ninety-seven million pounds in thirty years. While Turkey supplied but a small percentage of this total, nevertheless this item was an important import from Turkey. The great variation in the quantity imported from the Ottoman state is explained by the new sources which were found during the period. For example, in 1840 Turkey supplied little more than half her 1835 figure; in that year more than a seven million pound increase appears in the total imported. Turkey ranked seventh after the East India Company, New South Wales, Cape Colony, Peru, Chile, Sweden. By 1855 Turkey held sixteenth place, the chief sources being New South Wales and British India.

[13] The years 1830 and 1850 were exceptions. Turkish raisins fell off in proportion to the total decrease in 1830, but dropped more severely in 1850. Cf. Appendix II, Tables 9 and 13.

[14] Except 1845, when Sardinia supplied a slightly larger quantity.

The one raw material of which Turkey had a virtual monopoly as far as Britain was concerned was valonia,[15] a byproduct of acorns, which was used by tanners in the English leather industry. While the total consumption of this article increased almost four-fold in the three decades, the quantity imported from Turkey increased more than six-fold. In the peak year, 1845, when Britain imported 381,154 cwt., 307,-080 cwt. came from Turkey. The falling off which shows up in the tables for 1850 and 1855 [16] was not caused by the opening of new sources, but by the fact that new processes made it less important.

Wool manufactures (i.e. carpets), olive oil, oil (otto of roses), and sponges were other items which Turkey sent to Britain in ever-increasing quantities. While three-fold increases are seen in both the total number of carpets imported and the number purchased in Turkey, olive oil and sponges increased twelve-fold each, while their respective totals increased six- and eight-fold. Turkey was the primary source of perfumed oil, known as otto of roses, throughout the whole period.

Though there was a general increase in Turkish products coming into the United Kingdom, there were some notable losses which should be recorded. During the three decades under study, certain items on the 1825 list fell off or disappeared entirely as imports into Britain. Cotton wool which was Turkey's chief export to England in 1825 (though only one-twelfth of the total imported by Britain) ranked thirty-eighth in the list in 1855, diminishing from almost nineteen million pounds to 5,700 pounds, when the Crimean War was in progress. This decrease is all the more remarkable when one notes that the total amount of cotton wool imported increased from 226,052,-135 pounds in 1825 to 796,207,100 pounds in 1855.[17] The only

[15] The name "valonia" was derived from the Albanian seaport of Valona, which was the outlet for this whole region, where oak forests abounded.

[16] In 1850 the total importation into Britain of valonia had dropped to 12,562 tons, of which 10,822 tons came from Turkey; in 1855 Turkey supplied 8,753 tons out of a total of 10,838 tons used. See Appendix II, Tables 13 and 14.

[17] Cf. Appendix II, Tables 8 and 14.

explanation is the fact that while the United States remained the principal source throughout the period, new sources such as Brazil, Egypt, and India appeared. Cotton yarn followed the same course as raw cotton, falling from 67,174 pounds in 1825 to 3,314 pounds in 1855 while the total increased from 67,228 to more than a million pounds.[18] Turkey's monopoly of this article lasted barely a decade, when she was superseded by Holland and Belgium in 1835.

Camel and mohair yarn was almost a Turkish monopoly as far as the United Kingdom was concerned in that almost 90 per cent of this product (and in 1845 more than 99 per cent) came from the Sultan's dominions. The years 1840 and 1850 show tremendous decreases in the quantity purchased in Turkey, but there is a corresponding decrease in the total amount imported. Opium was another item which showed fluctuation as far as the Turkish market was concerned. After a decade as the fifth most valuable import from Turkey, opium fell to thirteenth position, and though it came back to seventh place in 1845, the period closed with opium listed after seventeen other articles. This variation is partly explained by the presence of new items in the list, and partly by the fact that the demands of Britain for opium were not constant. In general, however, England depended on Turkey for this important drug; except for the year 1840,[19] when Turkey produced but 65 per cent of the British opium used, 90 per cent of all the opiates consumed in the United Kingdom were made from poppies grown in the Ottoman Empire, and in two of these years, 1825 and 1845, Turkey supplied 94 per cent.

Two items found in the table for 1825 are not found in the 1855 table: wet hides were no longer sold with profit to British traders by the Turks after 1840, because of the competition offered by Argentine, Brazil, and the United States, and goat's hair, after increasing steadily, suddenly ceased to appear in

---

[18] Cf. Appendix II, Tables 8 and 14.

[19] In 1840 the East India Company sent more than one fifth of all the opium used in Britain, valued at £2,629.

1845, except in very small quantities. But these losses and the decreases treated above were of no great significance, because they were replaced by many new articles: copper, brass, corn (wheat, barley, Indian corn), seeds, tobacco, figs, nuts, and other products of the soil. Further comment on the tabulated data seems unnecessary to emphasize the steadily increasing place of Turkey in the commercial relations of the United Kingdom. However, to complete the picture a brief survey of the principal ports of the Ottoman Empire through which this exchange of manufactured articles for raw materials went on seems appropriate.

Turkey's three thousand miles of coast line included many fine harbors which became entrepôts for exports and imports. During the first half of the nineteenth century the chief ports of the Ottoman Empire were Constantinople, Smyrna, Salonica, Beyrout, Alexandretta, Enos (Port of Adrianople), Galacz at the mouth of the Danube, Trebizond, and Scutari.[20]

Constantinople possessed a deep, sheltered harbor with anchorage for as many as twelve hundred ships. While more ships entered and cleared in the Golden Horn than in any other port of the empire,[21] Constantinople was by no means the most important commercial city of the empire. Because of its location many ships made it a port of call on their way to and from the Black Sea ports; also, it should be noted that the great majority of the vessels clearing at Constantinople were small coastwise vessels under Greek command. For example, in the year 1840, of the 5,630 ships arriving at Constantinople (5,499 departing) Greece led the list with 2,361 entering and 2,297 departing. Austria was second with 869 entering (133,878 tons) and 568 departing (134,710 tons), and England third with 567.[22] Goods

[20] *Pope's Yearly Journal* also includes Cisme, Larissa, Macri, Scalanova. Cf. *The Year Journal of Trade*, 1837–1839, ed. by Charles Pope, London, 1839.

[21] The year 1840 is used in several instances as an index year, because it falls midway in the period under study. 5,630 ships arrived at Constantinople in 1840, 969 at Smyrna, and 388 at Salonica; the departures were 5,499, 962, and 385 respectively. MacGregor, *op. cit.*, II, 79.

[22] MacGregor, *op. cit.*, II, 79. In 1846, 907 British vessels called at Constan-

brought to Constantinople ranged from corn, iron, timber, tallow, and furs from the Black Sea area to cotton stuffs, yarn, woolens, silks, coal, tin, cutlery, jewelry, paper, and glass from the European ports. Constantinople exported silk, wool, carpets, hides and leather, opium and drugs, and precious stones, but many of these were re-exports from other neighboring parts of the empire. In the period from 1825 until the middle of the century, in spite of the excellence of its harbor and the strategic location of the Ottoman capital between Europe and Asia, Constantinople was not a great distributing center; it cannot be compared with Smyrna, the great entrepôt for Asia Minor, or Salonica, the distributing point for the Balkan area. Constantinople imported little more than its population of about 600,-000 [23] could consume, the balance being re-exported to Odessa, Trebizond, or the Danubian ports,[24] while many ships cleared at Constantinople in ballast, picking up return cargoes at Smyrna or Salonica.

British trade with Constantinople in this period was not extensive. Consul Cartwright reported two hundred and eighty-nine English ships arriving at the Ottoman capital in 1835, as opposed to three hundred and fifty-three for Austria, and three hundred and ninety-seven Russian ships. More than half of these English vessels (one hundred and fifty-six, totaling 31,387 tons) merely touched at Constantinople on their way to or from ports on the Black Sea. The remaining one hundred and thirty-three (22,155 tons) brought goods for consumption in Constantinople. Of these the largest number (51) came from Liverpool bearing manufactures, general cargo, or coal, four of which went back to England laden with silk, wool, and mohair yarn, while nineteen vessels went to Smyrna in ballast or with the remainder of their cargo, thirteen to Odessa, and the rest to Galacz, Taganrog, Trebizond, or other minor ports. A similar

tinople and by 1851 England had second place with 1,156 ships. Michelsen, *op. cit.*, pp. 198–199.

[23] Estimate of Marshal Marmont in 1834; Marmont, *op. cit.*, p. 13. Ubicini estimates 891,000 ten years later (1844). Ubicini, *Letters*, I, 24.

[24] McCulloch, *op. cit.*, p. 395.

analysis was made for the ships from London and Cardiff with the same result, verifying the conclusion that few ships from English ports shipped their whole cargo to Constantinople. Moreover, few ships came directly to the Horn from England; the great majority, like those from Liverpool and London, made previous stops at Smyrna or Salonica, according to Cartwright.[25] By 1840 the number of British ships entering the Horn had risen to five hundred and sixty-seven, yet only one hundred and seventy brought English goods, valued at £1,189,-904, for consumption in the city or its environs.[26] The great majority of English bottoms (in 1840, 397) merely registered at Constantinople, and then proceeded to Russian or other ports on the Black Sea.[27] Scutari, on the Asiatic shores of the Bosporus about a mile from the Turkish capital, sometimes treated as a separate port, was really a part of Constantinople. It was especially noted for its corn warehouses and as the assembling point for caravans penetrating Persia and Armenia.

More important than Constantinople as a trading center in the first half of the nineteenth century was Smyrna in Asia Minor; in fact Smyrna might be called the first commercial city of the Near East. While the population of Smyrna [28] was not to be compared with that of Constantinople, its well-protected harbor and its connections with the interior gave it an advantage over the Turkish capital. A contemporary traveller

[25] B. T. 2/1. Cartwright to Palmerston, #10, 1836. The total tonnage of the English ships in Constantinople in 1835 was 54,148 tons; Cartwright was unable to report the value of their cargoes.

[26] In 1850 Constantinople imported manufactures from London, Liverpool and Southampton valued at £2,512,594. Michelsen, *op. cit.*, p. 212.

[27] MacGregor, *op. cit.*, II, 79 ff. MacGregor states that of the 4,133 ships arriving in Constantinople in 1841, 570 were British, but only 139 from English ports. The distribution of these was as follows:

From Liverpool	50 ships	— 10,075 tons
London	24	— 5,075
England (with coals)	54	— 13,760
Cardiff	11	— 2,374
TOTAL	139 ships	— 31,284 tons

[28] About 130,000, 50 per cent of whom were Turks. Cf. Juchereau de Saint Denys, *op. cit.*, I, 194.

in this part of the world, Marshal Marmont, described Smyrna in 1834 as "the greatest, and indeed almost the only place of commerce in the Turkish Dominions," [29] and he was convinced that it would retain its pre-eminence in spite of the efforts of the Turks to remove the trade to Constantinople.

Smyrna was located in the center of one of the most fertile districts of Asia Minor as well as on a direct line between the European markets and the distant East, and had been for many years the embarkation point for caravans en route to Syria, Bagdad, and Persia. Although the Sultan held a monopoly of certain articles bought and sold in Smyrna, the silk trade in particular, the absence of a strict trade policy on the part of the Turks made Smyrna almost a free port in the first half of the nineteenth century. Port dues were small (£1, 14 s. for deposit of papers, clearance, etc.; there were no light house or harbor dues), and the import and export duties were five and two per cent respectively.[30] The disorder which prevailed within the Sultan's government and the general unrest in the region did not affect the prosperity of the port of Smyrna. In 1833, the year in which Mahmoud's control of Asia Minor was seriously threatened by Mehemet Ali, Smyrna exported some 74,-692,129 piasters' worth of goods. Since goods valued at 50,359,-454 piasters were imported, a favorable trade balance of more than twenty-four million piasters or almost two and a half million pounds was shown. Trade balances of this kind over a period of years soon increased the total capital of the region until Smyrna was one of the wealthiest areas of Asia Minor.

Smyrna handled more foreign produce than any other port of the Empire. From Odessa Smyrna imported grain, furs, butter, and some iron, but the bulk of her trade was with western Europe, especially Britain, France, Italy, and even with the United States. These countries supplied manufactured cotton and woolen goods, tin, paper, glass, and other manufactured

[29] Marmont, op. cit., p. 177. MacFarlane reported the existence of twenty English business houses in Smyrna in 1828. MacFarlane, op. cit., p. 20.
[30] MacGregor, op. cit., II, 96.

products in return for raw wool, cotton wool, carpets, old copper, hides and skins, olive oil, madder root, drugs, sponges, dried fruits, and valonia. One of the most valuable exports from this port was manufactured silk, which was brought by caravan from Brusa, the Lyons of Turkey, some 200 miles distant. In 1839, for example, more than £15,000 worth of made-up silk was sent to England alone.

The number of ships entering and clearing at Smyrna is another proof of its importance as a trading center. In 1836,

TABLE 4

RETURN OF BRITISH TRADE, PORT OF SMYRNA, 1835 *

	Arrived		Departed	
	Vessels	Tons	Vessels	Tons
British	114	16,140	115	16,526
British, Ionian	37	2,272	37	2,272
British, Maltese	7	1,510	7	1,510
British, Hanoverian	1	90	1	90
Turkish	None		None	
American	27	4,448	27	4,448
Austrian	166	30,980	160	29,246
Dutch	7	970	7	970
French	53	7,768	37	5,175
Greek	770	44,430	751	42,956
Russian	44	5,118	41	4,638
Sardinian	29	5,139	27	4,992
TOTAL	1,255	118,865	1,210	112,823

* B. T. 2/1 Brant to Board of Trade, #6, Feb. 6, 1836. Invoice value of goods imported and exported not given. While the total number of ships entering and departing (and their total cargo) was greater than for the year 1834, the number of British ships arriving at Smyrna declined by fifteen, those departing by six. Cf. Brant's report for 1834, F. O. 78/261. For years 1848–1851 cf. Michelsen, *op. cit.*, pp. 208–209.

Consul Brant reported that 1,255 ships arrived at Smyrna in the previous year, bearing 118,865 tons of goods, while 112,821 tons were exported in 1,210 ships.[31] English ships ranked third after Greek and Austrian. The distribution of the vessels is shown by Table 4.

[31] B. T. 2/1 Brant to Board of Trade, #6, Feb. 6, 1836.

Consul Brant's report contains valuable information concerning the Anglo-Turkish trade in the port of Smyrna, in particular the home ports and cargoes; these facts are best presented in table form (Table 5).

TABLE 5
BRITISH SHIPS ARRIVING AT SMYRNA, 1835

	Ships	Cargo
From London	14	General
" Liverpool	25	"
" Constantinople	27	Ballast
" Beyrout	5	"
" Salonica	6	"
" Cardiff	8	Coal, Iron
" Other ports	29	

BRITISH SHIPS DEPARTING FROM SMYRNA, 1835 *

	Ships	Cargo
For London	18	General cargo, valonia, fruit
" Liverpool	30	" " " "
" Constantinople	4	Ballast
" Falmouth	2	Valonia
" Bristol	6	" , fruit
" Belfast	1	"
" Dublin	1	"
" Amsterdam	2	Raisins, opium, cotton, carpets
" Odessa	2	Ballast
" Other ports	49	

* B. T. 2/1 Brant to Board of Trade, #6, Feb. 6, 1836.

In the year 1839 Britain exported to Smyrna goods valued at £189,160, but her purchases there of £418,076 helped to offset Turkey's total unfavorable balance of more than two million pounds. Table 6 explains England's position in the commerce of Smyrna in that year. The principal articles imported from England were cotton goods, iron, hardware and cutlery, sugar, tin, and lead, while Britain purchased £138,760 of dyestuffs, large quantities of corn, valonia, dried fruits, carpets, silks, wool, and sponges.

Like Smyrna, another important link between Europe and Asia was Beyrout, the port of Damascus. Much of the overland trade to Bagdad, Bussora, and Persia went by way of Beyrout. Though Damascus was a large city of approximately

TABLE 6

TRADE OF SMYRNA, 1839 *

Country traded with	Imports	Exports
England	£189,160	£418,076
Austria	152,568	291,428
United States	132,924	174,432
Russia	46,984	56,756
France	45,376	306,372
Sardinia, Malta, Holland, Egypt, Syria, Tuscany, Belgium	114,152	187,176
TOTAL	£681,164	£1,434,240

* MacGregor, *op. cit.*, II, 100.

120,000 people,[32] Beyrout's population ranged between eight to ten thousand in the early thirties.[33] According to Consul Moore the number of ships under British colours arriving at Beyrout in the decade 1824 to 1834 varied from fifteen to twenty-eight, the latter figure being the number which arrived in 1833, the very year that Mehemet Ali was carrying his campaign against the Sultan for possession of that region.[34] The next year the figure dropped to thirteen but within six years it returned to thirty-five. Table 7 gives a good picture of the growth of British trade in this port.

English tonnage in the port of Beyrout increased more than three-fold (from 1,635 to 5,231 tons) in the six years 1835–1841, yet the total tonnage less than doubled.

The character of the British trade with Beyrout is shown by the Consulate's report for 1835; manufactured goods were ex-

[32] MacGregor, *op. cit.*, II, 135. Cf. also F. O. 78/380, Report on Syria for 1835, dated July, 1839.

[33] Marmont, *op. cit.*, p. 223.

[34] MacGregor, *op. cit.*, II, 151.

TABLE 7

BRITISH AND FOREIGN TRADE AT THE PORT OF BEYROUT, 1835 *

Nation	Arrived			Departed		
	Ships	Tons	Value	Ships	Tons	Value
British	13	1,635	Unknown	12	1,513	Unknown
French	26	2,017	£66,825	16	1,388	"
Austrian	20	4,153	Unknown	17	3,617	"
Russian	10	....	"	...	.....	"
Greek	104	7,993	£1,244	108	7,742	£2,466
Others	168	5,449	£57,380	63	4,852	£132,510
TOTAL	341	21,247	£125,449	216	19,112	£134,976

BRITISH AND FOREIGN TRADE AT THE PORT OF BEYROUT, 1841

Nation	Arrived			Departed		
	Ships	Tons	Value	Ships	Tons	Value
British	35	5,231	Unknown	35	5,231	Unknown
French	23	3,322	"	21	3,009	"
Austrian	26	3,966	£30,000	26	3,966	£20,000
Russian	4	326	£2,000	4	326	Ballast
Greek	68	5,576	£34,747	68	5,576	£5,128
Others	227	20,020	Unknown	227	20,020	Unknown
TOTAL	383	38,441	£66,747	381	38,128	£25,128

* MacGregor, *op. cit.*, p. 152. Similar data for years 1848–1851 will be found in Michelsen, *op. cit.*, pp. 226–228.

changed for raw materials for the most part. For example, eight vessels from Liverpool brought:

64	bales	cambric	130	bales	imitation Italian shawls
967	"	cotton twist	82	"	prints
151	"	calico	230	"	muslins
229	"	longcloths	81	"	handkerchiefs
54	cases	indigo	23	"	small shawls [35]

Five of these ships departed for Liverpool and London bearing:

20	bales	inferior silk	2230	bales	goat's skins
160	"	cotton	1	"	hare skins
10	"	sheep's wool	862	"	hides
15	"	sheep skins	75	bbls.	madder root

[35] MacGregor, *op. cit.*, II, 152.

1 bale carpets	12 cases fruit
275 cases soap	8 bbls. tobacco
4 bbls. oil	8 " sponges [36]

The trade of Beyrout and Damascus increased as interest in the overland route to India increased in the thirties, and it seems to have been little affected by the attempts of the Sultan's vassal to secure control of the region.

Approximately a hundred miles north of Beyrout lay the small port of Alexandretta (sometimes called Scanderoun). Trade reports are not listed under this name, but under Aleppo, a larger city some thirty miles inland, about half-way between the coast and the Euphrates River. Direct trade between Aleppo and the United Kingdom began in 1828, but owing to the disturbances of the early thirties, seven years elapsed before British concerns established business representatives in that city.[37]

The principal articles imported from England were textiles, sugar, and tin. Gray cottons more than doubled between 1830 and 1837, while printed cottons and printed handkerchiefs trebled. Woolens are not listed, except for 1836 when 200,000 piasters' worth were imported. The value of sugar imported increased from 96,000 piasters to 490,000 piasters in the same period. Tin increased somewhat less. MacGregor states that it is impossible to secure even approximate accounts of the exports of Aleppo, "because the exported goods come from several cities and the trade is carried on by natives, some of which is accomplished by means of exchanges in kind." [38] He reports five ships, 647 tons, sailing for England in 1836 bearing goods valued at £25,040.

While the figures noted above were but an infinitesimal part of Britain's total trade with the Ottoman Empire, it should be noted that the monopoly which English merchants maintained in some of these lesser ports was the factor which made their

[36] *Ibid.*, p. 151.
[37] MacGregor, *op. cit.*, II, 143.
[38] *Ibid.*

total trade with Turkey so important. The extent to which British imports superseded those of the other powers is shown by Table 8.

TABLE 8

BRITISH AND FOREIGN TRADE AT THE PORT OF ALEXANDRETTA
(CONSULATE OF ALEPPO), 1837 *

Nation	Arrived			Departed		
	Ships	Tons	Value	Ships	Tons	Value
British	13	1,720	£165,177	12	1,591	£1,710
French	7	1,017	15,439	6	887	8,865
Austrian	1	180	......	1	180	1,650
Tuscan	1	140	......	1	140	1,035
Sardinian	2	270	......	2	270	8,195
TOTAL	24	3,327	£180,616	22	3,068	£21,455

* MacGregor, *op. cit.*, II, 80. For years 1848–1851 cf. Michelsen, *op. cit.*, pp. 229–230.

British merchants met some competition from the other states in such items as Turkey red prints, which Switzerland provided at a much lower figure, handkerchief cassimeres, and cotton crepes from France, while Genoa and Leghorn provided the velvets consumed there. Though British paper was of a much better grade, Italy supplied Aleppo with larger amounts of this item because Italian traders could sell at least 15 per cent below the British figure.[39] MacGregor's conclusion to his survey of the Syrian ports is worth noting. "It is to be observed," he writes, "that the British vessels coming to the coast of Syria are all entirely loaded, their cargoes being nearly equally divided between Beyrout and Alexandretta, the larger portion rather for the latter place, and that of the fourteen vessels arriving during the year (1836), five only were enabled to find return cargoes, the remainder having recourse to Smyrna or Alexandria (eight to Smyrna, two to Alexandria), whereas the foreign vessels came out frequently with not more than two-thirds of a cargo. . . ."[40]

[39] MacGregor, *op. cit.*, p. 140.
[40] *Ibid.*, p. 144.

Of all the ports in European Turkey, Salonica was one of the most important. Salonica was to the Balkan region what Smyrna was to Asia Minor, ranking second to Constantinople in importance. Much of the overland trade from central Europe terminated at Salonica, and English goods were distributed from this point to Macedonia and even to the borders of Hungary. The make-up of the population suggests that it was primarily a trading center; barely 5,000 of the 70–75,000 population were Turks, the remainder being equally divided between the trading peoples of the East, the Jews, the Greeks, and the Franks. Salonica exported raw cotton, silk, tobacco, a high grade of sheep's wool, carpets, leather, wheat,[41] barley, and Indian corn. Her imports included sugar, coffee, dyewoods, indigo, muslins, calicoes, cotton twist, iron, lead, tin, and watches. Certain articles, such as salt, snuff, timber, staves, and abbas (a coarse cloth) were monopolies of the Turkish government and were thus subject to vexations at Salonica.[42]

England and Austria were the chief suppliers of Salonica with manufactured goods. In 1842 the importation of British manufactures increased more than two thirds, from £41,650 in 1841 to £73,165 the following year.[43] Imports from Britain were limited by the lack of capital in Salonica, which was quite the reverse of the situation in Smyrna. Exports to Britain from Salonica were trifling compared with the outlet for Asia Minor. For example, Consul Blunt reported seven British ships entering Salonica's harbor in 1835, all of which departed for Smyrna in ballast. Table 9, taken from Blunt's report in 1836, proves that British merchants sold more goods there than any others. Though only seven British ships took part in Salonica's trade

[41] The British Consul reported one cargo of wheat from Salonica to Liverpool in the year 1842, "the first that has been sent in many years." MacGregor, op. cit., II, 90.

[42] Ibid., p. 87.

[43]

	Imported Direct	Imported in Greek Ships	Total
1841	£ 6,380	£35,270	£41,650
1842	£61,165	£12,000	£73,165

Small quantities of British goods still continued to come in via Vienna, but from this time on the direct trade was by far the most important. Ibid., p. 88.

in 1835, British imports made up 29 per cent of the total imports.

TABLE 9

RETURN OF TRADE FOR SALONICA FOR THE YEAR 1835 *

	Arrived			Departed		
	Ships	Tons	Value	Ships	Tons	Value
British	7	1,072	£44,060	7	1,072	. . . . . .
Austrian	20	4,676	30,975	20	4,676	£8,700
Russian	6	1,140	2,050	6	1,140	720
Greek †	321	18,660	30,940	321	18,660	16,400
French	3	380	11,048	3	380	17,500
Turkish	93	18,010	21,748	93	18,010	22,000
Ionian Isles ‡ .	6	356	720	6	356	520
Sardinian	4	780	3,160	4	780	530
Various	13	495	3,400	13	495	2,000
TOTAL	473	45,569	£148,101	473	45,569	£68,370

* B. T. 2/1 Blunt to Board of Trade, #1, Jan. 31, 1836. Four of these vessels were from Liverpool with general cargo and manufactures, two from Cardiff with iron, and one from London with colonials. For 1848–1851 cf. Michelsen, *op. cit.*, pp. 200–203.

† "The cargoes of the Greek vessels from Syria, consist generally of goods, landed from British vessels direct, and left at that port to be forwarded to Salonica." B. T. 2/1 Blunt to Board of Trade, #1, Jan. 31, 1836. Consul Wilkinson verifies the above statement which would mean that British trade with Salonica was far greater than represented by the table. On Dec. 27, 1833 Wilkinson wrote Palmerston that Syria imported British cotton manufactures, iron, chain cables, cloths, and refined sugar, but that Syria was merely a depot, trading with the Ottoman Empire by means of a large number of small ships, most of them under the Greek flag. B. T. 2/6, Wilkinson to Palmerston, December 17, 1833.

‡ Since the Ionian Islands were British possessions until 1864, their exports to Salonica should also be added to the total British trade.

A study of the arrivals and departures of vessels in this port over a period of years shows that while Austrian and French commerce was fairly constant, and Russia's increased, Britain's fluctuated widely. For example, in 1837 five English ships entered and cleared at Salonica, bringing manufactured goods valued at £17,755, and returning with but £50 worth of local produce.[44] In 1840 Salonica was not graced with a single English ship, yet two years later, thirteen ships weighed anchor

[44] MacGregor, *op. cit.*, II, 86.

there, bringing goods to the amount of £61,165, and taking away £7,180 worth of raw materials.[45] Coal, iron, and manufactured articles were the principal imports from Britain, while wheat, bones, and manure were the chief articles imported by Britishers from Salonica. In 1847, for example, Salonica exported more than 20,000,000 francs' worth of agricultural produce, three fifths of which consisted of cereals and tobacco.[46] By 1851 thirty British ships were making Salonica their port of call annually, bringing cargoes worth more than £78,000, and returning to England with more than £15,000 of goods.[47] Because of these great fluctuations, as well as the quantity of English goods imported from Syria and other ports, generalization concerning the importance of Salonica as a trading center for British merchants in this period are to be avoided.

Salonica was the only Turkish port of real importance in the Balkans as far as British commerce was concerned. In 1836 Saunders reported for Albania (port of Prevesa in particular), that English trade which had flourished there in the decade of the twenties had declined steadily since that time. The Albanians were very near self-sufficiency, importing very little; there were no agents of British firms in this sector in 1836. The primary reason for this was that Britishers were loath to risk their persons and their property in the anarchical state in which Albania existed at that time.[48] The punitive expedition of 1831–32 had no lasting effect, and it was more difficult to enforce the decrees of the Sultan in this remote part

[45] MacGregor attributes the improvement in Salonica's commerce in 1842 to a more correct system of administering the local government, especially since "the same system of honesty and philanthropy is not general throughout the country." *Ibid.*, p. 89. That reform of the local government was necessary is proved by Consul Blunt's report in 1837. "Mustapha Pacha (Mouchire or Plenipotentiary of the province) will, it is to be hoped, My Lord, adopt measures to check the arbitrary powers of the Beys, who, to satisfy their heavy expenses do much damage to the country." In the same letter Blunt called the over-charge for Susamum (from which oil was made) "a system of plunder which no country can stand." B. T. 2/9 Blunt to Palmerston, Sept. 30, 1837.

[46] Ubicini, *Letters*, I, 316n.

[47] MacGregor, *op. cit.*, II, 90.

[48] B. T. 2/8, Saunders to Board of Trade, Nov. 20, 1836.

of the empire than in the provinces nearer to Constantinople.

Adrianople was not an important British trade center, because of its inland position [49] and its proximity to Constantinople. According to Consul Kerr's report for 1835, English and French trade with Adrianople had declined after 1817 when Enos harbor became blocked with sand brought down by the Maritza River.[50] A few small boats still brought foreign goods from Smyrna or Constantinople via Enos, though much of their supplies, especially cloth, came overland from Austria or Germany. Since duties on British imports were paid at Constantinople or Smyrna, it was almost impossible to secure a correct estimate of the quantity of British manufactures imported.

Adrianople's imports (for 1835) included coffee, fruits, handkerchiefs, coloured cambrics, English long cloths, cotton twist, and iron from both Britain and Russia.[51] These articles were distributed to the citizens of Adrianople and its environs through the medium of fairs which were held at intervals from May to October. Germany supplied most of the woolens sold at these bazaars, as well as some of the muslins, and Florentines, while the fine prints, not in great demand, came from Switzerland. Most of the cotton manufactures, however, were imported from Britain, and British traders led the Armenian, French, and Dutch merchants in other items imported.[52]

The exports from Adrianople were hare skins, hides, silk, sheep's wool, valonia, tobacco, and linseed, most of which went overland to Constantinople, or directly northward to the Danube and thence to the central part of Europe. England imported from Adrianople hare skins, silk,[53] yellow berries, and

[49] Located in the center of the province of Roumelia, this city of 90–100,000 people was connected with the sea through the port of Enos at the mouth of the Maritza River, which was navigable for 12–40 ton ships for six or eight months of the year. B. T. 2/1, Kerr to Palmerston, Dec. 2, 1835.

[50] As late as 1847 this was still a problem. Ubicini, *Letters*, I, 338n.

[51] The import trade was free except for coffee which was a government monopoly.

[52] B. T. 2/1, Kerr to Palmerston, Dec. 2, 1835.

[53] Adrianople silk was 10 per cent inferior to that of Brusa; much of the silk sold from Adrianople was manufactured at Constantinople.

valonia; sheep's wool was largely imported by France, and tobacco and wax by Germany. Kerr concluded his report by explaining that trade with that city had decreased within the last few years because the fairs were supplied from Bucharest and Galacz; he was sure that Adrianople would suffer should the direct trade between England and the Danubian region continue to increase.

Kerr reported but one English ship arriving at Enos in 1835, and that in ballast. It departed for Belfast with £1,046 worth of raw materials. The small Ionian and Greek ships engaged in the coasting trade "seldom discharge or load the whole of their cargoes there, . . ." "The cargoes loaded by foreign vessels are generally wool and the destination Marseilles." In 1835 "the only article loaded on this coast direct for England (valonia) was loaded at Macri on board of two English vessels," both of which returned to Smyrna to complete their cargoes.[54] Smyrna or Constantinople were the usual ports of embarcation for goods destined for Britain. Three small vessels, 426 tons, arrived at Enos in 1837 in ballast and cleared with cargoes worth £3,940.[55] The failure of the linseed crop and the inadequate supply of valonia in 1840 caused Enos to be passed by entirely by British traders, though three French and three Austrian ships called there in that year.

Toward the end of the period under discussion Galacz became an important trading center, though in the thirties it was about on a par with Enos. Located at the mouth of the Danube it served as outlet for the principalities and the whole Danubian region, yet the number of English ships visiting this port was not large, varying from one in 1834 to fifteen in 1837.[56] In the next decade, due partly to the repeal of the Corn Laws by Parliament in 1846, Galacz became an important source for grain. In 1843 seven vessels left Galacz for England bearing

[54] B. T. 2/1, Kerr to Palmerston, January 13, 1836.
[55] MacGregor, *op. cit.*, II, 84.
[56] Almost seven times as many ships (706 vessels) left Galacz in the four years 1846–1849 as in the eight year period 1837–1845. F. O. 78/977, Cunningham to Palmerston, September 16, 1830.

one thousand quarters of grain each; yet, three years after the Corn Laws were repealed, England imported some 298,392 quarters of grain.[57]

Galacz was never an important direct outlet for British manufactures, however. Most of the English goods consumed or redistributed at Galacz were brought in from other ports of the empire by Turkish, Russian, or Greek ships.[58] Its significance is shown by the fact that it was not included within the sphere of the Commercial Treaty of 1838.[59] How far the trade with Galacz was limited by Russia's extension of her quarantine area at the mouth of the Danube in June, 1836 [60] it would be difficult to measure, but there is little doubt but that it was a deterrent to foreign commerce. At least figures do show that it was not until the middle of the century that Galacz became significant in Britain's eastern trade.[61]

Of constantly growing importance, and eventually a dangerous rival of Smyrna in the trade with India, was Trebizond,[62] located in the northern and eastern portion of Asia Minor. From Persia and Afghanistan the caravans brought carpets, shawls, and silks which the *rayahs* exchanged with British and foreign merchants for cottons,[63] woolens, western silk, glass,

[57] F. O. 78/977, Cunningham to Palmerston, September 16, 1830.

[58] The British Consul reported that only six of the two hundred and two ships arriving at Galacz in 1835 were English; the remainder was divided as follows: 60 Greek, 49 Turkish, 45 Russian, 17 Austrian, 17 Ionian, 4 Sardinian, 2 from Samos, and 2 others (home-port not entered). These vessels brought goods valued at £3,149 and departed with £6,716 worth of materials. Iron was the principal import from England. B. T. 2/2, Report of Vice Consul Gesse, for Galacz, 1835; this report bears the date, March 1, 1836, and was enclosed in Colquhoun to Palmerston, 10, April 30, 1836.

[59] Galacz, which had maintained its own customs regulations since the principalities secured their partial autonomy in 1829, continued to do so after 1838. Puryear, *International Economics*, p. 187.

[60] Puryear, *International Economics*, p. 133.

[61] In 1851, 296 ships left Galacz for England bearing 35,368 quarters of wheat, 295,200 quarters of Indian corn, 15,664 quarters of rye, and 1,925 cwt. of tallow. The next largest number of ships destined for one port was 176, for Constantinople. McCulloch, *op. cit.*, p. 620.

[62] Population about 35,000; cf. Juchereau de Saint Denys, *op. cit.*, p. 196.

[63] Cottons made up approximately 90 per cent of all goods imported into Trebizond in the early thirties, 80 per cent of which came from England. Cf. Sir George Larpent, *Turkey, Its History and Progress, from the Journals and*

and sugar. Some tobacco, nuts, fruits, and other soil products were also exported from this region, but the transit trade was really more important in this port.

Figures are lacking for the early period due to the fact that Britain had no consuls in this part of the Ottoman Empire until 1829. The earliest extensive report was that of acting Vice Consul Suter in 1835. After reporting an ever-increasing consumption of British manufactures, Suter writes: "The direct trade from England has exceeded that of any former year, and there is an increase in the value of imports by British ships proportionate to that of their number." [64] Suter also reports a slight falling off of exports, but attributes this to the fact that the Turkish ships which plied the Black Sea throughout the winter had secured a large portion of the carrying trade between Trebizond and Constantinople. The quantity of goods which finally found their way to England by this route it is difficult to gauge accurately. In order to increase the direct trade with Britain, Suter plead for a reduction of the British duties on certain articles exported from this part of the Ottoman Empire, especially boxwood, one of the most important exports of Trebizond.

The number of British ships arriving in Trebizond in 1835 was eighteen, three times as many as the previous year.[65] These vessels, totaling 1,915 tons, brought cotton and woolen manufactures, iron, hardware, coffee, sugar, and spices. Only four came direct from English ports (London) while thirteen were from Constantinople, and one from Batoum. Seventeen English vessels (1,835 tons) cleared from Trebizond the same year, one for Batoum, one for Samsoun, two for Taganrog, and thirteen for Constantinople, one of which was proceeding directly to London. Silks, shawls, boxwood, tobacco, and galls from Persia were the principal goods exported in 1835, though four

Correspondence of Sir James Porter, fifteen years ambassador at Constantinople, continued to the present, 2 vols., London, 1854, I, 125.

[64] B. T. 2/2, Suter to Palmerston, #12, December 31, 1835.

[65] *Ibid.*, Return #1.

of the vessels cleared in ballast. The report for 1836 reads much the same. In spite of the plague which continued throughout the year, British trade increased after the first scare from

TABLE 10

BRITISH AND FOREIGN TRADE AT TREBIZOND, 1835 *

	Arrived			Departed		
	Ships	Tons	Value	Ships	Tons	Value
British	18	1,915	£155,260	17	1,851	£30,167
Turkish	113	16,644	619,336	102	15,212	602,854
Russian	16	2,651	157,439	14	2,275	34,084
Austrian	11	3,329	64,612	11	3,329	2,315
Greek	6	912	3,141	6	912	1,723
Sardinian	5	881	4,164	5	881	19,777
Samos	1	112	16,580	1	112	......
TOTAL	170	26,444	£1,020,532	156	24,572	£690,920

BRITISH AND FOREIGN TRADE AT TREBIZOND, 1836 *

	Arrived			Departed		
	Ships	Tons	Value	Ships	Tons	Value
British	27	2,591	£326,304	28	3,658	£69,876
Turkish	119	18,691	742,949	107	16,803	759,942
Russian	13	1,829	178,085	15	2,205	19,292
Austrian	6	1,680	97,050	6	1,680	9,977
Greek	5	538	83,985	5	238	286
Sardinian	1	233	200	1	233	......
Danish	1	156	23,220	1	156	......
TOTAL	172	25,718	£1,451,793	163	24,973	£859,373

* B. T. 2/2, Suter to Palmerston, December 31, 1835, Return #3. For years 1848–1851 cf. Michelsen, *op. cit.*, pp. 206–207.

£80,000 to £110,000. The number of British ships engaged was larger, yet, since most of these vessels were from Constantinople, a decrease in the direct trade with England is indicated.[66] The relation of British trade with Trebizond with that of the other powers is shown by Table 10.

[66] B. T. 2/8, Report on Trade of Trebizond for year 1836 by Henry Suter, Acting Vice Consul. The number of British ships arriving and departing increased from 18 and 17 to 27 and 28 respectively. The incoming ships (24 from Constantinople, 1 from London and Constantinople, 2 from London direct) brought 3,591

A hasty perusal of these tables denotes that Turkey was the largest carrier, importing more goods from Trebizond and making more sales there than any other power. It should be noted also that the number of British ships trading with this Black Sea port increased by one-third in the year 1836, while the value of British imports and exports here more than doubled. In 1835 British and Russian imports and exports were nearly equal, Russia's being but £3,000 larger in each case, but in 1836 British sales to Trebizond were almost twice that of Russia, and her purchases in that port more than three times that of the great Slav state. Undoubtedly the increased trade of England with Persia and the hinterland was responsible for this up-turn, but the exact relationship is difficult to measure.

According to Consul Brant's report, except for the year 1831 when Persia suffered from both cholera and plague epidemics, the quantity of goods in transit for Persia via Trebizond steadily increased after Britain established a consul there.[67] By 1836, 19,743 packages of goods were exported from Britain to Persia via Trebizond, while 27,039 packages were imported into England from this port.[68]

The transit trade via Trebizond was more significant than commerce with some of the other ports of the Turkish Empire because here certain obstacles had to be overcome before British trade could expand. The principal hindrance to trade with Persia through the Black Sea ports was that Turkey exacted the same tariff (3 per cent) on goods in transit (i.e. "without changing hand or without breaking bulk")[69] which in addition

---

tons of manufactures for Persia, sugar, coffee, iron, etc. valued at £326,304. The twenty-eight ships which left Trebizond carried 3,658 tons of galls, silks, tobacco, gum, and yellow berries worth £69,876. Twenty-five vessels went to Constantinople, one to Taganrog in ballast, and 2 to Odessa in ballast.

[67] Brant reports 7,000 packages imported in 1830; 4,730 in 1831; 9,189 in 1832; and 10,946 in 1833. B. T. 1/307, Brant to Palmerston, Sept. 10, 1834. In the next two years the figure rose to 19,743 packages or 7,666 more than in 1834 (11,661). B. T. 2/2, Suter to Palmerston, #12, Dec. 31, 1835.

[68] B. T. 2/8, Report on Trade of Trebizond, 1836, by Henry Suter, V.C.

[69] Definition according to C. H. Burgess, a practical business man, who had

to the 2 per cent levied at the Persian border raised the duty to 5 per cent. Burgess, in his report on the trade with Persia in 1835, requested that the British agents negotiating the new commercial agreements should suggest that Turkey adopt the same policy as the other European states, namely of levying but ½ per cent on goods in transit. He also urged upon the British ambassador at Constantinople, Lord Ponsonby, that he use his influence with the Porte to have the pashas in this region assist in keeping the routes from Trebizond open to British traders.

Another difficulty of which Burgess complained was the fact that Trebizond, the only port where it was possible to disembark goods and form caravans, was but ninety miles from the Russian border. In the previous fifteen years Russian merchants, unable to compete with English traders, had lost a valuable outlet in Persia. Burgess reported that Russia had made attempts to secure possession of Ghilan,[70] was doing all it could to prevent the conclusion of a commercial treaty between England and Persia, and since 1832 had extended its territory some 70 miles in the direction of Trebizond. The caravans passed within twelve miles of the Russian frontier, and it was feared that Russia might stir up the Caucasian tribes against the English to the detriment of the latter's trade.[71] Brant expressed somewhat the same feeling in his letter the year previous, 1834, asking for a vice consul for Ezeroum, from which point the English could better watch the activities of the Russians and more adequately protect the route to the east.[72]

---

been engaged in the Persia trade since 1829, several months before this route was officially opened. B. T. 1/316, Burgess Report on Trade of Persia, Sept. 5, 1835, encl. in Ponsonby to Palmerston, #189, October 14, 1835. Cf. also David Urquhart, *Portfolio*, V, 314 ff.

[70] Most of the silk produced here had been sent to Moscow in 1820, but in 1835 it found its way to Constantinople and into British hands. B. T. 1/316, Burgess Report on Trade of Persia, 1835.

[71] Ubicini estimates the transit trade with Persia at £1,800,000 in 1855. Ubicini, *Letters*, I, 352.

[72] B. T. 1/307, Brant to Palmerston, September 10, 1834.

Rivalry among the powers has long been considered one of the principal reasons for the continued existence of the Ottoman Empire. In the nineteenth century this rivalry was economic as well as political in scope. England's fears for the route to India and her trade with the Levant had their counterpart in Russia's anxiety lest another nation, especially England, become dominant in the Turkish Empire and thereby threaten her trade with middle Asia, i.e. Persia, Afghanistan, and northern India. English traders had little to fear from Russian competition in the Turkish markets, because Russia exported few manufactured articles; Russian exports [73] in this period consisted largely of grain, tallow, flax, linseed, leather, wool, and lumber, all articles which Turkey herself produced. If Russia won first place in the Asiatic markets, however, the transit trade through Trebizond would not only be destroyed, but also England might be cut off from her back-door entrance to one of her most valuable colonies, India, if political domination followed economic control of the region. These facts tended to strengthen Britain's determination to maintain the Ottoman state as a bulwark against Russian aggression.

Though French merchants sold the Turks goods worth twice that of the Russians,[74] Britain had less to fear from France than from Russia, because France had less to gain from economic or political domination of Turkey, and knowing that had earlier shifted her interest to the northern coast of Africa. Prior to 1800 French merchants had enjoyed a near-monopoly of the eastern trade, but this had been broken by the wars of Napoleon.[75] After 1815 France was at such a low point that

[73] In the year 1851, for example, the total Russian exports to Turkey amounted to only 27,000,000 frs. (£1,350,000) as compared with England's £5,333,374. Ubicini, *Letters*, I, 356 and Table 2, p. 74 (£5,333,374 represented real value — about 70 per cent of official value, which was £7,619,106.)

[74] The average of French exports to Turkey for the years 1849–1851 was 55,000,000 frs., Ubicini, *Letters*, I, 354. The average for the decade 1830–1840 was *c.* 21,000,000 frs., Juchereau de Saint Denys, *op. cit.*, I, 428.

[75] France exported but three-fifths as much to Turkey in 1850 as she had in 1789. One of the most important items which France had supplied, cotton, was taken over by the British, as were small wares by the Austrians. Ubicini, *Letters*, I, 354.

England soon superseded her in the eastern trade, until by 1829 French trading and diplomatic interests began to shift from Turkey to Egypt. For example, French trade with Smyrna, the principal depot for imports from Marseilles and other French ports as well as the point of departure for vessels returning to France, declined as England's progressed.[76]

Though it is true that France never recovered the losses suffered during the period of the revolution and Napoleon, and that her commerce with Turkey was small as compared with Britain's, nevertheless one cannot judge her whole trade on the basis of one port however important that may be.[77] Actually the total interchange of goods was more than double in 1850 what it had been two decades earlier,[78] and the gradual increase of French exports to Turkey caused Britishers to recognize France as a rival. In 1838, the *London Times* expressed the prevailing sentiment as follows:

> Let the merchants of Great Britain look around them. Let them turn their eyes to Senegal, Oran, Algiers, Constantine, Tunis, Greece, Naples, La Plata, the Amazons, the Gulf of Mexico, the Gulf of California, and they will perceive in each of these regions France established as the avowed enemy of British commerce.[79]

That this economic rivalry increased the political friction between the two powers interested in the Mediterranean there is little question.

Austria and the German states carried on an extensive trade with European Turkey in the first half of the century due largely to the proximity of the two states, the long connections between them, and above all to the fact that the Danube increased in importance as an avenue of trade. Iron, brass, linen, glass, porcelain, and other manufactured articles were sold to

[76] Imports from Smyrna fell off more than 25 per cent between 1834 and 1839, (i.e. from £62,416 to £45,376); French exports to Smyrna dropped from £325,968 to £307,372 in the same five years. MacGregor, *op. cit.*, II, 101.

[77] MacGregor maintained that "the direct trade between Smyrna and France exhibits the same variations as apply to the general trade" between France and Turkey. *Ibid.*

[78] Cf. note 74, p. 115.

[79] *London Times*, September 11, 1838. See also Hansard, 3 series, XLVII, 721.

the Turks [80] while Turkish products were marketed through the fairs at Frankfort-on-Oder and Leipzig. Tariff and quarantine regulations prevented any great development of this trade during the first four decades of the century, and by that time British traders had established themselves firmly in the chief commercial centers of the Ottoman state. The Austrians, together with the Greeks, continued to dominate the coasting trade, a field which the British never attempted to exploit.

American interest in Turkey was largely humanitarian and philanthropic. The American Bible Society began its work in the Near East in 1816 and three years later (1819) the American Board of Foreign Missions was established. From that time on the number of missionaries in this field increased rapidly. The American government sent out its first representative to Turkey, one David Offley, in 1830; after the consummation of a commercial treaty in 1831 David Porter was commissioned Chargé d'Affaires at Constantinople.[81] Protection of missionaries was only a part of these early representatives' duties. In 1829, the first year in which records were kept, the United States exported to Turkey some $27,660 worth of goods, and imported goods valued at $293,237. Within a year (1830) American exports rose to $75,801, imports to $417,392,[82] and by the outbreak of the Crimean War the total American-Turkish trade amounted to more than $934,000. In spite of the fact that these amounts were negligible compared to England's trade with Turkey, British observers recognized the United States as a competitor.[83]

Though neither Russian, French, German, or American traders individually endangered Britain's growing commerce

[80] Ubicini estimates the average annual Austrian trade at 91,000,000 francs at this period. Ubicini, *Letters*, I, 355.

[81] Porter was commissioned April 15, 1831 and remained at his post until 1843. N. Sousa, *The Capitulatory Regime of Turkey, Its History, Origin, and Nature*, Baltimore, 1933, p. 130.

[82] Gordon, *op. cit.*, p. 43.

[83] As early as 1834 Urquhart complained of the tactics of Americans, especially the fact that they undersold Britishers. Urquhart, *Turkey and Its Resources*, p 154.

in the Levant, nevertheless, their presence tended to keep the British government aware of what the loss of this valuable outlet would mean. English merchants not only urged the Foreign Office to assist in every possible way the maintenance and development of the Ottoman state, but they also sought to improve regulations within their own state which would make a freer exchange of goods possible.

As free trade [84] became more of a reality in Britain outlets for the increased production of the factories became more necessary.[85] In the late twenties individuals like C. H. Burgess and small companies such as the Bells or Briggs and Company assumed the role of the old Levant Company in the eastern trade. Greek middlemen became less important after 1830. The competition which developed between these individual traders themselves tended to increase the trade which the company had previously enjoyed, and many old ports were developed while new ones were established.[86]

The demise of the Levant Company in 1825 had a significant effect on the British government, in that the new obligations which the government was forced to assume brought it into closer touch with the Ottoman state and thereby increased its interest in preventing further disintegration. Prior to 1825, for example, the Company had appointed its own consular agents; [87] after the government assumed that task,[88] all the

[84] The Petition of the London Merchants (1820) was followed by a number of pamphlets on the subject of free trade, the most significant of which was Sir Henry Parnell's "On Financial Reform" (1830). Parnell argued that the only way to increase the national wealth was expansion of the overseas trade, and that this was best accomplished by a limitation of duties on goods entering the country. Villiers, Cobden, and Bright carried on the crusade until, by the middle of the century free trade in England was an accomplished fact.

[85] Puryear, *International Economics*, p. 181.

[86] The best example is Trebizond, the greatest development of which dates from 1830. "The entire prospects of our Turkey trade rest," . . . wrote Urquhart, "on these two points, the emancipation of commerce from the Levant company, and the emancipation of Greece from the Turkish sway." Urquhart, *Turkey and Its Resources*, p. 187.

[87] The government began to appoint its own representatives about 1800. John Barker was sent to Aleppo in 1799, and John Phillip Morier to Morea in 1804. Cf. Wood, *op. cit.*, pp. 184–185.

[88] For the Act authorizing this transfer, see *British Foreign and State Papers*,

ports of the Turkish Empire were in as close touch with London as Constantinople itself. Brant at Smyrna, Blunt at Salonica, and Kerr at Adrianople, to mention only three consuls, were invaluable aids to the British Ambassador at Constantinople in reporting conditions within the Turkish dominions. In 1836 Parliament passed an act "To enable His Majesty to make Regulations for the better defining and establishing the powers and jurisdiction of His Majesty's Consuls in the Ottoman Dominions." [89]

As British trade with Turkey continued to increase under these new conditions, attempts were made to extend it further. The old law requiring that all articles from Turkey must be imported in British bottoms had been annulled in 1822, and various prohibitions had been removed at the same time.[90] Among the obstacles to a free interchange of products that remained the most important were the high prices placed on English products. Urquhart was one of the first to perceive that a reduction in the prices of British goods would enhance the Turks' buying power, and thereby expand the Turkish markets for British manufactures. "Reduce prices," he said in 1833, "so as to make it to their interest to purchase — present the goods and the means of exchange, the whole scene instantly changes; communications are opened, connections established, desires created, energies raised, and progress commences." [91]

Yet complete emancipation of commerce from the Levant Company and a reduction of British prices were not the only obstacles to free intercourse, according to Urquhart; in his triumphant report on British commercial gains between 1827 and 1830 he regretted "no corresponding increase in returns." British import duties must also be lowered, if not abolished,

---

XII, 531–535, or Hertslet, *Commercial Treaties*, IV, 484–489. Had the Levant Company been a joint stock company, like the India Company, the transfer would have been more difficult.

[89] MacGregor, *op. cit.*, II, 30–32. This act was supplemented August 24, 1843 by the Foreign Jurisdiction Act which fixed consular jurisdiction in Turkey more definitely. Cf. Hertslet, *Commercial Treaties*, VI, 500–506, 840–841.

[90] Levi, *op. cit.*, p. 161.

[91] Urquhart, *Turkey and Its Resources*, pp. 142–144.

especially on such imports as valonia, fustic, madder root, galls, and shumac. He pointed out the almost incredible fact that for every £100 of English goods sold in Turkey, the Porte exacted but £3 in customs duties, whereas English duties on Turkish products of equal value amounted to £60.[92] "The quantity and quality of our imports from Turkey have greatly depended on our own duties," wrote Urquhart in 1833.[93] Naturally, however, the British merchant was less ready to grasp the significance of the changes in their own regulations proposed by Urquhart than to complain against the trade restrictions which existed within Turkey itself. Thus, one sees why, at least a decade before free trade was adopted in practice as well as in theory, commercial men had exacted from the Sultan the Anglo-Turkish Commercial Convention of 1838.

The principal restrictions against which British commercial men complained were transshipment duties (levied on goods transshipped across Turkey (and in some cases for goods shipped between Turkish ports), and the arbitrary levies of the local pashas.[94] All goods transported across Turkey were subject to a 2½ per cent duty, a tax which was a great handicap to trade between England and Persia, especially in the port of Trebizond where the transit trade was heaviest.[95] In some cases the transshipment fee was applied to goods transported between two Turkish ports, and often British vessels which touched at Smyrna or Beyrout to unload a part of their cargo before proceeding to Salonica or Constantinople were taxed as were the smaller carriers in the coastwise trade. Though these duties were not large, British merchants rightfully maintained that they were a restraint of trade.

[92] Urquhart, *Turkey and Its Resources*, p. 195. Urquhart was afraid that the Turks would one day perceive that their duties were too low in proportion to the British customs, and that if the Porte adopted England's tactics a valuable market would become worthless.   [93] *Ibid.*, p. 175.

[94] Memorandum of Grievances of British Merchants of Smyrna, July 25, 1829, P. R. O., *State Papers*, Foreign, 110/74. Cf. also Letters of Merchants to the *London Times*, August 28 and December 28, 1835, and January 12, April 4, and May 28, 1836.

[95] Exports to Persia amounted to almost £1,500,000 annually. Crawley, "Anglo-Russian Relations," *op. cit.*, p. 67.

In some instances the arbitrary levies of the government were no less significant. For example, there existed in 1829 a tax of 20 per cent on yellow berries transshipped at Enos for British ports, and Constantinople possessed a similar levy of 1¼ per cent on all silk sent to England from the capitol city. The *mirigi*, or license fees, levied by the local pashas were another source of complaint. Britishers regarded these as a surcharge in violation of the capitulations since they already paid the regular 3 per cent export duty. When English merchants were discriminated against while French and German traders enjoyed the most favored nation treatment, the government authorities were forced to protest.[96] Yet, these difficulties were of secondary importance compared to the monopolies which the Porte maintained. On December 6, 1833 Palmerston had declared for a definite policy with respect to the strengthening and up-building of the Ottoman state. In the same dispatch the Foreign Secretary instructed Ponsonby to remind the Porte that monopolies were "not only at variance with the engagements subsisting between Great Britain and the Porte, but tend necessarily to limit and contrast the commercial intercourse between the subjects of His Majesty and those of the Sultan in a manner and to an extent which cannot fail to be injurious to the Industry of both Nations, and in the end detrimental to the financial interests of the Porte."[97] Palmerston urged his ambassador to point out to the Sultan that the profits from the monopolies could not possibly compare with the enlarged revenues which a greater volume of trade would make possible; freer trade in Turkey would make for wealth and prosperity of a larger number of Turks instead of the few privileged monopoly holders.

Ponsonby, fully aware of the economic potentialities of the Ottoman Empire, needed little encouragement. On November 25, 1834 he wrote: "Protection given to our political in-

[96] B. T. 1/298, Granville to de Broglie, December 30, 1833.
[97] F. O. 78/220, Palmerston to Ponsonby, #22, December 6, 1833. Cf. also, Instructions relating to Commercial Convention proposed by Nourri Effendi, October 23, 1835, F. O. 195/130, Palmerston to Ponsonby, #59, July 28, 1836.

terests will throw open sources of commercial prosperity perhaps hardly to be hoped from our intercourse with any other Country upon Earth." [98] From the moment that he sent in his first complaint [99] he continued to work for revision of existing schedules, trusting that eventually the monopolies which were so detrimental to British commerce would be abolished entirely.

Finally, after years of urging, the Sultan was ready to negotiate, and in November, 1836 Ponsonby was given instructions regarding the appointment of commissioners to frame a new tariff treaty. [100] The three commissioners named were Messrs. Black, Farell, and Wright, and negotiations began at once with the chief customer, Tahir Bey. Early in 1837 Ponsonby gloomily reported that success could not be expected, [101] but six weeks later he hopefully informed his chief that the Sultan had consented "to abandon the Russian Tariff, and to content himself with the same Tariff as shall be agreed upon between Turkey and the other Great European Powers." [102] Negotiations were further delayed by the illness of the chief customer, and in the meantime the French Chargé d'Affaires began to make similar proposals which the British feared might foil their plans.

The Ottoman government hesitated to adopt the arrangements proposed by the British commissioners, because, as Ponsonby explained, "the Porte feels acutely the shackles imposed upon it by the conventions that exist." [103] The British ambas-

---

[98] F. O. 78/240, Ponsonby to Palmerston, #187, November 25, 1834.

[99] F. O. 78/224, Ponsonby to Palmerston, #46, August 26, 1833. Enclosures from Cartwright and Brant explain the difficulties under which British merchants worked in Galacz and Smyrna.

[100] B. T. 3/27, Marchant to Backhouse, April 3, 1837.

[101] B. T. 2/8, Ponsonby to Palmerston, January 4, 1837.

[102] B. T. 2/8, Ponsonby to Palmerston, February 18, 1837. Ponsonby reported, March 1, 1837, that "The Russian Agents and Partisans boast extremely of the Liberality of the Emperor of Russia in consenting to cancel the Russian Tariff. Well informed People seem to understand very well how little solid ground there is for such Boasts. The spell is broken by which Russia cheated the eye." Cf. B. T. 2/8, Ponsonby to Palmerston, #39, March 1, 1837.

[103] B. T. 2/8, Ponsonby to Palmerston, #103, May 9, 1837. The Porte was also anxious to raise its duties from 3 per cent to 5 per cent *ad valorem* in order to secure money to improve its regular army, and to make up the losses resulting from a depreciated currency.

sador countered "that if the Sublime Porte will not revise and ameliorate its system, the time will soon come when the country will no longer be able to support the expense of its army." [104] The British commissioners consented to the continuation of opium and corn as government monopolies, but all others must be abolished. Also, while recognizing the 3 per cent duties on exports and imports, they insisted on a strict definition of all other charges, and these were not to be altered without due notice.

The Committee of the Privy Council for Trade insisted upon the following stipulations being written into the proposed treaty:

Nothing beyond the 3 per cent duty on Imports and Exports to be acknowledged by us.

The British Merchants however are to be left at liberty to pay or not the duties imposed by the Porte in the Interior Trade on Turkish commodities which duties are paid by all Ottoman subjects, and thereby to obtain for themselves, having purchased these Commodities at the places where they are produced, and having paid this Interior Duty to export them at the 3 per cent under the privilege accorded by the stipulation.

That these duties shall be strictly defined and that the Foreign Merchants shall be at liberty to pay their whole amount at one time and in one place: that they shall not be altered in any way or degree without a previous notice of the alteration intended to be made in them, which shall be formally notified to the British mission several months previous to the operation of any alterations to be made.

That every monopoly or prohibition to export which the Porte may choose to enact shall be a real and effective Prohibition that no exemption whatever shall be allowed from its operation: that no one whatever shall be authorized or entitled to export the article so prohibited until the removal of such prohibition and that when removed the operation of the removal shall be universal and every British Subject shall be entitled to export it without exception.[105]

Ponsonby, the chief sponsor of the proposed convention, was frank to admit that Britain would gain from the treaty, but

[104] F. O. 78/330, Ponsonby to Pisani, April 17, 1838.
[105] B. T. 3/27, Marchant to Backhouse, July 20, 1837.

not at the expense of Turkey; Britain would gain by having a more prosperous customer.[106] He argued that monopolies weakened the country in that they were the principal cause of high prices [107] which in turn caused poverty and a falling off of the population. Aside from increasing the wealth of Turkey and thereby making for prosperity, the abolition of monopolies would "cut up by the roots the power of Mehemet Ali in Egypt and Syria. . . ." [108] Palmerston and Ponsonby were one in believing that if the Sultan adopted a new commercial code (without monopolies) and wrote it into a treaty with England, the latter could demand its execution in Egypt as a part of the Turkish Empire. By so doing the Sultan would not only ruin Mehemet Ali financially, but would also reassert his power over Egypt.[109] Thus, while Britain "took advantage of the Sultan's hatred for Mehemet in order to secure concessions favorable to English trade," [110] she really attempted more than that; Britain's aims were more far-reaching. Politically, anything which would free the Sultan from the Egyptian danger would make him less dependent upon Russia, in which case the Treaty of Unkiar Skelessi would become the desired dead letter, if it were not abolished completely. This is the thought behind the modern view that the political aspect of the monopoly question was far more important than the economic one.[111]

In return for the Porte's relinquishing monopolies, British

[106] In this he was strongly supported by the Foreign Secretary. Cf. F. O. 78/328, Palmerston to Ponsonby, #21, February 6, 1838.

[107] Necessities of life were six times costlier in Constantinople than in Adrianople, which did not suffer from the monopolies, according to Ponsonby. F. O. 78/331, Ponsonby to Palmerston, #119, May 10, 1838.

[108] F. O. 78/330, Ponsonby to Pisani, April 17, 1838.

[109] Mosely, *op. cit.*, p. 99. British policy in this respect proved to be a boomerang. Mehemet Ali agreed to apply the arrangements of August 16, 1838 to his territories, but he did not regard this as any surrender of his power to the Sultan. By a slight alteration of his economic organization, Mehemet remained master of industry and commerce. Thus, Egypt escaped unscathed, while the Sultan undoubtedly suffered considerably (until the readjustments began to show their effects) from decreased revenue. *Ibid.*, p. 101.   [110] *Ibid.*, p. 94.

[111] Puryear claims that by fostering the abolition of monopolies in Egypt as well as Turkey the British reopened the whole Near Eastern question once more. Cf. Puryear, *International Economics, op. cit.*, p. 84, and Mosely, *op. cit.*, p. 115.

merchants were to agree to export duties above 3 per cent, provided they were "settled between the two Governments," [112] and favorable arrangements in the interior trade were to be secured by individual traders, the Committee of the Privy Council for Trade [113] believing that this was beyond its sphere.[114] Though the Committee insisted on the right of transit, duty free, a right which had been violated by the local pashas in the past,[115] this was not granted by the Turkish commissioners. Thus, after much dickering, the treaty was finally signed on August 16, 1838.

The Convention of Balta Liman,[116] as this commercial treaty was called, written by Reschid Pasha and Lord Ponsonby, provided that all the old privileges and immunities be confirmed; that the monopolies be abolished, and that Britons be allowed to trade freely anywhere in the Turkish dominions; that British merchants would be subject to the same taxes in the internal trade; that the 3 per cent import duty be continued; and finally that the export tax be limited to 9 per cent *ad valorem*. The treaty was to become operative March 1, 1839.

Though all Britishers were not satisfied with the Convention,[117] Palmerston considered the treaty a success in that while some rights "supposed to have belonged to British Trade, are abandoned; . . . no real loss is sustained," and he expected

[112] B. T. 3/27, Marchant to Backhouse, July 20, 1837.

[113] The Committee of the Privy Council for Trade had supplanted the Council on Trade and Plantations in 1786; it was not known as the Board of Trade until 1861.

[114] The government could not recognize private bargains between merchants and the Porte, and the Committee frowned upon such bargains the purpose of which was to secure lower duties because the merchants were not guaranteed a fixed rate of exchange as they were under the regular system. Cf. Marchant to Backhouse, February 8, 1838, B. T. 3/27.

[115] *Ibid.*, April 3, 1837.

[116] *British Foreign and State Papers*, XXVI, 688–692. Cf. also F. O. 78/332, Ponsonby to Palmerston, #190, August 19, 1838, and "The Turkish Treaty," *British and Foreign Review*, London, July 1839, IX, 247–272.

[117] David Urquhart, who had urged a commercial agreement between England and Turkey, criticized the final draft of the treaty which he felt had been warped to England's disadvantage in the negotiations. For Palmerston's defense of Ponsonby's diplomacy, see Hansard, 3rd series, vol. 47, pp. 74, 76.

commerce to benefit.[118] Though the year 1839 showed increases
in British exports to Turkey in such articles as corn and flour,
sugar, and hardwares, while imports of wool, dyestuffs, oil, and
opium increased,[119] these do not represent the whole story. At
the same time there were slight decreases in the quantity of
indigo and cloth exported in 1839, and the value of dried fruits,
sponges, valonia, and gums, imported was less. It would be impossible to state definitely how far these gains or losses were
directly the result of the new convention, because the Near
East trade in general declined between 1839 and 1841 due to
the unrest in Egypt and Persia, and did not return to normal
until 1842.[120] Yet there is little question, as one surveys the
trade over the whole decade following, that both Britain and
Turkey (but especially Britain) benefited from the treaty of
1838.[121]

There were infractions of the Convention as it was undoubtedly expected there would be. For example, certain British cottons (grays) paid a duty of 7½ per cent, and occasionally as
much as 12 per cent, with the result that this type of goods was
sought in Switzerland, which was free from the heavy duties.
Yet British merchants had a new advantage which was a real
impetus to trade in that the monopolies were no more. Similar
conventions were arranged with Austria, France, and later with
Prussia, China, and Russia (1846),[122] all based to a great extent
on the Anglo-Turkish treaty.

From the political point of view the Convention of Balta
Liman was a significant step in the policy outlined by Palmerston in 1833,[123] because to strengthen the economic relations
of the two powers was to prepare the way for closer political
cooperation. Palmerston himself recognized this fact as early

[118] B. T. 3/28, Palmerston to Strangways, September 26, 1838.
[119] MacGregor, op. cit., II, 101.
[120] Cf. Table 2, p. 74, and Chart II, p. 75.
[121] B. T., G. 1550/54, Minute Paper, #1550, August 23, 1854, and Clarendon
to Canning, #698, November 13, 1854 (G. 1550/54). Cf. also Appendix II,
Tables 4–7, and 11–14.
[122] Ubicini, Letters, I, 349.
[123] F. O. 78/220, Palmerston to Ponsonby, #23, December 6, 1833.

as 1835. "An increase of the commercial intercourse between the subjects of the two states," he wrote, "must tend necessarily to strengthen the political union between the two governments."[124]

How far did the new commercial relations actually determine Anglo-Turkish political cooperation during the ensuing period? To state that "diplomacy . . . followed the British trader in the Mediterranean and attempted to promote his interests . . ."[125] is not a wholly satisfactory answer. In fact, there is no definitive answer, because it is impossible to measure precisely the direct relation between trade expansion and diplomatic policy. That Britishers were alarmed by the continued existence of the Treaty of Unkiar Skelessi, and that they made themselves heard there is little question.

How far Palmerston, having succeeded in breaking Russia's commercial advantages and substituting the convention favorable to Britain, was inspired to pursue the problem of strengthening Turkey is another question which cannot be accurately determined. Puryear maintains that the new economic concessions which threatened to replace Russia as the protector of Turkey "reopened the whole Near Eastern question."[126] Palmerston's success in this affair may well have increased his determination to make Turkey a strong state, entirely free from Russian domination, not only to further insure access to India by the land routes, but also because Turkey was a profitable outlet for British manufactures.[127] It was no mere historical coincidence that the period during which Britain developed and pursued a definite policy with respect to the maintenance of the territorial integrity and independence of the Ottoman Em-

---

[124] F. O. 195/122, Palmerston to Nourri, October 23, 1835.

[125] Swain, *op. cit.*, p. 54.

[126] Puryear, *International Economics*, p. 84.

[127] "The protection of trade interests was the key note to British interests in the Mediterranean." Swain, *op. cit.*, p. 108. In a speech in Parliament on March 22, 1849, Palmerston defended the independence of the Ottoman Empire for both economic and political reasons, stating that he believed that trade with the Turks could be greatly improved if certain internal reforms were carried out in the Sultan's dominions. Hansard, 3rd series, CIII, 1144.

pire (i.e. 1833–1853) was also the era in which Britain increased her commerce with Turkey most rapidly and profitably.

For a time after the conclusion of the commercial treaty
Palmerston continued his former tactics of subtly undermining
Russia's prestige and increasing that of his own nation. He was
not yet ready for the bold policy. To attempt openly to undo
in 1839 the harm which had been done in 1833 would have
caused a definite rupture between England and Russia, if not
in the whole international structure. Two years elapsed before
Palmerston administered the *coup de grâce* to Russian interference in Turkish affairs. In the interim he continued his
policy of freeing the Sultan from his difficult position. What
that policy was and how he promoted it from 1834 until he fell
from power in 1841 will be considered in subsequent chapters.

CHAPTER IV

PALMERSTON AND TURKISH REFORM, 1834–1839

AN INTERESTING counterpart of the expansion of British commerce in the Near East is the development of a foreign policy, the aims of which were two-fold, namely; to preserve the territorial integrity of the Ottoman Empire against foreign aggression and, secondly, to encourage the internal development of that state so that it would become free and independent. That the year 1833 and the Treaty of Unkiar Skelessi between Turkey and Russia marks the beginning of this new policy has already been suggested. Prior to 1833, the British Foreign Office did not consider Russia a dangerous rival in the Near East. France, which had just begun to establish a great overseas empire in Algeria, was regarded as the more dangerous to British trade and the new trade route to the East via the Mediterranean. The Foreign Office, slow to recognize Britain's interests in the Levant, continued its semi-defensive policy in that region until 1834. In order to understand fully why Palmerston was so slow in recognizing the significance of the Near East in British policy and to what extent his policy once adopted was a distinct departure from that of his predecessors, a brief review of the Eastern policy which he inherited is worthwhile.

Viscount Castlereagh had little interest in the welfare of Turkey, except in so far as a Russian invasion of the Sultan's domains in the interests of the Greeks might lead to general war in Europe.[1] His successor in the Foreign Office, George Canning, whose view of British policy was more worldly, less continental, looked upon Turkey as of secondary importance compared with the South American states with whom trade had

---

[1] C. K. Webster, *The Foreign Policy of Castlereagh, 1815–1822*, London, 1925, pp. 255, 343.

increased tremendously in the preceding decade. Canning refused to guarantee the independence of Turkey against aggressors; as for Russia he preferred to foil her intentions by acting in concert with the Tsar. England's entrance into the Greek trouble in 1827 was the result of two accidents, one diplomatic, the other military, namely Wellington's unfortunate visit to St. Petersburg in 1826, and the battle of Navarino, October 20, 1827, just two months after Canning's death (August 8, 1827). Whatever Turcophil tendencies Canning possessed were tempered by the wave of Philhellenism which swept across Britain during his term in the Foreign Office. In short, Canning pursued a frankly opportunist policy,[2] realizing that Turkey was but one, and perhaps a minor one, of Britain's many interests abroad.

In the troublesome interlude which followed, before the Foreign Office acquired a worthy successor to Castlereagh and Canning, Wellington, realizing that Britain had steadily declined in the Porte's favor since Navarino, was anxious to re-establish British influence at Constantinople more securely, yet he was not enough of a diplomat to know how to do it. Wellington opposed the French expedition to Algiers on the ground that any change in the *status quo* in the Mediterranean would menace the integrity of Turkey.[3] Aberdeen, the Foreign Secretary in the Wellington Cabinet, did not wholly share his chief's solicitude for the Ottoman Empire, believing that "the hour long since predicted" was at hand, and that "independently of all foreign or hostile impulse this clumsy fabric of barbarous power" was about to "crumble to pieces from its own inherent causes of decay." [4] Aberdeen at this time, as well as in 1844, was less interested in regenerating the Ottoman state than in determining what was to be done with the pieces

[2] *Cambridge History of British Foreign Policy*, II, 86.

[3] Swain, *op. cit.*, p. 60.

[4] Aberdeen to Gordon, November 31, 1828, F. O. 78/179. Quoted in A. H. Gordon, *Earl of Aberdeen*, London, 1893, pp. 85–86. Gordon regretted his chief's stand-off policy; he favored definite support by Britain to prevent Turkey's extinction. F. O. 195/85, Gordon to Aberdeen, #2, January 5, 1830.

when the inevitable crash came. His interest in the Algerian trouble was in checking the growing ambitions of France rather than in indirectly bolstering up a decadent Turkish Empire.

Through 1829 and 1830 Wellington continued his efforts to prevent the loss of Algiers to France. When intervention by France was certain, Aberdeen instructed Gordon, the British Ambassador at the Porte, to induce the Sultan to force the Dey of Algiers to settle his quarrel with the French.[5] Following the failure to prevent the expedition to Algiers, Britain then attempted to limit the extent and influence of its operations.[6] In March, 1830, Aberdeen complained to Polignac that French plans indicated destruction of the local authority "rather than the infliction of chastisement." [7] British protests against this violation of the Sultan's sovereignty continued, but Stuart's suggestion of a conference was not well received in Paris. In July, 1830, Charles X was overthrown by a revolution and French national aggressiveness turned to Belgium and the Rhine; interest in this quarter temporarily blinded the British Foreign Office as to what was really going on in the Mediterranean. These facts [8] are interesting in that they show a negative interest in Turkey's welfare. Palmerston's predecessors, far from having a definite policy as regards the strengthening of the Turkish state or of bolstering British influence at Constantinople, merely sought to delay the disintegration of the Ottoman Empire,[9] a process which not only endangered their interests in the Mediterranean, but also might lead to a general war.[10]

---

[5] F. O. 78/188, Aberdeen to Gordon, January 20, 1830.

[6] F. O. France 27/405, Aberdeen to Stuart, June, 1830.

[7] F. O. 27/405, Aberdeen to Stuart, March 5, 1830.

[8] For a more detailed account of English policy during this crisis, see Swain, *op. cit.*, ch. V.

[9] Gordon's belief that the regeneration of Turkey was feasible with outside assistance was not shared by either Wellington or Aberdeen. Cf. F. O. 78/181 Gordon to Aberdeen, November 11 and December 15, 1829; Wellington, *Despatches*, VI, 192.

[10] As late as March 7, 1832 Sir Robert Peel expressed great apprehension as to the maintenance of peace, if French aggression in the Mediterranean continued. Hansard, *op. cit.*, X, 1229.

The Englishmen who first went to the bottom of the problem of the Eastern question were Stratford Canning and David Urquhart. Canning's sojourn in Turkey in 1831 convinced him of the need of reform in the Ottoman administration, and he was anxious that England should assist the Turks in getting their house in order.[11] On March 7, 1832 he wrote Palmerston portraying the mildly successful attempts of the Sultan to reconstruct his dominion, and outlining the need of a new administrative system, an efficient army and an improvement in finances. "I think the time is near at hand, or perhaps already has come," he concludes, "when it is necessary that a decided line of policy should be adopted and steadily pursued with respect to this country. The Turkish Empire is evidently hastening to dissolution, and an approach to the civilization of Christendom affords the only chance of keeping it together for any length of time." [12]

Again on May 17, 1832 [13] Canning reported that "the Sultan and a few of his most favoured adherents are daily opening their eyes more and more to the weaknesses of the Empire, and to the necessity of seeking support in some well-chosen foreign alliance, in order to obtain leisure for completing their military establishments, and counsel for proceeding with their present system of improvement on sound principles." After reiterating his lack of confidence in Russia, Canning remarked, "If ever they form an Alliance with that Power, fear and helplessness will drive them into it." In view of events a year hence Canning appears to have had the gift of prophecy as well as diplomacy. Canning's lengthy memorandum of December 19, 1832 further outlined his views on the Eastern Question, but it failed to move the Foreign Secretary.[14]

About the same time Urquhart wrote, "The political state of Turkey is brought to a crisis, which if favourable will, I

[11] Lane-Poole, *op. cit.*, II, 74.
[12] F. O. 78/209, Canning to Palmerston, #12, March 7, 1832.
[13] F. O. 78/210, Canning to Palmerston, #34, *Confidential*, May 17, 1832.
[14] The marginal notes show how far Palmerston was from a definite Turkish policy. Cf. Appendix I.

believe, be the means of her speedy regeneration; and if un-
favourable, of her speedy dissolution; the long and industrious,
and hitherto eminently successful labours of Russia are therefore on the point of being crowned with complete success, or
of being entirely frustrated." [15] Yet even this failed to arouse
the Foreign Office.

As has been indicated in a previous chapter,[16] Russia's
domination over Turkey, as a result of the Treaty of Unkiar
Skelessi, roused many Englishmen to the significance of the
Eastern question in British policy.[17] In the years that followed,
many deplored the humiliating subserviency [18] of the Porte,
and although Palmerston did little, he was formulating a policy.
In the King's address on the opening of Parliament in 1834,
William IV stated that he hoped there would be no "change in
the relations of that Empire (Turkey) with other powers, which
might affect its future stability and independence." [19] Palmerston in reply to this address declared, "it was, . . . of the
utmost importance to the interests of this country, and to the
preservation of the balance of power in Europe, that the Turk-

---

[15] Urquhart, *Turkey and Its Resources*, p. 218.

[16] Cf. Chapter I, pp. 59 ff. Palmerston gained valuable experience and learned
many details about the troublesome Eastern Question in 1833. H. C. F. Bell,
Lord Palmerston, New York, 1936, I, 180.

[17] Prior to this time the majority of Englishmen were indifferent to the affairs
of Turkey or despaired of successfully influencing its reformation, believing that
the best policy was to let the Sultan travel by his own road, either to destruction
or enlightened despotism; either appeared more advantageous to Britishers than
the hopeless state Turkey was then experiencing. *Turkey and Russia* — By a
merchant, London, 1835 was a typical example of the new attitude toward
Turkey. The merchant concludes with the plea to "Let England declare to
Russia that the independence of the Turkish Empire is the *sine qua non* of her
friendship." *Loc. cit.*, p. 57.

[18] One example of Russian domination over the Porte was in their forcing
the Sultan to accept some honorary medals against the dictates of Moslem law.
The Sultan was forced to use the police, stimulating them with the threat of a
conspiracy, in order to keep his people quiet, at the acceptance of the proffered
medals. F. O. 78/252, Ponsonby to Wellington, #18, January 28, 1835 and #22,
February 11, 1835. For other descriptions of Turkey's subserviency see C. B.
Elliott, *Travels in the Three Great Empires of Austria, Russia and Turkey*,
2 vols., Philadelphia, 1839, I, 131; *London Times*, January 1, 1836, January 28,
1836, February 16, 1836, February 17, 1836, March 30, 1836.

[19] Hansard, *op. cit.*, vol. 21, February 4, 1834, p. 3.

ish Empire should be maintained in its integrity and independence." [20] Yet the year 1834 finds the Foreign Office
resigned to the fact of Russia's power in the East. The next
year, 1835, the reaction to Russia's aggressiveness came more
in the open. The press provided an outlet [21] for pent-up feelings. The *Times* since 1833 had been outspoken in its demand
for adequate defense against Russia.[22] India not Turkey was
in the minds of many of these men. While they felt certain
that Russia was in no position to deprive England of her
Indian possessions, . . . "nevertheless the security of our Indian territory should be placed beyond all doubt, by the adoption of every safe-guard that the wisdom of our statesmen can
devise, . . ." [23]

To demand a policy and to prepare one were two different
things. Palmerston proceeded with the utmost caution, and
more than two years passed before his intentions were obvious
to everyone. Supported by DeBroglie he declined to recognize
the treaty of Unkiar, intimating that further aggressive acts
by Russia would be resisted by force, if necessary.[24] He then
negotiated "the Quadruple Alliance of 1834, which grouped the
Constitutional Governments of Britain, France, Spain, and Portugal in mutual defence against the autocrats of Russia, Austria
and Prussia," [25] . . . who had revived the Holy Alliance the
year before by the Münchengrätz Convention (September,
1833).

At the same time he strengthened the Mediterranean squadron and ordered the Levant fleet to act upon the authorization
of the British ambassador at the Porte should the Sultan need

[20] Hansard, *op. cit.*, vol. 21, p. 105.
[21] Ross, *op. cit.*, p. xi.
[22] Cf. Chapter I, pp. 56, 59.
[23] Marmont, *op. cit.*, p. 307. According to Bell, Palmerston was worried as
much by Mehemet Ali's aims as by those of the Tsar. Mehemet must not be
allowed to control both the Suez and the overland route; modernization of
Turkey's army and navy was the best way to prevent Egyptian aggression.
Thus the news of Koniah was partly responsible for Palmerston's new policy of
active intervention in the Near East. Cf. Bell, *op. cit.*, I, 181.
[24] F. O. 65/206, Palmerston to Bligh, #101, December 6, 1833.
[25] *Cambridge History of British Foreign Policy*, II, 289.

assistance against Russia.[26] Palmerston did not expect war,[27] but he did wish to be ready for any eventuality.

> With Russia we are just as we were, snarling at each other, hating each other, but neither wishing for war. Their last communication on Eastern Affairs is anything but satisfactory. However, there is nothing at present to be done by us, because there is no danger of anything being done by them. They cannot return to Turkey unless invited by the Sultan, and the Sultan will not invite them unless he is again attacked by Mehemet Ali; but Mehemet Ali will not stir as long as we beg him not to do so, because he knows that our fleet could effectually prevent him. . . . Our policy as to the Levant is to remain quiet, but remain prepared.[28]

Eventually this pacific policy of watchful waiting became a positive policy of action. That he disapproved of the 1833 settlement, there is no doubt,[29] and he was determined that

[26] Secretary Stanley to Vice Admiral Rowley, January 31, 1834, enclosed in F. O. 78/234, Palmerston to Ponsonby, March 10, 1834. Cancelled by Wellington 1835; cf. F. O. 78/251, Wellington to Ponsonby, March 16, 1835; renewed on successive occasions until 1840. Cf. Crawley, "Anglo-Russian Relations," *op. cit.*, p. 62.

[27] Palmerston was neither an "alarmist" nor a "false-alarmist" as far as the Russian menace was concerned. *Ibid.*, p. 52.

[28] Henry Lytton Bulwer, *The Life of Henry John Temple, Viscount Palmerston*, 2 vols., Philadelphia, 1871, II, pp. 182–183. This statement is interesting, not only because it outlined British policy during the ensuing months, but because it proves that Palmerston perceived the importance of the fleet in foreign affairs, and finally because Palmerston realized that a general war could be prevented by working on Mehemet as well as upon the Sultan. Palmerston had no fear of Russia's power. On March 10, 1835, he wrote to his brother William: "The fact is that Russia is a great humbug, and that if England were fairly to go to work with her we should throw her back half a century in one campaign. But Nicholas, the proud and insolent, knows this, and will always check his pride and moderate his insolence when he finds that England is firmly determined and fully prepared to resist him." Palmerston to Temple, March 10, 1835, Bulwer, *op. cit.*, III, 5. Lord Durham after traveling to St. Petersburg from Constantinople during the summer of 1835 was "convinced that the Tsar did not have the power, even if he had the will, to call suddenly into action a sufficient force to take Constantinople." Durham's Report on the State of Russia 1836 in S. J. Reid, *Life and Letters of the First Earl of Durham, 1792–1840*, 2 vols., London, 1906, II, 29 ff. After 1833 Palmerston held the "balance between Durham at St. Petersburg and Ponsonby at Constantinople." Crawley, "Anglo-Russian Relations," *op. cit.*, p. 49.

[29] In general instructions to Colonel Campbell, February 4, 1833, Palmerston expressed regret that territorial cessions on the part of the Sultan had been necessary. F. O. 78/226, Palmerston to Campbell, February 4, 1833.

further disintegration of Turkey must not be allowed. More-over, Palmerston perceived that British influence in Turkey could not be enhanced without a limitation of Russian domina-tion there, and the best way to wean the Porte away from the Tsar was to assist in the reformation of Turkey, because only a strong state could assert its independence in the face of a powerful Tsar.[30]

After the destruction of the Janissaries in 1826, the Sultan had continued his efforts to reform his state, but not with great success because of the war with Russia 1827–1829, which re-sulted from Navarino and the Greek trouble. Following the signing of the treaty of Adrianople (1829) which concluded the Russo-Turk War and established the independence of Greece, Mahmoud again took up the cause of reform. He abol-ished feudal officials in the provinces. He established the begin-nings of a modern cabinet in which officials could be held more responsible for their particular tasks. He took steps to over-come bribery.[31] A passport system was established. Light-houses were built at certain dangerous points on the coast to protect shipping. Improved methods of controlling cholera and other diseases were established by the inauguration of a more rigid quarantine. In 1830 a military college and a college of medicine to train for the army and navy were established.[32] Mahmoud encouraged the introduction of new printing presses in order that his people might become educated up to his reform ideas.[33] With the aid of a French publisher, Monsieur Alex-

[30] Though this policy was conceived in 1833 and 1834, it was not executed forcibly until 1838. Cf. Mosely, *op. cit.*, p. 93.

[31] Mahmoud refused fees on the appointment of pashas and forbade subordi-nates to do so. Walsh, *op. cit.*, II, 307; *A. B. C. F. M. Report*, 1839, p. 64. He also fixed salaries for officers of central government. Rosen, *op. cit.*, I, 271. Fixed salaries were extended to pashas December, 1839. Cf. *supra*, Chapter V, p. 198.

[32] Rosen, *op. cit.*, I, 205–207.

[33] Books previously imported from abroad were now published in Constanti-nople. Emin estimates that but eighty works were printed in Turkey to 1828; between 1830 and 1842 one hundred and eighty-eight were published there. Cf. A. Emin, *Development of Modern Turkey as Measured by Its Press*, New York, 1914, pp. 25, 27. Contemporaries were most enthusiastic at these attempts

ander Blacque,[34] an official gazette, *Le Moniteur Ottoman*, was begun in 1831.

While these improvements demonstrated the wide variety of interests as well as the tireless energy of the Sultan, they did not materially improve the unhealthy condition of his Empire.[35] These reforms merely glossed over some of the surface cracks without removing the real source of the decay within. The complete absence of a well organized program on the part of the Sultan is significant throughout Mahmoud's reign.

Turkey had been left bankrupt by the Russian war,[36] which came at a time when she was just beginning to show life.[37] Her finances were disrupted; the army which Mahmoud had created following the destruction of the Janissaries needed reorganization. For these reasons the Sultan's authority was not respected in the provinces. In 1831 the Albanians revolted, but in spite of Mahmoud's inadequate military means, these haughty mountaineers were broken and humbled by the Grand Vizir. Many Turks, overlooking their own weakness or the strength of the enemies, attributed the disasters which had befallen their state to the hasty, ill-conceived reforms of their chief, in whom they had momentarily lost faith.[38] The great

---

to create an enlightened public opinion. Cf. *Missionary Herald*, vol. 28, 1832, p. 244, and Walsh, *op. cit.*, II, 279.

[34] Blacque went out to Smyrna in 1825 where he established the *Spectateur d'orient* (later called the *Courrier de Smyrne*). His friendship with Sultan Mahmoud lasted until his death at Malta in 1836. Another journal, the *Echo de l'orient*, was founded by M. Bargigli in 1838.

[35] F. O. 195/86, Gordon to Aberdeen, #66, August 21, 1830. Gordon deplored Mahmoud's lack of a basic plan for reforming the state.

[36] Not until January 29, 1834, was a treaty signed between the Tsar and the Sultan freeing Turkey from bondage exacted by Treaty of Adrianople five years before. By the new arrangement the Tsar relinquished all but four million ducats of the indemnity in return for the cession of the Pashalik of Akisla. Russia retained Silistria as pledge of final payment. *British Foreign and State Papers*, XXVI, 1245–1248.

[37] Reform would have been easier before Navarino. Cf. F. O. 352/24, Canning to Palmerston, "Private," February 14, 1832.

[38] Ross, *op. cit.*, pp. 231–232. Marmont, an observer who had a reputation for his precision, gave a gloomy picture of Turkey in 1834. "Formerly the abuses were greater than at present, and the exactions more frequent, but Christians alone were then the victims of these evils, for until the destruction

majority, however, were attached to the ruler who was also defender of their faith and on this assumption, Mahmoud went ahead with his plans.

Mahmoud's many reforms were nibbling attacks [39] on the great problem. This was Mahmoud's great weakness. Too inconsistent to adopt a definite program of westernization such as Mehemet Ali had done, he wasted his energy on many minor reforms, and he was too obstinate and pig-headed, too bent on reasserting the declining power of Constantinople to see how he might benefit more from less effort. Here was where the assistance of some foreign power could be important. The need of outside support was recognized by Englishmen both at home and abroad. In 1834 after commenting on the increases in commerce due largely to reduced duties on silk, figs, currants, and oils, McCulloch significantly added: "nothing, however, would contribute so much to its (i.e. commerce) extension, as the establishment of order and tranquillity throughout the country. But this, we fear, is beyond the ability of the Ottoman government. The abuses which have reduced the empire to its present state of degradation seem to be inherent in the structure of Turkish society, and to be in harmony with the habits and prejudices of the people. And if such be the case, that reform, which is so much to be wished for, must come from without, and not from within." [40] If Palmerston, through

---

of the Janissaries, the Turks preserved their power and retained their wealth; but now they are joint sufferers with the other inhabitants, living in equal wretchedness and degradation. The natural result of the present condition of the people is, that the cultivation of the land is neglected, and the Turks merely sow sufficient to produce a crop for the immediate support of their families and the payment of their taxes." Marmont, *op. cit.*, p. 190.

[39] The changes decreed in dress, for example, appear of no significance, yet "oriental dress was a great barrier which separated the people from Europeans, . . ." Walsh, *op. cit.*, II, 318.

[40] McCulloch, *op. cit.*, p. 395. See also "The Diplomacy of Russia," *British and Foreign Review*, Vol. I, #1, 1835, p. 129. Foreign intervention in Turkey's behalf was suggested as early as May, 1833, not by Ponsonby, but by one of his subordinates, James Brant, Vice Consul at Trebizond. "It is easier to point out an evil than to suggest an appropriate remedy," he wrote, "but I cannot refrain from remarking that in order to strengthen the Sultan's Government its system must be changed. It should be placed under the tutelage of an enlightened power, and be constrained to do what its own interests so imperatively demand.

his agents could convince the Sultan of the need of concentrating on one or two problems, Turkey would again become a strong power.

The crisis of 1832–33 was in reality a blessing in disguise, partly because it stimulated action on the part of Britain, and also because it made the Sultan realize that his reform policy to date had not been very successful and thereby made him more amendable to foreign advice. Thus when the British Foreign Minister suggested through his ambassador that what Turkey needed was, not constitutional reform, but an immediate strengthening of the civil service, the army and navy, and above all the financial administration, the Sultan was more ready to accept British suggestions than ever before.

One of the most difficult obstacles to good government in Turkey was the problem of the civil service. While its condition was worse in the provinces, even the central administration was honeycombed with bribe-taking officials. Mahmoud was usually able to keep these men from rising to the highest positions in his government, thereby keeping his cabinet and council clean; nevertheless, they were a hindrance to reform, as Urquhart unwillingly admits:

If, indeed, the re-organization of Turkey depended on the skill, the intelligence, and the honesty of any central administration, the case

The Country is rich almost beyond example in everything, but its resources are fritted away, and the treasures it should produce, are not brought into use through want of proper management on the part of the Government and the deplorable system of monopoly and oppression exercised as well by the Government itself, as by all its subordinate Pashas, Governors, and Employes. I am aware how difficult it would be to induce the Porte to submit to the necessary tutelage, and how impossible to introduce an enlightened system of Government without it. I am not less aware how delicate a thing it is to dictate the adoption of a particular line of conduct to an independent Sovereign. But I feel a strong conviction that such an interference as will produce good Government can alone save the Country from serious internal dissensions and ultimately from falling into the possession of Russia. If therefore interference should not be considered proper or convenient to be adopted, it is at least time to reflect how British Interests may be affected by the Country becoming Russian, and how they can best be secured whenever that event may take place." Observations on the supposed views of Russia, etc., by James Brant, Vice Consul at Trebizond, dated March 26, 1833, enclosed in F. O. 78/223, Ponsonby to Palmerston, #1, May 22, 1833.

would be hopeless. Shameless venality, unblushing ignorance, inveterate corruption and favouritism, are its characteristics, without a shadow of patriotism or a spark of honor.[41]

Also it should be noted that the Sultan, like many another absolutist ruler, kept to himself the plans he had for his state and in this way the few able, ambitious, and honest officials became disillusioned and used their positions for their own betterment. What was needed was a group of enlightened men who would follow Mahmoud's leadership to the new day.[42] Until these appeared Mahmoud would have to direct the reforms himself. Had he attempted to create an intelligent civil service he would have been less spectacular but more genuinely a reforming Sultan because he would have laid the basis for a truly modern state. Unfortunately Mahmoud was primarily interested in the army.

Following the disasters of 1829 and 1833, a new army was recruited and equipped, but it lacked training. This army was forced by the Sultan to adopt European dress and tactics, a policy which was repugnant to all but the younger men who had little prejudice toward the former system. When old soldiers were mixed with the new recruits, this merely made the situation worse. The Turks were naturally good fighters, especially when they were attacking a power which threatened the existence of their state, but they lacked leadership. Time was needed to train the fighting forces, but what was more important were officers to instruct the recruits and to lead them in battle. Mahmoud appreciated this weakness and had established a few military schools. After 1829 he continued the process and improved the instruction in those already functioning, in order to provide officers of ability and intelligence.[43]

[41] Urquhart, *Turkey and Its Resources*, p. 117. The above sentence is crossed out by ink lines in the revised version.

[42] Marmont claimed Turkey had none of these. While this was an exaggeration, it probably was true that "an administration calculated to create and husband resources does not exist in Turkey." Marmont, *op. cit.*, p. 101.

[43] "The great end and aim of the Sultan's exertions is the formation of a military force, capable of maintaining his authority at home, and of enabling him to recover the station, which he has lost for the present, with respect to

Marmont, whose observations of the military organization were especially cogent, described the situation in 1834 as follows:

The inefficiency of the Turkish army is admitted, and it is conceived to be the result of the three following causes:

1st. An injudicious system of recruiting; [44]

2nd. A deficiency of intelligent officers; and

3rd. An erroneous system of tactics.

These defects are remediable, and remembering the gallant feats of the Turks in former days, when they threatened all Christendom, we may rest satisfied that if their army were well organized, and skillfully employed, they would soon be able to defy their Northern neighbors, for there is no reason to question the bravery of the Turkish people, however unsuccessful in their recent wars.[45]

In the troops of all the other powers of Europe there are two admitted titles of precedence: birth and merit. The former has its basis on a higher social grade, which, by giving opportunities for better education leads to the expansion of the mind; the latter, on the experience and information resulting from previous service. In Turkey there are no gradations in the social order and the son of a water-carrier is on a par with the Visier's child, having often the same education. Hence there is no admitted superiority in those invested with power, and the previous equality indisposes others to obey authority obtained through mere caprice.[46]

In Turkey it does not seem contrary to reason to invest with a military dignity requiring strength, energy, and courage, a degraded being whose condition implies weakness and pusillanimity, and who can never be supposed to acquire an ascendancy over the minds of other men.[47]

As a consequence of this state of things not only the private soldiers, but also the superior officers, are taken from among the mass of the people, the latter being selected sometimes in consequence of their higher attainments, but more frequently according to the caprice

---

Foreign countries." F. O. 78/209, Canning to Palmerston, #12, *Confidential*, March 7, 1832.

[44] The frequent levees made by the Porte to maintain the army ranks was a great source of irritation. F. O. 78/236, Ponsonby to Palmerston, #55, May 14, 1934.

[45] Marmont, *op. cit.*, p. 324.

[46] *Ibid.*, p. 63.

[47] *Ibid.*, p. 67.

of those in authority. Here is one great cause of the present defective state of the Turkish army; and if it be an evil to appoint incompetent persons to situations of responsibility, it is no less so to remove the deserving from such places from mere caprice or prejudice. This, however, is so frequently the case in the Turkish service, that the officers never feel secure in their position, and therefore neither acquire confidence in themselves, nor obtain the respect of their men. So long as this mode of treating the officers may continue, the Turkish army can never attain to any great degree of excellence.[48]

These defects in the Turkish army could be remedied, argued the Marshal,[49] first, by the creation of talented officers who could command the confidence and respect of their men; this was a prerequisite to obedience, discipline and order. Second, by placing promotions on a merit basis and eliminating excessive favoritism. Third, the establishment of a model battalion which could be split each six months into two regiments. These were the first steps which must precede the creation of a whole new army, and though the process might involve ten years, the result would be more satisfactory. The Turks followed the French system of field movements which according to military authorities was less suited to the Turks than that of the British or the Prussians. In short, the army needed a complete renovating in organization, personnel, tactics, and equipment. What has been said of the army was equally true of the navy, though that was but a small part of the Sultan's armed forces.

Early in 1834 the Sultan ordered formation of national militias (akaciri).[50] The objects of this plan of defense had been summed up months before as follows:

1st. To augment through the Empire the means of public security and comfort, which rest on the inviolability of the territory.
2nd. To attain this result without in any degree diminishing the agricultural wealth of the country.
3rd. To obviate, in the event of war, levies of troops made hastily and without discrimination; and to avoid all the inconveniences of precipitation.

[48] Marmont, *op. cit.*, pp. 328–329.
[49] *Ibid.*, pp. 64 ff.
[50] F. O. 78/236, Ponsonby to Palmerston, #55, May 14, 1834.

4th. To put a period to the fruitless expenses which burdened the inhabitants.

To relieve the people [says the manifesto] from those heavy burdens, to prevent disastrous depopulation, and at the same time to insure the integrity of the Ottoman territory by an imposing number of able and well disciplined troops, his Highness wishes that hence forward every Mussulman in the vigour of life should be instructed in the use of arms and military exercise: devoting to those exercises only his intervals of leisure, without quitting his native town, and without renouncing the labours of his profession.[51]

While this was a big step forward there was still much to be done to make the Sultan a worthy opponent of his powerful vassal in Egypt.[52]

When one scans the many evils in the Ottoman state, together with the interruptions which Mahmoud suffered, it is to be wondered that he accomplished anything in the way of reform. A less determined ruler would have been discouraged at the start as were many contemporary observers of the situation.[53] Urquhart was not very hopeful of regeneration in Turkey unless encouraged by some outside power. Marshal Marmont, after discussing conditions in Turkey, remarked that "there being no means in Turkey of establishing an improved and equitable system, the present course of disorder must continue." [54]

[51] *Le Moniteur Ottoman*, January 10, 1834, #82 quoted in Ross, *op. cit.*, p. 103. For the Imperial Firman establishing the Khavas (guards) directly responsible to Seraskier Pasha, see *Le Moniteur Ottoman*, #78, January 22, 1834 enclosed in F. O. 78/235, Ponsonby to Palmerston, #25, March 1, 1834.

[52] For the condition of the army and defenses of the state, see H. von Moltke, *Briefe über Zustände und Begebenheiten in der Turkei aus den Jahren 1835 bis 1839*, Berlin, 1841. Moltke estimates the Turkish army at 80,000 by 1839. Cf. also Slade, *Records of Travel in Turkey and Greece, op. cit.*, vol. II, Appendix I.

[53] "The destruction of the Janissaries dissolved its internal bond of union, relieved it from the pressure that had brought it so low, but threw off entirely the weight which had steadied so long the jarring elements of which it is composed. Rebellion has been successful, habits of resistance have been formed, the hands of the government have been weakened, its authority insulted, and it may be truly said at this moment, the political organization is in a state of paralysis; authority, under whatever name it is exercised, whether of the Sultan or Mehemet Ali, is only a form; and this vast body lies with life in each articulation, without corresponding sympathies, without a ruling mind, or the powers of common action." Urquhart, *Turkey and Its Resources*, advertisement.

[54] Marmont, *op. cit.*, p. 191.

The necessities of the government will become daily greater, forming an excuse for fresh exactions, which will increase proportionately with the capacity of the Sultan's agents, who, under the pretext of contributing to the wants of the state, will pillage from every one within their jurisdiction. To effect the required amelioration of these provinces the throne of Constantinople should be filled by a man of commanding genius, with sufficient energy of character to disengage himself from such a miserable throng as now surrounds the present Sultan; and even a sovereign so qualified would require the assistance of a number of enlightened and able men, not only well informed as to the feelings of the nation, but acquainted with its capabilities, and competent to apply the latter for the utmost advantage of their country. In short, the required combination of circumstances does not now exist and can not be created.[55]

That this was an overstatement of the problem, Marmont admits, when toward the end of his book he observes:

The regeneration of Turkey can only be effected by her acquiring such a physical force, as will enable her to become independent of Russia, and by her adopting such a system of civil government as will give security to life and property, and promote agriculture and commerce. When the occupiers of the land shall have a certainty, that no demand will be made beyond such a fixed tax, as will leave them a fair remuneration for their labour, agriculture will necessarily flourish; and in order to produce this certainty, little else appears to be requisite beyond the regular payment, from the public revenues, of the district pasha, with all their subordinates, and the establishment of severe penalties on any functionary, who may make exactions from the people.[56]

Obviously this reform had to begin in Constantinople and the nearby provinces where the population was predominantly Turkish and also free from outside interference.[57]

In conclusion, Marmont states that he was convinced that

[55] Marmont, *op. cit.*, pp. 190–191. Like most Frenchmen, Marmont favored Mehemet Ali, and the contrast between Turkey and Egypt impressed him. "All the requisites for organization of which Turkey is deficient, have suddenly sprung up in Egypt, . . ." Marmont believes that if Mahmoud were victorious over Mehemet, Egypt would soon revert to its old state. *Ibid.*, p. 102.

[56] *Ibid.*, p. 323. On page 319 he claims his object to be to prove that "Turkey may again become a formidable empire."

[57] Syria and Palestine were in Mehemet's grip at this time, while the northern provinces were subject to Russian or Austrian interference.

Turkey's "army and navy may be put upon a respectable foot-ing, that England is of all powers the most able to assist her in affecting these objects; . . . that from her interference, Turkey has nothing to fear, and everything to hope; and lastly that no other power can fairly impugn the motives of Eng-land." [58]   At the very moment that these observations were being made by Marshal Marmont, Palmerston was consider-ing the situation, and he too concluded that it was to England's interest to assist in the creation of a new army by means of which Turkey could assert herself against Russia and Mehemet.

Convinced that the best way to assist Turkey was to help her reform herself,[59] Palmerston urged the Sultan to keep peace with Mehemet until he had put his army and finances in order.[60] At this time Palmerston appears to be less interested in the constitutional development of Turkey than in her military and financial reform, in short in that which would make her inde-pendent of Russia's domination and insure Britain freedom of intercourse in the Near East. In view of this, Ponsonby was instructed to exhort the Turkish ministers to pursue "with in-creasing energy and perseverance that wise system of organiza-tion, military, naval, financial and administrative which had already been so successfully begun." [61]   How far Palmerston's interest in the military development of Turkey was a result of his recognition of this as the basic problem and how far it was

---

[58] Marmont, *op. cit.*, p. 333. "England is, of all powers, the most able to exercise an influence in the regeneration of Turkey, and from her position is perhaps the least likely to have the honesty of her intentions either doubted by the Porte, . . . If she will therefore exert her energies in such a cause, Turkey can still be saved from the grasp of Russia, whose future interest, whatever may be her present wishes and professions, will be advanced by destroying the Turk-ish Empire." Statement of Lt. Colonel Sir Frederick Smith, K. H., in 1839. *Ibid.*, Introduction, p. iv.

[59] Harold Temperley, "British Policy towards Parliamentary Rule and Con-stitutionalism in Turkey (1830–1914)," *Cambridge Historical Journal*, vol. IV, #2, London, 1933, p. 156.

[60] F. O. 78/251, Palmerston to Ponsonby, #40, November 4, 1835. Palmerston also advised Mehemet not ot disturb the *status quo* by separating from the Porte and declaring himself independent. F. O. 78/244, Palmerston to Camp-bell, #14, October 26, 1834.

[61] F. O. 78/251, Palmerston to Ponsonby, #3, December 8, 1835.

a result of his interest in military affairs, a result of his war office experience, is hard to determine.

The natural aversion of many Turks to any new thing demanded the greatest subtleness on the part of foreign powers advocating reform of Ottoman institutions. That sheer necessity was the strongest force which caused the Turks to change their system no one appreciated more than Palmerston. In 1834 and 1835 he was a little uncertain how British assistance could be most effective, but he wisely chose indirect rather than direct action. Since the Porte was powerless against outside powers or obstreperous pashas within the empire, Palmerston advised a complete reorganization of the Turkish army. After Koniah it was not difficult to convince the Turkish authorities of the necessity of modern equipment and trained leaders; that disaster was standing evidence of the superiority of Mehemet, who had adopted western methods.

Though Palmerston offered to furnish muskets and supplies to the Sultan for his new army,[62] it was quite another thing to supply the Turks with military instructors without seeming to interfere too much in the Sultan's affairs. Palmerston's first offer to furnish officers to train the army was turned down by the Reis Effendi.[63] In December 1834 Palmerston went out of office and was succeeded by Wellington in the conservative Peel ministry. Five months later the Whigs returned to power and Melbourne restored Palmerston to the Foreign Office. In February 1835 the Turkish Seraskier requested through the Turkish ambassador at London, patterns of muskets used in the British service,[64] and the following month for permission for a number of qualified students to enter the academies at Woolwich, Portsmouth, and Sandhurst.[65] Though the second

[62] "If the Turkish government should be in want of muskets with which to arm its new levies, His Majesty's Government could supply them with any quantity out of His Majesty's stores in this country, and at a very moderate price." F. O. 78/234, Palmerston to Ponsonby, #24, June 1, 1834.

[63] F. O. 78/237, Ponsonby to Palmerston, #115, August 16, 1834. On the need of trained officers for the Turkish army, see Marmont, *op. cit.*, pp. 329–330.

[64] F. O. 78/268, Namic to Wellington, February 3, 1835.

[65] F. O. 78/268, Namic to Wellington, March 28, 1835.

request was refused because the Turks were too old,[66] it did show the Porte was ready to be advised. Upon his return to the Foreign Office Palmerston decided to try an experiment. Not knowing what his reception would be, in 1835 Palmerston sent one Chrzanowski, a Polish officer in the British service, to Constantinople with the suggestion that he be attached to the quartermaster's division of the Sultan's staff. Through Chrzanowski Palmerston hoped to be kept informed of developments in Turkey and to prepare plans for "reorganization of the militia." [67]

About the same time the request of Nourri Effendi, that several young Turks be allowed to study at Woolwich, the request which Wellington had refused, was granted with pleasure by the Foreign Minister.[68] Captain DuPlat and Lieutenant Colonel Considine followed Chrzanowski to Turkey to assist in the military reorganization. But Palmerston's plans did not meet approval in Constantinople. Though Chrzanowski stayed on for some time,[69] he was not received with enthusiasm.[70] A few months after he landed in Constantinople, Considine returned to England upon being informed that it was impossible to become more than an instructor of the Turkish forces. Palmerston persuaded him to return to Turkey, but he did no more than make a tour of inspection of Asia Minor. DuPlat made a report of conditions in European Turkey, but he accomplished little. Mahmoud was more ready to accept the assistance of Helmuth von Moltke whose character and approach to the problem had won the confidence and admiration

[66] F. O. 78/268, Wellington to Namic, April 8, 1835.

[67] F. O. 78/271, Palmerston to Ponsonby, March 7 and 29, 1836. For detailed discussion of these reforms cf. Rodkey, "Lord Palmerston and the Rejuvenation of Turkey," *op. cit.*, Part I, pp. 570–593.

[68] F. O. 78/268, Palmerston to Nourri, May 26, 1835.

[69] In 1836 Chrzanowski was ordered to Asia Minor. F. O. 78/271, Palmerston to Ponsonby, March 7 and 29, 1836.

[70] Chrzanowski reported "that the influence of England in this country, however fluctuating or depressed before, has never been at so low an ebb as at this moment, . . ." F. O. 78/309, Fraser to Backhouse, February 3, 1837. Cf. also Chrzanowski's Memorandum, F. O. 196/145, Palmerston to Ponsonby, #8, January 6, 1838.

of the Sultan.[71] By the end of 1837 it was evident that Palmerston's military missions were of little value. How far the Russians may be blamed for this failure to accept Palmerston's proffered assistance it would be difficult to gauge accurately, but there is little question but that they were in part responsible.

Yet Palmerston was not one to lose hope at once; [72] there were other means of enhancing the recuperation of "the sick man." The Ottoman fleet at this time was in more deplorable condition than the army.[73] Ponsonby requested from the Sultan (May 10, 1838) two ships of the line over which English officers would have absolute command and upon which young Turks could learn the business of naval officers.[74] This request was not granted. In July, 1838, Palmerston suggested the assistance of a naval mission to strengthen the naval power.[75] The Porte agreed but when the British naval officers, Messrs. Walker, Legard, Massie, and Foote, arrived they were received much as the army men had been.[76] A portion of the Turkish fleet cruised in the Eastern Mediterranean with the British Mediterranean squadron but little else was accomplished.

Failure in this particular endeavor did not discourage Palmerston. Confident of ultimate success his most immediate concern was that war should not break out in the Near East; war must be avoided because not only would it destroy all that had been accomplished, but with Russia in alliance with the Sultan, and France favorable to Mehemet Ali a general conflict might

[71] Moltke and his Prussian companions served without military titles. Other reasons why the Porte refused to employ English officers were: first, it had no desire to change its system; second, it was afraid Russia and France would make similar demands. Cf. F. O. 195/142, Ponsonby to Palmerston, #272, November 7, 1837.

[72] F. O. 78/300, Palmerston to Ponsonby, #62, August 4, 1837.

[73] F. O. 78/328b, Ponsonby to Palmerston, #12, January 8, 1838.

[74] F. O. 78/331, Ponsonby to Palmerston, #119, May 10, 1838.

[75] F. O. 78/329a, Palmerston to Ponsonby, #146, July 25, 1838, and F. O. 78/349, Foreign Office to Admiralty, August 3, 1838.

[76] Russian protests were partly responsible for this reversal of attitude. Cf. Mosely, *op. cit.*, p. 113.

ensue. With these thoughts in mind the Foreign Secretary again urged the Porte's representative in London, Achmed Fethi Pasha, to caution the Sultan to abstain from attacking Mehemet whose army was superior in every department. He argued that if the Porte was not disastrously defeated in such a war, his Empire would be weakened and more subject to Russian domination. "The Sultan ought to employ himself in organizing his Army, and Navy, and in improving his revenue," suggested Palmerston, in order to "make himself strong enough to be able to beat Mehemet Ali by his own means."[77] Specifically Palmerston advised the Porte to substitute for a conscripted[78] army an army of voluntary recruits, Christian as well as Turk. Such a national army would be more efficient in rendering real security to the state, if the Sultan became embroiled with his vassal.[79]

Though improvement of the military status of Turkey was Palmerston's primary interest, he did not lose sight of the other needs from which the Porte suffered. In fact a reorganization of the Turkish army could not be achieved unless certain other changes were brought about simultaneously. To equip, feed, and clothe an army of even moderate size in ordinary times was expensive,[80] and as has already been pointed out the last dec-

---

[77] F. O. 78/329a, Palmerston to Ponsonby, #185, September 15, 1838.

[78] Conscription was not given up, nor was it made efficient until 1843. Cf. Temperley, *The Crimea, op. cit.*, p. 404, note 48.

[79] Mahmoud had established a reserve corps (redif mansouri) in 1834 to keep order at home when the national army was at the front. F. O. 78/236, Ponsonby to Palmerston, #55, May 14, 1834, and #95, July 24, 1834 (F. O. 78/237). E. Cadalvène and E. Barrault, *Deux Années de l'histoire d'orient*, 1839–1840, 2 vols., Paris, 1840, II, 49.

[80] Marmont reported that the Sultan never spared himself in his dealings with his army. In 1833, the Marshal observed: "The lot of the Turkish soldiers is a very happy one. They are better fed than any other troops in Europe, having an abundance of provisions, of excellent quality, and partaking of meat once, and of soup twice a day. Their magazines are filled with stores, and their regiments have large reserves. The pay of each soldier is twenty piasters per month; the whole of which he receives, as there is a prohibition against withholding from him any part of that sum. In short, everything has been effected that could promote the welfare of the soldier." Marmont, *op. cit.*, p. 61. This in addition to the new equipment needed, made the creation of a large national army a great burden on the already weakened treasury.

ades of Mahmoud's reign were far from normal. Palmerston recognized that the Russian war had left a great burden on the Turkish treasury which was in no way eased by the revolutions which followed it, particularly the struggle with Mehemet in 1833. Turkey was a wealthy country, yet such a small proportion of the taxes collected ever reached the Sultan's coffers, he barely had enough to meet the ever-increasing costs of administration.[81] More than once the Foreign Secretary pointed out that financial reform was as necessary as military reorganization.

That the Sultan recognized the deficiencies in his tax system is shown by his ordering that imposts should be collected by officers cooperating with, yet independent of the Pashas.[82] This decree was never carried out, "whether from a difficulty of finding persons calculated for the office, or from other causes, . . . and the cupidity and injustice of the Pashas and Mutzelims were never greater than at present." [83] These injustices were a direct cause of under-production, and tended to keep the population in poverty. "Turks as well as Christians neglect the cultivation of the land," writes Marmont, "knowing that others will reap the fruits of their labour, and in every direction the population is diminishing." [84]

In April, 1834 another firman was issued abolishing the col-

[81] Financial difficulties, brought on by ancient fiscal evils, such as *avanias* (extortions by the pashas), was one of the causes for the promulgation of the Hatti Sherif de Gulhané in 1839. A stronger government was necessary to overcome the critical financial situation faced by the Sultan in 1838–1839. MacGregor, *op. cit.*, II, 166. Ponsonby reported in 1837 that "the Ottoman Treasury is empty, . . . that the work at the new palace, . . . had been suspended for want of money — that orders on the Treasury granted by heads of Departments in payment to Merchants for goods, etc. have been left unpaid, and the reason assigned was want of money." F. O. 78/306, Ponsonby to Palmerston, #298, November 21, 1837. On the income and expenditures of the Porte, see Ubicini, *Letters*, I, #13 and #14. Temperley estimates the total revenues in 1837 at £8,000,000. Cf. Temperley, *The Crimea*, p. 405, note 53.

[82] *Le Moniteur Ottoman*, #78, January 22, 1834, enclosed in F. O. 78/255, Ponsonby to Palmerston, #25, March 1, 1834. This Imperial Firman and the one of February 21, 1834 were intended to correct some of the worst abuses which had developed among the provincial tax-collectors.

[83] Marmont, *op. cit.*, p. 92.

[84] *Ibid.*

lectors of the *Kharatch,* and instituting in their place a commission made up of both *rayahs* and mussulmans. All collection
charges were abolished since the commission was to serve without pay. At the same time the *rayahs* were divided into three
classes and a definite quota was established for each class.[85]
That this firman was joyously received by the *rayahs* goes without saying. Between 1834 and 1839, through his ambassador,
Lord Ponsonby, Palmerston continually encouraged the Sultan
to make further improvements in his finances, pointing out that
this was necessary before the army and navy could be placed
on a firm basis.[86]

To erect and maintain a strong state more was required,
however, than merely a renovation of the military and financial
systems. A complete change of the methods of administration
in the central government was also necessary.[87] In the sum-

---

[85] *Le Moniteur Ottoman,* #81, April 26, 1834, quoted in Ross, *op. cit.,* p. 88.
The tax was fixed at fifteen, thirty, or sixty piastres according to class. Ubicini,
Letters, I, 269.

[86] The first warning of this kind came in June, 1834. "The financial arrangements of the country are no less important than the military; and it is to be
hoped that the Porte will direct its attention to that subject with a view to
establish some order and system in the collection of the revenue, and to secure
the means of maintaining the military force in a state of efficiency." F. O.
78/234, Palmerston to Ponsonby, #24, June 1, 1834.

[87] Juchereau de Saint Denys, *op. cit.,* IV, 310–311. Canning perceived that
administrative reform was basic as early as 1832. Writing in March of that year
he stated: "The main, and perhaps insuperable obstacle to the establishment of
a large national army in this country consists in the necessity of adopting at the
same time a totally new system of administration. Without a basis of this kind,
the Sultan will labour in vain to erect a military structure of any real strength
and utility; and, hampered as he is by the vices of a worn-out system founded
on religious faith, and by the incongruous elements, of which the population of
his Empire is composed, — to say nothing of his Commercial Treaties with
Foreign Powers, and more particularly of his various entanglements with Russia,
it is difficult to conceive by what means so great and perilous a task can be
achieved. . . ." "The great question to be resolved is this: how far is it possible
to introduce into the present system of administration those improvements,
without which the army and the finances of the Country must be equally
inefficient?" F. O. 78/209, Canning to Palmerston, #12, March 7, 1832. After
the 1833 crisis Palmerston was of the same opinion. In June, 1834 the Foreign
Secretary stated: "Anxious as the British government is that the Turkish Empire
should retain its integrity and independence, we must always see with pleasure
the development of its internal resources by which alone its independence can be
permanently secured." "Your Excellency is therefore instructed to use all the

mer of 1834 an assembly of notables was held at Constantinople
to examine this question. Following their deliberations the matter was taken up by the Council, but beyond gathering a great
quantity of information little was accomplished.[88] Attempts
to further restrict the power of the pashas and establish greater
administrative unity in the empire in 1836 were no more
successful.[89]

Many believed that the Municipal Principle of which Urquhart speaks so frequently had to be extended into the higher
organizations, if Turkey is to be regenerated; according to
Ross this was "as necessary as the admission of the blood of
the heart to circulation in the head." [90]

We are aware [he continues] that there are many persons in Europe, and even in Turkey, who express fears that from the development of this principle will result the subdivision of the Empire. We
answer, with the firmest conviction of the truth, that it is the development of this principle which had annihilated the Janissaries, and
therefore saved the empire; and that this very principle has alone
sustained the supremacy of the Sultan, when no'material force was
yet organized to replace that which had been destroyed.

Order in the public service could be secured only through a
proper distribution of authority and the abolition of favoritism.
The number of men who held government posts and received
their share of the treasury's outgo was appalling. Abolition of
these offices was necessary before economies could be effected.
Moreover most of the officials were attended by the *Kavasses*,
police officials, who should have been abolished for the way

means in your power to encourage the Turkish government to persevere in the
course of improvement which it has begun, in spite of all the endeavors which
jealousy or interested views may prompt other powers to make for the purpose
of paralyzing the efforts of Turkey to place her internal organization upon a
respectable footing." F. O. 78/234, Palmerston to Ponsonby, #24, June 1, 1834.
[88] *Le Moniteur Ottoman*, #86, August 30, 1834, quoted in Ross, *op. cit.*, p. 105.
[89] Cadalvène and Barrault, *op. cit.*, II, 49. "The great fault of the Ottoman
Government is its want of power to secure a pure and uncorrupt administration,
. . . it should be strengthened at the core, and so enabled to acquire a more
efficient control over the administration of its distant representatives, pashas,
and other functionaries, . . ." Ubicini, *Letters*, II, 439.
[90] Ross, *op. cit.*, p. 23.

in which they mistreated the people who failed to obey the laws; they were particularly hard upon the Jews, who were the most degraded of all infidels according to the Turkish code. Many other examples might also be cited.

In short, Turkey in the 1830's needed such a complete overhauling the Sultan could not be blamed for not having accomplished more than he had. *Le Moniteur Ottoman*, the official Turkish gazette, did not overstate the problem when it explained (1834):

> The dilatoriness of the Turkish Government in its work of reform is a consequence of the reforms required, being points of practice and detail and not theory, and no one well acquainted with the country will be disposed to reproach the government for its tardiness in this respect. Much more labour and consideration are required to restore an entire system to its primitive simplicity, than to build up the complicated systems, which exist in some countries; — it is more difficult to clear the ground than to encumber it. It is not our business to raise the veil which conceals the plans which are meditated on in silence by the government, but by taking a review of the principal acts done by it in these few years, we may be enabled to appreciate, by anticipation, the spirit in which all that remains to be done, will be conceived.[91]

While in no sense of the word an apology for the "dilatoriness of the Turkish government" the above statement describes the principal task of reform, namely, clearing the ground without encumbering it.

Why Palmerston did not openly encourage constitutional reform of the Ottoman state has long been a puzzling question to students of Anglo-Turkish relations in this period. Nothing in the documents gives a clue to this vital question. Palmerston, unlike his predecessor in the Foreign Office — George Canning — whose policies he admired, was an ardent advocate of constitutionalism in Europe,[92] but he never promoted the idea in Turkey, nor did he favor it in lands subject to Turkish rule. In 1835 Milos, the semi-independent Prince of Serbia, was

---

[91] *Le Moniteur Ottoman*, quoted in Ross, *op. cit.*, pp. 75–76.
[92] In Spain, Portugal, Greece, and Piedmont.

forced to promise a constitution for his state. Though the constitution was favored by both Tsar and Sultan, Palmerston supported Milos in his despotism.[93] In 1848, Palmerston supported the Hungarian demand for constitutional freedom and advised the Pope and others to grant constitutions to forestall revolutions, but his policy as regards Turkey remained constant.[94]

Palmerston's paradoxical support of reform and his indifference (if not real opposition) to a constitution for Turkey is explained by the fact that he believed an enlightened despotism, not parliamentary government, was the better remedy for the existing abuses in Turkey at that time.[95] Parliamentary government to function properly required honest, fearless, able leaders supported by an intelligent public opinion both of which were lacking in Turkey in the 1830's. Until these prerequisites were established, parliamentary government in Turkey was dangerous. David Urquhart was likewise disinclined to press for a constitution for Turkey. In 1833 Urquhart had put it as follows:

On the chances of reorganization of the Turkish empire, I have but one concluding but very important remark to make. A man who would be considered in Europe perfectly ignorant, may be in Turkey, if he is only honest, an able and excellent administrator, because he has no general questions to grapple with, no party opinions to follow — no letter of the law to consult, because not only is he never called on to decide on and interfere in questions of administration and finance, but his power is only honestly exercised when he prevents interference with the natural self-adjustment of interests. Therefore is it that Europeans form a false estimate, by an erroneous standard, of the administrative capacity of the Turks, and add to the real dangers which surround Turkey, others gratuitously suggested by their European prejudices. If a European thinks, with a minister of France, that the whole art of government resides in fixing a tariff, and "in

[93] Temperley, "British Policy," *op. cit.*, p. 158. Cf. also Harold Temperley, *History of Serbia*, London, 1919, pp. 222–23.

[94] "Her Majesty's Government have not advised the Sultan to follow the example of Pope Pius IX and to grant constitutional instructions in the Ottoman Empire." F. O. 65/360, Palmerston to Buchanan, #102, April 20, 1849.

[95] Temperley, "British Policy," *op. cit.*, p. 158.

reconciling the liberty which commerce requires with the prohibitions which manufactures require," he will set down the Turk as incapable, who looks on such science as childish nonsense. Others, perhaps, will consider this untutored conviction as a happy protection against proficiency in a science only to be acquired by deplorable experience. The same is to be observed in every other department of government. A Turkish reformer required no instruction in fund or bank monopolies, none in bankruptcy laws — not in the mysteries of conveyancing — none in corporate rights; there are no laws of entail or of primogeniture to be discussed or amended. In fact, there are no systematic evils; the reformer requires but honesty and firmness of purpose. Taking, in all things, the law as it is, he has to restore, or rather to fix, the currency — to separate the judiciary from the civil authority — to reduce the pashas to their real functions of prefects of police; he has to organize the army — and there all reforms ought to cease. Above all things, religiously abstaining from legislating for the municipalities or the rayahs. If the municipalities be found afterwards capable of forming higher representative combinations, the structure will be reared in its own good time, and on the sound foundation that already exists. That consummation will be little helped even by judicious forcing, and may be retarded by injudicious interference.[96]

Palmerston's interest in Turkish reforms is ably summed up by Temperley, who writes:

On the whole there does not seem much doubt that his (i.e. Palmerston's) chief interest in Turkey was to reorganize finances, and that his chief aim of such reorganization was to improve the army and navy. Now the army and navy was not likely to be improved by a Turkish Parliament. Hence, probably, one reason why Palmerston never advocated it. Another was his belief that it was wrong to encourage change in Turkey until it was absolutely necessary. . . . He was not of course anxious for parliamentary reform in England and he favored a complete *quieta non movere* in that respect in Turkey.[97]

Palmerston's indifference to constitutionalism in Turkey, an interesting attitude in itself, was noteworthy in that he established a precedent for the remainder of the century. Palmerston's successors in the Foreign Office, Disraeli, Lansdowne,

[96] Urquhart, *Turkey and Its Resources*, pp. 121–122.
[97] Temperley, "British Policy," *op. cit.*, p. 165.

Derby, Salisbury, whether liberal or conservative, following the same policy, believing with Gladstone that a constitutional regime would place Christians more at the mercy of the Moslem group. The first Foreign Secretary to sponsor a constitution for Turkey as the best method of correcting her backwardness was Sir Edward Grey in 1908.

While Palmerston's policy as regards internal affairs in Turkey was not as successful as his diplomacy in the years 1839–41, it was not without insight and showed a remarkable knowledge of the situation. It is interesting to speculate as to what might have been the outcome had Palmerston adopted earlier in his career as Foreign Minister such a policy as he pursued in 1834–41. While he might have forestalled Russia and prevented the Treaty of Unkiar, nevertheless his program might have been pursued with less vigour without the threat of Russia, and Turkey might have been even less receptive than she was. There can be little doubt but that while the sponsoring of internal reform in Turkey showed little outward results, it was the invisible item which made the Foreign Secretary's diplomacy between 1839 and 1841 successful and eventually freed Turkey from the Tsar's control. Yet, before discussing the Hatti Sherif de Gulhané and its accompanying events, an evaluation of Lord Ponsonby and David Urquhart's influence on the *tanzimat* is worth while.

Although the majority opinion is that Lord Ponsonby's influence on the internal reform of Turkey was negligible, one cannot disregard the ambassador at Constantinople entirely; his influence, while indirect was nevertheless significant, though because it was indirect it is much more difficult to measure. The absence of Ponsonby's original instructions dated December 11, 1832 [98] make it difficult to determine how far his accomplishments approach the hopes his chief had for him. Though specific instructions were sent to Ponsonby from the

[98] Lord Ponsonby, until then Ambassador at Naples, was appointed November 27, 1832. His instructions are not in Ambassadorial Archives, F. O. 78/220, nor in consular materials F. O. 195/109.

Foreign Office from time to time, the absence of the original orders is a distinct loss. To maintain British prestige while conducting the affairs of state, the fundamental purpose of any ambassador, was unquestionably Ponsonby's appointed task. "To destroy the adverse prepossessions of the Sultan and to establish in their place a large confidence in England" was by no means an easy task; however, by December, 1855 Ponsonby felt that he had partially achieved this end.[99]

As one studies Ponsonby's reports to his chief, one is impressed by the frank assertions of British self-interest in Turkey's welfare. In January, 1838 he informed Palmerston that he had "always told the ministers of the Sublime Porte, that I was of the opinion that the interest of my own Country required the prosperity and so forth of the Ottoman Empire and that the two countries were, to a certain degree, almost identified in policy, that, therefore, I was sincerely and warmly attached to the interest of the Porte, and desirous to assist in everything tending to its prosperous administration." [100] Again, in the months that followed when the commercial convention was being drawn up, Ponsonby insisted upon the rigid fulfillment of all the old engagements between the two powers,[101] until they were replaced by new agreements. And finally, the Commercial Convention itself, Ponsonby's greatest achievement, is another example of his anxiety to save Turkey for England's sake.

Another striking characteristic of Ponsonby's dispatches to the Foreign Office between 1833 and 1841, a natural corollary of the ambassador's determination to maintain Turkey as an outlet for British commerce, is the Russophobia of the ambassador. The fact that Ponsonby was more anti-Russian than he

---

[99] F. O. 78/256, Ponsonby to Palmerston, #23, December 29, 1835.

[100] F. O. 78/329b, Ponsonby to Palmerston, #10, January 8, 1838.

[101] "If the Sultan shall not concur substantially in the measures proposed by England for the amelioration of a system (i.e. monopolies) that will, if maintained, destroy the life of the Turkish Empire, Her Majesty's government must necessarily look to the protection of the commercial Rights and Interests of Her Majesty's Subjects and insist upon the rigid fulfillment by the Porte of all obligations derived under the Capitulations and Treaties between the two Powers." F. O. 78/330, Ponsonby to Palmerston, #101, April 21, 1838.

was pro-Turk tended to force him to use more direct methods
to break Russia's power in Turkey and at the same time raise
Britain's prestige to its rightful place. Shortly after his arrival
in Constantinople in May 1833, Ponsonby joined the French
Chargé in a protest against the prolonged stay of the Russian
fleet in Turkish waters. After the Treaty of Unkiar Skelessi
was known, Ponsonby was even more unwilling to credit the
Russians with any sincerity either in action or thought, insist-
ing that the treaty of 1833 confirmed Russia's mastery of the
Straits as well as giving to her a dominating position in the
Near East.

Ponsonby's policy seems to have but two aims: first, to dis-
credit Russia in the eyes of the Turks; second, to arouse the
Foreign Office against the Tsar. He forwarded evidence to
show that Russia was becoming entrenched in the principalities,
that the Tsar was cooperating with Mehemet Ali to thwart
Colonel Chesney's efforts to survey and establish the Euphrates
as a possible alternative to the Red Sea route. He attempted
to make the arrest of a British merchant a test of strength
between Britain and Russia. He encouraged Bell and Company
to send the Vixen to Soujouk Kale in order to raise the question
of Russia's claim to Circassia, but when war with Russia seemed
certain, the Foreign Office peacefully smoothed out this affair
with the Tsar,[102] showing its unwillingness to become the victim
of its agents' trickery, a policy which might have led to war
between the Russian and the English people.

The Foreign Office was never as firmly convinced of the Russian menace as was its agent; nevertheless Ponsonby's continued reiteration of the Russian danger was a potent influence
in stimulating new methods to reestablish Britain's favor at
the Porte. Ponsonby's arguments [103] were studied and sup-

---

[102] For details of this affair, cf. Puryear, *International Economics*, pp. 49 ff.

[103] Ponsonby maintained that Turkey would be a strong bulwark in what he
regarded as the inevitable Anglo-Russian conflict. If Turkey were "well managed," he wrote in 1834, after pointing out the potentialities of the Sultan's state,
"we shall find abundant power to give us all the support we should desire or
want in a struggle against Russia." F. O. 78/240, Ponsonby to Palmerston,
#187, November 25, 1834. "Turkey may be easily managed by England when-

ported by King William IV, but the Foreign Office clung to its more pacific policy [104] which further exasperated the Ambassador. As far as reform of the Turkish state was concerned, Ponsonby felt Britain would be more successful in her own aims if she allowed the Sultan to pursue his own course, assisting when called upon.

For the foregoing reasons, Ponsonby did not support Palmerston's military missions, knowing perhaps how they would probably be received by the Turks. After three years, discouraged by the ineffectiveness of Palmerston's attempts to reform the Turkish army and navy, the British Ambassador reverted to other methods. In 1838 Ponsonby used his influence to establish closer relationship of Turkey and Britain by means of a loan of £3,000,000 which British capitalists were then negotiating. If the Sultan could be definitely obligated to Britain, British prestige might be raised, argued Ponsonby. Nothing came of this, however, because although the Foreign Secretary did not object to this transaction, he finally refused to guarantee the loan,[105] and without this the English bankers refused to risk their money.

In 1834 and again in 1837 Ponsonby urged his government to accept a proposal for an Anglo-Turkish alliance against Mehemet Ali, arguing that if Britain assisted the Sultan in

---

ever England may think proper to manifest her determination to defend and direct Turkey." F. O. 78/255, Ponsonby to Palmerston, #178, September 27, 1835. ". . . the true interest of England is to consolidate and increase the power of the Ottoman Empire, . . ." Ponsonby to Pisani, May 17, 1835 enclosed in F. O. 78/253, Ponsonby to Palmerston, #110, June 30, 1835. If Russian aggression could not be checked by a joint statement of England and France (to which Austria would very likely agree) then Britain must be prepared to use force to maintain Turkey's integrity. F. O. 78/277, Ponsonby to Palmerston, #194, October 19, 1836.

[104] In 1836 Palmerston instructed Consul Brant to "watch with vigilance any proceedings on the part of that (i.e. the Russian) Agent which may have a bearing either upon the commerce of Russia, or upon that of other nations; or which may indicate an attempt to have the way for eventually extending the political influence of Russia in the districts in which you reside." But he thoughtfully added not to commit the government in any way. F. O. 78/289, Palmerston to Brant, #7, November 19, 1836.

[105] F. O. 78/391, Palmerston to Ponsonby, #279, December 30, 1840.

crushing his vassal, British influence would become supreme at Constantinople, and the Tsar would be compelled to relinquish control of the Straits. An English fleet in the Black Sea would effectively prevent Russia from helping Mehemet Ali, Ponsonby contended.[106] Though nothing came of this, Ponsonby increased his efforts toward that end, as the Sultan became more aware of the Russian danger.

Ponsonby is sometimes erroneously given credit for the maintenance of peace in the Levant 1833–1839. A study of the dispatches to and from the Foreign Office, however, shows that the Ambassador carried out his chief's instructions in this direction very reluctantly, believing that a Turkish assault (supported of course by the British fleet) upon Egypt would not only raise Britain's influence but possibly break the domination of the Tsar.[107]

Only on one occasion and that before his Eastern policy had been fully worked out did Palmerston seem to adhere to the war policy of Ponsonby. In January, 1834 Vice-Admiral Sir Joseph Rowley was secretly instructed to assist in defending Constantinople against a Russian attack, should the Turkish government require such assistance, and request the same through the British Ambassador, Lord Ponsonby.[108] The Tsar, however,

[106] F. O. 78/238, Ponsonby to Palmerston, September 15, 1834 and F. O. 78/305, Ponsonby to Palmerston, #182, August 8, 1837.

[107] Metternich stated that Ponsonby was partly responsible for the Sultan's war-like attitude in 1838–1839. Metternich to Apponyi, May 2, 1839. Prince de Metternich, *Mémoires*, 8 vols., Paris, 1844–1846, VI, 365–366. Temperley does not agree with those who say that Ponsonby encouraged the Sultan to attack Mehemet in 1839. Ponsonby, maintains Temperley, was not satisfied with the *status quo* and did promote unrest in Syria against Mehemet Ali, but did not actually favor the war until it had been begun. Temperley, *The Crimea*, pp. 423–425.

[108] F. O. Turkey 78/234, Palmerston to Ponsonby, March 10, 1834 ('Secret'). In July, Ponsonby reported that Russia was encouraging the Sultan to renew the struggle in order to be able to apply the Unkiar alliance. The ambassador sought power to use the fleet to prevent this action as well as to protect Turkey if war did break out. F. O. 78/224, Ponsonby to Palmerston, #35, July 12, 1834. A year later these general instructions regarding the use of the fleet were countermanded by Wellington when the great fear of Russia's designs had lessened after Russia had refused to support the Sultan in his meditated attack upon Mehemet Ali in the autumn of 1834. F. O. Turkey 78/251, Wellington to Ponsonby, March 16, 1835.

was too wise a diplomat to attempt to cash his blank check with Turkey; [109] aware that such a policy would stir England to the point of war, not to mention what France, Austria, and Prussia might do, Russia determined to sit quietly until Turkey disintegrated of itself.[110] In short, Russia pursued in the 1830's a form of "peaceful penetration" so popular during the decades after 1870. For the moment (1834) Palmerston was taken in by the war group who saw advantages for Britain in a Russian war,[111] but before he did or said anything which might cause war with Russia, he reverted to a wiser, more subtle policy.

Thus, the most reasonable conclusion is that while Ponsonby's contribution to the *tanzimat* was of no importance, the audacity of some of his schemes caused a more subtle policy to emanate from the Foreign Office which in the long run was more effective. As has already been pointed out, the Balta Liman Convention of 1838, so significant in strengthening Anglo-Turkish friendship and economic relations, was Ponsonby's work. Ponsonby also was partly responsible for Reschid Pasha's journey to London in 1838, the Ambassador believing that Reschid's presence there "would be a guarantee of close accord between England and Turkey and might render the Russo-Turkish treaty of 1833 void in fact." [112] But if British prestige with the Sultan gained steadily during Ponsonby's stay in Constantinople, this was due less to Lord Ponsonby than to skillful direction from London.

[109] Russia could succeed in Turkey "only by preventing any collision from taking place." *British and Foreign Review*, quoted in Ross, *op. cit.*, pp. 480–482. Mosely, *op. cit.*, p. 20.

[110] "Russia dare not proceed to any overt act against our Indian possessions, until she has rendered Turkey so completely subservient to her, as to be compelled to co-operate in shutting out the British fleet from the Dardanelles and the Bosphorus. For if, as we contend she ought to do, England were to send a formidable fleet into the Black Sea, she might then threaten the line of operations of the Russians, and check their advance towards the Indus. But so long as the Treaty of Unkiar Skelessi is respected, so long will the English fleet be prevented from passing through the Bosphorus, and Russia will be at liberty to pursue her course of conquest and aggression." Marmont, *op. cit.*, pp. 319–320.

[111] "To England a war opens up positive advantages, independent of the object," *British and Foreign Review*, quoted in Ross, *op. cit.*, pp. 480–482.

[112] Mosely, *op. cit.*, p. 94.

Another Britisher, whose influence on the *tanzimat*, though equally indirect, is nevertheless worthy of note, was David Urquhart (1805–1877). From the time that he was first sent out (in 1831) as a commissioner to help complete the separation of Greece from Turkey until his death he was a specialist in Eastern affairs. The fact that he had the absolute confidence of the Turks [113] placed him in a strong position as a go-between between London and Constantinople. In 1832 and 1833 Urquhart explored the commercial possibilities of Turkey at Palmerston's request and his report,[114] published under the title *Turkey and Its Resources* (1833),[115] was widely read.

Like Ponsonby, Urquhart suffered from Russophobia but his campaign in Turkey's interest with the British public was more pro-Turkish than it was anti-Russian.[116] More than anyone else he appreciated the fact that Turkey was an almost limitless market which Britain might exploit to her advantage. He warned that if Russia gained Turkey she would be in a position to acquire world dominion. As a result of his writings Englishmen began to ask "shall Turkey, with its space, and seas, and positions, and wealth, materials and arms, be used for aggressive or conservative purposes? Is Turkey to be placed in the scale of Russia, or in the scale of England?" [117]

Urquhart also recognized the relation of the survival or decay of Turkey to the maintenance of the *status quo* in Europe.[118]

---

[113] Urquhart was called "Daoud Bey" by his Turkish friends.

[114] F. O. 78/239, Ponsonby to Palmerston, #159, October 11, 1834, enclosure #1.

[115] Urquhart's thesis was that Mahmoud's destruction of the Janissaries rendered reform of Turkey possible, if principles of self-government already existent in Turkey were developed; that Turkey needed help in regeneration and England was best qualified to give it; England would profit from trade if Turkey's resources could be developed.

[116] "While Urquhart became anti-Russian mostly because he was pro-Turk, Palmerston and Ponsonby became pro-Turk only because they were anti-Russian." G. H. Bolsover, "David Urquhart and the Eastern Question, 1833–1837," *Journal of Modern History*, December, 1936, p. 466. Cf. also Crawley, "Anglo-Russian Relations," *op. cit.*, pp. 62–66.

[117] "The Diplomacy of Russia," *British and Foreign Review*, *op. cit.*, p. 133.

[118] "Its position implicates its interest with those of all the great states of Europe, or at least of four out of five. One has for its chief end, to create

His attempts to embroil England with Russia, in addition to his inability to cooperate with Ponsonby,[119] caused him to be removed as first secretary to the Constantinople Embassy in 1837.[120] Back in London he continued the *Portfolio*, a journal which aimed to promote British activity in the Eastern Question. The articles which appeared therein were most influential with British public opinion. According to Ross, Urquhart's "laborious researches shed an entirely new light on the subject, before so obscure, on the institutions of the Ottoman Empire, on the causes of the decline and on the means of its regeneration." [121]

David Urquhart's greatest contribution to the regeneration of Turkey, however, was his firm conviction that the decadent Empire could be given new life. Writing in 1833, he said:

In 1831, after visiting Albania and the greater portion of European Turkey, during the struggle between the Porte and the Albanians, I returned to England with very little hope of seeing the country tranquillized, or the Turkish rule prolonged; but a few months afterwards, returning to that country, I visited almost every portion of it, and was perfectly amazed at the incredible change which had taken

---

anarchy in Turkey; one that order and tranquility should be maintained, but under the most despotic form of government; the third endeavors in vain to conciliate a general system of support with a particular scheme of dismemberment; and the fourth, which alone has a direct and philanthropic interest in preserving its integrity and in reforming its abuses, unfortunately, by the very absence of specific and interested object, is either unprepared, or interferes too late. It is the deep conviction, that the future condition of Turkey hangs at this moment on foreign policy, and that to this country will belong, as the event will decide, the honor or the reproach, nay, more the profit or the loss, of her preservation, or her destruction, that induces the writer of the following pages, at so critical a moment, to publish his opinions on the elements of re-organization which Turkey possesses. . . ." Urquhart, *Turkey and Its Resources*, p. vi. In the edition revised by Urquhart there appears above the word "anarchy" a pencilled R, over "one" an A, after "third" an F in parentheses and over "fourth" a B. After reading this and other books by Urquhart, the abbreviations for the countries seem superfluous.

[119] Ponsonby thought Urquhart "mad" and demanded his removal. F. O. 78/301, Ponsonby to Palmerston, February 10, 1837.

[120] Urquhart was made the goat in the Vixen affair, but Ponsonby was equally responsible. Cf. Bolsover, "David Urquhart," *op. cit.*, p. 466.

[121] Ross, *op. cit.*, p. 27. Bolsover maintains his lack of restraint which prevented him from being a great diplomat was an asset as a publicist. Cf. Bolsover, "David Urquhart," *op. cit.*, p. 467.

place. It was then that I set myself seriously to inquire how the misfortunes of Turkey might be remedied; how the Sultan could attach himself to the Greek and Raya population, the proofs of which attachment met me at every turn. It was then that I clearly saw the value of the elementary municipal institutions, and the facilities for political reorganization which they afforded.[122]

Such faith was sure to win new converts and helped to insure the support of Britain which Urquhart believed indispensable.

The frankness of the arguments set forth by Urquhart for the regeneration of the Ottoman state appealed alike to both manufacturer and worker. His report makes no attempt to shroud his real aims, but, on the contrary, states most succinctly that to unloose "those administrative chains, those commercial prohibitions that lock its resources from the light" might render Turkey "the largest mart in the world for English manufactures." [123] To achieve this end he not only favored the abolition of the Turkish system of monopolies, but he also made a plea for the reduction of prices on English goods so that it would be advantageous for the Turks to buy from English merchants.[124] Probably no Englishman exhibited Britain's

[122] Urquhart, *Turkey and Its Resources*, pp. 1–2.

[123] "A manufacturing people our first element of prosperity is abundant and cheap materials, what unlimited supplies would this country not afford? What natural facilities of transport by sea and on her now unfrequented road — What bounds to the production of cotton, of the finest qualities of silk, of tobacco, of wool, drugs, of corn, oil, hemp, tallow, floss — The facilities of exchange render production comparatively cheaper, than in any other of the countries from which these articles are at present exported in quantities. Her forests and inexhaustible mines, offer richer natural sources than are elsewhere to be found —, . . . Were the commerce of Turkey thus emancipated (i.e. from the administrative chains) so immense would be the production that the price of raw materials would fall throughout the world and a revolution in commerce would take place similar (since there is nothing greater to which to compare it) to that produced by the discovery of America." Urquhart's Report enclosed in F. O. 78/239, Ponsonby to Palmerston, #159, October 11, 1834.

[124] "Were England to make some concession in favor of the produce of Turkey in return for the facilities Turkey affords for the introduction of our manufactures, these results whether as to the strengthening of Turkey, our controul over her counsels, the production of a greater supply of cheapened raw materials or greater demand for our wares — would be greatly hastened — but above all things, would such a measure be advantageous as the means of preserving to ourselves the chief benefits of her future prosperity, if anticipating a conexion the advantages of which no other nation forsees at present but which will hereafter become the object of rivalry and competition." Urquhart's Report, *loc. cit.*

material interests in Turkey more than David Urquhart, yet this fact in no way detracts from his own, or that of his followers' determination to reform the Ottoman Empire.

Urquhart preached that Russian aggression was the greatest menace to the Levant trade and to the route to India. Like Ponsonby he believed, and he tried to convince others that Russia constantly encouraged Mehemet Ali to revolt in order to further enfeeble the Turkish state.[125] These ideas were accepted by a great body of the English public who regarded him as an authority on Eastern Affairs. As far as the government was concerned, the unfriendliness which eventually resulted in a complete breach with the Foreign Secretary was apparent two years before he was dismissed from the diplomatic service (1837), though Urquhart still influenced his chief's eastern policy, by means of his close friendship with Sir Henry Taylor, secretary to William IV.

Close economic relations with the Ottoman Empire were favored by Urquhart for three reasons: first, because the British manufacturer would benefit; second, because Turkey would be strengthened; and finally, because a strong Turkey would act as a buffer state to Russia in the eastern Mediterranean.[126] Needless to say the editor of the *Portfolio* regarded the Convention of 1838 as a triumph for Britain, a triumph in which he was proud to have had such a large part.[127] When the dispute over Persia occurred the same year, Urquhart took a much stronger position against Russia than did the Foreign Minister. Palmerston accepted Nesselrode's explanations, while Urquhart maintained that England was unjustly accused.[128]

[125] *Portfolio* I, #7, p. 16. Urquhart maintained that Russia in one way or another always managed to retard Turkey's growth, if she seemed to be progressing too rapidly, as in 1833. The mere presence of an English fleet in the eastern Mediterranean would have stopped Russian aggression in that crisis, he was convinced.

[126] "Sur le contrôle commercial que l'Angleterre posséde vis-à vis de la Russie," *Portfolio*, II, 37–44.

[127] Urquhart's ideas were the basis for the treaty though Ponsonby received credit for it because he negotiated it. Bolsover, "David Urquhart," *op. cit.*, p. 462. Cf. also Temperley, *The Crimea*, p. 406, note 62.

[128] Analysis of the Note of the Russian Cabinet of October 20, 1838, appended to David Urquhart, *An Appeal against Faction*, London, 1843.

Thereafter the Foreign Secretary and his former agent remained at odds, yet Palmerston never absolutely disregarded Urquhart's opinions.

While Urquhart and Ponsonby continued to cry out against Russian aggression, Palmerston believed the most formidable enemy of the Sultan was not the Tsar but Mehemet Ali. Throughout the thirties Palmerston did everything he could to prevent the seemingly inevitable collision between Mahmoud II and his insubordinate vassal, a policy difficult to pursue because of Ponsonby's personal conception of the Near Eastern problem. Ponsonby was of the opinion that the Ottoman state would "crumble to pieces" if the Egyptian menace continued. The ambassador looked upon war between the Sultan and Mehemet Ali as a "fever which the Turks might easily recover from." [129] All Turkey lacked for complete recovery was "moral force" which Britain could supply by assisting the Sultan against his subjects.[130] Again and again Palmerston instructed his agents in the Levant to use their influence on both Mehemet and the Sultan to prevent the renewal of hostilities.[131]

In July, 1834 Ponsonby reported that the Sultan had resolved to renew the struggle regardless of the dangers involved. Palmerston not only ordered his ambassador to forestall the conflict,[132] but in September requested the Admiralty to have a British fleet maintain a watch for the Turkish fleet and turn it back should it attempt an engagement with Mehemet's force.[133] Conflict must be avoided in the Near East, for even though

[129] F. O. 78/255, Ponsonby to Palmerston, #186, October 11, 1835.

[130] F. O. 78/277, Ponsonby to Palmerston, #194, October 19, 1836. Cf. also F. O. 78/332, Ponsonby to Palmerston, September 5, October 3, 13, November 9, and December 31, 1838.

[131] Palmerston also dangled an alliance before the Sultan's eyes but refrained from consummating it in order to keep Mahmoud from declaring war on Mehemet Ali. Mosely, op. cit., p. 123.

[132] F. O. 78/234, Palmerston to Ponsonby, #41, August 23, 1834.

[133] F. O. 78/250, Foreign Office to Admiralty, September 19, 1834. Prince Metternich also thought that the best way to assist reform of the Sultan's administration was "removing from him the distraction of external politics; that for this purpose it is necessary that the dispute between England and Russia should cease. . . ." F. O. 195/130, Lamb to Palmerston, #6, August 5, 1836.

the Tsar did not become involved, and general war did not upset the balance of power, Turkey could ill afford a war of any kind until the reforms begun by Mahmoud had progressed further.

As has been already indicated, the material value of British assistance to a reforming Sultan was not great. There is little question but that the Prussians under the direction of Moltke were more effective in improving the Turkish army than the combined efforts of both the British and Russian commissions. The moral support of the British Foreign Office, however, was very important.[134] When Mahmoud became convinced that Britain was definitely favorable to his policy he set to work with increased vigor to correct the faults in his army, navy, and financial system. Mahmoud's aim in all this was quite different from Palmerston's. While the Foreign Secretary had aimed to strengthen Turkey in order to free it from Russia, the Sultan's great purpose had been to become strong enough to beat Mehemet into submission. Within four years Mahmoud thought himself ready.

By 1837 the grouping of the powers on the Eastern Question had changed. With both Austria and Prussia becoming more suspicious of Russia the Münchengrätz Convention showed signs of weakening. Likewise the western powers, France and England, were further apart than before, France definitely leaning in the direction of Mehemet. Aware of these changes in April 1837 Mahmoud appealed to Britain for an alliance against the Egyptian.[135] Palmerston rejected this proposal but indicated in his reply that he hoped to see Turkey strong enough to recover Syria unaided.[136] Mehemet sensing trouble countered by increasing his defenses in Syria.

---

[134] Britain had strengthened the fleet at Malta in order to insure the security of Turkey, a fact which Ponsonby frequently reminded the Sultan. F. O. 78/331, Ponsonby to Palmerston, #119, May 10, 1838.

[135] G. H. Bolsover, "Great Britain, Russia, and the Eastern Question 1832–1841," thesis, summarized in Institute of Historical Research, *Bulletin*, vol. XI, #32, November, 1933, p. 131.

[136] Though Palmerston understood Mahmoud's predicament he refused to support the Sultan against his vassal lest he involve his state in war. Instead he

Early in 1838 Palmerston instructed the British Consul-General in Egypt, Colonel Patrick Campbell, to warn Mehemet against attacking Turkish territory, and to seek an explanation of his extensive military preparations.[137] When Russian intervention seemed imminent (May 1838) Palmerston revived his friendship with France, and reminded the Tsar's government that England would not fail to object, by force if necessary, to a repetition of Russia's acts of 1833.[138] Palmerston was afraid that hostilities between Mahmoud and Mehemet would be an opportunity for Russia to seize the Straits.[139] Finally Palmerston proposed a five power conference to meet in London to settle the whole question of the Near East.[140] Such were Palmerston's methods of forestalling application of the treaty of 1833. The conference idea failed because Mehemet gave up his demand for absolute independence [141] whereupon Russia

---

advised the Porte to construct new forts and train its army officers more efficiently. F. O. 78/307, Palmerston to Vaughan, #29, May 11, 1837.

[137] *British Foreign and State Papers*, XXVI, 694. Palmerston's disfavor of Mehemet was obvious. He was irritated with the Egyptian because his armaments had delayed reform in Turkey, and because Mehemet's conquests on the Red Sea and Persian Gulf threatened Britain's control of India. Palmerston wrote Granville June 8, 1838 that he was determined to support the Sultan vigorously against Mehemet. E. Ashley, *The Life and Correspondence of Henry John Temple, Viscount Palmerston,* 2 vols., London, 1879, I, 355.

[138] F. O. 78/272, Lamb to Palmerston, #72, September 8, 1838.

[139] Mosely, *op. cit.,* p. 71.

[140] Palmerston believed that the threats made by Mehemet Ali were sufficient to allow the Porte to appeal to England, France, Austria, Prussia, and Russia "to enter jointly into engagements with the Porte with a view to maintain the integrity and independence of the Turkish Empire." Russia could not object to this as a violation of the Treaty of Unkiar Skelessi, maintained Palmerston, because the Sultan could reply to all objections that the dangers demanded as many friends as possible. The real aim of this proposal, however, was to prevent the Russians from invoking the Treaty of 1833, and possibly to substitute another arrangement for it. The best way to devalue the Russo-Turkish alliance, thought Palmerston, was "to merge it in some more general compact of a somewhat similar nature . . ." F. O. 78/329a, Palmerston to Ponsonby, #185, September 15, 1938. Cf. Bell, *op. cit.,* I, 294. Palmerston thought a conference would be embarrassing to Russia. Mosely, *op. cit.,* p. 93.

[141] Mehemet hoped to enlist the support of the arbiters of European affairs by a show of moderation, so he offered to withdraw his troops from the contested area, provided the Turks would do likewise, and provided he were granted Egypt and a major portion of the occupied territory in hereditary possession. This was practically what he secured in 1841.

took the stand that now there was nothing to discuss.[142] Moreover, since the Sultan was unwilling to make concessions of
any kind, successful discussion of the Eastern question was un-
likely. That the failure of compromise in 1838 was largely the
result of the lack of agreement of the Sultan's foreign advisors,
there is no doubt. Ponsonby, who was as much opposed to
Mehemet Ali as he was anti-Russian, did not discourage Mahmoud's aggressive demands, even though he recognized the
Sultan's weakness, the incapacity of his ministers, and Russia's
aims.[143] Roussin, the French admiral, tried to hold the Sultan
back. If these two men had cooperated in trying to prevent
trouble, the disaster of 1839 might never have taken place.

In the spring of 1839 war at length broke out between Sultan
and Pasha. Metternich immediately suggested an informal conference at Vienna, while Britain and France cooperated to
prevent Russian intervention at Constantinople. Austria's vacil-
lating policy left Russia more or less isolated, fearful of taking
definite action in the face of Anglo-French opposition. Mehemet's victory on land at Nezib, June 25, 1839,[144] the surrender
of the fleet at Alexandria, and the death of the Sultan almost
spelled complete defeat for Turkey.

Palmerston was no idle spectator in 1839 as he had been in
1833. The Foreign Secretary immediately came forward with
the dictum that only the restoration of Syria would guarantee
peace in the East. This declaration was accompanied by an
order that the fleet return to the Straits.[145] On July 27th the
Ambassadors of the powers at Constantinople issued a joint
declaration favoring the independence and territorial integrity
of Turkey. France's sympathies were so strongly on the side

[142] Bolsover, "Great Britain, Russia, and the Eastern Question," *op. cit.*, p.
131. Russia had accepted the conference idea because to agree with Palmerston
would prevent him from allying with France. The Tsar knew he could not
maintain the Unkiar Treaty without war with England and it wasn't worth the
price. Bell, *op. cit.*, I, 298.

[143] F. O. 195/159, Ponsonby to Palmerston, #149, June 19, 1839. Cf. note
107, p. 160.

[144] Full details of Turkish side of this battle in Moltke, *op. cit.*, #64, pp.
378–401.   [145] Rodkey, *op. cit.*, p. 111.

of Mehemet that she could not agree with Palmerston's declaration with regard to the restoration of Syria. The Tsar sensing division in the ranks of his opponents sent Brunnow to London to support the plan of the English Foreign Minister. Nicholas expressed his willingness to surrender the Treaty of 1833, provided Palmerston would recognize the Black Sea as a "mare clausum." Palmerston, supported by Austria, was willing to back such a proposal.[146]

But the Foreign Minister did not have the support of his own nor of the French government. He was unable to persuade his colleagues in the cabinet to go forward without France, and he found it impossible to induce France to coerce her protégé, Mehemet Ali, to cease his attacks against the Sultan. The question of the closure of the Straits was as baffling as ever. Finally he was forced against his will to suggest partition of Syria. Austria supported this, but France remained adamant. Palmerston then persuaded Austria, Russia, and Prussia to sign with England (July 15, 1840) a convention promising Mehemet Ali hereditary control of Egypt, and Acre for life, but Syria was to be retained by Turkey. The Straits were to be closed when the Sultan was not at war. It was not easy to force this through, but when Palmerston presented his colleagues [147] with the dreaded either-or, either this or continued trouble in the East, not to mention a renewal of the Unkiar Treaty, he secured the backing of his cabinet. The Straits Convention was finally signed July 13, 1841.[148]

While the war of 1838–1839 and the crisis following it was generally regarded as a set-back to the reform movement in the Ottoman state, the death of Mahmoud II (June 29, 1839),[149]

---

[146] "In 1839, Palmerston, like a true Canningite, found in cooperation with Russia the means of freeing the peace of Europe from the threat of independent Russian action in Turkey under the terms of the Treaty of Unkiar-Skelessi of July 8." Baker, *op. cit.*, p. 84.

[147] Some of whom wanted an alliance with Mehemet.

[148] For Palmerston's triumph over obstacles at home and abroad, see Bell, *op. cit.*, I, ch. 14; Temperley, *The Crimea*, bk. II, ch. 4 and 5.

[149] Mahmoud was fifty-four when he died. His premature death (the result of lung and liver complications) was undoubtedly hastened by the failures of

which occurred within a week after the catastrophe at Nezib, at a time when the status of Turkey was at one of its lowest ebbs, was looked upon with mixed feelings. While some regarded the death of this extraordinary Sultan [150] as a calamity, others were hopeful of greater reform under another type of ruler. Mahmoud's chief minister, Reschid Pasha, who was at that time on a mission to London, looked upon the death of the proud, vain, flattery-loving Sultan as somewhat of a blessing in disguise. "Il est à croire que la mort du Sultan Mahmoud," wrote Reschid, "apportera du soulagement à cet ancien mal du Gouvernement de la Sublime Porte." While not denying that Mahmoud at times showed great energy and power, Reschid resented the fact that Mahmoud was wont to deal harshly with those who disagreed with his policies, and Reschid Pasha was more than once one of that category. As for Mahmoud's reforms, Reschid felt that they were mere pretensions which added "nouvelles vexations aux tyrannies du passe." [151] Mahmoud's lack of good judgment, wrote Reschid, prevented him from becoming a great administrator, and after his destruction of the Janissaries in 1826, reform was retarded by the Sultan's refusal to adhere to the advice of his agents. In no other way could Reschid explain the general discontent in the Empire in 1839, except as the result of the Sultan's "tyrannie insupportable." [152]

Yet one must not accept uncritically Reschid's opinion of Mahmoud II, since it is well known that his travel and study in western Europe had enlightened him to the extent that he could not accept his chief's absolutism; one must weigh his conclusions with those of other contemporaries who had less

his last years and his addiction to liquor. "Sultan Mahmoud hat ein tiefes Leid durch Leben getragen: die wiedergeburt seines volks war die grosse Aufgabe seines Daseins, und das Misslingen dieses Planes sein Tod." Moltke, *op. cit.*, p. 407.

[150] Juchereau de Saint Denys, *op. cit.*, V, 204. Moltke did not regard Mahmoud as outstanding; thought his reforms a failure. Moltke, *op. cit.*, Letter #66, pp. 407-420. Cf. also Spencer, *op. cit.*, I, 260-261.

[151] Reschid Pasha's Memorandum, Appendix III, p. 271.

[152] *Ibid.*

personal interest in the Ottoman Empire. The man who was perhaps more responsible than anyone else for the Sultan's low estate, Ibrahim Pasha, son of Mehemet Ali, maintained that Mahmoud failed because, unlike his father, he had "taken civilization by the wrong side." [153]

An indefatigable worker, though not always free from favorites,[154] maintaining a self-possession "which neither the reverses of fortune nor the injustice of cabinets could vanquish," [155] Mahmoud II pointed the way to a more efficient state, though he achieved little during his reign.[156] The Sultan's reforms would have been more effective had he developed a more specific program once the Janissaries were destroyed. In 1839 Marmont wrote:

> Their fame (i.e. the reforms) has resounded throughout Europe, and it has been thought that the Sultan has created a new order of things, and commenced an era of civilization in Turkey, whereas in reality, little more has been effected than the destruction of the Janissaries, and the establishment of a new military force. The former

---

[153] "Turkey still possesses in itself seeds of improvement and strength, but they must be well directed. The Porte have taken civilization by the wrong side; — it is not by giving epaulettes and tight trousers to a nation that you begin the task of regeneration; — instead of beginning by their dress, and dress will never make a straight man of one who is lame, they should endeavor to enlighten the minds of their people. Look at us — we have schools of every description — we send our young men to be educated in Europe. — We are also *Turks*, but we defer to the opinions of those who are capable of directing our own, — whereas no regard is paid by the Porte to advice that is not their own. — Their men would make very good soldiers, but their officers. . . . — The only man they had, capable of conducting their affairs, is the late Grand Vizir, Reschid Pasha. . . . You see the treatment which he experienced at their hands. . . ." Memorandum of M. Alexander Pisani's report of his interview with Ibrahim Pasha at Kutaya, dated March 10, 1833, enclosed in F. O. 78/209, Canning to Palmerston, #12, March 7, 1832.

[154] F. O. 78/209, Canning to Palmerston, #12, March 7, 1832.

[155] Ubicini, *Letters*, II, 110.

[156] "Dennoch lebt sein Werk weiter und wird leben, so lange es ein türkisches Reich gebt. Nicht dass Vollbrachte, sondern das Erstrebte und muthig Begonnene ist der Massstab. den ihm die Nachwelt anzulegen hat, und dieser Massstab wird ihn immer zu einer ausgezeichneten Erscheinung stempeln." Rosen, *op. cit.*, II, 301. Cyrus Hamlin, missionary and founder of Robert College, wrote November 1, 1839, regretting that Mahmoud "had carried none of his reforms to that point where they did not still need his singular and fearless energy to sustain and perfect them." *Missionary Herald*, vol. 36, 1840, p. 173.

was an useful and important act, for which the Sultan is deserving of the highest praise; but the troops by which the Janissaries have been replaced, are far from realizing the hopes that were conceived of them; and as to the boasted reforms, they bear only on matters of a frivolous nature, such as the change of titles, or of dress. Thus the turban has been proscribed; the Reis-Effendi has changed his name to that of "Minister of Foreign Affairs;" the power of the Grand Vizir has been curtailed; the extent of some of the provinces altered; and the army is recruited by conscription, according to the arbitrary will of the Pashas. . . .[157]

Another resident in Turkey during Mahmoud's reign wrote:

During the reign of Mahmoud have been abolished the state and etiquette which were formerly the occupations of the court. An economy and simplicity have been introduced into several departments of the state, which is really surprising. The expenditure has been reduced to one-fifth of the former charges. The power of life and death has been withdrawn from the pashas. The Christians have been relieved from those burdens and prohibitions which galled them before. The revenue, notwithstanding the deficiencies caused by the loss of the contributions of Greece, Albania, Wallachia, Moldavia, and Servia — for many years of Egypt, Syria, Candia, Bagdad, Akhaltzik, and lately of Kars and Erzeroom, that is of nearly one half of the empire — is yet in a state to meet the increased demands of the new organization. Political culprits and rebels have not only been pardoned, but trusted according to their political capacity. The prisons of Constantinople are empty. There are no heads on the seraglio

[157] Marmont, *op. cit.*, p. 91. About the same time (1833) David Urquhart, to be sure an admirer of Mahmoud II, observed: ". . . the extirpation of the Janissaries — fell like a thunderbolt on the nation. Their sultan appeared in the character of an avenging angel; with the most extraordinary good fortune seemed combined in him the utmost fertility of resources, sternness of purpose and sanguinariness of disposition; so far his character was only calculated to strike terror; but when the ruthless executioner was seen entering the cot of a peasant, inquiring into his condition, asking for plans for its amelioration, subscribing for the erection of schools and churches, (or at least, reported to have done so), is it to be wondered at that he became the object of the idolatry of the Greek and Christian population, or that the measures which he adopted for thoroughly breaking the pride of the Turks, gained him the confidence and attachment of the rayas — much more important than the applause either of the stubborn Turk or of his European judges? He has effected three things, which have each been the principal objects of every sultan since Mahomet the Fourth: the destruction of the Janissaries, the extirpation of the derebeys, and the subjugation of Albania, which has not admitted the supremacy of the Porte, even in its days of conquest." Urquhart, *Turkey and Its Resources*, p. 115.

gates. Numerous academies have been built and endowed by the Sultan; and there are now seven thousand young men receiving in these establishments an education which, without pretending to embrace the higher branches of science, is exceedingly well calculated to make them useful and respectable members of society, and efficient servants of the government. In some of the regiments, the whole of the men have been taught handicrafts, in the exercise of which they are made to occupy their spare time; the profits of their labour are applied to the improvement of their own condition. These are facts which do not cease to be so, because they are not known in Europe because Europeans will not take the trouble to know them.[158]

These are the views of contemporaries. Historians have been more kind to Mahmoud II. Present-day scholars, viewing his reign from the vantage point of a century, seem in general agreement that more than any other Sultan of the 19th century he aroused the thought, especially among the more enlightened Turks, that reform was possible and this new spirit was responsible for significant changes later in the century. The destruction of the Janissaries, the creation of a new army, and the extension of civil rights were real accomplishments; the development of roads, a postal service, and improved revenues were steps in the direction of a more modern state. Had he lived longer there seems to be little doubt but that he would have learned to construct as well as destroy. All recognize today that before constructive reform was possible "the various forces within the Empire, . . . which hampered the omnipotence of the central power," [159] had to be destroyed, and this was the work of Mahmoud II.

[158] Ross, *op. cit.*, p. 233n. "Turkey participates in the renovating movement which toils everywhere. She does not plunge herself blindly into an adventurous course, but she studies herself, tries her forces, and will apply them with energy as soon as she has discovered, on mature consideration, the end she should have in view, and the means by which she is to arrive at it. Let her abstain from the honied poisons of Europe. Let her place once more confidence in her ancient institutions, and in the moral character of her children. Let her give to the former, vigour and efficiency for the direction of society, and to the latter, the free possession of all those riches on which their feet tread; and soon, in spite of the predictions of genius itself, she will see grandeur and power return to her hands, and then there will be no question of a partition of her empire, but of imitating her example, and conciliating her friendship." *Ibid.*, p. 130.
[159] *Cambridge Modern History*, X, 548.

But Mahmoud was not destructive alone, nor did his reforms merely correct the worst abuses in the state. On the other hand some of his reforms, though very inadequate, did foreshadow some of the promises of the Hatti Sherif de Gulhané. Two examples stand out; his attempt to prevent the muzzellims, agas, and pashas from inflicting punishment on their subjects, unless authorized by the cadi and signed by a judge,[160] was fostered by his desire to protect the lives of his subjects; also the Sultan's respect for property as well as life is shown by his refusal to confiscate the property of condemned men.[161] Mahmoud never gave expression to these sentiments with high-sounding words as did Abdul Medjid on November 3rd, 1839, but his own personal actions speak what was in his mind. His institution of the French language in the army, and in the military schools which he had established,[162] and his changing the titles of two members of the Divan in 1836,[163] although minor changes, did express his anxiety to improve his state along western lines.

According to Temperley, Mahmoud was "a genuine reforming sovereign" who accomplished what he did "by his own vigour and energy." [164] Few are willing to concede that Mahmoud was one of the great Sultans because his reforms were so "ill conceived and poorly coordinated." [165] Yet, ". . . apart from an occasional excess of fanatic rage, he was a man of good judgment, . . ." who ". . . scorning the slippered ease of the palace compound, . . . had the unusual energy to shoulder the heavy burden imposed upon him by his autocratic inheritance." [166] That he strengthened that inheritance in spite of the fact that it was actually diminished in size by the loss

[160] Walsh, op. cit., II, 307.
[161] Ibid., p. 308; Ubicini, Letters, I, 129n.
[162] Missionary Herald, vol. 33, 1837, p. 403.
[163] Kahlia Bey was henceforth called Minister of Interior and Reis Effendi was changed to Minister of Foreign Affairs. A.B.C.F.M., Report, 1837, p. 50.
[164] Temperley, "British Policy," op. cit., p. 158; cf. also La Jonquière, op. cit., II, 429.
[165] F. Schevill, History of Balkan Peninsula, New York, 1933, p. 348.
[166] Ibid., p. 345. Mahmoud essentially a military man cared not for costly style or pretense.

of Greece, Syria, and Egypt, there is little doubt, and he did this against great obstacles,[167] — the insurgent pashas, the rebellious *rayahs*, the old Turks, not to mention the greed and avarice of the neighboring states. No Sultan in the nineteenth century applied more thought and energy to the problem before him than Mahmoud II, and in that sense he was a true reformer and a great Sultan.[168] This Peter the Great [169] of the Ottoman Empire paved the way for the real *tanzimat* some forty years later, even as Peter's accomplishments made the glories of the reign of Catherine II possible a century earlier.

In conclusion, what may be said as to the real effect of Palmerston's policy on Turkey and the *tanzimat* to July 1839? Palmerston's refusal to agree to even the most limited defensive alliance unless that could be "interpreted by Britain in any given contingency" and his offer of "advice on the introduction of reforms, . . . thus helping the Turks to help themselves" may be regarded as not squarely meeting the issue. One writer terms his policy "near-sighted" and not "permanently constructive." [170] Generalizations of this type should be avoided in dealing with a policy as subtle as Lord Palmerston's. The only adequate yardstick for measuring Palmerston's success is a comparison of the situation in Turkey in 1839 with Palmerston's hopes five years before. As had been pointed out, following the crisis of the 1833 Palmerston sought both to prevent a renewal of Russian intervention in Turkish affairs, and, if possible, undermine the dominating position acquired by Russia in the treaty of Unkiar Skelessi. To accomplish this, peace must be maintained in the Near East and British prestige must be raised. In these respects Palmerston's policy must be judged successful. The inevitable struggle between Mahmoud and

---

[167] Ubicini maintained Mahmoud was greater than Peter I of Russia because the obstacles which he had to overcome were greater. Ubicini, *Letters*, pp. 8–9.

[168] "As long as Mahmoud lived he was the best proof of the argument that the Sultan was the best reformer." Temperley, "British Policy," *op. cit.*, p. 159.

[169] Walsh maintained that Mahmoud was greater than Peter the Great, because he not only subdued his subjects, he subdued himself (after 1826). Walsh, *op. cit.*, II, 319.

[170] Puryear, *International Economics*, pp. 102, 12.

Mehemet Ali was postponed until 1839 due largely to Palmerston's efforts, and Britain's friendly attitude went far toward making the Sultan look more to London than to St. Petersburg.[171]

On the other hand the plans which Palmerston worked out for the rejuvenation of Turkey however did not meet with the unqualified approval of the Sultan and hence were not successful. Though England stood ready to help in every possible fashion (except a binding Anglo-Turkish alliance), the reforms of the thirties were definitely Mahmoud's reforms. Within the next two years Palmerston was finally successful in breaking Russia's authority in Turkey, thereby prolonging Turkey's existence as an independent state, a fact which not only tended to raise Britain to first place in the favor of the Porte, but also make further reforms possible.[172]

The success of Palmerston's policy between 1839 and 1841 was directly proportional to his accomplishments of the five years previous. Between 1834 and 1839 Lord Palmerston had learned to appreciate the significance of Turkey's continued existence to British prosperity.[173] During this same half decade the Porte became fully aware of the power of England and her anxiety to maintain the unity of the Turkish state.[174] Thus, it was the period in which the integrity of the Ottoman Empire became a definite part of British foreign policy.[175] Thereafter Turkey was an important factor in the balance of power which England sought to maintain.[176] That this was the most lasting

[171] Even Mr. Puryear admits that 1838 was "one of British ascendancy at Constantinople, . . . in sharp contrast to the preceding five years. . . ." Puryear, *International Economics*, p. 71.

[172] This was undoubtedly one of the Foreign Secretary's aims, for Palmerston did not believe the Turkish state "a sapless trunk," "a dead body." If Turkey could have "ten years of peace," "there is no reason whatever why it should not become again a respectable power, . . ." Bulwer, *op. cit.*, II, 298–299.

[173] Puryear, *International Economics*, p. 11.

[174] Baker, *op. cit.*, p. 84.

[175] Temperley, "British Policy," *op. cit.*, p. 156.

[176] "In a short, but notable speech, delivered on March 1, 1848, in reply to an attack of the Russophobe Urquhart, he (Palmerston) said he held that the surest guarantee of peace was the establishment of a permanent balance of power; that is, stated differently, the prevention of any one State from assum-

achievement of Lord Palmerston, few will deny, but there were others also. The Foreign minister's influence on the Hatti Sherif de Gulhané of 1839 deserves a separate chapter.

---

ing a position of hegemony in the World. Now, the States whose ambitions he most dreaded were Russia and France. In order, therefore, to place a curb upon Russian aggression he felt it desirable that Denmark and Germany in the north, and still more the Austrian and Turkish Empires in the south, should be strong and in agreement." *Cambridge History of British Foreign Policy*, II, 336.

CHAPTER V

REFORM AS GOOD POLICY, 1839–1841

THE DEATH of Mahmoud II and the defeats at Nezib and Alex-andria did not have the disastrous effect on the reform move-ment in Turkey that one would normally expect. The apparent failure of Mahmoud's policies together with the accession of a young, rather incompetent ruler would normally mean a reac-tion in favor of the old Turks; yet such was not the case in 1839. To explain the developments of the next two or three years with the statement that the *tanzimat* fever had not yet run its course, or that the opposition forces were too divided to present a united front against the tendency toward western-ization is to undervalue the strength of the reform group in Turkey and above all their realization that internal reform was the best means of insuring the favor of western nations, par-ticularly Britain. In short, reform became good policy during the first years of the new Sultan.

Abdul Medjid, who succeeded Mahmoud July 1, 1839, was not prepared to carry on where Mahmud left off. Not yet seven-teen years of age, physically weak,[1] he was further handicapped by the fact that under Mahmoud II he had been allowed few opportunities to develop his natural limitation of powers,[2] a policy which rendered him incapable of pursuing an energetic policy. Well-intentioned, if not brilliant[3] Abdul's greatest

---

[1] "La nature l'avait peu favorisé et l'éducation n'avait pas corrigé l'œuvre de la nature." Engelhardt, *op. cit.*, I, p. 35. Cf. also Moltke, *Briefe*, Letter #65 (August 10, 1839), pp. 406–407.

[2] Juchereau de Saint Denys, *op. cit.*, V, 217.

[3] Lane-Poole, *op. cit.*, II, 80. Canning wrote to Lord Aberdeen January 28, 1842, after his first audience with Abdul Medjid "the graciousness of his manner, and the intelligent, though gentle and even melancholy expression of his counte-nance, warrant a hope, perhaps a sanguine one, that with riper years and a more experienced judgment he may prove a real blessing and a source of strength to his country." *Ibid.*, p. 81.

weakness was instability; [4] the fact that he was easily swayed by divergent councilors endangered the security of all his ministers. Moreover, since so much power was concentrated in the hands of the Sultan, Abdul Medjid's accession might well be regarded as an absolute barrier to further progress and the beginning of a reactionary policy.[5] The British theory that "reform was to be achieved through the Sultan," [6] would have had to have been revised, if not discarded completely, had not this weak Sultan been dominated by a few strong men who appreciated the gains of the previous decade and wished to go further.

The first problem to be faced was the Egyptian question, a favorable solution of which depended on the good offices of the powers, especially Britain. France at this time definitely favored Mehemet Ali; Russia might be expected to use the crisis as a pretext for strengthening her hold on the Sultan's power, provided it did not lead to war with England; Austria was not particularly interested in Turkey at this stage. Thus, Turkey turned more definitely toward reforms which would win the favor of her most logical ally, England.

Abdul Medjid was convinced by his minister of foreign affairs that he could not expect effective assistance from without until he adopted a policy for correcting abuses within his state. In this way, reform became a political lever by means of which enlightened ministers attempted to raise Turkey from the low state to which it had fallen. Now that Mahmoud was gone,

[4] ". . . the government of his (Mahmoud's) successor has not profited by the errors of the late Monarch; we see the same indecision in his acts, the same absence of sound enlightened policy — now truckling to the Rayah by granting some half measure of reform, and then stopping short to calm the effervescence of the privileged class — a system of governing which can never permanently succeed in attaching any." Edmund Spencer, *Travels in European Turkey in 1850*, 2 vols., London, 1851, I, 261.
[5] "The main obstacle to the growth and permanence of reforms in Turkey, . . . [has been] the absolutism of the Sultan, . . ." *Fortnightly Review, op. cit.*, p. 653. ". . . the old imperial prerogatives of deceiving or over ruling his ministers behind their backs, or rating them in his presence, or dismissing them individually at a moment's notice, were fully retained by Abdul Medjid." Temperley, "British Policy," *op. cit.*, p. 161.
[6] *Ibid.*, p. 167.

reconciliation with Egypt was much more likely, but at least
one of the Sultan's advisers appreciated that the Egyptian problem was only one danger, the solution of which *per se* would
not make Turkey a strong state.[7] No man was more aware of
the necessity of permanent reforms for the Turkish state, nor
more convinced of what the effect a definite reform program
would have on the powers at this time than the Foreign Minister, Reschid Pasha.[8]

Reschid Pasha was a statesman of high caliber,[9] one of the
few which Turkey produced in the decades prior to the Crimean
War; more far-sighted than most of his colleagues, he is today
regarded as one of the most outstanding Turkish statesmen
of the nineteenth century. Little is known of Reschid's early
life; he was probably born in 1802 at Constantinople, where he
died in 1858 at the age of fifty-six.[10] It may be assumed that
he was given the usual education of a well-to-do Turkish family,[11] and prepared early for the government service. His first

[7] Reschid Pasha's Memorandum, Appendix III, p. 272.

[8] "Ces moyens qui causeraient évidemment une amélioration sensible dans la
position de tours, présenteraient aux hommes actuellement à la tête des affaires
une occasion de gagner la bienveillance des puissances Européennes." Reschid
Pasha's Memorandum, August 12, 1839, Appendix III, p. 274. The Hatti Sherif
was promulgated on November 3, 1839. Two days after its promulgation Reschid wrote Baron von Sturmer, Austrian Internuncio at the Porte: "Le Gouvernement de S. H. espère que les puissances amies apprécieront le bien qui doit
résulter de ces institutions dans l'intérêt de l'humanité et de l'Empire Ottoman
et qu'elles y verront un nouveau motif de réserver les biens qui les unissent à
la Turquie." Reschid à Sturmer, le 5 Novembre 1839, H. H. u. St. A., Wien,
Türkei VI, fasz. 51. According to Rosen, to set forth a definite program of
reform would place Turkey "in die Reihe des liberalen Reiches." Rosen, *op. cit.*,
II, 14–15. Cf. also, Engelhardt, *op. cit.*, I, 29; A. Du Velay, *Histoire financière
de la Turquie*, Paris, 1903, p. 89; F. Rouvière, *Essai sur l'évolution des idées
constitutionelles en Turquie*, Montpellier, 1910, p. 56; C. R. von Sax, *Geschichte
der Machtverfalls der Türkei bis ende des 19. Jahrhunderts*, Vienna, 1913, p.
278; Soubby Noury, *Le Régime représentatif en Turquie*, Paris, 1914, p. 39; G.
Franco, *Développements constitutionels en Turquie*, Paris, 1925, p. 15.

[9] F. O. 78/225, Ponsonby to Palmerston, December 19, 1833. Missionaries
regarded Reschid as "one of the most enlightened and liberal men in the Empire." Cf. *Missionary Herald*, vol. 42, 1846, p. 97.

[10] Not to be confused with Reschid Pasha, the general, who was defeated and
captured by Ibrahim's forces at Koniah in 1833; the general later committed
suicide to atone for his disgrace.

[11] Reschid's father was an official in one of the many bureaus of the Porte.
Cadalvène and Barrault, *op. cit.*, II, 272.

position was that of secretary to Ali Pasha; later he was taken over by Izzet Pasha, the Grand Vizir, in the same capacity. Reschid's ability was recognized early, and he held various positions in the Sultan's bureaucracy; here he became acquainted with the intricacies of the Turkish governmental system, noting the strong but especially the weak spots which needed strengthening. This experience proved invaluable later when he became leader of the reform movement under Abdul Medjid.

Reschid's shrewd, yet honest, approach to the problems of the Porte inspired confidence and eventually made him a popular figure with the more broad-minded Turks. "A just, though severe man, . . . highly respected," [12] he had "that kind of moral authority with them (i.e. the clerks and officials in the government) which a leading man in any profession exercises over its inferior members." [13] As far as the Sultan was concerned, Mahmoud did not always agree with Reschid's policies, but he never questioned his fidelity. [14]

Reschid Pasha's courage, his natural calm in a crisis, not to mention his mastery of languages, qualified him particularly well for diplomacy and foreign affairs, in which field he later so distinguished himself. In 1833 he assisted in the arrangement of the Peace of Kutayia, and during the next four years was ambassador both at London (1834–1836) and Paris (1836–1837). [15] After Pertew Effendi's fall (1837) Reschid was recalled from Paris to become Minister of Foreign Affairs under Grand Vizir Raouf Pasha. [16] Reschid held this post several times before attaining the highest position offered by the Porte, namely that of Grand Vizir. However, it was as minister of

[12] F. O. 78/276, Ponsonby to Palmerston, #116, July 15, 1836.
[13] Ashley, *op. cit.*, II, 347.
[14] F. O. 78/276, Ponsonby to Palmerston, #116, July 15, 1836.
[15] Cadalvène and Barrault, *op. cit.*, II, 272; Du Velay, *op. cit.*, pp. 91–92. Reschid was ambassador at Paris a second time, 1840–1841, and again at the Court of St. James, 1843–1845. He frequently relinquished his portefolio of Foreign Affairs to go on special missions for Mahmoud II.
[16] Pertew Effendi was an honest, straightforward minister, yet his devotion to the old Turkish principles made him insufferably intolerant. Ubicini, *Letters*, II, 113. Pertew was particularly fanatical against Christians. Juchereau de Saint Denys, *op. cit.*, V, 211.

foreign affairs that he performed his greatest service toward the establishment of a reformed Turkey.

Though Reschid fully appreciated the significance of the abolition of the Janissaries and the other reforms of Mahmoud II, Turkey's defeat in 1833 convinced him that the Ottoman Empire could never become a strong state until it adopted European methods. He was cautious, however, about expressing his views to the Sultan, knowing only too well the fate of over-zealous advisors. In the years that followed, his plans were modified from time to time by the realization that Turkey was not France or England, and that, even though the Sultan were won over, the people were not able to manage western institutions.

The only accomplishment for which Reschid was primarily responsible prior to 1839 was the reorganization of the Council and bureaus of the Porte. Instead of one council, three were established in 1838; [17] the *Medjliss Cumouri Askerize*, composed of the Seraskier and ten army officers, was set up to manage military affairs; at the same time a council for finance and interior civil matters, the *Medjliss Cumouri Naziri*, came into being; but most important was the *Medjliss Ahkiami Adlie*, a committee of eight men who examined all proposals of the two lower councils; all laws had to be passed by this group, which corresponded to the old Privy Council, before being submitted to the Sultan. Unfortunately these councils, while a real step forward, did not function well because of the jealousy of the personnel. Within two months Reschid's colleagues were intriguing against the Minister of Foreign Affairs because of his creation of these chambers of divided power "in imitation of England," though Ponsonby maintained that the cabal was managed by Russians, especially a Mr. Stepowitch, Chief Dragoman of the Prussian Mission, "indubitably an agent of the Russians." [18]

---

[17] F. O. 78/330, Ponsonby to Palmerston, #79, March 26, 1838 and *Le Moniteur Ottoman*, #131, May 5, 1838.

[18] F. O. 78/331, Ponsonby to Palmerston, #125, May 21, 1838.

For these reasons Reschid never fully outlined his whole reform program, even to his foreign friends, until after Mahmoud died in July, 1839. Reschid Pasha was at that time in London, to which place he had gone late in 1838 [19] with the hope of negotiating an Anglo-Turkish alliance against Mehemet Ali.[20] Though unable to secure definite support from the British Foreign Office, he stayed on in London until the middle of August, 1839; when, after Mahmoud's death, Abdul Medjid became Sultan, Reschid was called to Constantinople to resume the office of Foreign Minister.[21]

Reschid was somewhat dubious of the future of Turkey under Abdul Medjid, fearing that his extreme youth and inexperience would cause him to become the tool of the reactionary forces already at work in Turkey.[22] For this reason he hoped to obtain assistance from the friendly powers, believing that the new ruler would perhaps be more amenable to advice than the older, more experienced Mahmoud. If the powers intervened in Eastern affairs, he hoped they would do so through the usual channels, and that such intervention would be jointly undertaken by all the powers. Reschid did not wish the precedent of 1833 to be repeated, both because it was a bad precedent and because he was genuinely afraid of the motives of Russia "dont l'intérêt serait l'affaiblissement de l'empire Ottoman." [23] These ideas were recorded in a memorandum in Palmerston's handwriting, dated August 12, 1839, undoubtedly written immediately after an interview with Reschid at which the status of Turkey was the principal topic of conversation.

[19] Reschid presented his credentials, November 29, 1838. *London Gazette*, vol. 166, p. 2777.

[20] F. O. 78/460, Ponsonby to Palmerston, #322, November 30, 1839. Rouvière maintains that he was sent on this mission partly because his ideas were too liberal for the aging Sultan. Rouvière, *op. cit.*, p. 56. Cf. also *Manchester Guardian*, September 5, 1838.

[21] Reschid left London August 17, 1839, returning via Paris and Marseilles. *London Times*, August 19, 1839. He arrived in Constantinople September 4, 1839. F. O. 78/358, Ponsonby to Palmerston, #243, September 5, 1839.

[22] Before Reschid returned from London Nourri Effendi and Sarim Effendi attempted to prevent him from becoming foreign minister, but Raouf Pasha was firm. Khosrew then tried to delay his return. F. O. 78/357, Ponsonby to Palmerston, #176, July 12, 1839.

[23] Reschid Pasha's Memorandum, Appendix III. p. 275.

In Reschid Pasha's opinion the immediate crisis in the Levant was not the central issue. With the friendly offices of the powers, especially England, Mehemet Ali could be returned to his place in the empire without weakening the structure. What was more fundamental was to strengthen the Sultan's waning power so that the process of disintegration would not continue in the future. Reschid had been considering genuine reforms for several years; after Mahmoud's death he was less fearful of expressing and more hopeful of effecting them than before.

Reschid sought a remedy which would not weaken in any way the power of the Sublime Porte, because such a reform would meet the immediate disapproval of the majority of his countrymen.[24] He favored the establishment of a fixed governmental system as the best means of insuring permanent reform. That he meant by "un système immumablement établi" government based on well-established principles rather than the arbitrary will of the Sultan, there is little question. The difficulty of affecting genuine reforms as long as each minister's tenure depended on the good will of the Sultan was an experience with which he was thoroughly acquainted. Moreover a fixed system based on law would be the best guarantee of life and property which he held sacred. Execution of opponents and the confiscation of their property was one of the most deplorable of the Sultan's prerogatives argued Reschid. Equality before the law, public trials for offenders, quick and sure sentence for convicted criminals, — all were impossible under the existing regime, and unless these weaknesses were corrected, the Sultan could not expect his people to support the state in a crisis. Such was Reschid's philosophy of government as he outlined it to Palmerston on August 12, 1839.[25] Three months later the

---

[24] "Mais, dira-t-on peut-être, le remède à ce mal ne sauroit être apporté sans une sorte d'invasion sur le terrain de l'administration intérieure de la Sublime Porte, une semblable conduite serait contraire aux droits respectifs des nations; d'ailleurs la soumission aveugle des musulmans aux lois du Coran, et leur fanatisme reconnu, ne manqueraient pas de leur faire repousser toutes propositions dictées par les puissances Européennes." Reschid Pasha's Memorandum, Appendix III, p. 273.

[25] Reschid Pasha's Memorandum, Appendix III.

Sultan issued the famous Hatti Sherif de Gulhané (November 3, 1839). The similarity of the ideas of these two documents is convincing evidence that Reschid was the author of the "Hat," and causes one to wonder how far Englishmen were responsible for the proclamation and the ideas it contained.

A wide variety of opinion exists as to who among the British statesmen interested in Turkey was more important in encouraging Reschid in his desire to westernize Turkey. Lane-Poole insists that Stratford Canning was the original sponsor of the decree of 1839, having advised it as early as 1833. Yet, there is an admission in the quotation from Canning's memoirs that Reschid merely sought the advice of Canning on means of affecting an idea which was really his own. Recalling a conversation he had with Reschid in 1832, Canning writes: "I remember that he opened himself to me on the subject of reforms in Turkey. It was evident that he looked to taking an active part in the new policy inaugurated by the overthrow of the Janissaries, and stimulated by the example of Mohammed Ali in Egypt." [26] It seems more than probable that Lane-Poole, realizing that Reschid and Canning had known each other since 1832, read back into their early relationships the friendly advice which Canning offered so freely at the time of his ambassadorship in Constantinople.

Although Lord Ponsonby was close to Reschid, a study of the ambassador's reports after 1833 reveals little evidence that he was in any way responsible for Reschid's determination to reform the Turkish state; [27] nor did he assist in the execution

[26] Lane-Poole, *op. cit.*, II, 105.

[27] Ponsonby applauded the Hat after it was proclaimed, however. On November 5, 1839 he wrote Palmerston: "What has been done is excellent in conception and execution. It is in perfect unison with the religion and interest and feelings of the people, and at the same time provides security for the great interests of every class of subjects, whilst it infringes no right or privilege of any. It is a victorious answer to those who say that this empire cannot be saved by its ancient government, and that the spurious regeneration to be worked out by the Pasha of Egypt is its only preservative." F. O. 78/360, Ponsonby to Palmerston, #301, November 5, 1839. Palmerston received the news of the Gulhané decree with equal enthusiasm. Cf. F. O. 78/353, Palmerston to Ponsonby, #181, December 2, 1839.

of Hatti Sherif, though he remained in Constantinople until 1841. As has already been stated, Lord Ponsonby's principal contribution to the betterment of Turkey was the Commercial Treaty of 1838, which provided for the abolition of the monopolies, and in this he was motivated largely by selfish interests. Eighteen months before the promulgation of the Gulhané decree when Reschid outlined his plans for the reform of the Turkish administration, his proposals met with little enthusiasm from the English ambassador.[28] Ponsonby was primarily interested in undermining Russian influence at the Porte and in convincing the Sultan that Britain was his only true friend.

While Ponsonby's advice on diplomatic affairs was frequently sought by Reschid Pasha, it was not until September, 1939, after the reformer had returned from his mission in England, that he requested Ponsonby's support for alleviating the predicament of the Turkish state. When Ponsonby visited Reschid, September 10, 1839, to congratulate him upon his return, the minister of foreign affairs expressed "his entire confidence in the good will and friendship of England" and stated that he hoped the British government would "do some *act* that would confirm . . . the kind intentions of that government, for it was the constant endeavor of the Russians to persuade the Porte and the world that England would do nothing, whatever England might say, . . ."[29]

When Reschid disclosed his plans for effecting measures to give security of life and property to all Turkish citizens, Ponsonby recommended that "caution should be united with energy in the pursuit of such inestimable ends." Ponsonby suggested that the civil and military powers in Turkey vested in the Pashas be separated, that the imposts be uniform for all districts and be collected by a new official, and that the Convention of 1838 be strictly executed because this "would tend

[28] F. O. 78/331, Ponsonby to Palmerston, #119, May 10, 1838.
[29] F. O. 78/358, Ponsonby to Palmerston, #249, September 10, 1839. Two weeks later Ponsonby reported that one of the chief Mollahs was anxious to have a foreign power intervene to ameliorate the situation in Turkey. F. O. 78/359, Ponsonby to Palmerston, #264, September 24, 1839.

forcibly to establish security of property amongst the Turks as well as the Rayahs;"[30] Ponsonby's statements, carefully guarded lest he involve his government, were of little value to the reformer.[31] As one reads Ponsonby's dispatches during these months, one longs for an ambassador who, though he might at times act on his own initiative counter to the Foreign Office, would not have let slip such an opportunity to strengthen the Ottoman state. Lord Ponsonby was no Stratford Canning; perhaps it was fortunate he recognized his limitations and merely carried out the commands of his chief.

Of all English statesmen, Palmerston was probably closer to Reschid in the 1830's than any other Englishman. The Foreign Secretary's influence is most difficult to gauge, however, because his and Reschid's remedies did not always coincide. Palmerston was not ready to sponsor the constitutional ideas which Reschid entertained for Turkey, and Reschid for his part could not avoid the belief that Palmerston's military and naval missions were not striking at the real root of the problem. Though their solutions varied, they did agree on the fundamental difficulties in the Ottoman state. In fact, the similarity of the ideas of the memorandum in Palmerston's handwriting and the decree of November 3 is most striking.[32]

Both documents speak of Turkey's advantageous geographical position, the fertility of her soil, and the aptitude and intelligence of the people. Both deplore the excessive burdens placed on the people, the mismanagement of finances, and the arbitrary exercise of authority by the Sultan and his agents, which have broken the spirit of all but the official class. Both

[30] F. O. 78/359, Ponsonby to Palmerston, September 30, 1839. Palmerston approved all these suggestions. Cf. F. O. 195/158, Palmerston to Ponsonby, October 23, 1839.

[31] On October 22, 1839, after reporting that the chief ministers of the Porte had prepared a plan for securing the subject against capital punishment without a trial, and for protecting property from arbitrary power, the ambassador added: "I do not know how they intend to proceed to establish such a vast good, nor to secure it. I think it prudent not to enquire much into the matter lest I should incur responsibility." F. O. 78/359, Ponsonby to Palmerston, October 22, 1839.

[32] Cf. Appendices III and IV. Cf. also P. Imbert, *La Rénovation de l'Empire Ottoman, affaires de Turquie*, Paris, 1909, p. 190.

documents are certain of the future welfare of the Ottoman state if institutions guaranteeing the lives, honor, and fortune of its citizens can be established. Internal reform was necessary if Turkey was to stand alone. Yet, the mere fact that the two statesmen generally agreed on the problems to be solved is no proof that the British Foreign Secretary was Reschid's principal sponsor and guide. That Palmerston rendered moral support to the hopes and plans of the Turkish statesmen no one can deny, but there is nothing in the documents to show any positive influence of the Foreign Secretary on the Hatti Sherif de Gulhané. Of course the documents do not provide the complete story of Palmerston's attitude toward Reschid's reform program, but they are indicative of the attitude of the Foreign Secretary toward the reformer in the twelve months before the Hat was issued.

Reschid arrived in London on November 24, 1838. A fortnight later (December 8, 1838) he wrote Palmerston asking for an interview. The repetition of the request ten days later would indicate that the first request had been ignored. On the same day Palmerston refused to accept the Turkish order Reschid wished to confer upon him by order of the Sultan.[33] No further communications between the two men appear in the documents until March, 1839. On the eleventh of that month Reschid sought an interview with the Foreign Secretary; that Palmerston planned to grant him an audience is shown by the note on the back of the letter in Palmerston's hand "Tomorrow at ½ past Two. P. 11/3/39;"[34] no details of the discussion show up in any later dispatches. Late in April Reschid asked Palmerston for a draft of the treaty which would put an end to Mehemet's desire for independence.[35] Palmerston did not reply until May 6, saying that he would send it in the course of a few days.[36] Reschid's request for an interview on May 3, 1839

---

[33] F. O. 78/347, Palmerston to Reschid, December 18, 1839.
[34] F. O. 78/383, Reschid to Palmerston, March 11, 1839.
[35] *Ibid.*, April 26, 1839.
[36] *Ibid.*, Palmerston to Reschid, May 6, 1839.

was not answered for a week.[37] Another conference was probably held on May 30th.[38] Insufficient as these letters are to draw any general conclusions, they do impress one with a certain indifference and coolness on the part of the Foreign Secretary toward Reschid. During the first six months of Reschid's stay in London it appears from the official documents that only three of six interviews requested were granted. Whether private unreported meetings were held is not known, but it does seem that if the Foreign Secretary was seriously interested in improving Turkey's status, more details would show in the records.[39] In 1839 Palmerston was no more interested in administrative reform than he had been five years before; his interest still centered on the army.

But if there is no proof that Palmerston inspired the proposals outlined in the Hatti Sherif de Gulhané, like many Englishmen he did applaud Reschid's efforts to establish a firmer basis for the Turkish state. As soon as he learned of the promulgation of the decree of Gulhané he wrote Ponsonby to congratulate the Porte "upon a measure which is fraught with incalculable advantage to the Ottoman Empire, and which redounds highly to the honor of the Statesmen by whom it has been framed." [40] Palmerston promised support in carrying out "the excellent principles which are set forth in the Hatti Sherif." But in another dispatch written the same day he instructed Ponsonby "to point out to the Turkish government how much it would be to their advantage to profit by the military skill and acquirements of a few European officers, for the purpose of reorganizing their army." Palmerston favored the Porte's

[37] Palmerston's notation: "Tomorrow at Four, and tell him the messenger is delayed. P. 10/5/-39." F. O. 78/383, Reschid to Palmerston, May 3, 1839.

[38] *Ibid.*, May 29, 1839. Palmerston's note: "Tomorrow at ½ past 3. P. 30/5/39."

[39] No further communications appear until just before Reschid left London for Constantinople. Reschid had an audience with the queen to announce the accession of Abdul Medjid, August 9, 1839. On the 10th he had a conference with Palmerston and the next day sent the Foreign Secretary the Memorandum on the state of Turkey. Cf. *ibid.*, August 9, 1839; F. O. 78/387, Domestic various July–September, 1839.

[40] F. O. 78/353, Palmerston to Ponsonby, #181, December 2, 1839.

granting "actual command of troops to some few good European officers, either English or German," as well as the creation of a small model corps the example of which "would spread the spirit of improvement through the rest of the Turkish army." [41] While aware of the many evils which existed in the Turkish administration, Palmerston felt these were problems which would have to be solved by the Turkish statesmen themselves.[42] Yet, this is not to deny that Palmerston had no part in the improvement of Turkey's status in 1839–1840. By effecting a reasonable solution of the Egyptian crisis and by forcing the Russians to limit their influence in Turkey with the forfeiting of the Unkiar Treaty, Palmerston exerted indirectly more influence on the reform movement than any other person.

The reconciliation of Mehemet Ali and the Sultan, the scrapping of the Russo-Turkish treaty of 1833, and the establishment of the Straits Convention were accomplishments [43] which insured the freedom and independence of Turkey in the future, and thus placed internal reform, which was primarily the business of Turkish statesmen, within the range of possibility. Since this appears to have been Palmerston's primary aim, the success of his Eastern policy cannot be questioned. The settlement of the Eastern Question must be regarded then as more than a purely diplomatic triumph for Palmerston; it was also his greatest contribution to the reform movement in Turkey between 1833 and 1841.

From another point of view, the fact that Britain had assisted Turkey at one of the most critical periods of her history was a triumph for Reschid as well. In a word, his reform pro-

[41] F. O. 78/353, Palmerston to Ponsonby, #182, December 2, 1839.

[42] Palmerston felt in 1839 in much the same way as he later expressed himself to Lord Russell. "Our power (in maintaining the Turkish Empire) depends on Public Opinion in this country, and that Public Opinion would not support us unless the Turkish Government exerts itself to make reforms." Palmerston to Russell, December 13, 1860, Russell Papers, G. D. 22/21.

[43] For a complete account of the crisis and its settlement, see Rodkey, *The Turco-Egyptian Question;* Vicomte de Guichen, *La Crise d'Orient de 1839 à 1841 et l'Europe*, Paris, 1922; A. Hasenclever, *Die orientalische Frage in den Jahren 1838–1841*, Leipzig, 1914.

gram had proved to be good policy.[44] Yet, this is not to question the sincerity of that Turkish statesman's motives. Reschid Pasha's attempts to make real the promises of November 3, 1839 during the years that followed is sufficient proof that he regarded the *tanzimat* as more than a diplomatic gesture to curry the favor of the western nations.

Almost any study of great reform movements furnishes sufficient proof for the fact that the essential qualifications of a successful reformer are patience and political opportunism. These qualities were especially necessary for anyone who hoped to improve a state as backward as Turkey in the nineteenth century. The great protagonist of Turkish reform was richly endowed with both these prerequisites. Much as he chafed at Mahmoud's inability to make substantial reforms, Reschid seldom gave vent to his irritation; instead he patiently awaited the time when the need of reform would make agitation unnecessary. The defeat of the Sultan's army at Nezib, followed immediately by the surrender of the fleet at Alexandria and the death of Mahmoud II, seemed to Reschid the long sought opportunity to come forward with a definite program of reform.

To most Turks these losses were no more than the normal risks of war, which, if they did not prove fatal, could be made up for at a later date. To Reschid however these defeats had a deeper significance; they were the result of Mahmoud's failure to make his state the equal of that of his vassal. Moreover, the problem could not be rectified merely by a reasonable settlement with Mehemet; [45] unless these defeats were to be re-

[44] The impression which the Hatti Sherif created both at home and abroad corresponded with the aim of its creator. "Die Verherrlichung des freisinnigen Ministers Abdulmediids in der europäischen Presse, vor allen in England, fing an, dem Lobe Mehmed Alis die Wage zu halten." Rosen, *op. cit.*, II, 18. The *Journal de Constantinople* stated that "il semble ouvrir réellement une nouvelle Ère à l'Empire Ottoman." *Journal de Constantinople*, #2, 27 Novembre 1839, p. 1. The *London Times* of November 28, 1839 carried a lengthy description of the preparation and promulgation of the Hat as well as a translation of the decree itself, while the Mehemet crisis was treated in three short paragraphs.

[45] "Le véritable but ne saurait être atteint par le simple fait de la garantie de l'intégrité et de l'arrangement de l'affaire d'Egypte." Mémoire, 10 Mars, 1841. Appendix V, p. 280.

peated, — if not in Egypt, in other parts of the empire, — real reform of the civil and military organization of the state was needed at once. Reschid was convinced that to delay longer in presenting his program would spell defeat. Now the Porte would be forced by the failures of the armed forces and the near-bankruptcy of the treasury to use its reason to mend its ways. Moreover, the young Sultan, untainted by having experienced the old regime, would be more amenable to reform than his predecessor.

Little is known as to the preparation of the reform program issued on November 3, 1839.[46] Letters from newspaper correspondents indicate that daily councils of the Divan were confined to the discussion of administrative measures.[47] Army reorganization was put off since the leaders believed that if new taxes were levied upon the exhausted people revolt might result.[48] Officials who opposed reform were sent off on special missions,[49] while Reschid concentrated on the best form in which the program might be announced. The result was the Hatti Sherif de Gulhané of November 3, 1839.[50]

Probably few nineteenth century documents have been more misunderstood or misinterpreted than this first decree of Abdul Medjid. Yet, even the most cursory examination of the document convinces one that it was not, as it is so often sentimentally labelled, a constitution. Though there is little doubt but that constitutional forms had been considered by the author of the Hat, Reschid never regarded it as anything more than an outline of the necessary reforms toward which the Porte should strive.[51] Reschid knew only too well that the slightest imitation

[46] Ponsonby reported November 1, 1839, that he and the Austrian Internuncio were "indefatigable in our endeavors to encourage Reschid Pasha and his colleagues to persevere in the wise policy they have adopted," but he did not give any details of that wise policy. F. O. 195/150, Ponsonby to Palmerston, November 1, 1838.

[47] No reports were made public. *London Times*, October 13, 1839, p. 4.

[48] *Ibid.*, October 8, 1939, p. 4.

[49] Nourri Effendi was sent to Paris as Envoy Extraordinary, and Keani Bey was made Mousselim of Brussa. *Ibid.*, October 14, 21, 1839.

[50] For a description of the promulgation of the Hat, see Engelhardt, *op. cit.*, I, 35 ff.; Ubicini, *Letters*, I, 28.

[51] Wholesale adoption of western forms would have met with strong opposi-

of the constitutional governments which existed in western
Europe was impossible in Turkey in 1839 where the great majority of the people were entirely ignorant of the purposes and
advantages of a parliamentary system.[52] Reschid was too clever
a politician to even vaguely mention a constitution, a word
which he realized was anathema to all the old Turks. The promises of security of life, honor, and property have led scholars
to misinterpret the decree as the Magna Charta of modern
Turkey.[53] The Hatti Sherif was neither a constitution, nor did
it provide the basis for one.[54] In only one respect did this decree
limit the arbitrary power of the Sultan,[55] which from some
points of view was its principal weakness.[56] The sanction of the
Sultan was necessary for all laws; without it a law did not
exist.[57]

On the other hand, it is unfair to regard the Hat merely as
an expedient method of renewing the faith of the citizens in
the Turkish Empire, in order to prevent complete collapse following the disastrous defeats at Nezib and Alexandria. There
is no doubt but that Reschid recognized the moral effect the
promulgation of this "charte des libertés" [58] would have on

---

tion, Reschid knew. His task was to convince the people that the proposed
changes were a return to the old principles, and did not controvert the Koran.
Ibid., I, 133.

[52] Mémoire, 10 Mars 1841, Appendix V, p. 285.

[53] Lane-Poole, *op. cit.*, II, 82n.

[54] "Der Hattisherif von Gulhane nicht selber ein Gesetz war, sondern nur die
Grundsätze darlegte, nach welchem eine Reihe organischer Gesetze erlassen
werden sollte." Rosen, *op. cit.*, II, 24.

[55] The guarantee of security of life was a renunciation of the hereditary right
of life and death over every subject. Though this was the only limitation, it was
a significant one, because it foreshadowed the end of the old power of the Sultans. *L'Empire Ottoman*, p. 74. In this sense it may be considered "une des
révolutions les plus mémorable du 19ᵉ siècle." J. Pharon, et T. Dulau, *Études
sur les législations anciennes et modernes*, Paris, 1839, p. 467. The Hat was revolutionary in that it removed all religious distinctions wherever life, honor and
fortune were involved. Engelhardt, *op. cit.*, I, 37; Rouvière, *op. cit.*, p. 60.

[56] For this reason one writer calls it "la première parodie constitutionelle."
L'Empire Ottoman, p. 65.

[57] Rouvière, *op. cit.*, p. 59.

[58] Engelhardt, *op. cit.*, I, 36. Franco describes the Hatti Sherif as "une expression indiquant un état d'esprit, une attitude politique." Franco, *op. cit.*,
p. 13.

the oppressed peoples as well as upon friendly powers, but he expected far more from it than that. The most reasonable interpretation of the Gulhané decree is that it established a program which if carried into execution would make Turkey once again a strong state. A glance at the Hat itself is the best proof of this fact.

The Hatti Sherif de Gulhané promised to establish the security of all Turkish subjects, regardless of religious belief, against all violations of their honor, life, and property.[59] Criminal as well as political offenders were to be protected henceforth by public trial before being sentenced. As regards the excessive taxation, an insufferable burden to the majority of the Turks, the decree provided that in the future all taxes would be more equally distributed over all classes in the population, and that the method of collection of these taxes would be less arbitrary. The third outstanding plank in the new platform was that a systematic method of recruiting soldiers for the army would be created and enforced in the future. Beyond these three points the decree is hardly more than an expression of a more hopeful future. The ideas of the Hatti Sherif were not new, having been expressed by Mahmoud II,[60] but never had they been set forth as a definite program of reform, since he was too much of an absolutist to admit any limitations to his power.[61] Promulgation of a reform policy was but the first step, and no one realized more than the author, Reschid Pasha, that it was one thing to set forth a policy, and quite another thing to effect it in the Turkish state.[62]

[59] Such a declaration provided the basis for political equality in Turkey. If fully carried out, it would break down the old religious prejudice and create in its place a genuine feeling of national unity. Rouvière, *op. cit.*, p. 60.

[60] Rosen, *op. cit.*, II, 16. "Reschid ist weder Begründer noch der erste Adept der neuen Türkischen Staatsweisheit, aber ihm gebührt das Lob, selbständiger, durchgreifender und mit mehr Verständniss des wirklichen Bedürfnisses vorgeschritten zu sein, als seine unwissenderen Collegen." *Ibid.*, p. 272. Cf. also Ubicini, *Letters*, I, 27; Ubicini, *État présent de L'Empire Ottoman*, p. 1; Cadalvène et Barrault, *op. cit.*, II, 287; Rouvière, *op. cit.*, p. 7.

[61] Mahmoud "restait turc avec le désir de ne plus l'être." Engelhardt, *op. cit.*, I, 23.

[62] Cf. J. A. Blanqui, *Voyage en Bulgarie pendant l'année 1841*, Paris, 1843, p. 344.

Reschid immediately recognized his chief opponents with the Council itself. Khosrew Pasha, the Grand Vizir, leaned definitely toward Russia.[63] Halil Pasha, the new Seraskier, had long been a personal enemy of Reschid, and was likely to be an obstacle to reform.[64] Raouf Pasha, President of the High Council, Minister of Commerce Said Pasha, and the other ministers, Nuri, and Riza Pasha were less outspoken, and Reschid hoped that they might counter-balance Khosrew and Halil Pashas in effecting the pledges of the Hatti Sherif.[65]

Though Reschid was aware of the difficulties, he went ahead with a confidence based on the knowledge of certain advantages in his favor. His long service in the Turkish government provided him with a better understanding of the difficulties to be overcome than most Turkish statesmen; he thought he understood the psychology of the Turkish people; and finally, his study of European systems of government, finance, and army organization prepared him for the great tasks ahead. Yet, more important than any of his own personal qualifications was the framework of the Turkish government. The Sultan was the final authority; he possessed both legislative and executive powers.[66] The fact that the present Sultan was a young man, without any experience in ruling such a large empire, was another advantage. For more than a year Khosrew and Halil held second place to Reschid Pasha in the young Abdul Medjid's favor, and the Minister of Foreign Affairs made the most of his position. As long as that situation continued what did it matter that many of the reforms which he hoped to establish ran counter to Moslem law and tradition? If the Sultan could

---

[63] Cadalvène and Barrault, *op. cit.*, II, 270. Khosrew and Reschid had formerly been friends, but the elder statesman's jealousy of Reschid's courage and intelligence forced him to oppose whatever Reschid favored. Juchereau de Saint Denys, *op. cit.*, IV, 239.

[64] Ponsonby reported September 22, 1839 that Khosrew and Halil Pashas were supporting Reschid, but that they were unstable and likely to shift, as they did as soon as Turkey's condition improved. F. O. 195/160, Ponsonby to Palmerston, #257, September 22, 1839.

[65] The reactionaries were motivated for the most part by self-interest and prejudice. Temperley, *The Crimea*, p. 245.

[66] Ubicini, *Letters*, I, 33.

be won over, he could force the *ulema* to promulgate the new decrees.[67]

Reschid Pasha did not overlook the fact that the arbitrary authority of the Sultan might be advantageous to the opposition as well. Abdul Medjid's inability to appreciate the power in Reschid's reform policy, and his lack of courage to maintain the Minister of Foreign Affairs in the face of old Turk opposition actually did terminate Reschid's career abruptly and thereby retarded the reform movement. Aware of the possibility of such an outcome Reschid attacked the problem of effecting the promises of 1839 with vigor and enthusiasm, determined that the Gulhané decree should not become a dead letter. Reschid knew that he must act quickly if he was to accomplish anything before the inevitable reaction thwarted his plans. Delay in execution of the Hat would be an admission of defeat, whereas an immediate success would win converts to his cause.

Simultaneous with the promulgation of the Hatti Sherif an investigation was ordered to determine the actual amounts paid by each district in taxes, and how this money was spent for the upkeep of the army, navy, and civil administration.[68] At the same time the Porte decided to affect in the two provinces nearest the capital, Broussa and Gallipoli, the following system:

That a table shall be constructed exhibiting the sums received. 1. For the Treasury. 2. For the valis and voivodes. 3. For the expenses of travelling functionaries. 4. The amount of contributions in kind to different departments, paid in saltpetre, corn, timber, etc. 5. The value of labour to which certain towns and districts were liable under the denomination of Angaria (corvée). 6. The sums paid for local police, judges, etc.

It was also resolved by the Council:

That an exact statement or balance sheet be prepared of the whole revenue, fixed and casual, of the state. Henceforward every tax unauthorized by the ancient canon shall be abolished.

[67] Abdul Medjid by his personal leadership inaugurated "une ère nouvelle à l'église." *L'Empire Ottoman, op. cit.*, p. 45.
[68] MacGregor, *op. cit.*, II, 178–179.

The properties of the high functionaries of the state, whether military or civil, and the persons attached to the services shall be equally assessed with those of the nation. Every exemption from taxation, and every privilege through which the common burdens were avoided shall cease. The imposts shall be imposed with complete impartiality, at a rate of so much per thousand, which shall yearly be settled in the month of March, according to the new ordinance.

Each individual shall receive a ticket bearing the seal of the community, stating the amount of his contributions, and these sums shall be entered in the public register of each municipality. Men of recognized probity and intelligence shall be commissioned, at the public expense, to prosecute the necessary inquiries throughout the empire. . . .

From the date of the execution of this order, the two provinces designated (Broussa and Gallipoli) shall be exempt from the payment of the impost termed "Ichtisab," i.e., internal customs.

Such a proposal affected many Turks so directly, it was no wonder that they believed that a new era had begun for Turkey.[69]

In December, 1839 the Council decreed that beginning March 1, 1840, governors of provinces, cities, and burghs were to be paid fixed salaries, that promotion to more important governments would be made on the basis of merit, and that governors should exact only the established imposts; [70] the people entered upon their tasks with new vigor following this announcement. Though a costly reform,[71] it immediately changed the spirit of the Turks from one of hopeless desperation to one of optimistic progress. Vice Consul Suter, after visit-

[69] Ponsonby described the Hat as "a victorious answer to those who say that this Empire cannot be saved by its ancient Government, . . ." F. O. 78/360, Ponsonby to Palmerston, #301, November 5, 1839. He later reported that it was "universally approved of, and that Ottoman and Rayah subjects desire with equal anxiety to see it carried into execution." F. O. 78/360, Ponsonby to Palmerston, #313, November 24, 1839 and #334, December 17, 1839.

[70] F. O. 78/360, Ponsonby to Palmerston, #346, December 31, 1839. Iltizam (sale to the governor of the revenue levied within his government) had been one of the worst abuses of the old regime. The Kharatch (head tax on Christians) was abolished January 9, 1840. Cf. F. O. 78/392, Ponsonby to Palmerston, #15, January 16, 1840, and *London Times*, February 7, 1840.

[71] The immediate deficit occasioned by the abolition of the sale of offices was made up by a loan raised among the monied men of Constantinople. F. O. 78/392, Ponsonby to Palmerston, #46, March 3, 1840.

ing Smyrna reported January 5, 1840 that "it had already produced so much greater feeling of confidence in the security of property, that purchases of land had been made, and additional impulse had been given to the extension of cultivation in many parts of the Country." [72]

A Supreme Council of State and Justice (Medjliss Aali) was established in December, 1839 to frame the laws which were to be decreed by the Sultan. All laws were discussed by this body, and no decree was to be made without the approval of a majority of its members.[73] The president of this council, Raouf Pasha, was also a member of the Privy Council. Raouf was encouraged by Reschid to begin a study of the codes and to continue the investigations already begun on the tax system. The Supreme Council was not taken seriously,[74] however, and was little more than an investigating and drafting committee. The real power in Turkey continued to remain with the Sultan and the Privy Council, in which Reschid Pasha was still the dominating influence.

Upon learning of these reforms, Palmerston ordered Ponsonby to congratulate Reschid Pasha "upon the perseverance he had shown in his systematick endeavors to reorganize the Country, and upon the success with which those endeavors have already been attended." [75] The Foreign Secretary stated that "H. M. Gov't also take the deepest interest in the regeneration of Turkey, are delighted to find that Reschid Pasha is going to work in so wise and judicious a manner; and that instead of endeavoring to set up prematurely new Institutions, which would be repugnant to the habits and prejudices of the Turkish Nation, He is progressively improving and developing the old Institutions of his Country, and in truth bringing them back to their ancient purity and vigour. Reschid Pasha seems

---

[72] F. O. 78/392, Suter to Ponsonby, January 5, 1840, enclosed in Ponsonby to Palmerston, #4, January 7, 1840. This information was derived "from native agents engaged in the sale of British goods and the purchase of produce, and who had the opportunity of observing these improvements, . . ."

[73] *London Times*, January 6, 1840, p. 4.

[74] Engelhardt, *op. cit.*, II, 17.

[75] F. O. 78/389, Palmerston to Ponsonby, #17, February 4, 1840.

to understand the force of the well known maxim that they who wish to improve things should preserve ancient names, and by that means avoid rousing needless jealousy, and exciting unnecessary distrust." [76]

Reschid was quick to perceive that the principles laid down by the Gulhané decree could not be achieved without revision of the ancient codes, especially the separation of the civil and criminal codes from the religious and moral codes. Before life, honor, and fortune could be made secure a revision of the penal code, in particular, was necessary. This task was undertaken in February, 1840 by the Council of State and Justice,[77] and in May (1840) the new penal code, *Kanouni Djeraim*,[78] was ready for promulgation. The *Kanouni Djeraim* established equality for all subjects regardless of race or faith; it further decreed that all trials terminating in capital punishment should be reviewed by the Supreme Council of Justice and that no capital sentence could be effected without the signature of the Sultan. While these decrees were not always completely fulfilled, the mere fact that they existed was a great advantage over the previous system of arbitrary arrest and punishment. It was no wonder that contemporaries regarded this and other reforms promulgated between 1839 and 1841 as inaugurating a new era in the history of the Ottoman Empire.

Since all of Reschid's reforms limited the power of those who had formerly been in authority, the inevitable reaction showed itself sooner than he himself expected.[79] When Khosrew Pasha was ousted from the council (July 8, 1840) for embezzling public money, his friends conspired against Reschid, but

---

[76] F.O. 78/389, Palmerston to Ponsonby, #18, February 4, 1840.

[77] Assisted by Reschid, Riza, Halil, and Achmed Fethi Pashas. Ubicini, *Letters*, I, 163.

[78] F. O. 78/394, Ponsonby to Palmerston, #110, May 26, 1840. Printed in Ubicini, *Letters*, II, Appendix I.

[79] Ponsonby reported more than a year before Reschid finally resigned that "the state of Society in this Country has not prepared it for the transformation of a Theocratic Despot into a Constitutional Monarch, and the apeing the forms of Representative Governments may produce worse things than the ridicule it excites here." F. O. 78/393, Ponsonby to Palmerston, March 16, 1840.

Raouf Pasha was made Grand Vizir at Reschid's suggestion and the conspiracy was quashed. From that time the anti-reform feeling spread rapidly among the old Turks who became fanatically anti-European, anti-Christian, and above all hateful of Reschid. The desire to return to Mahmoud's system of more gradual reform had been stimulated by the radical, sweeping nature of Reschid's improvements; [80] others tried to encourage the Sultan to pursue a strictly Turkish policy. Within a year Khosrew Pasha had united the moderates and the Turcophils in opposition to Reschid's policies. Eventually Raouf turned against Reschid in favor of Khosrew and the reactionaries.[81] Reschid concluded that it was useless to carry the fight further, and on March 29, 1841 he and Achmed Fethi Pasha, the Minister of Commerce and brother-in-law of the Sultan, resigned their positions.[82]

There is some reason to believe that this resignation was merely a Bismarckian attempt to force his policy through. Failing to find strong advisors, the Sultan would recall him, thereby making his position stronger than ever in Turkey. This policy is suggested by a letter from Reschid to Baron von Sturmer, Austrian Internuncio, dated March 7, 1841.[83] On that date he wrote as follows:

L'événement inattendu qui vient d'avoir lieu démentira et fera tomber, sans aucun doute, les bruits qui circulaient depuis quelques jours. Toutefois, je ne sais si ce qu'on a fait est vraiment *sincère* ou bien si cela n'est qu'une espèce de ruse pour me faire servir sans ralentissement de zèle jusqu'à la conclusion finale de la grande affaire qui nous occupé. Dans tout les cas, ce doute ne pouvant être éclairci que par les procédés dont on usera envers moi par la suite, ce ne sera que peu à peu que je saurai à quoi m'en tenir.

[80] Reschid's reforms were no more opposed to Islamic ideas than some of Mahmoud's. Temperley, *The Crimea*, p. 245. But Reschid's presentation of the reforms was suggestive of a complete revolution. Many liberals thought the best policy was to strive for justice, efficiency, and honesty within the old framework. *Ibid.*, p. 246.

[81] Khosrew Pasha was as much a power out of office as in it. Juchereau de Saint Denys, *op. cit.*, IV, 387.

[82] *Ibid.*, p. 305.

[83] Reschid to Sturmer, 7 Mars 1841, H. H. u. St. A., Wien, Türkei VI, fasz. 57.

Reschid also suggested that the powers be called in to force the necessary reforms on the Sultan, even as they had forced a settlement of the Egyptian question. At such a conference, at which Turkey would be represented, means of carrying out the reforms already proposed could be discussed. Reschid felt that the mere advice of the great powers would not be sufficient to make the Porte pursue the correct course; active intervention was what he desired more than anything else, but here Reschid overlooked the fact that for almost a decade Britain, the strongest supporter of the Turkish reform movement, though generous with advice had very definitely refused to intervene in the domestic affairs of the Sultan. Such a conference of the great powers, however, might have the effect of frightening the Sultan into pushing forward his reform policy, especially if the suggestion of a partition of the Ottoman state was brought forward, as it undoubtedly would be.[84]

These thoughts were expressed not from any personal desire to remain in office on the part of Reschid Pasha, but from the deep-seated conviction that his reforms could forestall the steady decline of Turkish power. They do suggest, however, that Reschid did not consider his labors at an end with his resignation, but continued to work toward his goal. When the conference idea did not meet with an enthusiastic response, Reschid finally resigned himself to his fate, accepted the Ambassadorship to France which he had been offered.[85] He remained at that post for two years, 1841–1843, during which time his political enemy, Rifaat Pasha, gained steadily in power.

The fall of Reschid Pasha is usually attributed to a cabal of the reactionaries led by Rifaat Pasha, but as one reads the dispatches one is convinced that agents of the foreign powers were also involved in his dismissal. In a letter to Baron von Sturmer,

---

[84] Mémoire, 10 Mars 1841, Appendix V.

[85] Reschid is described at this time as "grave, pensif, triste aussi des nombreux obstacles qu'avaient rencontrés ses efforts pour régénérer l'Empire, voyait alors très-clairement, sans en convenir, la faute qu'il avait commise de prêter son appui à la politique exclusive et violente de l'ambassadeur d'Angleterre." Blanqui, *op. cit.*, p. 345.

April 9, 1841, when all hopes of being restored to his position had faded, Reschid explained his fall as the result of Rifaat's intrigues with the Sultan through the English ambassador. According to the Reschid version,[86] he and Ponsonby had disagreed on a number of issues. Reschid had opposed Ponsonby in the settlement of the Mehemet affair; Ponsonby had complained of the use of Frenchmen in the service of the Porte, a policy which Reschid sanctioned. In the winter of 1840–41 Ponsonby became interested in the cause of a group of English Jews who wished to establish themselves in Jerusalem. The Turkish Council rejected the English ambassador's proposal because they foresaw political inconveniences. About the same time the Porte refused the advice of certain English officers who arrived in Constantinople, largely because to introduce a new system would disrupt this part of the service which seemed to the Porte satisfactory under the Prussian system then in use.[87]

Ponsonby regarded these refusals to cooperate as a personal affront, and complained of the treatment he had received, blaming Reschid. Reschid, unaware of Ponsonby's feelings toward him, continued his efforts to secure a house for the English ambassador nearer the Porte. This attempt to strengthen the relations of the Turkish government and the British representative was defeated by Riza Pasha. Ponsonby, disappointed at the outcome of events, instead of complaining to the Sultan, informed Riza of the affair, who thereupon established a liaison between himself, the English ambassador, and the Sultan through which he worked against Reschid. Finally, when Riza's efforts succeeded and Abdul Medjid decided to remove Reschid,

[86] Reschid to Sturmer, April 9, 1841, H. H. u. St. A. Wien, Türkei, fasz. 58.

[87] In October, 1840 Palmerston sent a group of medical men under Dr. Davy to improve the medical service in the Sultan's army. F. O. 78/415, Palmerston to Davy, October 27 and 30, 1840; F. O. 78/391, Palmerston to Ponsonby, #218, October 29, 1840 and #220, October 31, 1840. Recommendations of Davy were not accepted and he returned to England September, 1841. Captain Williams who went out to advise improvements in the artillery was likewise unable to overcome the reactionary conservatism of the time. Finally Ponsonby advised Palmerston not to send further missions without the Porte's consent. Cf. F. O. 78/431, Ponsonby to Palmerston, #70, February 21, 1841.

if he did not resign of his own accord, Ponsonby intimated
that this would not hurt the course of events in Turkey, though
he did believe that Reschid should be rewarded for his long
service to the Turkish state with some public award.[88]

Ponsonby's version of Reschid's dismissal is quite another
story. On April 7th, 1841 he wrote to Palmerston as follows: [89]

> On Sunday preceding the deposition of Reschid Pasha, and Ahmed
> Fethi Pasha; Reschid presented to the great Council a Commercial
> Code for approval. Somebody observed that the code ought to have
> been based upon the Seer Sherif (the Holy Law of the Koran). To
> this Reschid replied that the Holy Law had nothing to do with such
> matters; on hearing this one of the Cadeshew and others of the
> Ulema expressed great disgust at the want of reverence to the Holy
> Law, and some altercation ensuing then declared they would never
> again enter the council where like things were permitted; — there
> followed much upon this, and there was great confusion, Ahmed Fethi
> Pasha supporting Reschid Pasha. At last order was restored by the
> intervention of Riza Pasha and others. This affair was reported to
> the Sultan that night and His Highness immediately ordered the
> deposition of Reschid Pasha and of Ahmed Fethi Pasha, which order
> was carried into execution next morning.

From this dispatch one is led to believe that Reschid's dismissal
was an affair of the moment, the result of his lack of reverence
for the Moslem code, and an incident in which the British ambassador played no part directly or indirectly.

Whatever Ponsonby did or did not do, he was acting counter
to his chief's policy, though specific instructions from the Foreign Office regarding the intrigues against Reschid (under the
date of April 1, 1841) arrived in Constantinople several weeks
after the Turkish minister had been forced from office. In that
dispatch [90] Palmerston advised Ponsonby to cooperate with the
Austrian ambassador in supporting Reschid, whose loss at this

---

[88] Reschid claims he did not seek the ambassadorship; he would have been
happy to live a quiet life with his family during his remaining years, and finally
accepted the post in Paris only as a means of protection from his enemies in
Turkey. Reschid to Sturmer, April 9, 1841.

[89] Ponsonby to Palmerston, #128, April 7, 1841, F. O. 78/433.

[90] F. O. 78/427, Palmerston to Ponsonby, #54, April 1, 1841.

time would have been most regrettable, since he was the one man capable of effecting the reforms planned for in the Hatti Sherif de Gulhané. Palmerston's feeling for Reschid and the decree of 1839 was expressed as follows:

He [Reschid] is understood to have been the principal author of the Hatti Sherif of Gulhané, and to entertain liberal and enlightened views as to the Improvement which ought to be introduced into the general administration of the Turkish Empire, and especially into the practical dispensation of Justice between man and man with a view to affording to all classes of the Sultan's subjects, security for Person and Property; and Reschid seems to Her Majesty's Government the Person most likely to have the will and the means of enforcing practically throughout the Empire the faithful Execution of the Hatti Sherif of Gulhané, a Task which Her Majesty's Government are well aware is one of more difficulty and which will require more time than many People may be disposed to think.

This dispatch concludes with speculation as to who may succeed Reschid, should be be forced out, and with what consequences. Before Palmerston received Ponsonby's account of Reschid's dismissal the Foreign Secretary again (April 21, 1841) exhorted his agent to protect Reschid from injury if he was the victim of the opposition, but to do everything possible to maintain him at the helm of the Turkish state.[91] In short, Palmerston feared the dismissal of Reschid would be the end of the reform movement which was undertaken with the promulgation of the Gulhané decree two years before. How far he was correct will be treated subsequently.

[91] F. O. 78/428, Palmerston to Ponsonby, #91, April 21, 1841.

CHAPTER VI

BRITISH POLICY, 1842 TO THE CRIMEAN WAR

THE PRINCIPAL task of the historian is to determine how and why a particular policy emerges and to trace the development of that policy over a period of years until it is abandoned, or gradually merges into another policy. In absolutist states where ministers often remain in office during the whole life-time of a ruler, if not longer, this problem is much less difficult than in parliamentary or democratic states where party government causes frequent changes of personnel, and thereby makes for lack of continuity in the domestic or foreign policy. Though the historian may perceive certain tendencies or trends in the foreign policy of a parliamentary state over a period of years, nevertheless, it must be admitted that every new foreign minister, whether that be his intention or not, sees the problem before him from an individualistic viewpoint which makes absolute constancy impossible.

Lack of continuity is one of the interesting facts about British foreign policy in the decade prior to the Crimean War. In the short space of eleven years (1841–1852) four ministries rose and fell, and the war which followed was caused to a very great extent by an agreement made by one of those ministers, an agreement which, not recognized by his successors, created a misunderstanding which eventually led to war.[1] Yet, this is not an insurmountable difficulty in the study of Anglo-Turkish relations between 1841 and 1852, if one approaches the problem from Constantinople rather than from London. In Constantinople Britain had a most able representative in Stratford

---

[1] The agreement between Russia and England of 1844, made by Aberdeen, was never recognized by Palmerston, with the result that Nicholas I went ahead with his aggressive eastern policy believing that he had England's support. Cf. Puryear, *England, Russia, and the Straits Question*, ch. IV.

Canning, who in spite of the fact of the changes in ministries at home, remained at his post from 1842 to 1858; Canning provided the continuity of policy which was lacking in London.

Palmerston went out of the Foreign Office in September, 1841 with the resignation of the Melbourne ministry, and was succeeded by Lord Aberdeen who held the position of Foreign Secretary in the second Peel ministry from 1841 to 1846. In 1844 the fateful arrangement with Russia was negotiated, yet Stratford did not recognize it, and continued to regard the Sultan as though the agreement did not exist. Canning's anti-Russian policy received official support when Palmerston returned to the Foreign Office in 1846 where he continued under Russell (1846–1852), Derby-Disraeli (1852), and Aberdeen (1852–1855). When Aberdeen's cautious, pacifistic policy proved unpopular in 1854, he was forced to resign and Palmerston became prime minister in January, 1855. Lord Clarendon held the post of Foreign Secretary in the Palmerston cabinet until 1858.

Although Palmerston was the controlling influence in British foreign policy from 1846 to 1858, he was less active in the cause of Turkish reform in this period than he was from 1834 to 1841. The reform movement in Turkey had succumbed to reactionary influences, and the minister of foreign affairs was content to leave the matter up to his ambassador. Palmerston's and Canning's views upon the regeneration of Turkey were one and the same. For these reasons British policy, 1842–1853, can best be dealt with from the point of view of Constantinople, that is the policy of Stratford Canning, British Ambassador at the Porte, rather than that of either Palmerston or Aberdeen; after 1842, continuity was maintained by the Ambassador, not by the changing Foreign Secretaries.

The fall of Reschid Pasha in March, 1841, while a blow to the *tanzimat*, did not mean the complete cessation of all attempts to improve the state of Turkey, though it must be admitted that the driving force of the movement toward a well-organized state went out of Turkey when Reschid left Constantinople to take up his duties in Paris. In the following years the Sultan himself took up the cause of reform. Abdul Medjid tried further to Europeanize his army; [2] he encouraged the reform of education; and attempted to free commerce from some of the restrictions under which it still labored. In general, it must be said that Abdul's reforms were not the result of a definite well-thought out policy, and some of them show specific lack of advice and consultation. On the other hand his reforms being more gradual and less sweeping tended to arouse fewer people against him. But with Reschid out of power the support of friendly powers was more necessary than ever.

Though Ponsonby remained in Constantinople until November, 1841, he was no more sympathetic with the feeble attempts of the Padishah to carry out his promises of 1839 than he had been with Reschid.[3] Ponsonby's successor at the Porte, Stratford Canning, though he recognized the obstacles to reform, particularly the reaction which had set in,[4] was not discouraged at the prospects. As the reform movement showed signs of waning, Canning redoubled British efforts to keep it alive by winning the confidence of the Sultan who alone could restore to power the one man who could continue the work so well begun, Reschid Pasha. In this Canning was not only pursuing what he personally believed the right course; he had the support of his Government as well.

Canning's instructions [5] were written by Lord Aberdeen who became Foreign Secretary on Palmerston's resignation in Sep-

[2] N. Iorga, *Geschichte des osmanischen Reiches*, 5 vols., Gotha, 1908–1913, vol. V, bk. 3, p. 424.

[3] In March, 1842, Ponsonby wrote that "the measures taken by Reschid Pasha for carrying the Hatti Sherif into execution have always appeared to me to be very foolish and jejune, and the offsprings of frippery, French philosophy, and ignorant vanity." Ponsonby maintained that "Reschid's measures alarmed religion and often offended manners" while what Turkey needed was an efficient army. Lord Ponsonby to General Jochmus, March 23, 1842, A. Jochmus, *The Syrian War and the Decline of the Ottoman Empire, 1840–1848*, Berlin, 1883, II, 41.

[4] F. O. 352/26, Canning to Aberdeen, February 13, 1842.

[5] F. O. 78/439, Aberdeen to Canning, October 30, 1841.

tember 1841; from the content one might guess they were from Palmerston's own hand. After instructing his ambassador to do everything he could to maintain amicable relations between the Sultan, Mehemet Ali, and the recently recovered Syrian provinces, Aberdeen urged his ambassador to encourage by all means reform of the internal administration, especially of the army which was more important than in any other state due to the weaknesses of the civil administration and police system. Canning was also requested to seek real protection and security for the Christian population of Turkey, though nothing must be done to diminish their loyalty to the Sultan. Her Majesty's Government, wrote Aberdeen, hoped that ". . . by promoting judicious and well considered reform, to impart some degree of consistency and stability to the government which is threatened by so many causes of dissolution." Canning was warned by the Foreign Secretary against "pursuing a busy, meddling policy," since more could be accomplished with the Porte by informal concerted action of all the foreign representatives at Constantinople than by the direct intervention of any particular state. "The policy of Great Britain in the Levant," concluded the new Foreign Secretary, "has long been distinguished by a sincere desire to support the Turkish Power; and to avert the dissolution, either from the effects of internal convulsion or of Foreign aggression."

Canning's first report on the state of Turkey is at once a panorama of conditions in Turkey and a portrait of the new ambassador. While recognizing the desire on the part of many to return to the pre-Reschid regime, if not the pre-Mahmoud status, Canning felt that much could be accomplished in Turkey "by European influence and example, . . ." "The spirit and tendency of the present administrative system in Turkey are reactive," he wrote. "The elements of this reaction are a return to old abuses, hostility to Christian privileges, mistrust of Foreigners, and estrangement from European connection." [6] Pol-

---

[6] F. O. 78/476, Canning to Aberdeen, #67, March 27, 1842. "There is just now an apparent retrogression in the Turkish mind — possibly a reaction upon

icies composed of such elements weakened the state and hastened catastrophe unless more effective influence from without was forthcoming. Canning described the Grand Vizir, Izzet Pasha, as cruel and severe, strongly Mahometan and anti-foreign. The minister of Foreign Affairs, Sarim Effendi, was a follower of Reschid, but against so much reaction he was lost, while Riza Pasha maintained "an equilibrium between the opinions of the anti-reform party, and the personal inclinations of the Sultan, whose character is still but partially unfolded. The Sultan is told that the principles of Gulhané are respected, and that a revival of the old system in regard to the revenue [7] and to the Christians will not fail to replenish his coffers, and to repair his authority." Such was the hopeless state of affairs when Canning arrived in Constantinople. Though Canning admitted that conditions were in part the result of Reschid's "rapid and inconsiderate reforms" he feared "irremediable mischief" unless the Porte was given a new direction in its policy, and he considered it a great error "to suppose that the Porte is the best judge of her own interests." Men of less prejudice and more ability were needed in high positions.[8]

The absence of capable leaders was recognized by other observers. Writing in 1851, after travelling in European Turkey in 1850, Edmund Spencer described the Sultan's government as an anomaly — "the complete antithesis of our governments of

the forced reforms in manners and usages under the vigorous reign of Mahmoud, when, too, European diplomatic influence was more actively exerted at the Porte, than it is at present. Fanaticism is an essential element of the Mohammedan religion, and under its revived and baleful power, the famed Hatti Sherif, or charter of liberty for the rayahs, proves but a dead letter." *Missionary Herald*, vol. 38, 1842, pp. 104–105. Layard, *op. cit.*, II, 170.

[7] The barrenness of the Treasury was a powerful argument against further expensive reforms; the reactionaries also used the fear and jealousy of the Christians as a source of strength. The Kharatch was restored and *rayahs* were forced to wear old forms of dress. Cf. Memorandum, enclosed in F. O. 78/476, Canning to Aberdeen, #67, March 27, 1842.

[8] The character of the Turkish leaders in 1842 was anything but progressive. More than once the character and power of the British ambassador was unable to offset the reactionary forces which prevailed, and much that Canning had hoped for in 1842 was never attained. For this reason the accomplishments of the period 1842 to 1853 are more outstanding.

western Europe," because of the "absence of all hereditary rank and property." [9] "If the power of the Sultan is ever to be placed upon a secure foundation," he continued, "among other reforms, he must waive his title as sole lord of the soil, and create an independent aristocracy; this can only be done by separate allotments of land to the most deserving among his subjects, without respect to creed or race, and by establishing the law of primogeniture. . . ." [10] "The introduction of the wisest and most effective measures of reform," he concluded, "will, we fear, fail of success unless aided by the assistance of men endowed with more energy and intelligence than the inexperienced, indolent Osmanli. . . ." [11] By this statement he did not mean the introduction of foreign talent,[12] but the development of the best leaders which Turkey herself had available. Until these new leaders could be found, something had to be done to stem the tide of reaction; Canning recommended collective action by the five powers who had saved Turkey in 1840–1841.

The reactionary tendency so feared by Canning was stopped short, not by intervention of the Powers, however, but by a stiffening of the Sultan's will. In July, 1842, the Council was reorganized; [13] Izzet Pasha was replaced by Riza Pasha as Grand Vizir and Raouf Pasha became president of the Council in place of the bigoted, impractical Arif. These were hopeful

[9] Spencer, *op. cit.*, I, 267. "In a country where the unlettered son of a cobbler is eligible to the office of a Pacha or Vizier, according to the caprice of the sovereign, or the influence of bribery; a change in the authorities only adds to the evil, by substituting a poor man for a rich one, who must have recourse to extortion to support his new dignity. . . . This state of things cannot endure, an aristocracy of hungry officials, is one of the greatest curses that can be inflicted upon a country, and most assuredly has principally contributed to the decadence of the Turkish Empire, . . ." *Ibid.*, p. 269.

[10] Spencer, *op. cit.*, I, 270.

[11] *Ibid.*, p. 272.

[12] It was impossible to import foreign talent into Turkey, as the Russian rulers had enticed Germans in the 18th century, "so long as that absurd law of the Koran remained in force, which denies political rights to any but a member of the Mahometan creed." *Ibid.*, p. 272. Non-Moslems were not allowed to hold political office in the Ottoman Empire until after the Crimean War. Cf. Hamlin, *op. cit.*, pp. 224–226.

[13] F. O. 78/479, Canning to Aberdeen, #158, July 27, 1842.

signs, but the recall of Reschid Pasha [14] from Paris in December, 1842 seemed to point definitely to further improvements in the administration. Before Reschid arrived in Constantinople, Canning was able to report [15] that reform of the army, the navy, and the revenues were being considered by the Council. Since these were problems Canning had steadily pressed upon the Porte for discussion and action, he felt that his earlier optimism was vindicated, yet he could not be sure of success "until the Sultan exhibits a more decided character, or gives his confidence to some statesmen of higher qualifications than any who are now in power, . . ."

Reschid arrived in Constantinople late in February, 1843, but although he was not immediately restored to power in the Council, Canning felt that "his presence can hardly fail to promote the adoption of measures favourable to improvement, . . ." [16] Riza Pasha's jealousy of the reformer supported by those who foresaw the end of their opportunities to enrich themselves, if Reschid was restored, kept Reschid from returning to his old position of leadership. Hope for a strong administration vanished when Reschid was appointed Governor of Adrianople.[17] Thus, the first year of Canning's ministry at the Porte passed without any specific accomplishments [18] against the reactionary spirit. The ambassador's report toward

[14] F. O. 78/482, Canning to Aberdeen, December 18, 1842.

[15] F. O. 78/516, Canning to Aberdeen, February 18, 1843.

[16] F. O. 78/517, Canning to Aberdeen, #48, March 2, 1843.

[17] F. O. 78/518, Canning to Aberdeen, #107, May 17, 1843. The Sultan wished to place Reschid in Sarim Effendi's position (Minister of Foreign Affairs), but Rifaat Pasha was chosen instead, because of Riza Pasha's jealousy of Reschid's superior intelligence, according to Canning.

[18] Canning did ask that Reschid be relieved of his appointment to Adrianople, and this favor was granted by Riza Pasha. F. O. 78/521, Canning to Aberdeen, #183, August 31, 1843. Two months later Reschid was made ambassador to Paris. F. O. 78/523, Canning to Aberdeen, #238, November 17, 1843. Canning was certain that Riza removed Reschid from Constantinople in order to maintain himself with the Sultan. F. O. 78/523, Canning to Aberdeen, December 13, 1843. On the day that Reschid left to take up his duties in Paris, Canning wrote: "He represents a system of improvement and benevolence, which counteracts the more selfish and bigoted views of those who have obtained possession of the Sultan's authority." After reporting that Reschid's request to take some Turkish youths with him, but had been given some Armenian boys instead, the Ambas-

the end of 1843 shows his disappointment. "Experience taught me," he wrote, "to mistrust the favorable appearances, which occasionally gave promise of improvement in the Political System of the Porte, and the general condition of the Empire. . . . It is the prevailing opinion here that the Turkish government is committed to a false course of policy, and that system of reaction, begun more than two years ago, is still to be carried on, notwithstanding professions and some partial measures [19] to the contrary. . . ." [20] Continuation of present tendencies would not only be ruinous to commercial interests, but endangered the peace of Europe, if Turkey should crumble.

The year 1844 offered even fewer opportunities for Canning to prevent the steady decline of the Turkish state. While the Forign Secretary was negotiating with Russia the fateful agreement [21] concerning the ultimate disposition of the sick man's remains Canning turned from administrative reform to befriend persecuted Christians. Cases of proselytism, torture, and refusal to hear Christian evidence in the courts [22] were brought to Rifaat Pasha's attention, but Canning had to proceed carefully lest he irritate a large body of Turks or involve his government.[23] Oppression and intimidation, religious and political, continued unabated. "Every man according to his means and opportunities," wrote Canning, "gets what he can, commands whom he dares, and submits when he must. . . . There is no such thing as system in Turkey." [24] The reform movement was drawing to a close.

---

sador observed: "It would seem therefore to be a part of the prevailing policy to perpetuate the union of ignorance with power, and of knowledge with subjection." F. O. 78/523, Canning to Aberdeen, #265, December 17, 1843.

[19] The attempt to establish representative government in the provincial assemblies was unsuccessful, a fact more deplorable since the old officers in the provinces could defeat the ends of the central government.

[20] Cf. p. 206, note 1.

[22] The Firman of March 21, 1844 promising not to put Christians to death without proper trial was not strictly enforced in all the provinces. F. Eichmann, *Die Reformen des Osmanischen Reiches*, Berlin, 1858, p. 402.

[23] F. O. 78/558, Canning to Aberdeen, #112, June 1, 1844, and #128, June 25, 1844.

[24] F. O. 78/563, Canning to Aberdeen, #245, November 4, 1844.

By 1845 the *tanzimat* was given another setback by the Sultan's admission that Turkey was not yet ready for more advanced institutions. In an Imperial Rescript issued in January, 1845 the Sultan expressed his regret at the lack of progress [25] and argued that the ignorance of his people was the principal reason. The *tanzimat* was not supported by the people, because they did not understand it; they regarded it as foreign because it was encouraged by foreigners.[26] Tradition, religious prejudice, lack of leadership — the very factors which made violent revolution against tyranny infrequent in Turkey were also obstacles to progress. Abdul Medjid turned to the slower method of approach by way of education. He suggested that a committee of seven be chosen to consider plans for new schools throughout the Empire as well as investigate the instructions given in the existing institutions of learning.

The committee of seven which began its work in March, 1845 finally reported August, 1846. It was recommended that the Ottoman University established the year before be made a state institution, that a number of secondary schools be created, and that a Council of Public Instruction be set up to execute the foregoing suggestions.[27] The elementary schools needed little alteration except extension and further secularization according to the investigators. Fundamental as this program was it was not carried out; few secondary schools were established; the buildings for the university were still unfinished in 1852. In 1850 the Sultan's mother established the College of the Valideh Sultanah, and the same year saw the beginnings of an agricultural school and a veterinary college,[28] but these educational reforms were leavened by a too wide variety of interests.

Though Canning does not show any interest in the educational projects of the Sultan, he was not idle. His continued efforts with the Sultan for the return of Reschid were finally

[25] Cf. Rosen, *op. cit.*, II, 86 and Noury, *op. cit.*, pp. 43–44.
[26] Franco, *op. cit.*, p. 18.
[27] Ubicini, *Letters*, I, 197.
[28] *Ibid.*, pp. 204, 208.

successful. In January, 1846 he reported that Reschid had
been made Minister of Foreign Affairs, Kosrew Pasha was the
new Seraskier, and Sarim Effendi had been recalled from London to become minister of commerce.[29] The "unusual tranquillity in the Turkish Empire" he regards as ominous, but
there was little chance of a comprehensive scheme of improvement until Reschid checked the corruption in the state and
made himself solid with the Sultan [30] and the people. Canning
felt that the return of Reschid strengthened his own position
with the Porte sufficiently, so that he could again suggest
ameliorative legislation without threatening Anglo-Turkish relations.[31] The proclamation [32] of the Sultan defining and
limiting the powers of functionaries of the government, and
forbidding the controversion of law and justice renewed the
ambassador's faith. The cloud of reaction which had hung so
heavy over Turkey since 1841 appeared to be lifting.

In 1846 Canning was instrumental in the promulgation of
the decree providing for mixed tribunals [33] in which Christian
evidence had equal weight with that of Moslems, a most necessary measure if justice was to be secure, yet a most dangerous
one in that it might revive the old religious prejudices.[34] Both
Aberdeen and Palmerston, who returned to the Foreign Office
in July, 1846, approved Canning's attempts to promote prosperity in Turkey,[35] believing that security of person and prop-

[29] F. O. 78/637, Canning to Aberdeen, #8, January 19, 1846.
[30] Reschid did not have the complete support of the Sultan in 1845 as he
had five years before, largely because Abdul Medjid was more experienced and
because he feared the effect of Reschid's sweeping reforms.
[31] F. O. 78/638, Canning to Aberdeen, #41, March 18, 1846; F. O. 78/639,
Canning to Aberdeen, #73, April 30, 1846, enclosing two memorandums ad-
dressed to Sultan on needed reforms.
[32] Enclosed in Canning's #41. Cf. also Ubicini, Letters, I, 165.
[33] Precedent for these mixed tribunals was the Commercial Tribunal (Mehkeme-i-tidjaret) established in 1840 to care for all commercial litigations. This
tribunal was composed of the Minister of Commerce (established 1839), who
was president of the tribunal, and representatives of commerce, both Mussulmans and Europeans. The Commercial Tribunal was organized and officially
proclaimed January 10, 1848. Cf. A. Mandelstam, La Justice Ottomane dans
ses rapports avec les puissances étrangères, Paris, 1911, pp. 1–2.
[34] Ubicini, Letters, I, 179.
[35] F. O. 78/635, Palmerston to Canning, #27, August 6, 1846.

erty and equal rights for all was one of the prime necessities for strength and progress.[36] In May and June Abdul Medjid visited Roumelia, travelling as far as Varna; on several occasions he summoned before him the local officials admonishing them to respect his royal will by promoting justice with all his subjects.[37] Canning hoped that this step would be followed by practical reforms which would "diminish the burdens of the people, and promote the extension of commerce," [38] because Canning as much as Ponsonby, Urquhart, or Palmerston recognized the material value of Turkey to the British Empire.

The Porte had already moved to free commerce from some of its restrictions. In March, 1846 the duty on articles of Turkish produce purchased by British subjects for export (ehtipab) was abandoned,[39] and the next month the Porte abolished the symbol of distinction between Mussulmans and Christians engaged in commercial navigation. Moslems and Christians henceforth were to sail under a common flag and pay uniform charges for the privilege.[40] The monopoly enjoyed by a company of tanners was abolished in June, 1846,[41] and Canning reported after his interview with the Sultan, of July 11, 1846, that Abdul Medjid was determined to continue his enlightened policy.[42]

In 1846 the problem of the renewal of the Balta Liman convention of 1838 [43] arose. Canning arbitrarily continued the treaty, but Prince Kallimaki, the Turkish minister in London, proposed that certain changes be made so as to "approximate the Russian convention of April 30, 1846, by which certain articles were excepted from the principle of freedom of trade. . . ." Palmerston felt that although this would work no injury to

[36] F. O. 78/636, Palmerston to Wellesley, #46, October 24, 1846.
[37] Sultan's statement to Council, June 20, 1846, enclosed in F. O. 78/640, Canning to Aberdeen, #112, June 25, 1846.
[38] F. O. 78/640, Canning to Aberdeen, #113, June 25, 1846.
[39] F. O. 78/638, Canning to Aberdeen, #44, March 18, 1846.
[40] F. O. 78/639, Canning to Aberdeen, #70, April 30, 1846.
[41] F. O. 78/641, Canning to Aberdeen, #119, July 4, 1846.
[42] Ibid., #121, July 11, 1846.
[43] The commercial convention of 1838 ran until March 1, 1846.

British subjects resident in Turkey, he could not agree "to record in a convention with a Foreign Power doctrines of restriction and monopoly so entirely at variance with those principles of free trade, which can alone form an advantageous basis for the commercial intercourse of nations." [44] The Lords of Trade opposed any modification of the treaty which might prove unfavorable to England,[45] so Palmerston suggested a reconsideration of tariffs of 1839 (since prices had changed) by a joint commission of English and Turkish merchants. Finally in October, 1850 a new treaty was arranged with a few minor changes most of which were beneficial to British merchants.[46]

The strength of Reschid's position and the "unexampled tranquility" which prevailed in Constantinople in July, 1846 allowed Canning to take leave from his post and return to England.[47] A few days before leaving he wrote the Foreign Secretary, now Lord Palmerston, that he feared Riza Pasha's appointment as Minister of Commerce [48] was due to the Sultana Validha's influence and that it weakened Reschid's power in the government; [49] later his fears for Reschid were so great he advised Palmerston to send a note to the Sultan supporting Reschid and advising that he be maintained in a strong position.[50] Canning's fears were justified; while Canning was away Reschid was raised to Grand Vizir, suddenly dismissed entirely from the Privy Council, and finally restored to his seat in the Council of State and Justice.[51] During the ambassador's absence the reactionary forces had retrenched themselves so firmly that reform became increasingly difficult. Lord Cowley,

[44] G. 1823/46, Addington to MacGregor, October 10, 1846.
[45] G. 1823/46, Stanley to MacGregor, #2363, December 21, 1846.
[46] Puryear, *International Economics*, p. 213.
[47] F. O. 78/641, Canning to Aberdeen, #121, July 11, 1846. Mr. Wellesley took over the embassy during Canning's absence.
[48] *Ibid.*, #123, July 20, 1846. Canning left Constantinople July 26.
[49] F. O. 78/641, Canning to Palmerston, #132, July 25, 1846.
[50] *Ibid.*, "Private," September 22, 1846.
[51] F. O. 78/733, Canning to Palmerston, #1, June 26, 1848 The ambassador did not think Reschid would remain long unless he secured "a more complete renewal of the Sultan's favor."

who was acting ambassador while Canning was on leave, did secure the recognition of protestanism in Turkey,[52] though Canning had prepared the way for this step, and deserves whatever credit there is for it.[53]

After almost two years away from his post, Canning arrived back in Constantinople June 24, 1848. Palmerston's instructions to Canning on his resumption of his post stated that he should assist Reschid in all ways, since Turkey could become independent and prosperous only under the leadership of enlightened ministers. Palmerston further stated that he hoped the equality of Christians and Mussulmans could be made more secure in the army, in taxation, and in legal affairs.[54] Canning did not take over his duties with the same enthusiasm with which he had in 1842; for six years he had worked for these very ends, and his achievements did not warrant optimism for the future.

In 1850 Canning reported [55] little progress or improvement in comparison with the needs. The same elements which hindered him in 1842 were again in power. The revenue was small, the army weak, the frontier provinces unruly. Stratford stated that he believed Riza Pasha and other malcontents were supported by Russian agents in their intrigues against Reschid Pasha, but that merely necessitated increased efforts on his part, because "the interests of British commerce no less than those of humanity, of civilization and of a sound European policy are indeed too deeply engaged in the advancement of this country and in the establishment of independence on a solid basis to warrant any indifference to such matters on the part of Great Britain and its agents." By this statement he seems to justify his action of calling up the fleet into the Dar-

---

[52] Firman, signed by Reschid Pasha, November 15, 1847 printed in *Missionary Herald*, vol. 44, 1848, pp. 98–99. See also letter signed by American missionaries in Near East to Lord Cowley congratulating him on his success and his reply. *Ibid.*, pp. 157–158.

[53] Dwight, *op. cit.*, pp. 205, 225.

[54] F. O. 78/691, Palmerston to Canning, #1, October 30, 1847.

[55] F. O. 78/822, Canning to Palmerston, #261, August 22, 1850.

danelles the year before. Canning's despatch [56] enclosed a long
memorandum on the state of Turkey's finances and the possibility of their improvement. The ambassador advocated a loan
of three or four million pounds (at 4%) to improve Turkey's
buying power and thereby increase commerce. Turkey needed
a definite system of government and finance and honest officials
to execute it; Canning regretted she had not continued the
strides made in 1838 and 1839.

The events of 1848, especially Russia's entrance into the
principalities while the rest of Europe suffered from national
and social uprisings, tended to shift Englishmen from the
thought of reform in Turkey to the maintenance of its independence. In short, the situation was just where it had been
ten years before; the slightest disturbance in the Near East
would be used by Russia to attempt to partition the Ottoman
Empire, and general war was inevitable if this were tried. Lord
Dudley Stuart speaking in the House of Commons on March 22,
1849 [57] pointed out that while English exports to Turkey increased five-fold between 1827 and 1846, English goods sold
to Russia merely increased from £1,200,000 to £1,700,000. In
fact, England had only three better customers than Turkey:
Germany, Holland, and Italy. English exports to Turkey
equalled her exports to France and were one third greater than
those to Russia. Fearing Russia's aims in the Near East, Stuart
hoped England would assist Turkey in every possible way.
David Urquhart was another who thought Palmerston had been
too lenient with respect to Russia's occupation of Moldavia and
Wallachia. It hardly need be said that the same fears for the
safety of Turkey were being raised in Constantinople.

In such an atmosphere reform was difficult even if Reschid
had been in a stronger position and the Sultan was favorable.
In 1850 a new commercial code was adopted,[58] and a charter
was secured for the protestants promising non-interference in

[56] *Ibid.*
[57] Hansard, *op. cit.*, vol. 103, 1849, pp. 1138 ff.
[58] Mandelstam, *op. cit.*, p. 5.

their religious affairs, tax-free marriages, and a separate pass-port bureau.[59] But this decree was not fully enforced as is shown by the Imperial Firman of 1853 demanding that the earlier decrees be carried out to the letter by all officials. On October 28, 1852 the Sultan issued a firman organizing his Empire into districts and asking them to send representatives to Constantinople to take part in the government,[60] but in the warlike atmosphere which already prevailed nothing could be accomplished in the direction of more centralized control of the state. By 1852 it was more a question of Turkey's survival than one of improvement of her institutions or strengthening her power.[61]

What then is the final estimate of the reform movement begun by Reschid Pasha in 1839? A comparison of the reform program as outlined in the Hatti Sherif with the accomplishments of the next decade has caused many critics to make the most disparaging remarks about the whole *tanzimat*. One writer facetiously states that the Hat of 1839 "smelt as sweet and withered as quickly as the flowers" [62] after which it was named. The fault, however, was not entirely with the decree itself; [63] the real explanation is that the weak Sultan became a tool of the reactionaries in defeating Reschid's plans. The Sultan, like many of his predecessors, was most susceptible to the wiles of women, and this was used to advantage by those who wished to control his politics.

To evaluate the reforms of the year 1839 and following is by no means an easy task, because the available materials are

[59] Eichmann, *op. cit.*, p. 411. Protestants were incorporated as a community in November, 1850. Cf. *Missionary Herald*, vol. 47, 1851, pp. 81, 114–115; see also letters of American missionaries congratulating Stratford Canning and his reply, *ibid.*, pp. 197–198.

[60] Franco, *op. cit.*, pp. 17–18. Mahmoud in 1834 established 28 provinces (Eyalets), 31 Sandjaks, and 54 Voivodes. Ubicini, *Letters*, I, 41. In 1852 the number of Eyalets was increased to thirty-six and a large number (1347) of smaller districts (casas) were established. Besse, *op. cit.*, pp. 93–94.

[61] An excellent description of the waning of the reform movement will be found in Temperley, *The Crimea*, pp. 239–247.

[62] Temperley, "British Policy," *op. cit.*, p. 159.

[63] DuVelay, *op. cit.*, p. 704; Ubicini, *Letters*, II, 417.

most biased. Contemporaries looked upon the Hatti Sherif with prejudice, either for or against. Missionaries, for example, were loud in their praises of this decree of November 3rd, because it placed all the subjects of the empire on an equal plane, and by putting the Christian and the Jew on a par with the Turk, it paved the way for subversion of the Mahometan religion, which was their special interest.[64] Missionary material must be used with caution for this reason. On the other hand there were others who condemned the Hatti Sherif because it did promise equality. Spencer maintained that the Hatti Sherif, "which invested Christian and Mussalman with equal civil rights, has only had the effect of making an enemy of the Mahometan and a discontented subject of the Rayah! . . ."[65]

One of the best methods of judging the *tanzimat* is to study diaries and travel literature of the period, of which there is a great abundance, particularly after the Crimean War had called men's attention once again to the Near East. The pictures of actual conditions here portrayed, however, are as discouraging to the modern reader as to the reformers who witnessed them.[66] Layard reports (1845) that the Pashas around Mosul were enjoying the old privileges of life and death over their subjects with impunity; [67] that the Ghega chiefs in northern Albania were in revolt against conscription,[68] and the whole *tanzimat* which had so limited their power. In 1848 the revolutions which shook the foundations of many of the western states of Europe had their counterpart in portions of the Ottoman Empire.[69] Spencer reported (1850) after a tour through Upper Moesia, Bosnia, and Albania that "the discontent of the Rayahs and the disturbances of the Mussalmans, appear increasing instead of diminishing, and might be attended with fatal consequences

---

[64] Dwight, *op. cit.*, p. 89.
[65] Spencer, *op. cit.*, pp. 261–262.
[66] Temperley, *The Crimea*, p. 244.
[67] Layard, *op. cit.*, II, 158, 159.
[68] The Ghegas would gladly serve as irregulars, but they would not submit to being forced into the regular army. *Ibid.*, II, 127, 131.
[69] Temperley, *The Crimea*, pp. 214–225.

to the Sultan's government in these provinces, should he be
forced into a war with any of his powerful neighbors, . . ." [70]
Finally, persecution of the Armenians and other Christians did
not seem to abate as a result of the *tanzimat*.[71]

The weakness of the Sultan is the most popular explanation
for the failure of the reform movement to achieve its purposes,
but more fundamental reasons also exist. Most significant was
the fact that after 1841 the real motive for permanent reforms
had been eliminated. By that time pressure both within and
without the empire for a stronger, more efficient state was
diminished by the settlement with Mehemet. During the previous decade the constant prospect of a new war with the Egyptians had been a powerful factor in encouraging Mahmoud to
modernize his civil as well as his military organization.[72] In
large measure his failure to effect permanent reforms had been
the cause of Turkey's defeat in 1839, which in turn made the
Hat necessary. With the assistance of the great powers, though
it was largely directed by Lord Palmerston, the Egyptian Question was brought to a reasonable conclusion, with the result
that reform ceased to be an immediate need,[73] but became a
luxury which might be acquired at some future date. Thus,
Palmerston's removal of the greatest dangers to the Turkish
state weakened the challenge to reform.

Absence of internal pressure was equally important, though
this had never been as driving a force as the dangers from the
outside. Reschid Pasha and his colleagues [74] continued to work
alone as individuals, rather than as leaders of an efficient organization or party. Of course Reschid did not expect support
for his program from the mass of Turks; that was too much to

---

[70] Spencer, *op. cit.*, I, 255–256.

[71] *Missionary Herald*, vol. 42, 1846, pp. 195–200, 202–203, 228–229, 269–273.

[72] Cf. note 51, p. 143.

[73] "The plans of Reschid Pasha, the regulation of Gulhané, the improvements
introduced from Europe went out of favour with the settlement of Egypt, and
the recovery of Syria and Caudia. The Porte gradually relapsed into most of
her old ideas. . . ." F. O. 78/523, Canning to Aberdeen, #260, December 13,
1843.

[74] Ali Pasha, Fuad Effendi, and Achmed Fethi Pasha.

expect from a people as ignorant as the Turkish populace was at that time. Though the people complained of the high taxes and other grievances, they were far from being of a revolutionary frame of mind, largely because of their loyalty to the protector of their faith. Reform in Turkey, as in Russia (until the mid-nineteenth century), came from above, because the rulers were more revolutionary than their conservative subjects.[75] Progress could be made while there was a strong ruler such as Mahmoud II at the head of the state, but when that leadership was removed, the state drifted. What was essential for Reschid Pasha was the support of a well-organized minority group of intellectuals who could bring pressure to bear on the Sultan. The absence of such a party made it a comparatively easy matter for the reactionary forces, who steadily increased their control of the Ruling Institution through Abdul Medjid's help, to disperse the individual leaders, and thereby defeat the cause of reform.

Moreover, public opinion had not kept pace with the reform movement; all criticism came from foreigners or from the rayahs; the attempts made to create an intelligent Turkish public opinion were far from successful. Without the support of the lawyers, journalists, and men of letters Reschid was lost.

In large measure the weakness of Reschid himself,[76] which showed up during his last years in the Divan, was a cause of the failure of the Hatti Sherif, and the reform movement which it inaugurated. Reschid did not know how to face the opposition. It is hard to believe that the greatest protagonist of reform in Turkey was naturally a timid person who in his later years cringed before the withering opposition of such men as Khosrew Pasha, Riza, and others.[77] Yet, it is even more difficult to understand why this opponent of corruption in his prime should himself become a party to shady dealings with the Armenians,[78]

[75] Cf. Moltke, *op. cit.*, p. 408.
[76] Temperley, *The Crimea*, pp. 244–245.
[77] Ashley, *op. cit.*, II, 327.
[78] F. O. 78/858, Canning to Palmerston, #307, October 16, 1851.

and later to cooperate with the Russians whom he had earlier looked upon as the foes of Turkey.[79] When one examines these facts one wonders that the forties were as fruitful as they were.

It is to deny the facts, however, to say that because the Crimean War showed up a wealth of corruption, bribery, and inefficiency, the whole reform movement was a failure.[80] Without the start which had been made in the thirties and forties, the later attempts at reform would have been impossible. A beginning had to be made, and though it was soon overshadowed, this first period of reform prepared the way for later progress.[81] Moreover, a comparison of the state of Turkey in 1853 with the conditions existing in 1825 shows that progress had been made. Arbitrary confiscation of property by the Sultan or his agents, the use of torture to secure an admission of guilt from a criminal, and resort to the death penalty had become more rare. Christians were recognized as equals with Mussulmans before the law, and their testimony was accepted in all legal adjudications.[82] It could be reasonably expected that the new educational facilities as well as the development of an intelligent public mind through the press would reap a rich harvest in a later period.[83] A perusal of the Hatti Humayoun of 1856 is

[79] Temperley, *The Crimea*, p. 310, and note 467, p. 471.

[80] Ubicini maintained that the great progress in Turkey between 1839 and 1853 was one of the principal reasons why Nicholas I undertook the Crimean War. Ubicini, *Letters*, II, 430.

[81] "The true value of this document (Hatti Sheriff de Gulhané) is to be sought in its effects on the people. More than in the administration of government; it awoke the slumbering East to the true objects of government." Cf. Hamlin, *op. cit.*, p. 56.

[82] "Compared with the first years of Sultan Mahmud's reign the present times have a decided advantage. A certain progress has been made; the avenues to further improvement are more free; life and property are more secure; the number of educated Turks is increased; the popular prejudices are generally softened; and the Porte's Christian subjects have rather to complain in common with the whole population, than on account of any flagrant grievances to which they are exclusively exposed. The establishment of the Quarantine; the use of Steam Navigation, the recognition of some milder principles of government, the introduction of European manufactures, and the increase of communication with the states of Christendom are so many steps in the road of civilization, . . ." F. O. 78/523, Canning to Aberdeen, #260, December 13, 1843. Cf. also *Missionary Herald*, vol. 38, 1842, p. 274.

[83] Cf. Hamlin, *op. cit.*, ch. XXIII, "Signs of Progress."

another significant piece of evidence in support of the early reform movement. The decrees of this Hat were not new by any means; in large measure they were a reaffirmation of the reforms which had been attempted in the two previous decades.[84]

What was the influence of Britain on the reform movement after 1839? According to Lane-Poole, the execution of the Hatti Sherif would have been even less successful had it not been for England. Lane-Poole believes that Stratford Canning, the Great Elchi, was most influential in all the reforms of this period. From the foregoing survey one can but conclude that there is little evidence to bear out this interpretation. In fact, after examining all the existing material concerning Canning's policy, the only conclusion that can be fairly maintained is that he was less successful than Palmerston had been in the previous decade. Canning's lack of success is explained largely by the fact that the Turks resented his methods, methods which were not dictated by the Foreign Office, but which were primarily the result of his own dominating character.

A more vigorous, aggressive, and able statesman Britain had never sent to the Porte. Canning's long experience in Turkish affairs well qualified him for the position he occupied from 1842 to 1858, and whether one agrees with his policy or not, one is forced to admire the energy with which he tackled his problems. Canning was shrewd beyond measure, yet it would be an exaggeration to say that this shrewdness smacked of dishonesty. His greatest weakness was his intimate knowledge of the workings of the Sultan's government, and his absolute frankness in expressing his opinions about those weaknesses. At times he was so arrogant and overbearing in his dealings with the Sultan's ministers that he created in their minds fear and contempt rather than genuine good feeling and respect. On one occasion the Turkish Council refused to recognize an official mission from France, because it knew that the English Ambassador was not favorable to it.[85] Even Reschid Pasha at times longed to be

---

[84] Cf. Appendix VI.   [85] Hoskins, *op. cit.*, p. 308.

free from the influence of Canning and his agents. Canning would have been more successful in promoting reform had he been less overbearing in his demeanor.

Canning's attitude toward Turkey after 1841 is another explanation why he was not more successful in furthering reform. More of a Russophobe than his predecessor, Ponsonby, his primary aim was to maintain the freedom from Russian domination which Palmerston had acquired for Turkey in the two years prior to his entrance on the scene. Canning's policy was more anti-Russian than it was pro-Turkish. Anxious to strengthen Britain's position in the Near East, he sympathized with reforms which would raise the prestige of his country, and allow his countrymen to increase their trade with Turkey. Canning believed that the greatest needs in Turkey were a purified civil service, reasonable laws, fair taxation, and a balanced budget. These changes, he argued, would guarantee the continuation of Turkey as a power in Europe, and incidentally would prove a boon to English commercial men.

Canning's policy was not entirely selfish however. He lent his support to any efforts which would improve the condition of non-Mussulmans in the empire because he was convinced that Turkey could never develop a real national spirit until the distinctions between the Mohammedan and Christian peoples were broken down. As the best means of limiting these distinctions he favored the acceptance of Christians in the military, naval, and civil service, the admission of Christian children to the state schools, and the recognition of evidence of Christians in the law courts. It is undoubtedly true that Canning would have been more successful with the Turks had he disguised this phase of his policy; his support of administrative reforms, and the improvement of the army and finance was weakened by his humanitarian program which the Turks did not understand and with which they could not sympathize.[86]

Like Palmerston Canning did not favor the establishment of parliamentary institutions in Turkey. "There is no question of transferring any portion of power from the (Turkish) sovereign

[86] Temperley, *The Crimea*, p. 454, note 366.

to his subjects," [87] he wrote in 1848, and that policy he had pursued long before he actually put it into words. Canning was a firm believer that the Sultan was the best reformer. Moreover, the ambassador was convinced that the inauguration of a new system with which the Turks were not familiar would cause a dislocation of the political machinery in Turkey which might prove fatal to the state. If the Ottoman Empire was to continue, more could be accomplished by guiding the Sultan along the right course, but he became less optimistic as to the value of this policy after he had been in Constantinople for a few years.

Canning's influence on the Turkish reform movement should not be discounted too much however. Like Palmerston he exerted considerable influence indirectly on the Sultan. When he arrived at the Porte, Reschid Pasha, Canning's friend and protagonist of reform, had been sent off to Paris. Canning, on every possible occasion, pointed out to Abdul Medjid the mistakes he had made in deferring to the dictates of the other party. By every possible means he tried to undermine the power of Riza Pasha and his colleagues at the Porte and restore Reschid to his rightful position. Finally in 1846, largely through Canning's efforts, Reschid returned to the leadership of Turkey, but by that time the reform movement had run its course.

From the moment Canning returned from his leave, in 1848, his chief task was to protect Turkey from complete destruction at the hands of the Tsar. Russia's declaration of war, November 1, 1853, was the culmination of a policy begun nine years before. Had it not been for Canning and Palmerston Russia might have achieved her aims. The Treaty of Paris did not solve the Eastern Question, but it did recognize Turkey as one of the great powers of Europe. The Hatti Humayoun forced upon the Sultan was general recognition that Turkey could be saved. Thus, began a second phase in the life of the Ottoman state in the nineteenth century, a phase incontestably dominated by what had been attempted in the two previous decades.

[87] F. O. 78/773, Canning to Palmerston, #84, March 12, 1848.

CONCLUSION

It is obvious from the foregoing chapters that the period 1825–1853 was merely the beginning of the *tanzimat*. The reforms of these years, though not far-reaching in themselves, did pave the way for the more extensive reforms of a later period. Mahmoud II and Reschid Pasha by their successive improvements undermined the old order which had existed until that time, and thus rendered possible the development of a genuine national feeling for the Turkish state without which progress could not be made.[1] The short-lived constitutional regime, 1875–1876, was constructed by Midhat Pasha and the Young Turks on the foundations laid in the pre-Crimean period, and this constitution of 1876 was the goal for which the reformers worked in the revolution of 1908, and again in the final breakdown of the old empire in 1918. Thus, in the last instance, the *tanzimat*, a step away from the old autocratic feudal order, has a much closer relationship with the modern Turkey than has heretofore been recognized; though the old bonds were merely loosed, not broken, nevertheless it was a move in the direction of modernization which has eventually culminated in the respected national republic which Turkey is today.

A second important feature of the reform movement in the two decades after 1825 was that it was essentially Turkish in origin. Beginning with the destruction of the Janissary Corps in 1826, the Sultan set in motion a reform movement years before the powers recognized the feasibility of rejuvenation. The *tanzimat* was motivated not by the desire for an improved order for its own sake, but by the sheer necessity of self-preservation. Turkey's failure to prevent the loss of Greece proved that she could not continue without accepting western ideas.

[1] The development of Turkish nationalism, which reached its maximum after the World War, made it possible for the late Mustapha Kemal, Ataturk Ghazi, to create from the remnants of the old empire a truly modern state.

Moreover, the success of the Sultan's vassal Mehemet Ali, was unquestionably a significant factor in turning Mahmoud in the direction of reform. While his program was not well conceived and very inadequately executed, he did establish a precedent for improvements in the military and civil administration. Codification of these ideas in the Hatti Sherif de Gulhané of 1839 (as well as the addition of many unknown to Mahmoud) was the work of Reschid Pasha, a genuine Turkish patriot and statesman, who was determined to preserve what remained of the Ottoman Empire, and build thereon a modern state worthy of its subjects' support. Unfortunately for Turkey westernization was not desired by many in the first half of the nineteenth century; the number who sympathized with Reschid Pasha's aims in 1839 was small. However, in spite of the fact that the Hatti Sherif de Gulhané, dictated as it was by the pressure of the moment, was not of great significance *per se*, it did become the goal of all reformers in the succeeding decades, until it was finally replaced by the Constitution of 1876.

The most significant facts with respect to British influence on the reform movement after 1825 were its tardiness and its ineffectiveness. Genuine interest in the welfare of the Ottoman state was slow to develop in the British Foreign Office. The "maintenance of the independence and territorial integrity of the Ottoman Empire" was merely a theory until the threat of Russia in 1833 caused it to become the basis for future action. Had Britain's interest in Turkey developed earlier, the problems which she aimed to correct would have been less difficult, if not absolutely non-existent. Had the Foreign Office adopted a strong pro-Turkish policy immediately after the Congress of Vienna, Mehemet Ali might never have become powerful enough to defy the Sultan successfully, and Russia would thereby have been deprived of an adequate pretext for intervention in 1833; moreover, Russia might never have ventured to intervene in a state where the British were already firmly established. But these hypothetical historical "ifs," so fascinating to the historian, should not be allowed to efface the fact that as a result of

Britain's late awakening with respect to the Near East, in the half decade after 1833 the British Foreign Office faced the very difficult task of strengthening Turkey without appearing to do so. Knowing that open intervention in Turkey's behalf would cause a break with the Russian state already established there, Palmerston proceeded with the utmost caution. By the time that he finally began to advise the Sultan to reform his military organization, his finances, and his civil administration, the British Foreign Secretary discovered that his advice was not well received, because the Sultan had already become accustomed to French, Russian, and Prussian advisors. Because of these facts it cannot be over-emphasized that Palmerston was only in part responsible for the Hatti Sherif of 1839. In fact, the decree issued by Abdul Medjid was less the result of British influence than of Reschid Pasha's knowledge of western systems which he attempted to force upon the young Sultan when the latter's state was hard pressed and needed the backing of western nations, especially England.

If Palmerston was slow to awaken to the importance of Turkey's continued existence, and if his policy designed to preserve Turkey against further Russian encroachment was not effective when applied in 1837–1838, what then was his importance to the Turkish reform movement? Palmerston's chief contribution was his effective settlement of the Egyptian question in 1840–41, a settlement which gave Turkey a breathing spell to recover its strength after the disasters of 1839. Palmerston never favored extensive constitutional development in the Ottoman Empire. In this he was supported by both his Ambassador at Constantinople, Lord Ponsonby, and by David Urquhart; the primary aims of both of these men were not internal reforms for Turkey but improved economic relations between Turkey and England. To achieve this end Ponsonby worked to forestall further aggrandizement in the Near East by Russia, while Urquhart tried to convince influential Britishers of the importance of Turkish trade to Britain's prosperity. Through their combined efforts both the Foreign Office and the English people at large learned in the 1830's how important Turkey's future existence was to them both as a trade outlet and because of its geographic position.

As for Stratford Canning, there is no evidence to prove that he was any more successful in strengthening the Ottoman state than Lord Palmerston, Ponsonby, or David Urquhart. Canning, like Palmerston, did not press for constitutional development in Turkey, realizing that the Turks were too backward, too lacking in enlightened leaders as well as in intelligent followers, to assimilate such a system. Instead Canning worked for the execution of the Hat of 1839 within the existing framework of government, and his interest was less with the Turkish populace than with the Christian population there. Canning was instrumental in securing more liberty for these subjects as well as special concessions for the missionaries there. By the time Canning arrived in Constantinople (1842) the reform movement had given way to a reactionary policy, and though he was influential in obtaining Reschid's restoration to authority, his efforts in the years that followed were not as significant as Mr. Stanley Lane-Poole, his biographer, would have us believe. Moreover, by 1845, the need of reform was not as great as it had been six years before, and the opposition of the old Turks was stronger.

Yet, because both Palmerston and Canning were late in promoting reforms in the Ottoman Empire, and because their achievements failed to measure up to their high hopes at the beginning, one cannot maintain that the Foreign Office had no influence on the *tanzimat* prior to 1853. On the contrary, by his breaking the force of the Treaty of Unkiar Skelessi, and finally substituting for it the Straits Convention of 1841, Palmerston made the reform movement of Abdul Medjid and Reschid Pasha possible. When Canning arrived in Constantinople he faced the task of maintaining the freedom which had just been achieved, and no one can deny that he was not successful in this respect. When, as a result of the Crimean War, Turkey was at last recognized as one of the great European powers,

both men felt repaid for their efforts; independence and territorial integrity, hollow words twenty years before, had finally
come to mean something both to Turkey and England.

Though England steadfastly refused to enter into a definite
alliance with the Porte, as a complement to her policy of freeing Turkey from Russian domination, Britain indirectly fostered the reform movement to an immeasurable degree. The
moral support of such able Britishers as Palmerston and Canning was invaluable to Mahmoud and Reschid in their attempts
to rebuild the former power of the Turkish state. The support
of the richest and one of the most powerful states in the world
aroused a feeling of confidence in the Turks which showed itself in the attempts of the Turkish statesmen to rebuild Turkey,
not only for its own sake, but also to please their powerful
friend, England. When Russia was supreme in Turkish affairs,
the desires of the Tsar's government were carried out because
the Porte feared the consequences; when the English influence
became dominant, loyalty and gratitude replaced fear as their
principal motives.

The motives of Britain in her attempts to establish new
vigour in the Ottoman Empire are equally varied. That she
wished to strengthen Turkey in order to maintain the balance
of power in the Mediterranean there is little doubt; since France
supported Mehemet Ali, Britain was forced to back the Sultan.
Humanitarian interest in the subjects of the Ottoman state was
undoubtedly another reason. But in large measure Britain's
policy was motivated by purely selfish aims. The trade routes
to India had to be protected from the steady encroachment of
Russia, and the best means of protection was a strong Turkey,
a Turkey loyal to, if not absolutely dependent upon, England.
In this sense, British policy in the Near East was less pro-Turk
than it was anti-Russian.

Moreover, foreign trade was the basic factor in English life.
Without markets her factories would close, and closing of the
factories meant both ruin to the owners and poverty for the
laboring classes. Although England's Near Eastern trade was

but a small proportion of her total commerce, and though this was never seriously threatened by the powers before 1853, the constant penetration of the Caucasus region by Russia and the close relations of France with Egypt were warnings which could not go unheeded in London. As Anglo-Turkish commerce became more extensive, Britain's original anti-Russian policy became sincerely pro-Turkish. These economic factors must be kept in mind in order to appreciate fully the policy of Britain in the Near East during the years under surveillance.

Thus, in the two decades prior to the outbreak of the Crimean War, a new facet was added to the many-sided policy pursued by the British Foreign Office; though at times it did not seem to follow any specific policy with respect to Turkey, it never ceased to recognize the importance of that state in its larger European and world policies. Later under Disraeli and Salisbury Britain's Near Eastern policy became even more significant in relation to her maintenance of the balance of power in Europe; this subject has been thoroughly treated by Professor Sidney B. Fay in his *Origins of the World War* and especially by Professor W. L. Langer in his *European Alliances and Alignments*. Until the formation of the *Entente Cordiale* in 1904 France remained suspicious and resentful of English success in the eastern Mediterranean. Moreover, there is no doubt that British friendship for the Sultan was one of the reasons for Anglo-Russian animosity until 1907. For the remainder of the century after 1833 the Mediterranean, and especially the eastern half of the Mediterranean, was the focal point of the interests of these three powers. Austria's interest in the Balkans after 1878 and Germany's entrance into the Turkish question with the Bagdad railway project further complicated the problem and contributed to the inevitable clash. During this period British policy varied with successive foreign ministers, but English interests in Turkey remained constant after 1833.

APPENDICES

APPENDIX I

CANNING'S MEMORANDUM, DECEMBER 19, 1832

F.O. 78/211. *Memo.*, on the Turco-Egyptian Question, by Sir Stratford Canning: encld. in: Canning, Paris, Dec. 19/32; to Palmerston.

The Turkish Empire has reached, in its decline, that critical point, at which it must either revive and commence a fresh era of Prosperity, or fall into a state of complete dissolution. To Great Britain the fate of this Empire can never be indifferent. It would affect the interests of her Trade and East Indian Possessions, even if it were unconnected with the maintenance of her relative Power in Europe. Nearer and more pressing Duties may forbid His Majesty's Government to take an active part in the Contest which now agitates Turkey; but the issue of a struggle so likely to prove decisive of the Sultan's independence, can hardly be overlooked and left to chance on any sound Principles of English Policy.

Often as the Sultan and his Predecessors have had occasion to maintain their Authority by force of Arms, they have always done so with ultimate Success, except in the recent instance of the Greeks. But the Egyptian War, though originating in the same vicious system of government, which has caused so many Convulsions in Turkey, is far more dangerous to the Porte than any preceding Rebellion, whether it be considered with reference to the Character and Resources of Mehemet Ali, or to the difficulties of the Sultan's Position. The Pasha, however, if he succeed in the end, will not be able to carry his point without a severe and protracted Contest. Already overstrained by his exertions, he can only sustain them by imposing Additional Burthens on Egypt and Syria, increasing thereby the hazard and odium inseparable from the prosecution of his enterprise. His Sovereign, who has publicly branded him as a Rebel and Outlaw, is urged by the strongest motives to reject such terms of compromise as, on any probable supposition, it would agree with the views or safety of the Pasha to offer of his own accord. If Mehemet Ali be superior in point of capacity, if he can dispose more completely of the resources of his Country, and exhibit a higher degree of discipline in his Fleet and Army, the Sultan, on the other hand, has those advantages, which belong to an acknowledged Right, and a greater extent of Territory. He cannot be blind to the consequences of allowing his Vassal to form a separate Sovereignty within the Limits of his Empire. The Erection of Syria and Egypt into an independent State would in fact cut off the communication between Constantinople and Mecca, and while it weakened Mahmoud's Title to the Caliphat, would place the most important Parts of Arabia and Mesopotamia under the controul of his Enemy.

The extraordinary Progress made by Ibrahim Pasha during the last Campaign has given rise to an idea, that the Capital itself is not beyond his reach. In Turkey no kind or description of Revolution is impossible. But the Egyptian Army has paused in its Career. The Sultan has had time to repair, in some measure, his losses; and the Grand Visir at the head of a considerable Force, composed in part of new Levies, and partly of the Albanian Troops, which he commanded with so much credit in Bosnia, will afford a rallying point for the remains of the Army defeated under Hussein Pasha, and, if not strong enough to attack the Egyptian cantonments, will at least be able to make a stand in the fastnesses of Mount Taurus. But let us suppose an extreme case. The Vizir, no doubt, may experience the fate of his Predecessor; his Army may be dispersed; the country may rise in favour of the Egyptians; and Ibrahim Pasha, encouraged by these circumstances, may possibly follow up his Victory even to the Shores of the Bosphorus, and dictate the most humiliating Terms to the Sultan.

In this case one of two results would be unavoidable. The Sultan must either abandon his Throne altogether, or consent to such a reduction of his Empire as would leave Mehemet Ali in permanent Possession of Egypt and Syria with all the Country behind those Provinces as far as the Persian Frontier. Supposing the triumphant Viceroy to occupy and maintain himself on the vacant Throne of Constantinople, it is evident that he would be placed towards the Powers of Europe in the same position as the Sultan, with the additional weakness belonging to an usurped Title, and the necessity of flattering the religious prejudices of the Turks. The Interests of England and of Christendom would gain little by such a change. Whatever price the Chief of a new Dynasty would be willing to pay for recognition, could equally be obtained from the reigning Sultan in return for support and coöperation. Supposing the contest to terminate in the formation of a separate Government under the Sceptre of Mehemet Ali or of Ibrahim Pasha, the Sultan, deprived of so large a Portion of his Empire, and degraded in the opinion of his Subjects, would find it more difficult than ever either to make head against the encroachments of Russia, or to carry on that system of improvement, which is become essential to the maintenance of his Independence.

If the contending Parties were left to themselves it is but too probable that a long and arduous War would drain their respective resources, and, by adding another cause of desolation to those which have long worn down the Turkish Empire, render it an easy prey to the first Invader. Nor is it in this respect alone that a protracted Contest in the Mediterranean Provinces of Turkey would be detrimental to European Interests. The necessities of both Parties would oblige them to employ every kind of extortion and violence injurious to life and property, and it is difficult to conceive how Commerce more than civilization could expand, or even exist, under such a pressure.[1]

So many indeed and great are the Evils which this Contest is likely to generate in its Progress,[2] that it becomes a duty to enquire by what means Great Britain, either alone or in concert with any of her Allies, may best contribute to hasten its Termination. No pretext for interference is wanting. The Sultan and the Pasha have both appealed to the friendly and equitable disposition of the British Cabinet, but with this difference, that the former applies for our assistance, and the latter for our mediation. It is not surprising that the Sultan, whose Honour and Independence are at stake, should look for succour to that Power, which has once already been the instrument of restoring Egypt to the Porte; nor is it less natural, that Mehemet Ali should reckon, however erroneously, upon Great Britain for the means of securing to him that independence, of which the Greek Insurrection has probably given him the idea and the occasion.

Unfortunately this very consideration indisposes the Sultan to every kind of foreign interference unaccompanied with a moral or physical coöperation in his favour. He must necessarily feel that his plain unquestionable Interest is to put down the Pasha of Egypt, and to reestablish his own Authority in that Province and Syria. What he wants is the effectual aid of Great Britain for the accomplishment of this purpose, and there is little doubt, that, if His Majesty's Government could find in the present circumstances of the

[1] *Marginal note by Palmerston:* Is not the unwieldy extent of the Turkish Empire one great check to the improvement of its industry and resources and possibly one great cause of its external weakness? Is it quite clear that war on an extensive scale in an Empire which at all times & during what is — (?) peace is the Theatre of perpetual turbulence & petty disturbances is really so injurious to its commerce & improvements as this paragraph supports?

[2] *Marginal note by Palmerston:* This assumes more than is proved.

Turkish Empire adequate motives for acceding to this request, the presence of a British Squadron would suffice to ensure success.[3]

The principal difficulties, with which the Sultan has to contend in directing his operations against Mehemet Ali, arise out of the distant and insulated position of Egypt, the ease with which Syria can be defended against an Army invading it from the North, and the disadvantage of having a Fleet, which though superior in numerical Force to that of Egypt is by no means so well manned and manoeuvred.

With the assistance of a British Squadron there is great reason to believe, that the Sultan would easily surmount these obstacles. Instead of attacking the Egyptian Forces in Syria, he might send an Expedition by Sea against Egypt itself. To the East of Damietta the Coast affords Facilities for landing Troops, and an invasion properly directed on that side would not only compel Ibrahim Pasha to retreat, but would also menace Cairo, and bring into the field all those, who, secretly attached to the Sultan's Cause, are nevertheless kept down at present by the want of support and the fear of Punishment.

Whatever just or insuperable objections may be raised on the score of expense, or on any other account, to the participation of Great Britain in this measure, the probable result of it would be beneficial in no small degree to her interests. The very attempt, indeed, would give her an important Influence in the Counsels of the Divan. That Influence would operate most powerfully in promoting the Progress of reform and civilization throughout Turkey; and the spirit of improvement, thus encouraged and directed, could hardly fail to revive the overlaid resources of a Country so rich in natural advantages.[4] The Treaty of Alliance, which would naturally be formed to regulate the operations of the combined Forces, and to provide for the reception and refreshment of the British Squadron, might also contain Stipulations in favour of any specific concession desired by His Majesty's Government, as well as an engagement to indemnify our Merchants at Alexandria for any losses arising out of the participation of Great Britain in the Contest. The Sultan's Pardon and a suitable Provision for Mehemet Ali and his Son Ibrahim, in the event of their overthrow, might be secured by means of the same Instrument.

[3] *Marginal note by Palmerston:* Or. Is even this quite certain?

[4] *Marginal note by Palmerston:* We rescued Egypt once for Turkey. We acquired, or supposed that we acquired influence in this Divan. What was the beneficial result? Certainly no progress in civilization or Reform nor any such improvement of Turkish measures as is here contemplated.

It is obvious, that, as far as Great Britain is concerned, the only ground on which this plan could be recommended, is the necessity of interfering to rescue the Turkish Empire from a War, which threatens to lay it at the feet of a Power already too great for the general Interests and Liberties of Europe.[5] It is impossible at the same time to contemplate such a necessity without an encreased Feeling of regret that a Contest fraught with such consequences should ever have commenced; and hence arises an anxious desire to discover some means of restoring matters, as nearly as may be practicable, to the state in which they stood before the Pasha's attempt upon Acre.

If it be true, as the Sultan alleges, that Mehemet Ali has embarked in an enterprize or mere Ambition; if he has taken advantage of his Sovereign's embarrassments with the sole view of establishing an independent Sovereignty for himself and his Family, there is evidently no middle course; he must either succeed altogether or fail altogether.[6] The question in that case is, whether the object of enabling the Sultan to hasten the conclusion of the War by an attack upon Egypt, be sufficient to overbalance the objections which His Majesty's Government may entertain in general to extending their interference in foreign quarrels. Of their right to interfere upon an invitation from the Sultan there can be no doubt; and it is probable that the mode of interference suggested above would prove effectual.

But to judge impartially of the Viceroy's motives, we must call to mind the situation in which he was placed before his Expedition into Syria. The main object of the Sultan's internal Policy throughout his Reign has been the Suppression of all minor Authorities, which had acquired in any degree an abusive power of checking his own.[7] Having destroyed the Janissaries, who formed the great obstacle to his designs, and having reconciled himself to the loss of Greece, — that perilous bone of contention between him and Christendom, his views were turned to the establishment of a more regular system of administration in the Provinces of his Empire, and to the cultivation of a better understanding with the Powers of Europe, and principally with Great Britain. Such being the case, it is far from improbable that Mehemet Ali may have looked with apprehension to the moment, when measures arising out of this policy would be applied

[5] *Marginal note by Palmerston:* This is most just and true.

[6] *Marginal note by Palmerston:* Do not see that this conclusion follows from the premises.

[7] *Marginal note by Palmerston:* Is authority built on the forcible suppression of minor authorities — (?) and if not, in what would the Pasha's usurped authority differ from the Sultan's, if successful, but in degree? Both would be usurpation.

to Egypt, which he had advanced, during an administration of twenty years, from a state of confusion and comparative poverty, to a degree of improvement, in point of order and production, which filled his Coffers, and placed him at the head of a considerable military and naval force. He might have thought that the Sultan's designs, coinciding with his necessities, would shortly lead to the spoliation of these fruits of his eminent capacity for government, and therefore that it would be better to avail himself of the latter, while there was yet time, in order to increase his means of resisting the execution of the former at his expence. Upon this supposition prudence and not ambition would be the motive of his conduct; — security, rather than aggrandizement, his object. In a question of so much difficulty and complication, it may, therefore, be worth while to ascertain how far a reasonable security, consistent with what is due to the rights and character of the Sultan, might by possibility be obtained from him by means of British interference.

To go at once to the point, — it is clear that the Pasha cannot be left in possession of Syria, on any imaginable terms whatever, without a considerable loss of credit, if not of actual strength, to the Sultan's Government. His right to retain possession either of Syria or of Egypt without the Sultan's consent can only be the right of force.[8] The obvious inference is that no arrangement intended to give security to the Pasha can be fairly proposed to the Porte, unless it be attended with the recall of the Egyptian forces from Syria. Nor is it likely that any proposal would prove effectual, which should not be accompanied with a distinct understanding as to the amount of revenue, and the contingent of troops and ships that the Pasha would be ready henceforward to hold at the Sultan's disposal, in consideration of his continuing to hold the Viceroyalty of Egypt for life, and cooperating with the Sultan for the advancement of those plans of reform, upon the execution of which the best and only hope of maintaining the independence of the Turkish Empire, and improving the condition of its inhabitants, may be truly said to depend. An arrangement comprizing these points, and concluded under the sanction, though not necessarily with the guarantee, of Great Britain, might be expected to allay the Pasha's apprehensions, supposing his present conduct to have originated rather in them than in any ambitious impulse. But in order to reconcile the Sultan's mind to a transaction which, at best, would be far from palatable to a Prince of his temper and policy, something more than the recollection of his disasters in the late campaign would be necessary. He would no doubt expect

[8] *Marginal note by Palmerston:* What other has the Sultan?

of Great Britain to declare Herself openly in favour of his cause, and to follow up that declaration with measures tending to uphold his authority in the eyes of his subjects, and to facilitate his operations against the Egyptian forces. The most obvious measures of this description are a prohibition to His Majesty's subjects to convey provisions or warlike stores to Egypt and Syria,[9] the establishment of Cruizers on the Coast to prevent the importation of those Articles, the recall of all British Subjects serving under the Pasha, an arrangement for introducing Engineers and Naval Officers into the Sultan's service, and a refusal to acknowledge the Egyptian Flag. To these might be added such diplomatick proceedings at The Courts of Persia and Greece, and at Bagdad, and in those parts of Syria which are not actually occupied by Ibrahim Pasha, as would counteract the intrigues of Mehemet Ali, and contribute to the promotion of the Sultan's interests in those Quarters.

Great Britain by adopting these measures, or measures like these, might perhaps be able to gain in a sufficient degree the confidence of the Sultan; but much would still remain to be done in order to bring the Viceroy of Egypt into an arrangement on the above mentioned terms. It would be necessary, in the first place, to extinguish his hope of our ever consenting to the accomplishment of his schemes of independence, in the second, to provide in some degree for Ibrahim Pasha's interests, — and, in the third, to soften his mortification at the loss of Syria by making some change in the Authorities of that Country more acceptable to him than the reinstatement of those whom he has forcibly removed. On the second and third of these points, it would of course be advisable to consult the views and feelings of the Viceroy himself, but as far as a conjecture may be hazarded, it is not impossible that an immediate transfer of the government of Candia to Ibrahim Pasha, or a promise of the reversion of that of Egypt to him during his life time on the same conditions under which it is proposed that Mehemet Ali should hold it in future, would be satisfactory on that point; and that as to Syria, the Sultan might be induced to consign the Pashalick of Acre to one of Mehemet Ali's grandsons, — provided no Egyptian Troops were allowed to remain there, and that the Fortress of Acre were garrisoned by a detachment of the Sultan's Guard, and commanded by a governor enjoying his confidence.

The effect of this plan, if it were carried into execution, would be

---

[9] *Marginal note by Palmerston:* i.e. with a view to remote and precarious advantages to our commerce, to begin by cramping and prohibiting that which exists with Egypt and Syria.

to restore the matters in question as nearly as possible to their former state. It is grounded on the threefold persuasion that nothing but absolute necessity would induce the Sultan to consent to the union of the two Provinces of Egypt and Syria under Mehemet Ali; that his efforts to avert that necessity would exhaust his resources, and render the independence of his Empire still more precarious than now; and, finally, that His Majesty's Government might either find insuperable objections to cooperating with the Sultan by means of an auxiliary Squadron, or, at all events, that they would prefer withholding that kind of assistance until the experiment of milder measures had been made without success. The very apprehension of their recurring eventually to such an extremity would doubtless contribute to produce in the Viceroy's mind a disposition favourable to the acceptance of their proposals.

How far it may be practicable to render the proposed Alliance respecting Egypt, on either of the preceding suppositions, available to the acquisition of any exclusive advantage for Great Britain, is by no means so clear as the benefit which would in all probability accrue from it to the general interests of Europe and of Turkey itself. It is not to be doubted that our support, and more particularly our assistance under such circumstances, would secure the confidence and gratitude of the Sultan, and that he would be ready to make any reasonable sacrifice in return for such important aids. But the Porte is so bound by her Treaties with the principal European Powers, that no commercial privilege granted to one could long be withheld from the others, and it would be difficult to point out any special object of interest not coming under that head, unless it were the grant of certain facilities for navigating the River Euphrates by steam, with a view to the promotion of a more direct intercourse with India; the feasibility of which very important project, though probable in the highest degree, has not yet been submitted to actual experiment; or the privilege of obtaining ship-timber from the extensive forests of Turkey, which could only be of value to Great Britain in the event of Her being engaged in a naval war in some degree similar to the last. But it stands to reason that the same motives which induce the Sultan to court an Alliance with Great Britain would render the existence of that Alliance favourable to the promotion of our interests in Turkey. Nor can it be necessary to repeat that if it be a British and an European object to uphold the Turkish Empire as a barrier against encroachments from the North, and if the Sultan's independence be endangered by the chances of a contest indefinitely prolonged against Egypt, and the consequent interruption of measures essential to its maintenance, there are sufficient motives for acceding, under proper restrictions, to the Sultan's overture without the additional inducement of a special or exclusive British interest.

Another part of the subject remains to be examined, and it is one which embraces such various and extensive considerations as scarcely to find place in a memoir grounded on the presumed facility of access to local information. The question of British interference in the Egyptian contest is, however, indissolubly connected with the policy of other Courts respecting Turkey. Nor is it possible to arrive at a satisfactory conclusion on the subject, without referring in some measure to the opposition or concurrence which Great Britain would have to expect from them in the event of her determining to support the Sultan's cause, or to offer her mediation between him and the Pasha of Egypt. But it is by no means necessary to go over the whole ground of inquiry on this occasion. What can be stated with some degree of confidence, or prospect of utility, it is not difficult to bring within a narrow compass.

There is no doubt that the Sultan would in any emergency look with preference to the Counsels or assistance of Great Britain. No Christian State ranks so high in his estimation either for power, or for good-faith. If England were to take up the affair of Egypt in concert with France He would not perhaps reject their joint interference accompanied with the support of his cause, but in all probability he would only consent to it from deference to His Majesty's Government. Many acts of France during the last forty years, concluding with the occupation of Algiers, have rendered the Porte extremely mistrustful of the Power. The concurrence of France in the supposed case could therefore be desirable to Great Britain, only as it might tend to allay jealousy, or enable her to operate more effectually on the Pasha of Egypt. The motives which at present prevail with the French Ministers to cultivate the good-will and confidence of England, might possibly suffice to reconcile them to her single interference in the Affairs of Turkey; but the counteraction, however disguised, of a Power like France could hardly fail to increase the difficulties already existing, and it is well known that the French Cabinet has long regarded the Levant, and Syria and Egypt in particular, with more than common interest.[10]

Of the two remaining Powers, whose disposition with respect to

[10] *Marginal note by Palmerston:* Surely it would be very strange if it did — should we be easily reconciled to the *single* interference of France? Yet France is not by position and actual connection more directly interested in Turkish affairs than ourselves?

Turkey is of any immediate consequence, Austria would no doubt behold with satisfaction the influence and energy of Great Britain employed in support of the Sultan's authority and the preservation of His empire from dismemberment. It is equally clear that a similar interference for such purposes could never be agreeable to Russia, although the feelings, which it would be likely to excite in that quarter, might soften in proportion as British influence was pointed to the overthrow of rebellion; and the Court of St. Petersburgh, though no less adverse to our interference than to the Sultan's application for it, could hardly, with due regard to its own principles and professions of peace, step forward to *oppose* its exercise.[11]

To return to the main question, there is no denying that whether it be contemplated with reference to a single or to a joint interference, the difficulties are great, the hazards considerable. In one respect, however, the prospect is clear. Let Mehemet Ali succeed in constituting an independent State, and a great and irretrievable step is made towards the dismemberment of the Turkish Empire. That Empire may fall to pieces at all events; and he must be a bold man who would undertake to answer for its being saved by any effort of human policy. But His Majesty's Government may rest assured that to leave it to itself is to leave it to its Enemies.

[11] *Marginal note by Palmerston:* Perhaps not, but would she or could *she* be entirely neutral and passive on such an occasion — America is not glanced (?) at but she has commerce in those parts and by interfering we sanction her right of interfering too.

APPENDIX II

EXPORTS TO AND IMPORTS FROM TURKEY, 1825–1855

TABLE 1

DECLARED VALUE OF GOODS EXPORTED FROM THE UNITED KINGDOM COMPARED WITH THE EXPORTS TO TURKEY [1]

1825

ARTICLES		QUANTITY EXPORTED		VALUE OF EXPORTS	
		Total	To Turkey	Total	To Turkey
Cotton mfgrs. (Calico)	Yds.	132,129,625	3,578,575	£4,865,224	£103,012
Cotton Twist	Lbs.	35,344,127	557,584	3,420,575	48,886
Total Cotton Goods	....	....	....	18,788,016	490,413
Sugar, refined	Cwt.	389,783	10,930	929,495	25,786
Tin, unwrought	Cwt.	34,237	2,592	154,568	12,687
Iron & Steel (excl. of ore)	....	....	....	1,355,379	12,527
Gunpowder	Lbs.	3,033,224	470,350	82,642	12,418
Woolens, yarn & mfgrs.	....	....	....	7,328,841	8,318
Ordnance of Iron	Tons	6,959	509	117,868	7,112
Hardware & Cutlery	Cwt.	251,353	914	1,656,039	6,784
Tin Plates	....	....	....	206,970	6,079
Apparel	....	....	....	317,444	4,967
Lead & Shot	Tons	9,589	176	239,788	4,495
Leather Goods	....	....	....	401,511	4,328

TABLE 1 (*Continued*)

ARTICLES		QUANTITY EXPORTED		VALUE OF EXPORTS	
		Total	To Turkey	Total	To Turkey
Watches	No.	8,038	755	44,329	3,261
Machinery	......	......	......	144,640	3,077
Military Stores	......	......	......	72,098	2,773
Coal, Culm & Cinders .	......	......	......	463,656	2,388
Silk goods, total	......	......	......	311,592	1,695
Stationery	......	......	......	216,238	1,640
Glassware, total	......	......	......	700,519	963
Haberdashery & Millinery	Cwt.	24,481	20	737,765	692
Beer & Ale	Tons	9,027	25	186,588	610
Cabinet & Upholstery wares	Cwt.	......	......	108,667	599
Books, printed	Cwt.	10,717	38	186,086	543
Linen mfgrs.	......	......	......	2,185,491	474
Cordage & Cables	Cwt.	88,398	133	207,104	336
Painter's Colours	......	......	......	171,971	226
Slops & Negro Clothing	......	......	......	206,585	223
Plate, wrought of silver	Oz.	171,912	414	77,367	188

¹ Customs 9/12.

TABLE 2

DECLARED VALUE OF GOODS EXPORTED FROM THE UNITED KINGDOM COMPARED WITH THE EXPORTS TO TURKEY [1]

1830

ARTICLES		QUANTITY EXPORTED		VALUE OF EXPORTS	
		Total	To Turkey	Total	To Turkey
Cotton mfgrs. (Calico)	Yds.	219,355,817	15,940,910	£5,786,107	£351,173
Cotton Twist	Lbs.	64,645,342	1,528,271	4,133,740	86,147
Total Cotton Goods	.....	.....	.....	19,428,633	947,906
Sugar, refined	Cwt.	607,580	27,282	1,288,077	58,133
Iron & Steel (excl. of ore)	Tons	117,419	6,223	1,078,523	37,900
Woolen yarn & mfgrs.	.....	.....	.....	4,851,096	19,970
Tin, unwrought	Cwt.	30,425	3,659	106,134	12,821
Cordage & Cables	Cwt.	35,658	5,081	84,084	12,712
Hardware & Cutlery	Cwt.	267,731	1,073	1,412,107	7,915
Tin plates	.....	.....	.....	231,922	6,083
Watches	No.	10,942	1,326	46,461	5,054
Linen mfgrs.	.....	.....	.....	2,066,424	2,853
Glassware, total	.....	.....	.....	401,542	1,961
Leather, wrought & unwrought	Lbs.	1,405,003	9,197	257,129	1,109
Silk goods, total	.....	.....	.....	165,219	1,056
Apparel	.....	.....	.....	206,137	993
Lead & Shot	Tons	7,442	50	106,789	795
Stationery	.....	.....	.....	171,847	530
Machinery	.....	.....	.....	64,532	155
Military Stores	.....	.....	.....	33,471	124
Coal, Culm & Cinders	Tons	504,419	218	184,463	97

[1] Customs 9/17.

TABLE 3

DECLARED VALUE OF GOODS EXPORTED FROM THE UNITED KINGDOM COMPARED WITH THE EXPORTS TO TURKEY [1]

1835

Articles		Quantity Exported		Value of Exports	
		Total	To Turkey	Total	To Turkey
Cotton, mfgrs. (Calico)	Yds.	256,606,641	17,033,138	£6,253,142	£485,334
Cotton Twist	Lbs.	83,214,198	1,575,400	5,706,589	89,404
Total Cotton Goods				22,128,304	1,062,780
Sugar, refined	Cwt.	349,370	30,267	852,487	83,762
Iron & Steel (excl. of ore)	Tons	199,006	8,734	1,643,741	58,964
Woolens, yarn & mfgrs.				6,840,511	41,498
Hardware & Cutlery	Cwt.	403,939	1,104	1,833,042	7,106
Tin Plates				367,055	7,089
Watches	No.	19,484	1,574	84,312	6,573
Linen, mfgrs.				3,208,777	5,324
Earthenware	No.	45,893,446	330,776	549,420	4,960
Copper (excl. of ore)	Cwt.	237,682	962	1,063,931	3,361
Silk Goods, total				973,785	3,291
Coal, Culm, Cinders	Tons	736,060	6,097	244,898	2,301
Apparel				269,627	2,045
Glassware, total				640,409	2,024
Tin, unwrought	Cwt.	7,765	451	32,289	1,895
Lead & Shot	Tons	11,081	56	195,143	1,002
Stationery				259,105	878
Machinery				197,742	402
Leather, wrought & unwrought	Lbs.	2,104,318	888	285,933	165
Military Stores				11,703	80

[1] Customs 9/22.

TABLE 4

DECLARED VALUE OF GOODS EXPORTED FROM THE UNITED KINGDOM COMPARED WITH THE EXPORTS TO TURKEY [1]

1840

ARTICLES		QUANTITY EXPORTED		VALUE OF EXPORTS	
		Total	To Turkey	Total	To Turkey
Cotton, mfgrs. (Calico)	Yds.	421,122,838	25,692,589	£7,491,974	£348,569
Cotton Twist & Yarn	Lbs.	118,470,223	3,272,805	7,101,308	152,774
Total Cotton Goods				24,668,618	895,888
Sugar, refined	Cwt.	235,178	33,376	440,892	63,608
Iron & Steel (excl. of ore)	Tons	268,327	7,010	2,524,858	56,646
Woolens, yarn & mfgrs.				5,327,853	25,587
Coal, Culm, Cinders	Tons	1,606,313	27,536	576,519	11,047
Hardware & Cutlery	Cwt.	299,899	1,613	1,349,137	8,404
Watches	No.	8,918	2,086	43,382	8,226
Earthenware	No.	50,533,949	652,315	573,184	8,180
Tin, unwrought	Cwt.	36,884	2,078	138,786	7,808
Tin Plates				336,529	6,295
Steam Engines				294,147	6,200
Mill Work				39,570	3,280
Machinery				188,102	2,772
Linen, mfgrs.				3,306,088	2,914
Apparel				444,457	2,475
Mathematical Instruments				36,986	2,347
Sal Amonica	Cwt.	5,607	878	13,236	2,101
Glassware, total				417,177	2,020
Coal Pitch & Tar	Bbls.	63,316	4,600	18,383	1,755
Copper goods (excl. of ore)	Cwt.	304,081	241	1,406,815	1,201
Stationery				282,402	995
Silk Goods, total				792,648	791
Lead & Shot	Tons	13,223	26	237,312	487
Leather, wrought and unwrought	Lbs.	2,404,067	324	320,912	33
Military Stores				3,038	15

[1] Customs 9/27 and Customs 8/51.

TABLE 5

DECLARED VALUE OF GOODS EXPORTED FROM THE UNITED KINGDOM COMPARED WITH THE EXPORTS TO TURKEY [1]

1845

ARTICLES		QUANTITY EXPORTED		VALUE OF EXPORTS	
		Total	To Turkey	Total	To Turkey
Cotton, mfgrs. (Calico)	Yds.	673,268,356	46,793,211	£9,518,396	£653,789
Cotton Twist	Lbs.	135,144,865	5,830,328	6,963,235	229,917
Total Cotton Goods		. . . .	. . . .	26,119,331	1,820,282
Woolens, mfgrs.		. . . .	. . . .	7,693,117	120,844
Iron & Steel (excl. of ore)	Tons	351,978	8,343	3,501,894	76,659
Coal, Culm, Cinders	Tons	2,531,281	56,765	973,635	24,434
Sugar, refined	Cwt.	273,775	13,397	472,946	21,379
Hardware & Cutlery	Cwt.	415,092	3,063	2,182,999	21,165
Linen, Mfgrs.		. . . .	. . . .	3,036,369	15,167
Earthenware	No.	67,362,497	937,981	824,381	13,358
Tin Plates		. . . .	. . . .	615,729	11,755
Machinery		. . . .	. . . .	580,789	9,342

Tin, unwrought	Cwt.	11,525	2,125	48,776	8,346
Watches	No.	16,311	1,659	79,257	8,040
Apparel				528,371	6,982
Plate, wrought of Silver	Oz.	219,754	17,169	98,011	5,297
Gunpowder	Lbs.	7,905,061	149,160	160,829	4,408
Painter's Colours				221,514	4,355
Glassware, total				357,421	3,130
Silk Goods, total				766,404	2,458
Sal Amonica	Cwt.	9,353	1,149	19,128	2,263
Jewellery				78,099	2,179
Stationery				280,108	2,142
Coal Pitch & Tar	Bbls.	54,694	4,590	15,907	976
Mathematical Instruments			30,709	817	
Saltpeter	Cwt.	29,948	449	43,461	639
Steam Engines				324,171	602
Military Stores				18,806	547
Copper (excl. of ore)	Cwt.	360,781	84	1,627,833	494
Lead & Shot	Tons	1,092	14	23,445	333
Leather, wrought & unwrought	Lbs.	2,473,762	1,154	351,476	249

¹ Customs 9/32 and Customs 8/61.

TABLE 6

DECLARED VALUE OF GOODS EXPORTED FROM THE UNITED KINGDOM COMPARED WITH THE EXPORTS TO TURKEY [1]

1850

ARTICLES		QUANTITY EXPORTED		VALUE OF EXPORTS	
		Total	To Turkey	Total	To Turkey
Cotton mfgrs. (Calico)	Yds.	757,979,632	31,124,932	£9,597,169	£472,226
Cotton Twist	Lbs.	131,370,368	2,384,075	6,383,703	80,758
Total Cotton Goods		. . . . . .	. . . . . .	28,257,401	1,975,060
Woolens, yarn & mfgrs.		. . . . . .	. . . . . .	8,588,690	143,379
Iron & Steel (excl. of ore)	Tons	783,423	15,332	5,350,056	93,052
Hardware & Cutlery	Cwt.	514,921	6,448	2,641,432	39,603
Coal, Culm, Cinders	Tons	3,351,880	86,692	1,284,223	32,750
Sugar, refined	Cwt.	209,147	16,119	344,498	29,109
Linen, mfgrs.		. . . . . .	. . . . . .	3,947,681	21,346
Tin, unwrought	Cwt.	31,761	4,804	124,798	19,183
Tin Plates		. . . . . .	. . . . . .	16,556	16,557
Earthenware	No.	75,939,818	1,174,015	999,458	14,705
Silk Goods, total		. . . . . .	. . . . . .	1,255,640	12,801
Steam Engines		. . . . . .	. . . . . .	423,977	10,610
Watches	No.	20,567	2,125	85,784	9,707
Apparel		. . . . . .	. . . . . .	652,879	6,424
Jewellery		. . . . . .	. . . . . .	102,899	6,095

Ordnance of Iron	Tons	2,532	290	34,222	5,700
Haberdashery & Millinery				1,470,301	5,523
Glassware, total				307,754	5,215
Stationery				408,380	4,855
Guns, muskets	No.	213,059	6,042	176,437	4,554
Gunpowder	Lbs.	8,501,274	143,630	207,819	4,001
Painter's Colours				248,493	3,953
Cabinet & Upholstery wares				102,283	3,643
Copper (excl. of ore)	Cwt.	426,153	723	1,851,495	3,562
Beer & Ale	Bbls.	182,479	966	558,792	3,533
Machinery & Mill work				618,189	3,488
Plate wrought of silver	Oz.	117,449	6,062	64,184	3,066
Umbrellas & parasols				82,587	2,263
Coal Pitch & Tar	Bbls.	75,692	7,814	21,617	2,111
Fuel	Tons	39,977	2,524	31,005	1,807
Apothecary Wares	Cwt.	80,257	211	363,142	1,475
Wooden house frames				6,565	1,358
Alum	Cwt.	55,877	2,815	23,439	1,307
Sal Amonica	Cwt.	7,885	711	13,412	1,159
Saltpeter	Cwt.	30,544	456	45,697	700
Mathematical Instruments				35,036	561
Leather, wrought & unwrought	Lbs.	5,257,563	3,801	484,905	347
Lead & Shot	Tons	1,750	8	36,534	179
Military Stores				11,109	12

¹ Customs 9/39–40 and Customs 8/71.

TABLE 7

Declared Value of Goods Exported from the United Kingdom Compared with the Exports to Turkey [1]

1855

Articles		Quantity Exported		Value of Exports	
		Total	To Turkey	Total	To Turkey
Cotton mfgrs. (Calico)	Yds.	1,230,827,458	132,605,467	£14,259,328	£1,688,095
Cotton Twist	Lbs.	105,493,598	8,446,792	7,200,395	313,946
Total Cotton Goods				34,763,792	3,722,983
Coal, Culm, Cinders	Tons	4,986,902	462,549	2,446,341	230,585
Iron & Steel (excl. of ore)	Tons	1,092,667	20,439	9,485,030	187,017
Woolens, yarn & mfgrs.				9,599,463	142,772
Provisions (not described)				332,052	116,823
Beer & Ale	Bbls.	384,414	25,969	1,398,885	95,575
Linen, mfgrs.				5,047,164	94,354
Pork, salted	Bbls.	37,076	15,947	174,753	75,691
Telegraph wires				163,737	71,000
Hay	Tons	21,311	9,208	132,243	65,609
Wooden house frames				157,008	60,984
Apparel				989,207	57,109
Hardware & Cutlery	Cwt.	530,958	8,330	2,959,610	50,678
Butter	Cwt.	120,098	10,308	570,506	47,804
Corn, Grain, total				1,002,633	47,217
Stationery				593,206	36,885
Glassware, total				507,332	36,066
Sugar, refined	Cwt.	43,881	14,149	99,916	33,708
Corn, oats	Qts.	152,769	15,853	255,333	31,492

Item	Unit				
Tin plates	Cwt.	....	....	1,110,843	28,900
Tin, unwrought	Cwt.	26,826	5,006	151,505	28,251
Copper (excl. of ore)	Cwt.	333,166	4,047	2,004,122	24,319
Spirits	Gals.	3,762,087	95,907	829,101	24,271
Earthenware	No.	72,286,191	1,622,422	983,834	21,512
Gunpowder	Lbs.	8,546,430	537,500	251,763	19,344
Apothecary Wares	Cwt.	98,618	3,432	492,593	18,660
Machinery & Mill Work	....	....	....	1,359,796	15,395
Ordnance of Iron	Tons	3,252	1,018	50,314	14,737
Haberdashery & Millinery	....	....	....	2,682,537	14,110
Bread & Biscuit	Cwt.	42,731	12,278	70,202	13,625
Corn, wheat flour	Cwt.	71,999	9,008	96,070	13,047
Pickles & Sauces	....	....	....	325,731	11,169
Slops & Negro clothing	....	....	....	297,167	....
Soap	Cwt.	204,277	8,232	267,907	10,842
Silk Goods, total	....	....	....	1,524,343	10,376
Fuel	Tons	84,860	15,154	58,985	8,821
Cabinet & Upholstery Wares	....	....	....	178,299	8,679
Beef, salted	Bbls.	6,117	1,396	35,484	7,949
Naval stores	....	....	....	23,203	7,785
Painter's Colours	....	....	....	314,473	7,777
Bags	Doz.	407,443	13,696	233,101	7,303
Zinc, unwrought	Cwt.	36,021	4,489	51,160	6,575
Alkali soda	Cwt.	1,045,004	13,010	395,959	5,667
Tarpaulins	....	....	....	12,977	5,287
Cordage & Cables	Cwt.	99,315	1,549	261,117	4,915
Leather, wrought and unwrought	Lbs.	6,974,580	34,832	915,217	4,771
Bacon & Hams	Cwt.	40,012	1,048	149,370	4,460
Cheese	Cwt.	22,318	1,020	88,142	4,032

TABLE 7 (Continued)

Articles		Quantity Exported		Value of Exports	
		Total	To Turkey	Total	To Turkey
Saltpeter	Cwt.	52,649	2,060	81,062	4,006
Candles, Stearine	Lbs.	4,110,513	69,420	206,242	3,631
Saddlery & Harness				226,659	3,534
Brass, other than wire	Cwt.	12,859	238	83,384	3,483
Watches	No.	21,709	453	97,321	3,476
Steam Engines				872,110	3,330
Books, printed	Cwt.	24,844	241	370,922	3,266
Wood, boards & planks	Loads	4,555	1,394	16,005	3,096
Alum	Cwt.	57,698	7,249	26,633	2,973
Potatoes	Cwt.	51,014	10,249	12,911	2,937
Umbrellas & parasols				92,469	2,786
Confectionary	Cwt.	16,464	492	80,863	2,617
Sal Amonica	Cwt.	14,510	1,388	19,231	2,617
Plate wrought of Silver	Oz.	189,667	5,336	89,062	2,506
Sheathing felt & paper	Cwt.	5,875	2,383	7,161	2,342

Tobacco, mfged. in U.K.	Lbs.	19,437	10,362	4,609	2,118
Caoutchouc, mfgrs. of	Cwt.	……	1,874	65,982	2,091
Lead, white	Cwt.	60,173	28,824	76,243	2,089
Oil Cloth	Yds.	515,944	……	41,507	2,036
Felt	……	……	……	15,164	1,745
Jewellery	……	……	2,200	197,855	1,613
Brimstone	Cwt.	19,752	218	10,217	1,500
Twine	Cwt.	10,910	1,366	67,126	1,497
Fish, Red Herrings	Bbls.	29,706	……	31,209	1,475
Brushes & Brooms	……	……	8,914	26,307	1,432
Coal Pitch & Tar	Cwt.	67,840	9,214	16,806	1,420
Soda Water	Gals.	28,929	333	3,620	1,304
Corn, peas	Qrs.	5,400	104	17,667	1,293
Oil Cake	Tons	755	1,308	9,385	1,250
Pearl barley	Cwt.	12,134	688	12,157	1,066
Lead, red	Cwt.	35,637	……	43,850	1,052
Gunflints	No.	14,070,619	2,633,000	3,395	1,009
Lead & Shot	Tons	1,681	28	44,447	813
Mathematical Instruments	……	……	……	61,730	624
Bricks	No.	19,608,272	156,167	60,928	597
Military Stores	……	……	……	20,190	438

¹ Customs 9/49-50 and Customs 8/81.

TABLE 8

Official Value of Goods Imported Into the United Kingdom Compared with the Imports from Turkey [1]

1825

Articles		Quantity Imported		Value of Imports	
		Total	From Turkey	Total	From Turkey
Wool, cotton	Lbs.	226,052,135	18,938,246	£7,405,618	£611,537
Madder Root	Cwt.	46,414	21,910	410,849	198,231
Silk, raw	Lbs.	1,829,379	341,107	1,033,976	193,293
Raisins	Cwt.	83,266	76,673	58,282	53,671
Opium	Lbs.	122,754	115,124	16,878	15,829
Wool, sheep & lamb's	Lbs.	63,796,186	513,414	1,436,510	12,835
Oil, Otto of Roses	Lbs.	768	553	12,296	8,848
Yarn, Camel & Mohair	Lbs.	68,199	62,538	9,377	8,598
Valonia	Cwt.	51,966	28,640	12,991	7,160
Galls	Cwt.	7,541	3,376	13,199	5,734
Wool, mfgrs. (Carpets)	No.	1,963	1,938	5,643	5,571
Olive Oil	Tons	4,449	101	208,639	2,854
Yarn, cotton	Lbs.	67,228	67,174	2,521	2,519
Sponges	Lbs.	58,802	25,446	2,994	1,272
Hair, goat's	Lbs.	104,588	39,003	1,996	731
Hides, wet	Cwt.	174,353	93	493,766	281

[1] Customs 4/20 and Customs 5/14.

TABLE 9

Official Value of Goods Imported Into the United Kingdom Compared with the Imports from Turkey [1]

1830

Articles		Quantity Imported		Value of Imports	
		Total	From Turkey	Total	From Turkey
Silk, raw	Lbs.	3,440,638	463,307	£1,599,534	£262,540
Madder Root	Cwt.	37,074	27,183	333,611	255,023
Valonia	Cwt.	150,129	114,682	51,868	43,005
Raisins	Cwt.	108,514	46,198	74,386	31,598
Opium	Lbs.	209,076	192,136	28,751	26,418
Wool, sheep & lamb's	Lbs.	32,302,172	......	882,384	12,898
Wool, mfgrs. (Carpets)	No.			62,870	11,776
Figs	Cwt.	20,407	18,801	12,803	11,401
Wool, cotton	Lbs.	247,999,087	353,077	8,280,994	10,591
Oil, Otto of Roses	Lbs.	700	661	11,202	10,442
Yarn, Camel & Mohair	Lbs.	79,489	75,946	10,929	8,491
Yellow Berries	Cwt.	2,970	2,873	8,782	6,647
Hides, wet	Cwt.	176,851	2,215	507,533	5,734
Hair, goat's	Lbs.	315,000	305,864	5,906	4,604
Emery Stones	Cwt.	11,511	11,511	4,604	4,195
Yarn, cotton	Lbs.	195,396	111,884	14,971	3,145
Currants	Cwt.	113,891	2,996	119,584	2,862
Olive Oil	Gals.	2,791,057	21,467	374,956	1,903
Boxwood	Tons	335	237	2,716	1,513
Sponges	Lbs.		30,265	......	1,060
Gum, Fragacynth	Lbs.	26,449	21,200	1,322	451
Galls	Cwt.	1,967	258	3,684	

[1] Customs 4/25 and Customs 5/19.

TABLE 10

Official Value of Goods Imported Into the United Kingdom Compared with the Imports from Turkey [1]

1835

Articles		Quantity Imported		Value of Imports	
		Total	From Turkey	Total	From Turkey
Silk, raw	Lbs.	3,737,480	673,254	£1,780,752	£381,510
Madder Root	Cwt.	66,323	24,102	432,874	201,768
Valonia	Cwt.	182,081	149,141	69,114	59,815
Wool, sheep & lamb's	Lbs.	42,168,142	1,281,839	1,136,722	33,857
Raisins	Cwt.	168,893	47,559	119,625	32,591
Wool, cotton	Lbs.	320,716,021	557,949	10,710,357	18,017
Oil, Otto of Roses	Lbs.	1,926	1,120	30,825	17,922
Yarn, Camel & Mohair	Lbs.	92,729	91,497	12,750	12,580
Wool, mfgrs. (Carpets)	No.	.....	.....	96,935	12,155
Hides, wet	Cwt.	136,393	3,731	398,661	11,193
Yellow Berries	Cwt.	5,050	3,762	14,848	10,987
Figs	Cwt.	18,773	17,269	11,904	10,934
Opium	Lbs.	85,840	77,985	11,790	10,723
Galls	Cwt.	5,145	5,052	9,010	8,842
Hair, goat's	Lbs.	542,617	448,644	10,174	8,412
Hides, dry	Cwt.	135,350	2,187	408,070	6,561
Emery Stones	Tons	680	680	5,443	5,443
Olive Oil	Gals.	606,166	34,789	81,884	4,726
Sponges	Lbs.	47,557	35,046	2,516	1,752
Gum, Fragacynth	Cwt.	307	307	1,724	1,724
Yarn, Cotton	Lbs.	117,826	31,090	5,805	1,165
Currants	Cwt.	176,062	309	185,352	324
Boxwood	Tons	996	863	8,194	136

[1] Customs 4/30 and Customs 5/24.

TABLE 11

Official Value of Goods Imported Into the United Kingdom Compared with the Imports from Turkey [1]

1840

Articles		Quantity Imported		Value of Imports	
		Total	From Turkey	Total	From Turkey
Madder Root	Cwt.	109,414	66,528	£817,204	£562,017
Silk, raw	Lbs.	3,759,016	721,738	1,858,579	408,984
Valonia	Cwt.	163,983	143,094	54,306	48,533
Raisins	Cwt.	224,774	54,333	157,474	37,144
Wool, mfgrs. (Carpets)	No.	......	......	137,690	21,033
Hair, goat's	Lbs.	989,257	938,452	18,548	17,595
Wool, sheep & lamb's	Lbs.	49,393,967	655,964	1,327,807	16,399
Wool, cotton	Lbs.	514,978,471	463,978	17,070,383	14,982
Yellow Berries	Cwt.	6,232	5,049	18,204	14,657
Oil, Otto of Roses	Lbs.	825	774	13,207	12,389
Bones of Animals	......	......	......	262,334	11,184
Figs	Cwt.	36,063	17,863	18,988	11,181
Boxwood	Tons	1,609	1,356	12,959	10,880
Emery Stones	Tons	1,131	1,131	9,053	9,053
Corn, wheat	Qrs.	1,985,188	4,802	3,247,491	7,923

TABLE 11 (*Continued*)

Articles		Quantity Imported		Value of Imports	
		Total	From Turkey	Total	From Turkey
Opium	Lbs.	77,872	50,746	10,964	7,234
Saltpetre	Cwt.	304,817	6,554	188,463	3,932
Galls	Cwt.	6,446	2,229	11,310	3,901
Scammony	Lbs.	16,410	15,693	3,692	3,530
Olive Oil	Gals.	2,213,435	24,936	297,402	3,324
Sponges	Lbs.	68,878	48,186	3,832	2,459
Yarn, cotton	Lbs.	424,635	42,062	16,105	1,577
Gum, Fragacynth	Cwt.	318	259	1,784	1,453
Currants	Cwt.	221,118	343	231,733	360
Yarn, Camel & Mohair	Lbs.	2,630	1,251	361	172
Hides, wet	Cwt.	217,309	55	649,074	165
Hides, dry	Cwt.	63,966	47	193,310	141
Tobacco, un-mfg.	Lbs.	......	2,118	......	19

¹ Customs 4/35 and Customs 5/29.

TABLE 12

Official Value of Goods Imported Into the United Kingdom Compared with the Imports from Turkey [1]

1845

Articles		Quantity Imported		Value of Imports	
		Total	From Turkey	Total	From Turkey
Madder Root	Cwt.	147,590	66,755	£1,217,442	£654,203
Silk, raw	Lbs.	4,354,696	439,422	1,885,154	249,005
Valonia	Tons	19,077	15,354	124,442	101,666
Raisins	Cwt.	301,109	87,788	211,928	60,206
Wool, sheep & lamb's ...	Lbs.	75,551,950	1,639,450	2,011,737	52,727
Olive Oil	Tuns	12,315	1,461	422,134	50,218
Opium	Lbs.	259,644	244,644	35,701	33,638
Yellow Berries	Cwt.	9,372	8,681	27,983	25,923
Figs	Cwt.	47,357	33,900	29,814	21,229
Oil, Otto of Roses	Lbs.	1,253	1,150	20,062	18,423
Wool, mfgrs. (Carpets) .	No.	....	....	195,033	17,149
Bones of Animals	Tons	37,410	3,504	177,701	16,647
Corn, barley	Qrs.	364,720	19,117	305,872	16,261
Tallow	Cwt.	1,113,154	14,802	1,202,856	15,542
Seeds, Millet	Cwt.	16,410	15,419	13,129	12,335
Boxwood	Tons	1,375	1,327	11,358	10,967
Stones, in lumps	Tons	3,048	1,711	17,835	10,013

TABLE 12 (Continued)

ARTICLES		QUANTITY IMPORTED		VALUE OF IMPORTS	
		Total	From Turkey	Total	From Turkey
Corn, wheat	Qrs.	820,170	5,842	1,322,524	9,639
Corn, Indian	Qrs.	51,960	11,551	30,292	9,255
Seeds, Linseed, Flaxseed	Qrs.	656,792	6,588	675,276	6,148
Sponges	Lbs.	290,026	122,998	14,501	5,649
Galls	Cwt.	8,195	2,715	16,627	4,758
Gum, Fragacynth	Cwt.	905	759	5,069	4,254
Wool, cotton	Cwt.	1,543,722	1,114	4,256,449	4,138
Yarn, camel & Mohair	Lbs.	26,295	26,102	3,615	3,589
Currants	Cwt.	352,705	3,387	369,201	3,556
Scammony	Lbs.	12,992	10,811	2,923	2,432
Leeches	No.	....	18,979	15,551	2,298
Skins, goat's	No.	329,623	18,979	27,471	1,581
Yarn, cotton	Lbs.	664,259	34,329	25,530	1,431
Tobacco	Lbs.	32,944,017	10,911	308,972	102
Hides, dry	Cwt.	181,758	9	580,614	28

[1] Customs 4/40 and Customs 5/34.

TABLE 13

Official Value of Goods Imported Into the United Kingdom Compared with the Imports from Turkey [1]

1850

Articles		Quantity Imported		Value of Imports	
		Total	From Turkey	Total	From Turkey
Madder root	Cwt.	161,637	109,312	£1,316,343	£922,856
Silk, raw	Lbs.	4,942,407	781,347	2,132,466	442,763
Corn, Indian	Qrs.	1,273,218	185,877	1,859,954	371,566
Corn, wheat	Qrs.	3,716,007	52,319	6,270,026	97,622
Valonia	Tons	12,526	10,822	75,132	66,613
Olive Oil	Tuns	20,783	1,788	710,415	61,285
Oil, Otto of Roses	Lbs.	1,847	1,592	29,567	25,480
Yellow Berries	Cwt.	8,290	7,920	23,926	22,816
Boxwood	Tons	2,463	2,360	20,030	19,192
Raisins	Cwt.	275,193	25,014	193,989	17,102
Figs	Cwt.	33,828	25,795	21,392	16,165
Opium	Lbs.	126,101	115,893	17,518	16,114
Stones, in lumps	Tons	3,403	2,099	20,012	12,377
Sponges	Lbs.	356,508	215,562	17,973	10,778
Wool, sheep & lamb's	Lbs.	72,674,483	416,375	1,912,029	10,718
Wool, mfgrs.				145,831	9,725
Galls	Cwt.	13,691	5,147	23,989	9,007
Seeds, not described	Qrs.	45,919	5,891	53,501	6,872

TABLE 13 (*Continued*)

Articles		Quantity Imported		Value of Imports	
		Total	From Turkey	Total	From Turkey
Corn, barley	Qrs.	1,035,902	6,245	873,943	5,464
Copper, old	Tons	431	72	32,307	5,400
Leeches	....	......	......	26,937	5,269
Sesamum	Qrs.	8,967	4,012	10,461	4,680
Seeds, Linseed, Flaxseed	Qrs.	608,984	4,902	658,584	4,575
Wool, cotton	Cwt.	5,924,793	1,300	21,531,806	4,340
Gum, Fragacynth	Cwt.	525	457	2,943	2,527
Nuts, small	Bus.	199,277	20,543	24,152	2,482
Bones of Animals	Tons	27,198	481	129,191	2,285
Yarn, cotton	Lbs.	905,966	52,047	34,236	1,951
Scammony	Lbs.	10,344	8,689	2,327	1,955
Currants	Cwt.	429,606	1,692	449,488	1,880
Tobacco	Lbs.	19,758,559	123,863	185,407	1,161
Seeds, Millet	Cwt.	92,188	1,166	73,750	993
Skins, goat's	No.	479,541	3,952	39,952	329
Yarn, Camel & Mohair	Lbs.	2,356	1,639	323	225

[1] Customs 4/45 and Customs 5/42–43.

TABLE 14

Official Value of Goods Imported Into the United Kingdom Compared with the Imports from Turkey [1]

1855

Articles		Quantity Imported		Value of Imports	
		Total	From Turkey	Total	From Turkey
Madder Root	Cwt.	175,046	93,775	£1,534,757	£862,069
Corn, wheat	Qrs.	2,643,610	80,687	4,326,753	147,498
Corn, Indian	Qrs.	1,209,507	64,325	1,428,433	112,375
Seeds, Linseed, Flaxseed	Qrs.	740,056	102,108	722,236	100,089
Silk, raw	Lbs.	6,618,862	153,892	2,686,515	87,205
Raisins	Cwt.	301,283	93,301	210,232	63,757
Valonia	Tons	10,838	8,753	62,053	51,628
Olive Oil	Tuns	25,449	1,221	862,782	41,489
Stones, in lumps	Tons	6,765	4,193	40,508	24,657
Figs	Cwt.	44,724	38,238	28,120	23,900
Seeds, Millet	Cwt.	47,093	22,684	37,675	18,101
Tallow	Cwt.	886,228	17,239	935,474	18,101
Sponges	Lbs.	471,871	309,445	23,601	15,472
Wool, sheep & lamb's	Lbs.	97,853,739	604,123	2,497,004	15,103
Oil, Otto of Roses	Lbs.	1,343	942	21,495	15,087
Wool, mfgrs.	Sq. Yds.	43,329	36,560	17,331	14,624
Copper, total (excl. of ore)	Tons	9,480	151	932,099	14,394
Opium	Lbs.	112,865	102,373	15,519	14,076
Yellow Berries	Cwt.	4,101	4,021	12,303	12,053
Boxwood	Tons	1,321	1,134	10,576	9,074

TABLE 14 (*Continued*)

Articles		Quantity Imported		Value of Imports	
		Total	From Turkey	Total	From Turkey
Copper, hammered	Tons	4,419	63	530,298	7,602
Liquorice paste	Cwt.	2,939	1,596	13,284	7,448
Bones of Animals	Tons	65,055	1,502	309,011	7,134
Brass, old	Tons	286	67	25,792	6,030
Copper plate & coin	Tons	269	63	24,284	5,718
Tobacco	Lbs.	21,479,906	509,445	201,514	5,526
Galls	Cwt.	11,341	3,055	21,837	5,346
Corn, barley	Qrs.	348,109	6,411	283,880	5,111
Nuts, small	Bus.	256,396	31,122	31,021	3,761
Copper, old	Tons	1,168	34	87,530	2,560
Copper, unwrought	Tons	3,624	25	289,987	2,074
Currants	Cwt.	163,728	1,466	171,914	1,540
Scammony	Lbs.	9,242	6,509	2,079	1,464
Gum, Fragacynth	Cwt.	300	239	1,680	1,343
Chromate of Iron	Tons	527	167	4,217	1,342
Hides, dry	Cwt.	188,844	280	566,924	840
Skins, goat's	No.	261,401	8,494	21,783	708
Wool, cotton	Cwt.	7,962,071	57	28,587,691	206
Yarn, cotton	Lbs.	1,029,237	3,314	38,745	124

[1] Customs 4/45 and Customs 5/42–43.

APPENDIX III

RESCHID PASHA'S MEMORANDUM OF AUGUST 12, 1839

Le sol de l'empire ottoman est extrêmement riche et fertile. Sa position géographique des plus heureuses, est surtout favorable au commerce. Ses populations par leur nature intelligente sont aptes à tous.

Lorsque ces populations s'attacheront au système nouveau, réclamé désormais par la nécessité, et d'où découlent de sages réformes et la civilisation, nul doute que dans un temps très court, elles n'en obtiennent les résultats les plus salutaires et les plus nombreux.

La mauvaise direction imprimée précédemment aux affaires intérieures de la Sublime Porte, a été pour ses sujets une calamité véritable. Depuis treize ou quatorze ans, loin qu'on vît naître le moindre bien de tout ce qu'on avait décoré pompeusement du nom de réforme, ces prétendues réformes n'ont fait que venir ajouter de nouvelles vexations aux tyrannies du passé. Il serait impossible de faire connaître dans toute son étendue l'excès du mécontentement général dans tout l'empire.

Le mécontentement du peuple n'est pas né, comme on le croit en Europe, de son peu de disposition à la civilisation ou de toute autre cause provenant du fanatisme, mais seulement de tous les maux d'une tyrannie insupportable, tandis que de l'intérieur et du dehors, des intrigues de toutes sortes venaient empêcher l'administration supérieure de rien entreprendre pour le bien du pays.

Cependant, alors que les institutions nouvelles seraient conduites avec sagesse et discernement, chacune éprouverait les avantages réels d'un système immuablement établi; à mesure que la tyrannie diminuerait, l'affection pour le gouvernement s'accroîtrait, les populations se rallieraient de toutes les forces de leur cœur à des innovations utiles et bienfaisantes. De là, par l'impulsion seule de l'amour des peuples, les progrès rapides d'une véritable réforme, et par suite, la régénération inévitable des forces de l'empire ottoman.

Jusqu'à l'époque de leur destruction, les Janissaires ont été la cause de la mauvaise direction des affaires publiques. Mais depuis, l'action du Gouvernement n'a été entravée en aucune manière par le peuple. Si les nouvelles institutions dont le Sultan Mahmoud s'est montré partisan ont rencontré quelquefois des difficultés; si presque toutes elles sont restées à leur point de départ, sans faire un pas en avant, la cause ne doit être attribuée qu'à l'orgueil du souverain que les a fait consister seulement dans de vaines démonstrations dont aucun fruit salutaire ne pouvait résulter pour le peuple.

Plus tard, les affaires d'Égypte au point ou elles étaient arrivées, ne devaient pas manquer d'être aussi une cause nouvelle de ruine pour l'empire. En présence d'obstacles aussi nombreux, sa mérite ne pouvait être marquée par aucun progrès; et lorsque son affaiblissement que chaque jour voyait s'accroître, provenait en grande partie des différens qui existent avec l'Égypte, ces différens prenant exclusivement leur source dans la haine réciproque et personnelle, du Sultan Mahmoud et de Mehmed Ali, aujourd'hui que l'un d'eux a cessé de vivre, l'autre abandonnant les ressentimens du passé, ne devra plus songer qu'au bonheur de la nation et à la prospérité de sa patrie. Désormais il semble donc que la réconciliation de la Sublime Porte avec l'Égypte doit être très facile.

Mais la question d'Égypte n'est en elle-même qu'un accident. Lui trouver une solution ne suffirait pas pour obtenir un résultat satisfaisant et définitif. Tant qu'il ne sera pas porté remède au véritable danger, au mal ancien de la Sublime Porte, il est impossible qu'elle puisse parvenir a se régénérer; un accident d'ailleurs cesse aujourd'hui, mille autres peuvent évidemment naître demain. Ce que nous devons considérer avant tout, c'est cet ancien mal de la Sublime Porte pour en faire connaître l'histoire, il ne faudrait rien moins que des volumes.

Mais pour l'intelligence supérieure de certains hommes il suffira de quelques mots qui donneront la mesure d'un tableau plus complet.

Les puissances de l'Europe savent à quel degré était progressivement parvenue la tyrannie des Empereurs Ottomans quand, depuis la destruction des Janissaires, le Sultan Mahmoud ne voulut désormais rien entendre, il ne [voulut] plus prendre conseil que de lui-même. Il serait injuste de lui refuser dans les grandes occasions de la force et de l'énergie, mais il n'avait aucunement les connaissances à l'administration des affaires; Son esprit manquait de discernement. Flatter son orgueil et sa vanité, c'était s'assurer son approbation et, par contre, si quelques courageux amis de la vérité croyaient devoir ouvrir un avis contraire au sien, la mort ou la confiscation était le prix de leur zèle audacieux. Le Sultan savait à la fois se débarrasser ainsi de leurs observations, et par l'effroi de semblables rigueurs, rendre désormais toutes les bouches muettes.

Telle était de plus l'instabilité de son opinion et de son esprit qu'on l'a vu déposer un ancien Ministre des affaires étrangères Saïda Effendi, le plus honnête homme de son empire, puis le faire empoisonner, et cela, pour avoir été d'un sentiment opposé à la guerre contre la Russie; tandis que son successeur Pertew Pacha qui souscrivit à cette guerre, quoiqu'il en vît bien tous les dangers, ne put échapper au cruel ressentiment dont les suites fatales furent différées, mais dont il devint enfin la triste victime sept à huit ans plus tard.

Les hommes dont la flatterie entourait le Sultan, et qui connaissaient le secret de son caractère, employaient, lorsque quelqu'un n'était pas des leurs, ou ne convenait par à leur vue, la manœuvre facile pour le perdre, de déverser sur lui la calomnie, tel était pour eux contre tout rival, le moyen certain de s'en défaire par le poison ou par une mort ostensible.

Le malheureux procédé n'était pas moins efficacement pratiqué pas les ennemis du départ qui désiraient l'affaiblissement de l'empire.

Quand un Ministre s'appliquait au bien du pays, les agents de l'étranger savaient aussitôt s'introduire habilement auprès de chacun de ces rivaux, pour prêter tout l'appui de leur force à sa jalousie, en même temps que par leurs intrigues multipliés auprès du Sultan ils parvenaient aisément à introduire mille funestes soupçons dans son âme.

Il est à croire que la mort du Sultan Mahmoud apportera du soulagement à cet ancien mal du Gouvernement de la Sublime Porte, mais la jalousie des grands de l'empire n'est pas éteinte. Par son jeune âge et son inexpérience, le nouvel empereur sera plus facilement accessible aux machinations de l'intérieur et du dehors, et l'on peut aussi redouter que sous son règne le mal ne devienne plus grand encore que dans celui de son père.

Il ne faut donc regarder l'état présent de la Sublime Porte que comme une crise extrêmement dangereuse. Si l'on se refusait à reconnaître l'imminence du péril pour ne s'occuper que de la pacification avec l'Égypte, en même temps que des seules questions de l'intégrité et de l'indépendance de l'empire, on manquerait le but qu'on se propose, c'est à dire que les puissances qui veulent le maintien de l'empire, ne verraient leur désir que très imparfaitement accompli, et qu'en résultat, tout ce qui serait ainsi tenté pour conjurer l'orage, ne ferait que retarder de bien peu son explosion.

Mais, dira-t-on peut-être, le remède à ce mal ne sauroit être apporté sans une sorte d'invasion sur le terrain de l'administration intérieure de la Sublime Porte, une semblable conduite serait contraire aux droits respectifs des nations; d'ailleurs la soumission aveugle des musulmans aux lois du Coran, et leur fanatisme reconnu, ne manqueraient pas de leur faire repousser toutes propositions dictées par les puissances Européennes.

Pour répondre à cette objection, il suffirait de demander si cette invasion sur les droits respectifs des nations, aurait pour but aucune action nuisible à un peuple, et si lorsque sa conversation serait reclamée par l'équilibre de l'Europe, il peut y avoir aucun mal et aucun inconvénient à s'attacher à tout ce qui doit faire la force et la prospérité de ce peuple, dût-on n'y parvenir sans cependant dépasser de certaines limites qu'en s'immisçant à son administration intérieure.

De plus, les propositions qui lui seraient faites ne venant pas d'une seule nation, mais bien de l'alliance de toutes les grandes puissances; par la suite, ce cas exceptionnel ne pourrait servir ni de prétexte ni d'antécédent à aucune d'entre elles pour s'ingérer seule dans les affaires intérieures de la Sublime Porte.

Le jeune âge du Sultan permet aux puissances amies de lui montrer la route à suivre; leur conduite à cet égard ne saurait être attribuée qu'à leur affection et à la sincérité de leur sentimens, le fanatisme de la nation musulmane n'est plus ce qu'il était, la force des Ulémas a cessé d'être la même, et les moyens à prendre pour remédier à l'ancien mal présentement signalé ne portent aucune atteinte aux lois du Coran. Ces moyens qui causeraient évidemment une amélioration sensible dans la position de tous, présenteraient aux hommes actuellement à la tête des affaires une occasion de gagner la bienveillance des puissances Européennes. Dans la pensée de s'en faire bien venir, ils s'empresseraient, on n'en peut douter, d'accepter sans difficultés toutes propositions faites par elles.

Dans ces derniers temps, lors de la question Grecque, et de plusieurs autres questions de ce genre, la Sublime Porte s'était retranchée, pour motiver ses refus et sa résistance derrière les lois du Coran, mais en réalité cette résistance ne s'appuyait véritablement sur aucun passage du livre saint; seulement, comme les propositions adressées au Sultan Mahmoud étaient opposées à sa volonté il invoquait la religion pour prétexte de ses refus, tandis qu'au contraire, il laissait constamment la loi du prophète en oubli, toutes les fois qu'il s'agissait pour lui d'obéir à ses penchans.

Tel est le véritable état des choses en Turquie, que toute disposition nouvelle adaptée par la Sublime Porte dans le but d'offrir des avantages réels au peuple, est certain d'obtenir l'assentiment général le plus complet. S'il est des contrées où les institutions nouvelles ont trouvé de la résistance, c'est qu'elles ne présentaient aux habitants la perspective d'aucun bien. La Bosnie, l'Albanie et le Curdistan, pays qui ne reconnaissent pas facilement le gouvernement tyrannique de la Porte, ont montré l'opposition du fanatisme à ces mêmes institutions, mais cette aversion contre elle venait surtout de la crainte qu'elles ne fussent plus tard l'origine d'une nouvelle source de persécution.

Que si les propositions à faire au Divan paraissaient se rattacher d'après le nom généralement reçu, à ce qu'on appelle des libertés, il n'y aurait point à se méprendre, et cela ne saurait assurément donner motif à aucune objection de la part des puissances dont les gouvernements sont absolus, car il ne s'agirait nullement d'obtenir des libertés, mais uniquement de la vie et la fortune. Les sûretés générales, consacrées déjà par les lois civiles et religieuses de l'empire, lois dont on ne ferait que conseiller à l'administration intérieure de la Sublime Porte, la salutaire exécution.

Verser le sang des hommes et les dépouiller de leur bien, sans autre motif que la haine ou la vengeance est un crime que ne saurait tolérer aucune loi des Etats absolus de l'Europe. Il ne saurait convenir à aucune nation, à aucun gouvernement de refuser son concours et son appui à une question toute d'humanité.

Que parmi les puissances il [vînt] à s'en recontrer une dont l'intérêt serait l'affaiblissement de l'empire ottoman, en présence de la solide alliance des peuples; l'humanité, la justice et la raison debout devant elle; aucune objection, ouvertement avancée lui serait impossible. Et de plus, lorsque, malgré la considération, si forte du voisinage, l'Autriche et la Russie, quelqu'en soit d'ailleurs le motif, permettent à la Valachie, à la Moldavie et à la Servie, d'adopter une constitution, aucune puissance saurait elle jamais vouloir empêcher que les populations musulmans obtiennent rien que de simples sûretés pour leur vie et pour leur fortune, c'est ce qu'on ne saurait jamais croire. Ainsi nul obstacle ne se rencontrerait au dehors contre les propositions qui peuvent être faites au Divan par l'Europe.

Les populations dont le coeur est ulcéré par la souffrance, appellent de tous leurs vœux cette première de toutes les améliorations; aussitôt que les puissances auraient seulement laissé entrevoir leur généreuse attention, les chefs du gouvernement, appréciant pour eux-mêmes toute l'importance d'une semblable conquête s'empresseraient de compléter des lois protectrices, dont le bienfait s'étendrait aux chrétiens sujets de la Sublime Porte qui trouveraient dans cette œuvre de justice l'élément le plus puissant de sa régénération.

Ce point obtenu, tout deviendrait facile, et comme pour assurer à la Sublime Porte son indépendance et l'intégrité de son territoire, il serait indispensable de l'appeler à la participation des droits politiques de l'Europe. Lorsqu'on lui soumettrait le proposition dont il est ici question, il faudrait alléguer toutes les considérations qui se rattachent à la jeunesse du Sultan, et la nécessité pour le Divan, placée sous le droit qui régit les puissances Européennes, d'adopter cette loi sacrée chez elles, de ne pas tuer les citoyens, et de ne pas les dépouiller de leur fortune, contrairement à la justice, ainsi que le préscrit le

Coran lui-même; de telle sorte que si un homme avait commis un crime qui mérite la mort, il dût être jugé publiquement devant les tribunaux, d'après les lois religieuses et civiles, les lois anciennes et celles nouvellement créées en cette occasion sans que l'accusé eût rien autre chose à redouter que la sentence de son jugement.

Mais s'il arrive que la politique des puissances dût recontrer dans l'exécution de semblables projets des difficultés et des inconveniens qui les empêchent de les mettre en œuvre, qu'alors au moins, elles adressant au Divan, par l'entremise de leurs ambassadeurs à Constantinople, des conseils qui, sans sortir d'une certaine limite, ne seraient cependant pas que de vaines représentations, des conseils non moins impérieusement réclamés par toutes les plus hautes et les plus utiles considérations, que par la voix et les cris de l'humanité.

Il faudrait dire à la Porte que, quand les populations si capables de ces provinces restent ainsi arriérées; que quand ces Pachas qui acquièrent au dehors la force, cessent du lui obéir; que quand la Valachie, la Moldavie, la Servie, ont toutes adopté divers gouvernements à part; que quand la Grèce est devenue indépendante, la cause en est au manque de sécurité de ses sujets pour leur vie et pour leur fortune: qu'au moment où elle est descendue à un si grand degré de faiblesse, si elle persiste dans des erreurs si funestes, son mal fera de rapides progrès: que les puissances qui veulent le maintien et la conservation de l'empire ottoman, désormais découragées et sans espoir, trouveront forcément dans ces fautes une excuse pour ne plus lui accorder le soutien de leur amitié: qu'au contraire, si la Porte suit désormais une meilleure route, si elle place la sûreté des personnes et des fortunes sous la garantie de sages règlements et des lois fidèlement exécutées en délivrant complètement sa population au juge de la tyrannie; qu'en retour de cette conduite, le secours des puissances ne lui faillira pas; que bien que depuis une certaine époque, la Sublime Porte se soit abstenue de toute exécution publique et avérée, qu'elle n'en a pas moins fait périr en secret de nombreuses victimes; tandis que ces Pachas dans les provinces n'ont cessé de même de verser de sang, toutes choses, qui ne sont point ignorées de l'Europe; que l'Europe sait comment Saïda Effendi a été empoisonné; comment il a été mis fin aux jours de Radandans Bey, d'Ali Bey d'Adana, et de Siliedat Pada [*sic*]; qu'elle n'a pas moins connu dans ces derniers temps de quelle manière s'est terminée la vie de Pertew Pacha, et celle de son gendre Vassaw Efendi; et que ces crimes sont de nature à aliéner à jamais d'elles, tous les peuples de l'Europe! Lui faire entendre ces représentations sévères et d'autres semblables serait un acte de la plus haute importance.

APPENDIX IV

HATTI SHERIF DE GULHANÉ (TANZIMAT)
NOVEMBER 3, 1839

All the world knows that in the first days of the Ottoman Monarchy the glorious precepts of the Koran and the Laws of the Empire were always honoured. The Empire in consequence increased in strength and greatness, and all her subjects, without exception, had risen in the highest degree to ease and prosperity. In the last 150 years a succession of accidents and divers causes have arisen which have brought about a disregard for the sacred code of laws, and the regulations flowing therefrom, and the former strength and prosperity have changed into weakness and poverty: an Empire in fact, loses all its stability so soon as it ceases to observe its laws.

These considerations are ever present to our mind; and, ever since the day of our advent to the throne, the thought of the public weal, of the improvement of the state of the Provinces, and of relief to the peoples, has not ceased to engage it. If, therefore, the geographical position of the Ottoman Provinces, the fertility of the soil, the aptitude and intelligence of the inhabitants are considered, the conviction will remain that, by striving to find efficacious means, the result, which by the help of God we hope to attain, can be obtained with a few years. Full of confidence, therefore, in the help of the Most High, assisted by the intercession of our Prophet, we deem it right to seek by new institutions to give to the Provinces composing the Ottoman Empire the benefit of a good Administration.

These institutions must be principally carried out under three heads, which are: (1) The guarantees ensuring to our subjects perfect security for life, honour, and fortune. (2) A regular system of assessing and levying taxes. (3) An equally regular system for the levy of troops and the duration of their service. . . .

As to the regular and fixed assessment of the taxes, it is very important to settle that matter, for the State which is forced to incur many expenses for the defence of its territory cannot obtain the money necessary for its armies and other services except by means of contributions levied on its subjects. Although, thanks be to God, our Empire has for some time past been delivered from the scourge of Monopolies, falsely considered in times of war as a source of revenue, a fatal custom still exists, although it can only have disastrous consequences; it is that of venal concessions, known under the name of 'Iltizam.' Under that name the civil and financial administration of a locality is delivered over to the passions of a single man; that is to say, sometimes to the iron grasp of the most violent and avaricious passions, for if that contractor is not a good man he will only look to his own advantage.

It is therefore necessary that henceforth each member of the Ottoman Society should be taxed for a quota of a fixed tax, according to his fortune and his means, and that it should be impossible that anything more could be exacted from him. It is also necessary that special laws should fix and limit the expenses of our land and sea forces.

Although, as we have said, the defence of the country is an important matter, and that it is the duty of all the inhabitants to furnish soldiers for that object, it has become necessary to establish laws to regulate the contingent to be furnished by each locality, according to the necessity of the time, and to reduce the term of military service to four or five years. For it is at the same time doing an injustice and giving a mortal blow to agriculture and to industry to take, without consideration to the respective population of the localities, in the one more, in the other less, men than they can furnish; it is also reducing the soldiers to despair, and contributing to the depopulation of the country, by keeping them all their lives in the service.

In short, without the several laws, the necessity for which has just been described, there can be neither strength, nor riches, nor happiness, nor tranquillity for the Empire; it must, on the contrary, look for them in the existence of these new laws.

From henceforth, therefore, the cause of every accused person shall be publicly judged in accordance with our Divine Law, after inquiry and examination, and so long as a regular judgement shall not have been pronounced, no one can, secretly or publicly, put another to death by poison or in any other manner.

No one shall be allowed to attack the honour of any other person whatever.

Each one shall possess his property of every kind, and shall dispose of it in all freedom, without let or hindrance from any person whatever; thus, for example, the innocent heirs of a criminal shall not be deprived of their legal rights, and the property of the criminal shall not be confiscated.

These Imperial concessions shall extend to all our subjects, of whatever religion or sect they may be; they shall enjoy them without exception. We therefore grant perfect security to the inhabitants of our

Empire, in their lives, their honour, and their fortunes, as they are secured to them by the sacred text of our law.

As for the other points, as they must be settled with the assistance of enlightened opinions, our Council of Justice (increased by new members, as shall be found necessary), to whom shall be joined, on certain days which we shall determine, our Ministers and the Notabilities of the Empire, shall assemble, in order to frame laws regulating the security of life and fortune and the assessment of the taxes. Each one in these assemblies shall freely deliver his ideas and give his advice.

The laws regulating the military service shall be discussed by a Military Council, holding its sittings at the Palace of the Seraskier.

As soon as a law shall be passed, in order to be for ever valid, it shall be presented to us; we shall give it our approval, which we will write with our Imperial sign manual.

As the object of these institutions is solely for the purpose of reviving religion, government, the nation, and the Empire, we engage not to do anything which is contrary thereto. In testimony of our promise, we will, after having deposited them in the Hall containing the glorious mantle of the Prophet, in the presence of all the Ulemas and the Grandees of the Empire, make Oath in the name of God, and shall afterwards cause the Oath to be taken by the Ulemas and the Grandees of the empire.

After that, those from among the Ulemas or the Grandees of the Empire, or any other persons whatsoever, who shall infringe these institutions, shall undergo, without respect of rank, position, and influence, the punishment corresponding to his crime, after having been well authenticated. A Penal Code shall be compiled to that effect.

As all the public servants of the Empire receive a suitable salary, and that the salaries of those whose duties have not, up to the present time, been sufficiently remunerated are to be fixed, a rigorous law shall be passed against the traffic of favouritism and of appointments (richvet), which the Divine Law reprobates, and which is one of the principal causes of the decay of the Empire.

The above dispositions being an alteration and a complete renewal of ancient customs, this Imperial Rescript shall be published at Constantinople, and in all places of our Empire, and shall be officially communicated to all the Ambassadors of the friendly Powers resident at Constantinople, that they may be witnesses to the granting of these institutions, which, should it please God, shall last for ever. . . .

APPENDIX V

MÉMOIRE DE BARON VON STURMER, MARCH 10, 1841

H. H. u. St. A. Wien. Türkei VI, fasz. 57

Traduction d'un mémoire sur la situation actuelle de l'Empire Ottoman

    (ad Bericht No. 472 E, Constantinople, 19 Mars 1841)

Le maintien et l'indépendance de l'Empire Ottoman étant essentiellement nécessaires à l'équilibre politique de l'Europe, les cours alliées, en faisant de grands et généreux efforts, ont assuré l'intégrité de son territoire et réglé convenablement la question Egyptienne.

Après cela, si la S. Porte adopte les principes nécessaires à une bonne administration, c'est-à-dire si, jouissant au dehors d'une sécurité parfaite, elle est en état de bien arranger ses affaires intérieures, il est indubitable que cela donnera de la force au gouvernement, assurera le bonheur et la tranquillité de ses sujets et consolidera ainsi la paix générale. Dans le cas opposé, il est évident, que la S. Porte s'avançant de jour en jour davantage vers sa perte et sa destruction, causera aux grandes Puissances une foule d'embarras et amènera même peut-être une guerre générale. D'après ceci, il est clair que le véritable but ne saurait être atteint par le simple fait de la garantie de l'intégrité et de l'arrangement de l'affaire d'Egypte.

C'est dans l'appréciation de cette vérité que l'on a publié les règlemens fondamentaux contenus dans le Hatti cherif de Gulhané, règlemens qui avaient pour but d'organiser, s'il était possible, la marche des affaires intérieures et de tirer la S. Porte de la situation périlleuse ou elle se trouve. Les motifs qui ont encouragé à entreprendre cette grande œuvre sont les suivans:

1°. le changement de règne et la facilité qu'on entrevoyait dès lors de faire entrer dans la bonne voie le nouveau Souverain qui ne connaissait pas encore les funestes maximes de l'ancien régime; —

2do. l'espoir que, par suite de la bataille de Nizib, de la défection de la flotte, de l'attitude formidable de Mehmed Aly, comme aussi de la pénurie du trésor et des embarras intérieurs de tout genre qui étaient arrivés à leur comble, les ministres de la S. Porte et les chefs de la nation écouteraient enfin la voix de la raison, et seraient dis-

posés à abandonner la poursuite de leur vues et intérêts particuliers
et à travailler aussi un peu pour le bien public; —

3°. l'espoir que, la question Egyptienne obligeant ce gouvernement
à avoir des égards pour les Puissances Européennes, cette circonstance
fournirait les moyens de combattre et d'extirper le fanatisme. Ces
nouvelles institutions n'étaient d'ailleurs qu'une sorte d'essai; on avait
considéré que si elles réussissaient, cela ferait infiniment heureux, et
que, dans le cas contraire, le gouvernement marcherait dans l'ancienne
voie de sorte qu'on se trouverait n'avoir rien gâté ni empiré. Ceux
qui ne connaissaient pas la pensée intime du fonctionnaire qui avait
suggéré le Hatt de Gulhané avaient conçu toute sorte de soupçons
parce qu'ils voyaient dans ces innovations une simple fantaisie d'imiter
les formes des gouvernemens constitutionnels de l'Europe. Mais cette
pensée ne lui avait jamais passé par l'esprit, vu qu'il serait de toute
impossibilité de gouverner dans les voies constitutionelles un peuple
aussi ignorant que le nôtre et aussi incapable de comprendre ses véritables intérêts. Les principales dispositions du Hatt de Gulhané
tendent à établir une sûreté parfaite par rapport à la vie, à la propriété et à l'honneur des individus, et à régulariser les dépenses intérieures et militaires de la S. Porte comme aussi les autres branches
de l'administration et nommément les impôts à prélever sur le peuple.
Dans les gouvernemens absolus de l'Europe le Souverain ne peut,
comme on sait, ni faire tuer personne sans qu'il ait été jugé et reconnu
coupable, ni attenter à la propriété ou à l'honneur de qui que ce soit.
Un peu d'attention suffit pour reconnaître que ce sont là les seules
privilèges que le Hatt de Gulhané est destiné à assurer au peuple.
Dans ces pays, non seulement le Souverain et ses Visirs, mais de
simples Musselims, Voivodes etc. infligent, à leur gré, la peine capitale,
et portent atteinte à la fortune et à l'honneur de leurs administrés.

Niera-t-on que la prospérité et la durée de cet Empire seront im-
possibles si on n'avise pas d'abord aux moyens d'abolir d'aussi détes-
tables abus? Et vouloir faire cesser un état de choses aussi funeste,
est-ce restreindre l'autorité souveraine du Sultan? N'est-ce pas plutôt
la ramener au point qui lui est indiqué par la saine raison et même
par les préceptes de l'Islamisme?

Quoi qu'il en soit, le but de l'acte de Gulhané est de procurer à
tous cette sûreté si désirable et qui sert de base à tout le reste. Le
Sultan lui-même l'a d'abord bien accueilli et s'est montré disposé à
l'exécuter; mais les choses sont bien changées maintenant, et en voici
à peu près les causes: *1°* la cessation de la position critique dans la-
quelle le Sultan se trouvait auparavant; —*2ᵈᵒ* le goût qu'il prend peu à
peu à faire tout ce qui lui vient à l'esprit sans réfléchir et sans con--

sulter personne; —*3°* les propos trompeurs de ceux qui ne pensent qu'à leurs intérêts personnels, ainsi que les flatteries et les insinuations des Oulémas; –*4°* l'influence déplacée des femmes. Il est évident que si le nouveau Souverain prend, dès à présent, les allures de son père, il sera plus tard impossible de le retenir.

Mais ici on pourrait nous adresser la question suivante: Supposé que les nouvelles institutions ne se consolidassent pas et que l'on retournât à l'ancien régime, la S. Porte ne pourra-t-elle pas continuer à gouverner ces pays de la même manière dont Elle l'a fait depuis si longtemps? — Voici la réponse.

La forme cohérente et la force irrégulière qu'on supposait à cet Empire à une époque où les Etats Européens n'étaient ni aussi forts ni aussi bien organisés qu'ils le sont aujourd'hui, ont, en raison des abus, éprouvé une décadence progressive depuis environ quatre vingts ans, et maintenant les forces vitales de ce pays sont menacées d'un anéantissement complet. Par conséquent, si on n'établit pas une force légale de nature à contenir le peuple et à empêcher en même temps tout acte d'injustice ou d'oppression envers qui que ce soit, la S. Porte ne pourra ni gouverner ses Etats ni sortir de la situation critique ou elle se trouve. Si dans les gouvernemens Européens, ou les Souverains et les ministres sont tous des hommes expérimentés et instruits, on a senti le besoin de lois tutélaires, pourra-t-on nier la réalité de ce besoin dans un pays tel que celui-ci? Nous pensons d'ailleurs que les temps sont passés où tout le monde supportait aveuglement les caprices d'un régime oppressif. On peut admettre que, vu la rareté d'hommes éclairés dans la nation Musulmane, les malheureux habitans de ces contrées, ne sachant où se réfugier, puissent patienter encore pendant quelque temps. Mais il n'en est pas moins certain que l'on verrait éclater tantôt ici tantôt là des séditions et des révoltes. Nous trouvons une preuve irréfragable de cette assertion dans la question d'Egypte, à peine terminée. Les premiers pas qu'a faits Mehmed Aly pour acquérir de la force lui ont été dictés par le peu de sécurité qu'il avait et par l'absence de principes et d'organisation dans le gouvernement de la S. Porte. Il tâchait simplement de pourvoir à sa sûreté personnelle. Que plus tard l'accroissement de son pouvoir lui ait fait concevoir d'autres idées et d'autres espérances, ceci est une question à part.

En outre, les sujets chrétiens de la Porte acquièrent tous les jours plus de lumières, ils ont devant les yeux, d'un côté, le royaume hellénique, de l'autre, les principautés de Valachie, de Moldavie et de Servie qui ont obtenu de grands privilèges et se sont affranchies de l'esclavage. Dans cet état de choses comment les sujets chrétiens pourraient-ils supporter la continuation d'un régime tyrannique et les traitemens avilissans dont ils sont l'objet? Et surtout, si les Musulmans continuent à croupir dans l'ignorance et le fanatisme, tandis que les populations chrétiennes s'éclairent nécessairement de plus en plus, si ces populations étaient de plus encouragées et excitées par quelque Puissance étrangère, le peu de force qui reste au gouvernement Ottoman pourrait-il résister longtemps? N'est-il pas, d'ailleurs, contraire à la saine raison qu'une nation ignorante puisse dicter la loi à des nations policées et instruites?

Mais admettons un instant que tous ces dangers ne soient pas encore imminens. Les gouvernemens de l'Europe, qui professent le plus grand respect pour les principes civilisateurs et pour les droits de l'humanité, regarderaient-ils comme conforme à leur dignité et à leurs sentimens philanthropiques d'abandonner froidement à leur sort tant de populations diverses, lorsque, avec un très léger effort, ils pourraient les délivrer des maux insupportables qui pèsent sur elles?

Ici on pourrait nous adresser quelques questions:

1ère question. Si les grandes Puissances s'occupaient des lois et des institutions de la S. Porte, cela constituerait une ingérence dans les affaires intérieures de ce pays. Ceci n'est-il pas contraire aux maximes des gouvernemens et aux droits des nations?

Réponse. Oui, cela y est contraire lorsqu'une semblable intervention est de nature à faire du mal à un pays. Mais quand on juge nécessaire l'existence d'un gouvernement incapable de compréhendre ses propres intérêts et qu'on intervient dans ses affaires intérieures à son avantage incontestable, on agit, selon nous, d'une manière tout-à-fait conforme aux droits des gouvernemens et des nations. C'est comme un malade frappé de démence envers lequel ses amis emploiraient la force pour le faire jeuner et lui faire prendre médecine.

2me question. Les conseils des grandes Puissances sont-ils suffisans pour faire entrer la S. Porte dans la bonne voie?

Réponse. Des conseils et même de légères menaces ne feraient ici aucun effet; car ces moyens ne font de l'impression que sur des hommes instruits, expérimentés et prévoyants. Il sera donc impossible de rien faire dans ce pays si on n'intervient pas *activement*.

3me question. D'après la seconde réponse, des conseils et des menaces ne sauraient être suffisans. Or, comme la S. Porte a coutume de régler toutes les affaires de l'Etat suivant la loi religieuse de l'Islamisme, dans le cas que les Puissances Européennes, intervenant activement, concertassent et proposassent quelques principes réglementaires, est-il probable que ces principes soient appréciés et adoptés par la nation Musulmane quand même ils le seraient par le Sultan? Et les mesures et menaces qui devront être employées pour faire adopter les réglemens proposés ne seraient-elles pas considérées comme des actes d'hostilité envers la nation Musulmane?

Réponse. La lois religieuse de l'Islamisme offrant à ceux qui sont appelés à l'interprêter une immense latitude, il n'est rien qu'on ne puisse faire adopter. Une mesure serait diamétralement opposée à la loi religieuse, qu'il serait permis de l'adopter dès qu'il y a force majeure.

D'ailleurs, lorsque les Souverains Ottomans ont sérieusement arrêté et adopté quelque chose, ni les Oulémas ni personne autre ne peuvent s'y opposer. La preuve en est que, sous le règne précédent, personne ne s'est opposé à une foule d'innovations qui ne consistaient qu'en de vaines formalités sans aucune espèce d'utilité réelle et qui même, sous certains rapports, étaient des actes de tyrannie et de vexation. Bref, les Sultans ne se soucient pas de la loi religieuse dans les choses qui leur conviennent; ils prétextent seulement cette loi pour empêcher et écarter plus facilement les choses qui ne leur plaisent pas. De même que les Sultans, regardant la loi religieuse comme un soutien de leur despotisme, sont obligés d'avoir des égards pour les Oulémas, ceux-ci désireux de se rendre nécessaires et de se donner de l'importance, s'appliquent à flatter les Sultans et à adopter à leurs goûts et à leurs penchans les dispositions de la loi religieuse. Il résulte de ces réflexions que dès que le Sultan a adopté une chose, il n'est nullement probable que les Oulémas ni l'ensemble de la nation s'y opposent. Pour faire adopter au Sultan les mesures dont il s'agit ici, il faut nécessairement qu'elles soient proposées avec vigueur et appuyées de menaces. Au commencement, il est vrai, le manque de lumières fera probablement que ces propositions et ces menaces seront considerées comme des procédés hostiles. Mais, vu le manque de tous moyens de résistance, il est à prévoir que ni le gouvernement ni la nation ne se porteraient à aucun acte inconvenant quelconque, d'autant plus qu'une fois que le Sultan, soit de bon gré, soit par crainte, aura adopté les mesures proposées, le peuple pourra être conduit dans tel sens qu'on voudra. En outre, ce que le peuple regarde avec répugnance, ce sont les règlemens qui ne consistent qu'en paroles et qui aboutissent à de nouvelles vexations. Mais quant aux véritables améliorations dont les avantages positifs sont évidents, tout le peuple les considéréra comme un grand bienfait, et les sujets chrétiens nommément non seulement ne s'y opposeront d'aucune manière, mais, dès qu'ils comprendront qu'il vont enfin être admis à la jouissance de droits égaux, ils seconderont de leur mieux les efforts des grandes Puissances.

APPENDIX V

Jusqu'ici il a été question des maximes actuelles du gouvernement Ottoman ainsi que des principes et des croyances de la nation Musulmane. Maintenant nous allons indiquer sommairement les mesures réglementaires dont l'établissement nous paraît le plus nécessaire.

1º. Renforcer par des lois sévères les articles du Hatt de Gulhané qui établissent la sûreté de la vie, de la propriété et de l'honneur.

2ᵈᵒ. Proclamer que désormais la différence entre toutes les classes de sujets ne consistera que dans la diversité de leur culte et des lieux où ils font leurs dévotions; abolir entièrement le Haradj (la capitation) qui aliène à la S. Porte les cœurs des populations chrétiennes et faire jouir ainsi toute la nation de droits égaux.

3º. Régler la fixation et la perception des impôts d'une manière satisfaisante et propre à prévenir toute vexation, et déterminer les dépenses pour l'armée et l'administration intérieure en les proportionnant aux besoins et à la position géographique de l'Empire Ottoman.

4º. Comme la S. Porte manque d'hommes versés dans les finances et dans l'administration militaire, faire venir d'Europe et employer des personnes capables qui puissent guider et instruire les fonctionnaires Ottomans.

5º. Etablir les écoles nécessaires pour que la S. Porte ne soit pas à la longue obligé d'employer des étrangers, et aussi afin que ses sujets ne restent pas dans l'ignorance et le fanatisme.

Tels sont les points qui devraient former la base des règlemens que nous avons en vue. En résumé, en faisant abstraction des institutions purement religieuses, la forme de gouvernement, les principes administratifs et la législation de l'Autriche conviendraient aux pays et aux sujets de la S. Porte. Il y aurait tout au plus à y apporter quelques modifications réclamées par les exigences locales et par les mœurs et les habitudes des Musulmans.

Si donc la manière de voir et les pensées des grandes Puissances s'accordaient pour arranger ainsi les affaires intérieures de la Turquie, et qu'on dût mettre la main à l'œuvre, il faudrait alors établir dans un point convenable de l'Europe une conférence composée des commissaires des grandes Puissances, inviter la S. Porte à y envoyer aussi deux hommes éclairés, et procéder ensuite à la discussion de l'affaire. Il y aurait, selon nous, trois avantages à y faire intervenir des commissaires Ottomans: *1°*. On aurait respecté l'indépendance de la S. Porte, puisqu'on ne déciderait pas l'affaire sans son concours; *2ᵈᵒ*. On mettrait à profit les connaissances locales des commissaires Ottomans, ce qui faciliterait beaucoup la grande œuvre dont s'occuperait la conférence; *3°*. Si les commissaires de la Porte se trouvent à Constantinople, il serait difficile et même dangereux pour eux de rapporter en entier et d'appuyer efficacement les décisions des grandes Puissances tandis que si ces commissaires se trouvent en Europe, ils écriront tout franchement et sans retenue. Dans tous les cas, si l'on entreprend l'œuvre de cette manière, il faudra outre le rapport des commissaires Ottomans, que les représentans des grandes Puissances à Constantinople proposent instamment et avec énergie tous les points fondamentaux qu'aura arrêtés la conférence. Si ces représentans remarquent de l'hésitation, ils auront recours aux menaces, et si la S. Porte refuse encore et montre de l'obstination, ils devront déclarer ouvertement que la non-acceptation des points proposés entraînerait le partage de l'Empire Ottoman.

Il y a d'ailleurs lieu d'espérer qu'il sera facile de faire adopter ces points fondamentaux, car comme à l'exception de l'abolition du Haradj, il n'y a rien que les Oulémas pussent repousser comme étant contraire à la loi religieuse, ils trouveront moyen de légitimer même cette abolition dès qu'on leur montrera un peu de fermeté et d'énergie, et le Sultan, de son côté, effrayé au seul mot de partage, se hâtera de céder également. Il faudra penser ensuite à assurer l'établissement solide et l'exécution des points fondamentaux adoptés et des détails qui s'y rattachent, comme aussi à se délivrer des intrigues des malveillans jusqu'à ce que, ces institutions une fois consolidées, l'opinion publique se prononce en faveur de leur maintien. A ce double effet, il nous semble nécessaire que, durant huit ou dix ans, les légations des grandes Puissances soient chargées de surveiller toutes les affaires, et même que ces Puissances pour assurer leur ascendant, fassent stationner dans le Bosphore chacune un ou deux bâtimens de guerre.

Si on n'entreprend pas de régler cette question, soit d'après le mode ci-dessus, soit d'une autre manière, et que les Etats de la S. Porte soient abandonnés encore quelque temps à leur sort, il y aura, prochainement et de tous côtés, de la confusion et des troubles de tout genre, et les grandes Puissances seront non seulement exposées à voir s'accumuler autour d'elles des embarras aussi sérieux qu'intempestifs, mais elles seront aussi responsables devant Dieu de la prolongation des maux et des souffrances qui affligent de si nombreuses populations.

Traduit par le Baron H. Testa.

APPENDIX VI

FIRMAN AND HAT–I–HUMAYUN (SULTAN OF TURKEY), FEBRUARY 18, 1856

The guarantees promised on our part by the Hat-i-Humayun of Gulhané,[1] and in conformity with the Tanzimat, to all the subjects of my Empire, without distinction of classes or of religion, for the security of their persons and property and the preservation of their honour, are to-day confirmed and consolidated, and efficacious measures shall be taken in order that they may have their full and entire effect.

All the privileges and spiritual immunities granted by my ancestors *ab antiquo,* and at subsequent dates, to all Christian communities or other non-Mussulman persuasions established in my Empire under my protection, shall be confirmed and maintained.

Every Christian or other non-Mussulman community shall be bound, within a fixed period, and with the concurrence of a Commission composed *ad hoc* of members of its own body, to proceed, with my high approbation and under the inspection of my Sublime Porte, to examine into its actual immunities and privileges, and to discuss and submit to my Sublime Porte the reforms required by the progress of civilization and of the age. The powers conceded to the Christian Patriarchs and Bishops by the Sultan Mahomet II and his successors shall be made to harmonize with the new position which my generous and beneficent intentions ensure to these communities.

The principle of nominating the Patriarchs for life, after the revision of the rules of election now in force, shall be exactly carried out, conformable to the tenor of their Firmans of Investiture.

The Patriarchs, Metropolitans, Archbishops, Bishops, and Rabbis shall take an oath on their entrance into office according to a form agreed upon in common by my Sublime Porte and the Spiritual heads of the different religious communities. The ecclesiastical dues, of whatever sort or nature they be, shall be abolished and replaced by fixed revenues of the Patriarchs and heads of communities, and by the allocation of allowances and salaries equitably proportioned to the importance, the rank, and the dignity of the different members of the clergy.

[1] Generally known as the Hatti Sherif de Gulhané. See Appendix IV.

The property, real or personal, of the different Christian ecclesiastics shall remain intact; the temporal administration of the Christian or other non-Mussulman communities shall, however, be placed under the safeguard of an Assembly to be chosen from among the members, both ecclesiastics and laymen, of the said communities.

In the towns, small boroughs, and villages, where the whole population is of the same religion, no obstacle shall be offered to the repair, according to their original plan, of buildings set apart for religious worship, for schools, for hospitals, and for cemeteries.

The plans of these different buildings, in case of their new erection, must, after having been approved by the Patriarchs or heads of communities, be submitted to my Sublime Porte, which will approve of them by my Imperial order, or make known its observations upon them within a certain time.

Each sect, in localities where they are no other religious denominations, shall be free from every species of restraint as regards the public exercise of its religion.

In the towns, small boroughs, and villages where different sects are mingled together, each community, inhabiting a distinct quarter, shall, by conforming to the above-mentioned ordinances, have equal power to repair and improve its churches, its hospitals, its schools, and its cemeteries. When there is a question of the erection of new buildings, the necessary authority must be asked for through the medium of the Patriarchs and the heads of communities from my Sublime Porte, which will pronounce a Sovereign decision according that authority, except in the case of administrative obstacles. The intervention of the administrative authority in all measures of this nature will be entirely gratuitous. My Sublime Porte will take energetic measures to ensure to each sect, whatever be the number of its adherents, entire freedom in the exercise of its religion.

Every distinction or designation tending to make any class whatever of the subjects of my Empire inferior to another class, on account or their religion, language, or race, shall be for ever effaced from the Administrative Protocol. The laws shall be put in force against the use of any injurious or offensive term, either among private individuals or on the part of the authorities.

As all forms of religion are and shall be freely professed in my dominions, no subject of my Empire shall be hindered in the exercise of the religion that he professes, nor shall be in any way annoyed on this account. No one shall be compelled to change their religion.

The nomination and choice of all functionaries and other employes of my Empire being wholly dependent upon my Sovereign will, all the subjects of my Empire, without distinction of nationality, shall be admissible to public employments, and qualified to fill them according to their capacity and merit, and conformably with rules to be generally applied.

All the subjects of my Empire, without distinction, shall be received into the Civil and Military Schools of the Government if they otherwise satisfy the conditions as to age and examination which are specified in the organic regulations of the said schools. Moreover, every community is authorized to establish Public Schools of Science, Art, and Industry. Only the method of instruction and the choice of professors in schools of this class shall be under the control of a Mixed Council of Public Instruction, the members of which shall be named by my Sovereign command.

All commercial, correctional, and criminal suits between Mussulmans and Christian or other non-Mussulman subjects, or between Christians or other non-Mussulmans of different sects, shall be referred to mixed tribunals.

The proceedings of these tribunals shall be public: the parties shall be confronted, and shall produce their witnesses, whose testimony shall be received, without distinction, upon an oath taken according to the religious law of each sect.

Suits relating to civil affairs shall continue to be publicly tried, according to the laws and regulations, before the Mixed Provincial Councils, in the presence of the Governor and Judge of the place. Special civil proceedings, such as those relating to successions or others of that kind, between subjects of the same Christian or other non-Mussulman faith, may, at the request of the parties, be sent before the Councils of the Patriarchs or of the communities.

Penal, correctional, and commercial laws, and rules of procedure for the mixed tribunals shall be drawn up as soon as possible, and formed into a Code. Translations of them shall be published in all the languages current in the Empire.

Proceedings shall be taken, with as little delay as possible, for the reform of the penitentiary system as applied to houses of detention, punishment, or correction, and other establishments of like nature, so as to reconcile the rights of humanity with those of justice. Corporal punishment shall not be administered, even in the prisons, except in conformity with the disciplinary regulations established by my Sublime Porte, and everything that resembles torture shall be entirely abolished.

Infractions of the law in this particular shall be severely repressed, and shall, besides, entail, as of right, the punishment, in conformity with the Civil Code, of the authorities who may order and of the agents who may commit them.

The organization of the police in the capital, in the provincial towns, and in the rural districts shall be revised in such a manner as to give to all the peaceable subjects of my Empire the strongest guarantees for the safety both of their person and property.

The equality of taxes entailing equality of burdens, as equality of duties entails that of rights, Christian subjects and those of other non-Mussulman sects, as it has been already decided, shall, as well as Mussulmans, be subject to the obligations of the Law of Recruitment. The principle of obtaining substitutes, or of purchasing exemption, shall be admitted. A complete law shall be published, with as little delay as possible, respecting the admission into and service in the army of Christian and other non-Mussulman subjects.

Proceedings shall be taken for a reform in the constitution of the Provincial and Communal Councils, in order to ensure fairness in the choice of the deputies of the Mussulman, Christian, and other communities, and freedom of voting in the councils. My Sublime Porte will take into consideration the adoption of the most effectual means for ascertaining exactly and for controlling the result of the deliberations and of the decisions arrived at.

As the laws regulating the purchase, sale, and disposal of real property are common to all the subjects of my Empire, it shall be lawful for foreigners to possess landed property in my dominions, conforming themselves to the laws and police regulations, and bearing the same charges as the native inhabitants, and after arrangements have been come to with Foreign Powers.[1]

The taxes are to be levied under the same denomination from all the subjects of my Empire, without distinction of class or of religion. The most prompt and energetic means for remedying the abuses in collecting the taxes, and especially the tithes, shall be considered. The system of direct collection shall gradually, and as soon as possible, be substituted for the plan of farming, in all the branches of the revenues of the State. As long as the present system remains in force, all agents of the Government and all members of the Medjlis shall be forbidden, under the severest penalties, to become lessees of any farming contracts which are announced for public competition, or to have any beneficial interest in carrying them out. The local taxes

---

[1] On January 18, 1867, a law was passed granting to foreigners the right to hold real property in the Ottoman Empire; and on July 28, 1868, a protocol was signed between the British and Turkish governments relative to the admission of British subjects to the right of holding real property in Turkey.

shall, as far as possible, be so imposed as not to affect the sources of production or to hinder the progress of internal commerce.

Works of public utility shall receive a suitable endowment, part of which shall be raised from private and special taxes levied in the Provinces, which shall have the benefit of the advantages arising from the establishment of ways of communication by land and sea.

A special law having been already passed, which declares that the Budget of the revenue and expenditure of the State shall be drawn up and made known every year, the said law shall be most scrupulously observed. Proceedings shall be taken for revising the emoluments attached to each office.

The heads of each community and a delegate designed by my Sublime Porte shall be summoned to take part in the deliberations of the Supreme Council of Justice on all occasions which might interest the generality of the subjects of my Empire. They shall be summoned specially for this purpose by my Grand Vizier. The delegates shall hold office for one year; they shall be sworn on entering upon their duties. All the members of the Council, at the ordinary and extraordinary meetings, shall freely give their opinions and their votes, and no one shall ever annoy them on this account.

Steps shall be taken for the formation of banks and other similar institutions, so as to effect a reform in the monetary and financial system, as well as to create funds to be employed in augmenting the sources of the material wealth of my Empire.

Steps shall also be taken for the formation of roads and canals to increase the facilities of communication and increase the sources of the wealth of the country. Everything that can impede commerce or agriculture shall be abolished. To accomplish these objects means shall be sought to profit by the science, the art, and the funds of Europe, and thus gradually to execute them.

Such being my wishes and my commands, you, who are my Grand Vizier, will, according to custom, cause this Imperial Firman to be published in my capital and in all parts of my Empire; and you will watch attentively, and take all the necessary measures that all the orders which it contains be henceforth carried out with the most rigorous punctuality.

10 Dzemaziul, 1272 (February 18, 1856)

BIBLIOGRAPHY

BIBLIOGRAPHY

I. UNPUBLISHED MATERIAL

Foreign Office Records. The British Public Record Office (Chancery Lane, London) now contains not only the out-going despatches of the Foreign Secretaries but also the in-coming ambassadorial and consular reports. In 1939 these were open for inspection through the year 1878. Out-going despatches to Turkey are indexed under F. O. 78/, in-coming reports under F. O. 195/. Despatches to and from ambassadors and consuls in other capitals are listed in the footnotes under the name of the country to which the representative was sent, as France, F. O. 25/, or Austria, F. O. 7/. In the Public Record Office are also preserved the reports of all military and naval commissioners. These are usually found with the covering letter in which they were forwarded to the Foreign Office, though sometimes the enclosures are filed separately in the War or Admiralty reports. Frequently, a whole series of despatches pertaining to a special subject will be bound separately and indexed under the name of the country and the attaché involved. While these variations in the cataloguing of material often proved troublesome to the investigator, the difficulties were outweighed by the fact that all the reports for the nineteenth century to 1878 were housed in the Chancery Lane repository.

Customs House Reports. Ledgers of imports and exports (Customs 5/ and Customs 4/ respectively) were available in the Chancery Lane repository through the year 1837. All customs reports after that date were preserved in H. M. prison at Canterbury, and special permission of the librarian of the Custom House was necessary to use them.

Board of Trade Records. The In and Out letters of the Board of Trade are now preserved in the Public Record Office. The Board of Trade archives (Gt. Russell Street, Whitehall) contain little material for the first half of the nineteenth century, the most important documents having been sent to the Foreign Secretary are now a part of the Foreign Office material.

British Museum. Aberdeen and Layard papers are available here in the Manuscript Division. The Library of the Museum contains a few of Ponsonby's letters, largely duplicates of those in the Foreign Office files and not particularly valuable. A large number of contemporary books and pamphlets, dealing particularly with the diplomatic aspects of the Eastern question, is also available here. The newspapers for the period are preserved in a separate repository at Hendon.

Palmerston Papers. These documents are most inaccessible, except to the most distinguished historians, since they are the private possession of

Sir Wilfred Ashley, proprietor of Broadlands, Romsey. However, it was gratifying to discover that Palmerston had not removed from the Foreign Office archives a large portion of his official correspondence, as was long believed. The despatches in the Public Record Office are most adequate, though one still cherishes the desire to peruse the private letters of the Foreign Secretary to his closest agents and friends.

Urquhart Papers. The Urquhart papers are now the property of Balliol College, Oxford. At least six large boxes exist, though few of the papers have been catalogued or systematically arranged. Though these documents undoubtedly contain valuable information as to David Urquhart's relations with Ponsonby and Sir Henry Taylor, private secretary to William IV, they were not examined for this work, since there seemed to be sufficient material on Urquhart in the Ambassadorial and Consular reports, and since the majority of his speeches and writings have been printed. Widener Library, Harvard University, possesses a very complete collection of Urquhart's printed works.

Canning Papers. The famous "Memoirs" which were the basis of the late Stanley Lane-Poole's biography of Stratford de Redcliffe are not to be found. All that remain of the Canning papers are several bundles of miscellaneous notes preserved in the Public Record Office and catalogued under F. O. 352/1–55. These miscellaneous papers are not particularly valuable except as an occasional supplement to his despatches in the Foreign Office reports.

II. PUBLISHED MATERIAL

1. BIBLIOGRAPHICAL GUIDES

Benegesco, G., *Essai d'une notice bibliographique sur la question d'Orient, 1821–1897*, Bruxelles, 1897.

Javanovic, V. M., *An English Bibliography of the Near Eastern Question, 1481–1906*, Belgrade, 1906.

Michoff, N. V., *Population de la Turquie et de la Bulgarie*, Sofia, 1915–1924.

2. DOCUMENTS

American Board of Commissioners for Foreign Missions, *Annual Reports*, Boston, 1834ff.

Annual Register; or a View of the History, Politicks, and Literature of the Year, London, 1761ff.

British Foreign and State Papers, London, 1832ff.

Hansard's *Parliamentary Debates*, Series III (1804–1920).

Hertslet, L., *A Complete Collection of the Treaties and Conventions and Reciprocal Regulations, . . . between Great Britain and Foreign Powers, . . . So Far As They Relate to Commerce and Navigation, . . .* 30 volumes, London, 1840–1924.

Hertslet, E., *The Map of Europe by Treaty*, 4 vols., London, 1875.

Holland, T. E., *The European Concert in the Eastern Question*, Oxford, 1885.

Jochmus, A., *The Syrian War and the Decline of the Ottoman Empire, 1840–1848*, 2 vols. in one, Berlin, 1883.

Martens, G. F. von, *Nouveau Recueil de traités d'alliance, . . . depuis 1808 jusqu'à présent*, 16 vols., Gottingue, 1817–1842.

Noradounghian, G., *Recueil d'actes internationaux de l'Empire Ottoman*, 4 vols., Paris, 1897–1903.

Parliamentary Papers, *Correspondence relative to the Affairs of the Levant*, Series I, London, 1841.

Shopov, A., *Les Réformes et la protection des Chrétiens en Turquie, 1673–1904, firmans, bérats, protocoles, traités, . . .* Paris, 1904.

Zambour, E. de, *Manuel de généalogie et de chronologie pour l'histoire de l'Islam*, Part I, Hanover, 1927.

3. CONTEMPORARY LITERATURE: BOOKS, PAMPHLETS, TRAVELLERS' ACCOUNTS, NEWSPAPERS, ETC.

Aubignosc, L. P. B., *La Turquis nouvelle, réformes du Sultan Mahmud*, 2 vols., Paris, 1839.

Besse, A., *L'Empire Turc, histoire et statistique, état politique et religieux, mœurs et usages, situation actuelle*, Paris, 1854.

Blanqui, J. A., *Voyage en Bulgarie pendant l'année 1841*, Paris, 1843.

Cadalvène, E., and Barrault, E., *Deux Années de l'histoire d'Orient, 1839–1840*, 2 vols., Paris, 1840.

De Kay, J. E., *Sketches of Turkey, 1831–1832, by an American*, New York, 1833.

Eichmann, F., *Die Reformen des Osmanischen Reiches*, Berlin, 1858.

Elliott, C. B., *Travels in the Three Great Empires of Austria, Russia, and Turkey*, 2 vols., Philadelphia, 1839.

Gilson, A., *The Czar and the Sultan, or Nicholas and Abdul Medjid*, London, 1852.

Hamlin, Cyrus, *Among the Turks*, New York, 1878.

Jouannin, J. M., *Turquie*, Paris, 1853.

Journal de Constantinople (as cited in footnotes).

Juchereau de Saint Denys, Le Baron Antoine, *Histoire de l'Empire Ottoman, 1792–1844*, 4 vols., Paris, 1844.

Kinglake, A. W., *Eothen: or, Traces of Travel Brought Home from the East*, London, 1844 (Everyman's edition, 1908).

Larpent, Sir George, *Turkey; Its History and Progress from the Journals and Correspondence of Sir James Porter, Fifteen Years Ambassador to Constantinople, Continued to the Present Time*, 2 vols., London, 1854.

Le Moniteur Ottoman (as cited).

London Daily Times (as cited).

London Morning Chronicle (as cited).

McCulloch, J. R., *A Dictionary, Practical, Theoretical, and Historical of Commerce and Commercial Navigation,* London, 1834.

MacFarlane, C., *Constantinople in 1828,* London, 1829.

MacGregor, John, *Commercial Statistics, a Digest of the Productive Resources. Commercial Legislation, . . . of all the Nations,* 5 vols., London, 1850.

Manchester Guardian (as cited).

Marmont, Marshal (Duc de Raguse), *The Present State of the Turkish Empire,* translated with notes and observations by Lt. Col. Sir Frederick Smith, London, 1839.

Marshall, John, *A Digest of All the Accounts Relating to the Population, Productions, Revenues, Financial Operations, Manufactures, Shipping, Colonies, Commerce,* etc., etc., *of the United Kingdom of Great Britain & Ireland, Diffused through More than 600 Volumes of Journals, Reports, Papers Presented to Parliament in the Last 35 Years,* London, 1833.

Michelsen, E. H., *The Ottoman Empire and Its Resources,* London, 1853.

Missionary Herald, 1821ff.

Morning Herald (London) (as cited).

Ohsson, M. de, *Tableau général de l'Empire Ottoman,* 4 vols., Paris, 1788–1791.

Pope, Charles, *The Yearly Journal of Trade, 1837–1839,* London, 1839.

Porter, G. R., *Progress of the Nation,* London, 1851.

Ross, David, *Opinions of the European Press on the Eastern Question,* London, 1836.

Slade, A., *Records of Travel in Turkey and Greece, 1829–1831,* 2 vols., London, 1833.

———, *Turkey, Greece, and Malta,* 2 vols., London, 1837.

———, *Travels in Turkey,* New York, 1854.

Spencer, Edmund, *Travels in European Turkey in 1850,* 2 vols., London, 1851.

Stockmar, Baron Ernst von, *Memoirs,* edited by M. Mueller, 2 vols., London, 1872.

Thornton, T., *The Present State of Turkey,* 2 vols., London, 1809.

Turkey and Russia; or Observations on their Political and Commercial Relations, by a Merchant, London, 1835.

Ubicini, M. A., *Letters on Turkey,* translated by Lady Easthope, 2 vols., London, 1856.

———, *État présent de l'Empire Ottoman,* Paris, 1876.

Urquhart, David, *Turkey and Its Resources: Its Municipal Organization,
. . . Prospects of English Commerce in the East,* etc., London, 1833.
——, *Portfolio,* 7 vols., London, 1836–1844.
——, *The Spirit of the East,* 2 vols., London, 1838.
——, *Sultan Mahmud et Mehemet Ali Pasha,* Paris, 1839.
——, *An Appeal against Faction,* London, 1843.
——, *The Military Strength of Turkey,* London, 1868.
Walsh, R., *A Residence in Constantinople,* 2 vols., London, 1836.
White, Charles, *Three Years in Constantinople, or Domestic Manners of
the Turks in 1844,* 3 vols., London, 1846.
Zinkeisen, Johann W., *Geschichte des osmanischen Reiches in Europa,*
7 vols., Hamburg, 1840–1863.

4. GENERAL HISTORIES

Ancel, J., *Manuel historique de la question d'Orient,* Paris, 1927.
Cambridge History of British Foreign Policy, 3 vols., Cambridge, 1922–1923.
Clapham, J. H., *An Economic History of Modern Britain,* 3 vols., Cambridge, 1930.
Cuinet, V., *La Turquie d'Asie,* 4 vols., Paris, 1892–1894.
Davis, W. S., *A Short History of the Near East,* New York, 1923.
Driault, Ed., *La Question d'Orient depuis ses origines jusqu'à la grande
guerre,* Paris, 1917.
*Encyclopedia of Islam, A Dictionary of the Geography, Ethnography, and
Biography of the Muhammedan Peoples,* edited by M. Houtsma, T. W.
Arnold, and A. Schaade, London, 1913–.
Jorga, Nicholas, *Geschichte des osmanischen Reiches,* 5 vols., Gotha, 1908–1913.
La Jonquière, A. Vicomte de, *Histoire de l'Empire Ottoman depuis des
origines jusqu'au traité de Berlin,* Paris, 1881.
Lavisse, E., and Rambaud, A., *Histoire générale du 4ᵉ siècle à nos jours,*
12 vols., Paris, 1893–1901.
Levi, L., *History of British Commerce, 1763–1870,* London, 1870.
Lipson, E., *Economic History of England,* 3 vols., London, 1915–1931.
Miller, William, *The Ottoman Empire, 1801–1913,* Cambridge, 1913.
Page, W., *Commerce and Industry, 1815–1914,* 2 vols., London, 1919.
Schevill, F., and Gewehr, W. M., *History of the Balkan Peninsula from the
Earliest Times to the Present Day,* New York, 1933.
Schiemann, T., *Geschichte Russlands unter Kaiser Nikolaus I,* 4 vols.,
Berlin, 1904–1919.
Stern, A., *Geschichte Europas seit den Verträgen von 1815 bis zum Frank-
furter Frieden von 1871,* 10 vols., Stuttgart, 1894–1925.

Verney, N., and Dambmann, G., *Les Puissances étrangères dans le Levant, en Syrie, et en Palestine*, Paris, 1900.

5. MONOGRAPHS

Arnold, T. W., *The Caliphate*, London, 1924.

Bastelburger, J. M., *Die militarischen Reformen unter Mahmoud II*, Gotha, 1874.

Blaisdell, N. C., *European Financial Control in the Ottoman Empire; a Study of the Establishment, Activities, and Significance of the Administration of the Ottoman Public Debt*, New York, 1929.

Bowley, A. L., *A Short Account of England's Foreign Trade in the Nineteenth Century*, London, 1905.

Crawley, C. W., *The Question of Greek Independence, a Study of British Foreign Policy, 1821–1833*, Cambridge, 1930.

Du Velay, A., *Histoire financière de la Turquie*, Paris, 1903.

Emin, A., *Development of Modern Turkey as Measured by Its Press*, New York, 1914.

L'Empire Ottoman, 1839–1877. L'Angleterre et la Russie dans la Question d'Orient, par un Ancien Diplomat, Paris, 1877.

Engelhardt, Ed., *La Turquie et le Tanzimat, ou Histoire des Réformes dans l'Empire Ottoman depuis 1828 jusqu'à nos jours*, 2 vols., Paris, 1882.

Franco, G., *Développements constitutionels en Turquie*, Paris, 1925.

Ghorbal, S., *The Beginnings of the Egyptian Question and the Rise of Mehemet Ali*, London, 1928.

Gordon, L. J., *American Relations with Turkey, 1830–1930, an Economic Interpretation*, Philadelphia, 1932.

Gorianov, S., *Le Bosphore et les Dardanelles*, Paris, 1910.

Guichen, Vicomte de, *La Crise d'Orient de 1839 à 1841 et l'Europe*, Paris, 1922.

Hall, Major John, *England and the Orleans Monarchy*, London, 1912.

Hasenclaver, A., *Die orientalische Frage in den Jahren 1838–1841*, Leipzig, 1914.

Headlam-Morley, J. W., *Studies in Diplomatic History*, London, 1930.

Hoskins, H. L., *British Routes to India*, New York, 1928.

Imbert, P., *La Rénovation de l'Empire Ottoman, affaires de Turquie*, Paris, 1909.

Lybyer, A. H., *The Government of the Ottoman Empire in the Time of Suleiman the Magnificent*, Cambridge, 1913.

Mandelstam, A., *La Justice ottomane dans ses rapports avec les puissances étrangères*, Paris, 1911.

Marriott, J. A. R., *The Eastern Question*, Oxford, 1917.

Miller, Barnette, *Beyond the Sublime Porte*, New Haven, 1931.

Morawitz, Charles, *Die Türkei im Spiegel ihrer Finanzen,* Berlin, 1903.

Mosely, P. E., *Russian Diplomacy and the Opening of the Eastern Question in 1838 and 1839,* Cambridge (Mass.), 1934.

Noury, Soubby, *Le Régime réprésentatif en Turquie,* Paris, 1914.

O'Rourke, V. A., *The Juristic Status of Egypt and the Sudan,* Baltimore, 1935.

Puryear, V. J., *England, Russia, and the Straits Question, 1844–1856,* Berkeley, 1931.

———, *International Economics and the Diplomacy of the Near East, a study of British Commercial Policy in the Levant, 1834–1853,* Stanford, 1935.

Rodkey, F. S., *The Turco-Egyptian Question in the Relations of England, France, and Russia, 1832–1841,* Urbana, 1921.

Rosen, G., *Geschichte der Türkei vom Siege der Reform im Jahre 1826 bis zum Pariser Tractat vom Jahre 1856,* 2 vols., Leipzig, 1866–1867.

Rouvière, F., *Essai sur l'évolution des idées constitutionelle en Turquie,* Montpellier, 1910.

Sabry, M., *L'Empire Egyptien sous Méhémed-Ali et la Question d'Orient, 1811–1849,* Paris, 1930.

Sax, C. R. von, *Geschichte des Machtverfalls der Türkei bis Ende des 19. Jahrhunderts,* Vienna, 1913.

Sousa, N., *The Capitulatory Regime of Turkey, Its History, Origin, and Nature,* Baltimore, 1933.

Swain, J. E., *The Struggle for the Control of the Mediterranean prior to 1848, a Study of Anglo-French Relations,* Boston, 1933.

Temperley, H. W. V., *England and the Near East, The Crimea,* London, 1936.

———, *History of Serbia,* London, 1919.

Wood, A. C., *The History of the Levant Company,* London, 1935.

Wright, W. L., *Ottoman Statecraft, The Book of Counsel for Vezirs and Governors,* Princeton, 1935.

6. BIOGRAPHIES, MEMOIRS, DIARIES, ETC.

Ashley, E., *The Life and Correspondence of Henry John Temple, Viscount Palmerston,* 2 vols., London, 1879.

Bell, H. C. F., *Lord Palmerston,* 2 vols., New York, 1936.

Bulwer, Sir Henry Lytton, *The Life of Henry John Temple, Viscount Palmerston with Selections from His Diaries and Correspondence,* 3 vols., London, 1870–1874.

Castille, H., "Réschid Pasha," in *Portraits politiques et historiques,* Paris, 1857.

Dodwell, H. H., *The Founder of Modern Egypt,* Cambridge (England), 1931.

Goodell, Wm., *Memoirs, or Forty Years in the Turkish Empire,* edited by E. R. G. Prime, Boston, 1891.

Gordon, A. H., *Earl of Aberdeen,* London, 1893.

Guedalla, Philip, *Palmerston, 1784–1865,* New York, 1927.

Hamlin, Cyrus, *My Life and Times,* Boston, 1893.

Lane-Poole, S., *The Life of the Right Honorable Stratford Canning, Viscount Stratford de Redcliffe, . . . from His Memoirs and Private and Official Papers,* 2 vols., London, 1888.

Layard, A. Henry, *Autobiography and Letters,* 2 vols., London, 1903.

Lieven, Princess Dorothea, *Letters, 1812–1834,* edited by L. D. Robinson, London, 1902.

Malcolm-Smith, E. F., *The Life of Stratford Canning,* London, 1933.

Metternich, Prince de, *Mémoires,* 8 vols., Paris, 1844–1846.

Moltke, Helmuth von, *Briefe über Zustände und Begebenheiten in der Türkei aus den Jahren 1835 bis 1839,* Berlin, 1841.

Reid, S. J., *Life and Letters of the First Earl of Durham, 1792–1840,* 2 vols., London, 1906.

Reminiscences of William IV, Correspondence between Lord Ponsonby and Mr. Urquhart, 1833–1836, London, 1891.

Robinson, G., *David Urquhart, Some Chapters in the Life of a Victorian Knight-Errant of Justice and Liberty,* Oxford, 1920.

Schauffler, W. G., *Autobiography,* New York, 1887.

Talleyrand-Périgord, C. M. de, Prince de Bénévent, *Mémoires,* 5 vols., New York, 1891–1892.

Temperley, Harold, *The Foreign Policy of Canning, 1822–1827,* London, 1925.

Webster, C. K., *The Foreign Policy of Castlereagh, 1815–1822,* London, 1925.

7. ARTICLES

Baker, R. L., "Palmerston on the Treaty of Unkiar Skelessi," *English Historical Review,* vol. 43, 1928, pp. 83–89.

Bérard, Victor, "Réforme Ottomane," *Revue de Paris,* vol. 5, September 1, 1908, pp. 188–224.

Bolsover, G. H., "Lord Ponsonby and the Eastern Question, 1833–1839," *Slavonic Review,* vol. 13, 1934, pp. 98–118.

———, "David Urquhart and the Eastern Question, 1833–1837: A Study in Publicity and Diplomacy," *Journal of Modern History,* December, 1936, pp. 444–467.

———, "Great Britain, Russia, and the Eastern Question, 1832–1841," Institute of Historical Research, *Bulletin,* vol. XI, no. 32, November, 1933, pp. 131ff.

Crawley, C. W., "Anglo-Russian Relations, 1815–1840," *Cambridge Historical Journal,* vol. III, pp. 47–73.

Milev, N., "Réchid Pacha et la Réforme Ottomane," *Zeitschrift für Osteuropäische Geschichte,* May, 1912, pp. 382–398.

"Reformen in der Türkei," *Preussen Jahrbuch,* vol. 112, Berlin, 1903, pp. 31–59.

Rodkey, F. S., "Lord Palmerston's Policy for the Rejuvenation of Turkey, 1839–1841," *Transactions of the Royal Historical Society,* 4th series, vol. XII, 1929, pp. 163–192.

——, "Lord Palmerston and the Rejuvenation of Turkey, 1830–1841," *Journal of Modern History,* December, 1929, pp. 570–593, and June, 1930, pp. 193–225.

——, "Views of Palmerston and Metternich on the Eastern Question, 1834," *English Historical Review,* vol. 45, 1930, pp. 627–640.

Temperley, H. W. V., "British Policy towards Parliamentary Rule and Constitutionalism in Turkey, 1830–1914," *Cambridge Historical Journal,* vol. 4, no. 2, 1933, pp. 156–191.

Turkish Patriot, A, "A Study in Turkish Reform," *Fortnightly Review,* vol. 61 (New Series) or vol. 67 (Old Series), May 1, 1897, pp. 639–659.

INDEX

INDEX

Abdul Medjid, character of, 179–180; reëstablishes Divan, 11n; restores Grand Vizir, 11n, 12n; favors reform to win British support, 180; reforms of, 208, 211, 214; fears "Old Turks," 197

Aberdeen, Lord, not interested in reform in Turkey, 130–131; instructions for Canning, *1842*, 208–209; and Agreement of *1844*, 206n, 207, 213

Administrative reform, need of, 151, 152n

Adrianople, Treaty of, 5, 36

Akaciri, defined, 142

Akerman, Treaty of, 5n

Aleppo, trade of, 103

American interests in Turkey, 117

Anglo-Russian Agreement of *1844*, 206n, 207, 213

Anglo-Turkish trade, increase in number of products *1825–1855*, 84; table of (Official Values) *1825–1853*, 74; analysis of table, 75–76; hampered by high prices of English goods, 119; limited by English import duties, 119–120; influenced by Balta Liman Convention, 126; influence of on British foreign policy, 127

Army, necessity for, 15; size and character of Turkish army, 15–16; development of *1829–1833*, 140; condition of in *1834*, 141–142, 143n; suggested reforms in, 142; changes instituted in *1834*, 142–143

Avanias, 16

Avarisi, 16

Balta Liman, convention of, based on Urquhart's idea, 165n; negotiation of, 122–125; terms of, 125; criticized by Urquhart, 125n; favored by Palmerston, 125–126; agreeable to Urquhart, 165; economic effect on Anglo-Turkish trade, 126; political

effect of, 126–127; renewal of, *1846*, 216–217

Berlin, Treaty of, 5

Beylerbeys, members of Divan, 11n; powers of, 13

Beyrout, trade of, 101–103

Blacque, Alexander, 137

Brant, James, Vice Consul at Trebizond, suggests foreign assistance in reformation of Turkey, 138n

Britain, economic needs of, 68–69; trade balances of (Official Values), *1825–1853*, 70; analysis of table of total exports and imports, 71–72; exports of, primarily manufactured goods, 85; textiles in the Turkish trade, 85–87; iron and steel exports to Turkey, 88; lack of interest in Turkish affairs, 39–41; failure to appreciate Koniah disaster, 47; anxiety for Turkey after treaty of Unkiar Skelessi, 38; new interest in Turkey after *1833*, reasons for, 61–62, 40–41, 232; fear of Russian aggression in Turkey, 61, 67; aims after *1833*, 129; foreign policy influenced by trade, 127; Near Eastern policy reverses itself, *1827–1853*, 63; and the territorial integrity of Turkey, 39, 64; Near Eastern policy based on self-interest, 82–83; influence on Turkish reforms *1834–1838*, 167, 176; influence on whole tanzimat evaluated, 229–230, 232

Bucharest, Treaty of, 5

Cadi, 22n

Caliphate, 20–21

Canning, George: reluctantly intervenes in Greek War, 63; attitude toward Turkey, 129–130; model for Palmerston, 64

Canning, Stratford: character of, 225; aware of Turkey's importance to Britain, 42; warns Britain of possi-

INDEX

Jews, number of, 8n; refugees in Turkey, 9

Kanouni Dzeraim, described, 200
Kavasses, defined, 152
Kharatch, 16n, 17n; collected by Rayah-Mussulman commission, 151; abolished *1840*, 198n
Khavas, guards, 143n
Koniah, battle of, 43, 46–47
Koreish, 20
Kutahia, treaty of, 49

Levant Company, 80–81; strengthens position in Turkey, 81–82; trade assumed by smaller companies, 118; effect of demise on British policy, 118–119
Livas, 13
London Times, demands defense against Russian aggression, 59, 134

Madder root, exports of to Britain, 91
Mahmoud II, character, 11n, 30–31, 138, 140; early life, 30–31; first years of reign, 11n, 29–32; attitude toward Janissaries, 29, 31; reform of military schools, 31; early reforms, 32; Europeanizing policy opposed by "Old Turks," 33, 38; imitates Mehemet Ali, 33n, 38, 229; destruction of Janissaries, 4, 35; attempts to defeudalize state, 36; other reforms, 37, 136–137; character of reforms, 138; absence of well-organized reform program, 137; reforms evaluated by Reschid Pasha, 192; effect of reforms, 38; military weaknesses of, 44; appeals for foreign aid after Koniah, 47–48; more amenable to foreign advice after *1833*, 139; makes war on Mehemet Ali *1839*, 169; estimate of policy, 37; death, 170–171; effect of death on reform movement, 179; estimate of reign, 171–176
Mediterranean, route to East secondary until 1830's, 64–65
Medjliss Aali, established *1839*, 199
Medjliss Ahkiami Adlie, described, 183

Medjliss Cumouri Askerize, described, 183
Medjliss Cumouri Naziri, described, 183
Mehemet Ali, character and career, 45; independence, 6; model for Sultan, 33n, 38, 229; fleet, 44n; expands eastward after *1830*, 46; feared by Palmerston, 134n, 135, 166, 168n
Mehkeme-i-tidjaret, 215n
Mejliss, 11n
Memorandum of August 12, 1839, summarized, 184; critical estimate of aims, 185; similarity to Hatti Sherif de Gulhané, 186, 188–189
Military: program *1834*, aims of, 142, 143; schools revised, 31; backed by Palmerston, 145–149; reforms opposed by Ponsonby, 159
Miri, 18n
Mirigi, 121
Mollahs, 22n
Moltke, Helmuth von, 147, 148n
Moniteur Ottoman, Le, official Turkish gazette, 137; on need of reforms *1834*, 153
Monopolies, opposed by Ponsonby, 122, 124; abolition urged by Palmerston, 124
Moslem Institution, relation to Ruling Institution, 19
Munchengratz Convention, 60n, 134; weakening of, 167
Murad IV, and Janissaries, 26
Mussulman(s), estimated number, 7; faults of rigid classification, 8–9
Mustapha III, and reform, 27n
Mustapha IV, reactionary policies of, 28
Mustapha, the Bairactar, 28; revolt of *1808*, 28–29; death, 29, 32
Mutzelim, control over local taxation, 18

Napoleonic Wars, and English economy, 67–68
Naval Aid to Turkey, 148
Navarino, battle of, 130, 137n
Near Eastern policy of Britain, reverses itself, *1827–1853*, 63; based on self-interest, 82–83

Reforms, administrative, 151, 152n; financial, 150, 151n; military, 31, 142, 149n; need of summarized, 23; need perceived by Stratford Canning, 132; of Mahmoud, 32, 37, 136–137, 183; favored by Abdul Medjid to win British support, 180; of Abdul Medjid, 208, 211, 214; influenced by Britain *1834–1838*, 167, 176; supported by Stratford Canning, 212–213, 215, 225, 227, 231

Reis Effendi, 11

Reschid Pasha, character and career, 181–183, 192; aware of need of reforms in Turkey, 181, 183; his opinion of Mahmoud's reforms, 192; reforms prior to *1839*, 183; an opportunist, 192; anxious to win European aid, 181n; in England, *1839*, 189–190; reforms of *1839–40*, 197–200; effect of his reforms, 200–201; supported by Palmerston, 199; Palmerston's estimate of, 205; reforms evaluated by Ponsonby, 208n; his policy described by Canning, 212n; opponents of, 196; suggests conference of powers to promote reforms, 202; resignation of, 201; fall climaxes tanzimat, 203; Ponsonby and fall of, 203; fall described by Ponsonby, 204; effect of his fall, 207; recalled, *1842*, 212.

Ruling Institution, 10; relation to Moslem Institution, 19

Russia, power of evaluated by Palmerston, 135n; domination over Sultan, 133n; British fears of further aggression in Turkey, 61, 67; menace of recognized by Palmerston, 135

Russo-Turkish war, economic and political effects on Turkey, 137

Salonica, trade of, 105–107

Sandjaks, 13; reduction in number by Mahmoud, 13n

Selem III, reorganizes council, 11n; as "reform sultan," 26, 27; hatred of Janissaries, 27; estimate of, 28; murder of, 29

Seraglio, defined, 10; storming of, *1808*, 29

Seraskier, 11

Sheik-ul-lslam, defined, 12, 19n; power of, 22; deposition of, *1808*, 28

Silk, Turkish, exported to Britain, 91–92

Sinecures, 19

Smyrna, taxation, 18; first commercial city of the Near East, 97–98; trade, 98–100

Spahis, destruction of, 36

Straits Convention, *1840*, 5n, 170

Suez Canal project, 65; opposed by Palmerston, 66–67

Suleiman the Magnificent, 3, 20

Sultan, relation with pashas, 14–15; relations with subjects, 14; position in Ruling Institution, 10

Supreme Council of the Empire, 10

Tanzimat, character of, 228; Turkish in origin, 38, 228–229; not supported by people, 214; its need of foreign support recognized, 138, 145n; evaluation, 220–222, 224–225; reasons for failure, 222–223; influenced by Palmerston, 230; Ponsonby's influence on, 156, 230; influenced by Urquhart, 162; British influence on, 229–230, 232

Taxes, need of, 16; direct taxes, 16; indirect taxes, 17; farming of, 17, 18; diversion of, 18–19; investigation of, 197; reforms begun, 197–198; inquiry demanded in Hatti Sherif, 18n

Timars, 36n, 37n

Tott, Baron de, 27n

Trebizond, trade of, 110–114; focal point of Anglo-Russian antagonism, 114–115

Tribute, of pashas, 14

Turkey, "the sick man of Europe," 3; causes of decline, 3, 4; and the trade routes to India, 41, 43; an agricultural country, 77–78; agricultural products, 84, 89–90; lack of industrialization, 78; indifference of Britishers until *1833*, 39–41, 133n; near bankruptcy, *1829*, 137; economic conditions, *1842*, 210n; hindrances to increased trade, 120–